The Jeffersonian Crisis

The Jeffersonian Crisis:
COURTS AND POLITICS
IN THE YOUNG REPUBLIC

RICHARD E. ELLIS

New York
OXFORD UNIVERSITY PRESS
1971

For my Mother
and
For the Memory of my Father

They gave me all that they had
and might have had

Preface

One of the best reasons I know for studying history is the need to keep the past inviolate. There exists a terrible tendency among people of all kinds of political persuasions to use what happened in the past to justify present-day actions. Sometimes this is done deliberately; more frequently, however, it is the inadvertent consequence of reading into the past the hopes, fears, and values of contemporary life. That people of a reactionary and conservative bent, people who are sometimes too mindful of the binding quality of the past, should commit this mistake is perhaps to be expected. But just as frequently, this error of reading present-day values back into the past is committed by radicals and other people who are bent on change and who, despite their seeming distrust and contempt of tradition, nonetheless look to history for justification.

Of course, certain parts of the past are more liable to misinterpretation than others. This is especially true of those subjects which tend to be fashionable or which appear to have particular "relevance" to present-day problems. One such subject is the question of the relationship of an independent judiciary, particularly the United States Supreme Court with its arrogated power of judicial review, to the development of American democracy. Since the Supreme Court has periodically come under attack from both the right and left, this question has become a kind of historical perennial and has been subject to all kinds of easy simplifications and overdramatized clichés. This book is an attempt to deal with the problem in one of its earliest phases: the struggle that took place over the judiciary on both the national and state level during the Jeffersonian era. And its main purpose is to describe, as much as the sources will allow, exactly what happened and the way it happened so that the reader will get a sense of the complex, halting, and at times irrational way that history is made.

Let it be said at once that my debt to a number of other scholars who have worked this field is great. Nonetheless, this is a revisionist study. Where previous scholars have tended to treat the subject in constitutional terms, I have emphasized complicated and subtle political considerations. Fundamental constitutional and even ideological issues were involved, to be sure; but these issues are, I believe, better understood when seen in a political perspective that was meaningful to the participants. While emphasizing politics I have de-emphasized the dramatic nature of the conflict between Thomas Jefferson and John Marshall; for it seems to me that those two men had more in common with each other than either historians or they themselves would admit. I have also rejected the traditional approach of viewing the court fight during Jefferson's first administration as simply a battle between Republicans and Federalists; because even though much of what happened can and has to be explained in these terms, it is my feeling that at this point in our study of the problem much more is to be gained by interpreting it as a struggle between moderates and extremists in both parties.

This book is in many ways a product of the historiographical debate between the so-called consensus historians and the so-called Progressive historians that has dominated American historiography since 1945. There is no question but that as a result of recent criticism much of the findings of the Progressive school can no longer be accepted. Nonetheless, despite their effectiveness as critics and their success at discovering new and sometimes ingenious ways at looking at old problems, the consensus historians, who emphasize shared values, compromise, and continuity—in contrast with the Progressive historians, who stress conflict—have not been successful in producing a meaningful reinterpretation of American history or in defining the nature of conflict in America's past. For example, Charles A. Beard's *An Economic Interpretation of the Constitution of the United States,* perhaps the most celebrated piece of Progressive scholar-

ship, has been attacked, and has been found almost totally wanting as a valid historical work. Yet all the serious and important
works that have recently been written on the period of the
Articles of Confederation and the adoption of the United States
Constitution, even those written by Beard's severest critics, have
contained points of view that are much closer to those of the
Progressive historians than to those of their consensus critics. The
crux of the problem, as I see it, is that the Progressive historians
rightly, at least for the post-Revolutionary period, recognized
that deep divisions existed in American society, but then defined
these divisions in a rigid and simplistic fashion. But questions
and answers are two different things; and because the answers
the Progressive historians posited to the questions they formulated have been found wanting, it does not necessarily follow
that the questions they asked were the wrong ones. Deep divisions
did exist in America during the early national period: over the
kind of society America should become, over whether economic
growth was good or bad and how it should take place, and over
the compatibility of skilled professionals with a republican form
of government, to name only a few areas. In the last two chapters
of this work I have tried, by building upon the work of both
recent and older scholars, to put my findings into a larger framework of meaning which I hope will offer a starting point or a
target for a long overdue re-evaluation of the Jeffersonian era.

In writing this book I have acquired a substantial number of
obligations. My debt is especially great to Charles Sellers, who
directed this as a dissertation, and whose support and encourage-
ment and gentle but thorny criticism have made this a much
better book than it ever deserved to be. When I first met him
others had already given me an enthusiasm for history, but it
was he who, by example and instruction, taught me to think
meaningfully. The book has also benefited from conversations
with and careful readings by William W. Abbot, Lawrence A.
Harper, Wythe Holt, Frederick Cople Jaher, Dumas Malone,
Merrill D. Peterson, and J. R. Pole. The responsibility for any
errors are, of course, my own. I am also deeply grateful to the
staffs of all the research libraries where I worked, but especially

to John Knowlton of the Library of Congress, who in numerous ways helped make my stay there a very productive one. Support for the research came from the Woodrow Wilson Foundation and the research funds of the University of California, Berkeley, and The College of the University of Chicago. Help for the typing came at a critical moment from Annie, Therese, and Sam Waldfogel.

Finally, to my wife, Sharon, who has been frugal, patient, and determined beyond belief, who taught me to write, and who has always been there when I needed her, I want to say thank you for everything.

R. E. E.

Charlottesville
February 1971

Contents

The Jeffersonian Crisis

I

An Unsettled Problem: The Judiciary and the American Revolution, 1776-1801

The American Revolution was the central event of the late eighteenth century, and it dominated United States history between 1776 and 1815. During those forty years two wars had to be fought to secure American independence, a foreign policy had to be forged to regulate the new nation's relations with the rest of the world, an economic policy had to be formulated to determine the direction of the young country's growth, and the problem of how and in what form the new country should be governed had to be resolved. Historians have now come to recognize what contemporaries understood quite well: that this last problem was what the American Revolution was all about. "It is a work of the most interesting nature," noted Thomas Jefferson, "and such as every individual would wish to have his voice in." He then added: "In truth it is the whole object of the present controversy; for should a bad government be instituted for us in future, it had as well to accept at first the bad one offered to us from beyond the water without the risk and expense of contest." [1] John Adams also appreciated the significance of the work to be done. Writing to a friend, he observed:

> You and I . . . have been sent into life at a time when the greatest lawgivers of antiquity would have wished to live. How few of the human race have ever enjoyed an opportunity of making an election of government, more than of air, soil, or

climate for themselves or their children! When, before the
present epoch, had three millions of people full power and a
fair opportunity to form and establish the wisest and happiest
government that human wisdom can contrive? [2]

Yet despite the awareness of many Americans of the momen-
tousness of the challenge before them, the establishment of a
viable system of state and national governments proved a long
and arduous task. There were, of course, a number of points on
which a rough kind of consensus had been achieved. There was
agreement that there should be a republican form of government,
that representation should be direct and not virtual, that all
constitutions should be written, and that ultimate sovereignty
should be in the people. However, these issues had been inti-
mately tied up with the causes and coming of the Revolution,
and they had already been widely debated.[3] There still remained,
as Americans soon discovered, a whole series of basic questions
about the nature, purpose, and correct institutional structure of
the government which had been raised as a consequence of the
Revolution; and to these questions most Americans did not
have any fixed answers, while even those who did could not
agree. As a consequence, the years following independence were
ones of continual debate over political and constitutional problems, and before anything resembling a consensus was achieved
many a battle had to be fought and won.[4]

In these encounters no branch of the government presented
as many problems that took as long to resolve, or were as
complex, as the judiciary. Before the break with England it was
only a peripheral issue. But afterward, during the 1780's, the
question of the role of the judiciary in a republic and its relationship to the other branches of the government became crucial.
Yet the political and constitutional questions raised by the
judicial branch of the government were never meaningfully
resolved during the confederation period. Even at the Philadelphia Convention of 1787, which hammered out the United
States Constitution and which offered a number of original and
precise answers to many complicated constitutional questions,
the thorny problems connected with the judiciary were generally
avoided. It was not until 1801, when political considerations,

coupled with the first change of government under the Constitution, pushed the judiciary issue into the forefront, that it became a problem which could no longer be put aside. And at this point, during the first decade of the nineteenth century, it took on such powerful and far-reaching implications that it threatened to upset, reverse, and even erase much of the constitutional development that had taken place since 1776.

I

By the eve of the American Revolution, in 1760, a basically uniform system of judicial organization had developed throughout the colonies, although different titles were frequently used to describe the same courts. At the apex was the King in Council. This court, which in practice was rarely used, had a veto over all provincial legislation and a right to review the decisions of colonial courts. In America the highest court varied from colony to colony, being either a special court or the governor sitting in council. Its main function was to hear appeals from the lower courts on writs of error. Below this there usually was a Superior Court that had original jurisdiction in high value civil cases and in criminal cases of serious consequence. In many colonies there were also courts of Admiralty, Chancery, Orphans, and Probate, in which special problems were determined. At the lowest level, the county, there were two kinds of courts: the Quarter Sessions, which dealt with criminal proceedings, and the Common Pleas, which handled most small value civil cases. These courts were usually presided over by local justices of the peace.[5]

No other branch of the government more directly affected the day-to-day lives of Americans than the judiciary. In addition to punishing criminals, deciding civil cases involving debtors and disputed land titles, and so on, the courts, particularly on the county level—even in New England, where the town meeting is generally thought of as the main unit of local government—had extensive administrative powers. They assessed local taxes and administered their spending on the building and repairing of roads, bridges, jails, workhouses, and courthouses. Their approval was necessary to establish a ferry, or to build a road or bridge,

and it was the neighborhood justice who determined over whose
land a road would pass. Courts set and paid bounties on wild
game, settled quarrels between servants and masters, and issued
licenses to innkeepers and merchants who wished to sell excised
goods.[6]

One of the most significant aspects of the colonial court system
was that, with the exception of the corporate colonies of Rhode
Island and Connecticut, where members of the judiciary were
elected annually, all the judges and justices of the peace held
their offices by appointment. Appointment to the judiciary by
the governor in royal and proprietary colonies was considered
a form of patronage made in order to secure political support.
The governor was usually so happy to have "respectable men"
from within the colony handle the problem of enforcing the laws
and policies of the provincial government on the county level
that few governors dared to interfere with the operation of local
government. The effect was that, prior to the Revolution, that
branch of the government which the Americans knew best was
run by a small oligarchy.[7]

Because of the influence that the courts held over their lives,
the colonists were sensitive to the way in which they operated.
At times, disputes over the operation or non-operation of the
judiciary even led to civil war within the colonies. The failure
of the English government to establish a court system for South
Carolina's rapidly developing western counties led to violence
in 1767. In North Carolina, abuses by corrupt court officials in
the western counties led to an open rebellion that lasted for
three years, between 1768 and 1771. Throughout the 1760's
English attempts to alter judicial commissions from "during
good behavior" to "at the King's pleasure," met with stiff resistance from colonial legislatures and pamphleteers. The Ministry's
decision in 1772 to remove control of the judges' salaries from
the Massachusetts legislature—called the Massachusetts General
Court—led to the establishment of local Committees of Correspondence; and the widespread bitterness of the American reaction to the Intolerable Acts was due in no small part to British
tampering with the Bay Colony's judicial system. Finally, the
closing of the courts and the suspension of the administration

of justice played an important role in bringing down the constituted authorities when the revolutionary movement reached its climax, 1774–76.[8]

During the colonial period the central problem involving the courts was the protection of the judiciary's independence from the encroachments of the Crown and Parliament. With independence the problem was reversed, for the establishment of republican governments with the people as the ultimate source of authority raised the radically new question of the extent to which the judiciary should be dependent upon and responsive to popular influence. Feelings differed sharply on this question; and with the writing of state constitutions, the main issue became whether the judges should be elected or appointed and whether they were to have a specified limited term of office or were to serve during good behavior.

The issue of judicial independence was more intensely fought out in some states than in others, and with very mixed results. In Massachusetts it took four years to resolve the struggle in favor of those who wished to see judges appointed by the executive and to hold their positions for life tenure during good behavior. Similar provisions, arrived at after much less debate, were included in the constitutions of Maryland, Virginia, New Hampshire, South Carolina, North Carolina, and New York. What was decided on in the other states, however, was very different. In Connecticut, Rhode Island, and Vermont judges were elected annually, in New Jersey and Pennsylvania they were elected for seven-year terms, and in Georgia the Chief Justice was appointed annually while the other judges and justices of the peace held office at the pleasure of the legislature. Aside from the tenure question, the new state constitutions said very little about the judiciary, leaving details to statutory arrangement, whereupon the existing colonial courts systems were generally continued with few changes in form.[9]

The state constitutions that were written in the years immediately following independence established the supremacy of the legislature, that branch of the government most directly responsive to the wishes of the people.[10] This was true even in those states where judges held their positions during good behavior, for the assemblies controlled salaries and fees and had at their disposal various procedures for the removal of judges. But by the 1780's the power of the legislatures began to be challenged. The most fundamental question raised was what could be done if the actions of a legislature exceeded the powers granted to it by the Constitution that created it? In several states, Rhode Island, New York, North Carolina, Virginia, Massachusetts, New Jersey, and Connecticut, a number of attempts were made to answer this question. The argument was that the judiciary had the right to declare the legislature's acts unconstitutional.[11]

The difficulties raised by this procedure and its relationship to the general democratic thrust of the revolution were clearly stated in an exchange of letters between Richard Spaight and James Iredell, following a ruling of a North Carolina court which in effect declared unconstitutional an act of the legislature. Spaight admitted that many of the Assembly's acts had been intemperate, but he questioned the authority of the courts to declare an act void. He opposed having political power entrusted to a branch of government that was not responsive to popular opinion. For if an appointed judiciary had the right to declare an act of the legislature unconstitutional, "the state, instead of being governed by the representatives in the General Assembly, would be subject to the will of three individuals. . . ." The important question to Spaight was: if the judiciary acted as a check on legislature, then who was to act as a check upon the judiciary? Spaight believed that the only way that the authority of the legislature could be safely controlled was through the annual election of the judges.[12]

Iredell's reply was a lucid presentation of the point of view of those in favor of judicial review. Under no circumstances was the legislature's power to be absolute. The Constitution, Iredell argued, was the fundamental law of the state, limiting the powers of the legislature. If an act of the legislature violated the Constitution it was up to the judges to declare it unconstitutional. As to Spaight's fear of tyranny by judicial rule, Iredell admitted it to be possible, but he felt it was not probable. Iredell was motivated primarily by a fear of unrestrained majority rule—tyranny by the majority. "If there be no check upon the public passions," he wrote, "it [government] is in the greatest danger. The majority having the rule in their own hands may take care of themselves; but in what condition are the minority, if the power of the other is without limit?" [13]

Although the concept of judicial review had the support of a number of important individuals, including Alexander Hamilton, who had used arguments similar to Iredell's in *Rutgers* v. *Waddington* in New York in 1784 and who reasserted the position in No. 78 of *The Federalist*, it was by no means a clearly accepted function of the courts. The various attempts made by the courts at judicial review during the 1780's either were ignored or brought forth statements of denunciation from the legislatures with threats to remove the judges. Indeed there are strong indications that a direct assault on the judiciary would have met with popular approval in many quarters. Yet opponents of judicial review tended to be more extreme in their rhetoric than in their actions, and in most ensuing battles only a stand-off was reached: the judges refused to recant, but their decisions were never really implemented. At best, the proponents of judicial review had stated a position; they had not won acceptance for it.[14]

Where the role of the judiciary was concerned, nothing was really settled during the 1780's. The only thing that appears clear is that, while most people were probably to be found somewhere in the middle, the debate over the judiciary did produce two fundamentally different and uncompromisable points of view. One placed final power in the legislature, which was regarded as the democratic branch of the government, and made the judges directly amenable to the public by having them elected or appointed for limited terms. The other opposed making the legislative branch supreme, believed in judicial review, and favored an independent judiciary based on executive appointment of judges who were to hold their offices during good behavior.

II

Equally indecisive were the results of the debate over the need for a national judiciary, which began with the drafting of the

Articles of Confederation and continued on through the 1790's.

The framers of the Articles of Confederation deliberately created a central government that lacked the authority to act directly upon its citizens. As a consequence it did not establish a national judiciary. It provided only for Congress to create courts on an *ad hoc* basis and only for the trial of felonies and crimes committed on the high seas, the determination of appeals in all cases involving captures, the final settling of disputes between states, and the resolving of private land controversies where grants from two or more states were involved. In every other way the central government was completely dependent upon the states and their judiciaries to protect its interests and enforce its laws.[15]

The need for a national judiciary was discussed at some length at Philadelphia in 1787. There, for the first time, the country's leading national-minded citizens deliberately set out to create a strong and energetic central government with the powers to assert its influence directly over individuals. Most of the delegates agreed that a Supreme Court was essential, but no concensus could be reached on the need for a lower court system. Some maintained that all that was required to secure a uniformity of decisions and to protect the interests of the national government was a Supreme Court which had the final word on appeals, and that on all other matters the federal government could use the state courts; while others argued that the federal government should have a completely separate judicial system "dispersed throughout the country." [16]

The final draft of the proposed Constitution provided for federal judges to be appointed by the President with the consent of the Senate, and to hold their positions during good behavior; for federal judges to be removable only by impeachment and conviction of "Treason, Bribery, or other high Crimes and Misdemeanors"; for federal courts to have jurisdiction in all cases of law and equity arising under the Constitution, the laws, and the treaties of the United States, in controversies involving different states, citizens of different states, or foreign citizens, and in certain other carefully defined instances; for the Supreme Court to have a limited original jurisdiction and broad appellate jurisdiction in many areas of both law and fact; and for all criminal cases to be tried by jury. On the question of a lower federal court system the Constitution simply allowed for "such inferior Courts as the Congress may from time to time ordain and establish." [17] The proposed Constitution also avoided the sticky question of whether any federal court, the Supreme Court in particular, had the authority to declare an act of Congress unconstitutional. The probable reason for the general looseness of the section on the judiciary was pointed out by Gouverneur Morris, a member of the drafting committee, whose account rings true to the proceedings of the convention even though he wrote it many years later. "On that subject conflicting opinions had been maintained with so much professional astuteness that it became necessary to select phrases, which expressing my own notion would not alarm others. . . ." [18]

In the struggle over the adoption of the Constitution, the Anti-Federalists stressed the dangers inherent in switching the locus of power from the states to the national government. Specifically, they warned against the central government's absolute control over taxation and the army, the inability of republican government to operate over a large area, the undemocratic nature of the three branches of the government, and the dangers of a national judiciary—which they predicted would swallow up and eventually destroy the state courts so that "an inhabitant of Pittsburgh, on a charge of crime committed on the banks of the Ohio, may be obliged to defend himself at the side of the Delaware, and so *vice versa*." [19] Of the seventy-nine different amendments proposed by the state ratifying conventions, sixteen were for changes in the judiciary article. The Anti-Federalists demanded that Congress's powers to establish a lower court system with any kind of original jurisdiction be eliminated or severely restricted, that the Supreme Court's appellate power be confined to questions of law and not include questions of fact, that jury trials be guaranteed in civil as well as criminal cases, and that there be a reduction of the Supreme Court's jurisdiction over cases involving diverse citizenship and foreigners. Although the Bill of Rights failed to prohibit the establishment of a lower court system and did not seriously circumscribe the substantive powers of the national government, it did in Articles V–VIII reflect somewhat the Anti-Federalist concern with the dangers inherent in a national judiciary.[20]

When the first Congress met, it immediately implemented the Constitution's provisions for a federal court system. After some wrangling, a compromise measure, the Judiciary Act of 1789, was agreed upon. It provided that the Supreme Court should consist of a Chief Justice and five associates, and it organized a lower court system consisting of district courts manned by separate judges and circuit courts made up of two Supreme Court justices and a district judge who were to meet in different locales across the length and breadth of the land. On this point there is substantial if indirect evidence to indicate that federal judges were expected not only to bring home the authority of the national government to the people, but also, by means of their charges to grand juries, to inculcate in their listeners an understanding of the intricacies of self-government and a respect for the Constitution. Although the Judiciary Act of 1789 was a victory for the advocates of a completely separate federal judiciary system, it was only a qualified victory; it did not grant the federal courts full jurisdiction in all the instances provided for in the Constitution and it gave the state courts broad powers of original jurisdiction in many vital areas involving federal law.[21]

Throughout George Washington's first administration the federal judiciary tried to avoid becoming engaged in political controversies or becoming entangled in questions outside its immediate jurisdiction. In the Hayburn case in 1792 a group of circuit court judges denied to Congress the authority to pass an act requiring federal judges to rule on the claims of disabled Revolutionary war veterans. The following year the justices of the Supreme Court refused a request from the Secretary of State for advice on questions of international law and neutrality. During these early years the federal court was not subject to criticism from the emerging Republican party, which, at this point in its development, did not have any sympathy for reforms along Anti-Federalist lines. In fact, some leading Republicans at first viewed the Supreme Court as a potential ally and hoped it would declare the act chartering the First Bank of the United

States unconstitutional and condemn other Federalist measures.[22]

Meanwhile the inadequacies of the Judiciary Act of 1789 were daily becoming apparent. The most serious criticism came from the justices of the Supreme Court themselves, who complained bitterly about having to ride circuit over bad roads in all kinds of inclement weather and having to spend long periods of time separated from the comforts of home, family, and friends. Frequently, because the judges would get sick, or because of bad weather and impassable roads, the circuit court sessions would have to be postponed. This delayed the dispensation of justice and caused added expense, inconvenience, and even hardship for suitors and persons awaiting trial for crimes. Another defect of the circuit court system was that it placed the justices of the Supreme Court in the embarrassing and difficult position of having to decide on appeals made from their own and their colleagues' rulings in the lower courts, thus allowing personal jealousies and antagonisms to play a role in the administration of justice.

In response to these complaints the Attorney General in 1790 prepared a sympathetic report strongly recommending to Congress that the Supreme Court justices be relieved of the duty of presiding over the circuit courts. He advised that the duty be given instead to the district judges who presided within each circuit. Congress, however, did not get around to acting on the matter until 1793, and then it only provided that the circuit courts be made up of one Supreme Court judge and one district judge. This, of course, scarcely solved anything. The justices of the Supreme Court were still required to ride circuit, though somewhat less frequently, and they were still forced to hear appeals from their own and fellow justices's rulings. The change also created the whole new problem of split decisions on the circuit court level. The position of the Supreme Court justices thus continued to remain, as John Jay was reputed to have said, "In a degree intolerable"; and throughout the 1790's they frequently resigned to take other, less demanding positions.[23]

The large turnover in the personnel of the Supreme Court coincided almost directly with the growth of political parties in America. The significance of this latter development was not understood by either the Federalists or the Republicans, both of whom shared and helped perpetuate the late eighteenth-century American belief that political parties were dangerous to the existence of the republic. Viewing their Jeffersonian critics as a morally reprehensible faction bent on overthrowing the government and destroying the constitution, Washington and his successor John Adams refused to appoint Republicans to any of the judicial offices under their control. Positions on the federal bench went only to men who were strong partisans of administration policy.[24]

Since appointments to the national judiciary went exclusively to members of the Federalist party, and since Federalists refused to recognize the legitimacy of Republican opposition, it is hardly surprising that the decisions handed down by the federal courts between 1796 and 1800 antagonized the Jeffersonians on many controversial issues. Republican resentment became aroused in 1796 by the Supreme Court's decision in *Ware* v. *Hylton* declaring invalid a Virginia statute of 1777 authorizing the confiscation of pre-Revolutionary War British debts. And the Republicans were further angered that same year, when the Supreme Court upheld, in *Hylton* v. *United States,* a law levying taxes on carriages, which the Republicans denounced as unconstitutional. They criticized federal court decisions which denied American ports to French privateers and supported Federalist claims that the Franco-American treaty of 1778 was no longer valid. And they were alarmed by the attempt of some federal judges to incorporate the English common law into American federal law. But what enraged and frightened them the most was the zeal and determination of many federal judges to uphold constitutionally and to enforce uncompromisingly the Alien and Sedition Acts.[25]

During the feverish eighteen months following the XYZ affair the dominant Federalist party turned its attention to the problem of making the federal judiciary stronger and more efficient, in order to bring home to the people the power of the national government and to suppress the Republican opposition. "We ought to spread out the judicial," wrote Theodore Sedgwick, who was soon to become Speaker of the House, "so as to render the justice of the nation acceptable to the people, to aid the national economy, to overawe the licentious, and to punish the guilty." [26] In this annual address to Congress in December 1799, President Adams urged that some kind of action be taken, but while various measures were debated and considered throughout the winter and spring of 1800 nothing was adopted.[27]

A judiciary act was finally passed on 13 February 1801. This was after the Republicans had captured the presidency and both Houses of Congress, but before the House had broken the tie in electoral votes by selecting Jefferson over Burr. The act's main features were the complete elimination of circuit court duty for Supreme Court justices; the creation of six new circuit courts, with sixteen judges; and the reduction of the number of Supreme Court justices from six to five, to take effect when the next vacancy occurred. The Judiciary Act of 1801 also contained provisions which made it easier to remove litigation from state to federal courts and sharply increased the original jurisdiction of the circuit courts, especially in cases involving land titles. This latter change was of great consequence to foreigners and other absentee landowners who were involved in land disputes and who were being harshly treated by state courts more responsive to local interests than to the technicalities of the law.[28]

On the one hand the Judiciary Act of 1801 was a purely partisan measure. Passed by a lame duck legislature and signed by a defeated President, all the judges appointed under it were Federalists. It also denied to the incoming Republican administration any opportunity of making an appointment to the Supreme Court until two vacancies occurred. The measure was necessary, Gouverneur Morris wrote, shortly after it was passed, because the Federalists "are about to experience a heavy gale of adverse wind; can they be blamed for casting many anchors to hold their ship through the storm?" [29] On the other hand, complaints had been made about the inadequacies of the Judiciary Act of 1789 for over a decade, and the Federalist program of judicial reform had begun in earnest before the results of the election of 1800 were known. Moreover, the broadened original jurisdiction of the lower federal courts was an important step forward in the establishment of a genuinely uniform land policy for all the states and not just for federal territories, and for the eventual development of a truly national commercial code.[30]

III

Between 1776 and 1801 a series of important questions was raised in connection with the judiciary. Should judges be amenable to or independent of the will of the people? What was the relationship of the courts to the other branches of the government? Did the judiciary have the right to determine the constitutionality of a legislature's acts, and if so, was its decision binding? Was a national judiciary necessary? How broad should its powers be? And what was its relation to state court systems? Although these questions were frequently raised, the answers to them tended to be evasive and incomplete, so that by 1800 nothing had been definitely settled.

Almost all Jeffersonians condemned the partisan manner in which the Judiciary Act of 1801 was passed and the appointments made under it. Many were also deeply concerned over the increased jurisdiction of the federal courts, for it was in the key Jeffersonian strongholds of Kentucky, Virginia, Georgia, North Carolina, and Pennsylvania that the most bitter battles between actual settlers and absentee landlords were being fought. Yet there were many Republicans, planters and other businessmen in the party, who were themselves absentee landlords, and who for other general reasons appreciated the need for a strong and active, though less partisan, national judiciary.

Finally, and perhaps most importantly, the judiciary issue by its very nature was related to the even more basic issue of constitutional reform. In 1801 this was an especially serious issue because the significance of the recent Republican victory was unclear. Did it simply mean a change of administrations? Or did it also mean actual changes in the government itself? It was soon to become clear that the Republicans themselves differed sharply over how to answer these questions. The judiciary issue, therefore, with its corresponding implications for constitutional change, became the overriding domestic issue of Jefferson's first administration; it became, in fact, the issue around which the meaning of the "revolution of 1800" was to be defined.

PART ONE

Politics and the Judiciary under Jefferson

party of George Washington by the excesses of Alexander Hamilton and his followers. Its most important members were James Madison, Wilson Cary Nicholas, Samuel Smith, Robert R. Livingston, James Sullivan, William Eustis, Thomas McKean, Alexander J. Dallas, and Pierce Butler. This group also included Albert Gallatin, whose politics had undergone considerable transformation since he had opposed the adoption of the Constitution in 1787.

The moderate Republicans had never been opposed to a strong national government *per se*, but only to the misuse of power to which such a government could be subject. They saw no need to amend the Constitution, for, in their way of viewing things, Jefferson's election was enough in itself to correct the evils of the previous administrations. Toward the defeated Federalist party they held mixed emotions, distrusting its leaders and not optimistic about conciliating them, but feeling that most of its followers were wise and virtuous men who would give their support to any reasonable administration that did not alienate them through radical innovations or mass removals. They hoped by a policy of moderation to encourage the virtuous and independent Federalists to join the Republican party. They believed that it was better "to Endeavor to Heal, Rather than Widen, the unhappy division in America, to reclaim rather than punish." [5]

An important source of the moderates' attitude was the fear that a continuation of the party battles of the 1790's would be hazardous to the survival of the American republican experiment in liberty. Dallas, for example, believed that it was possible "by a liberal policy, to secure for the Republican party, so great an accession of numbers, as will awe their opponents into silence . . . the door of reconciliation should be open:—open to excite their hopes, and to reward their penitence." At the same time he expressed the fear that if a different policy were adopted, "the parties will continue always equally to divide the nation; every Federalist will become a conspirator; every Republican will be a tyrant; and each general election will involve the hazard of a civil war." [6] Albert Gallatin was in complete agreement, for he wrote to Jefferson:

II

The Jeffersonians in Power

The passage of the Judiciary Act of 1801, coupled with the Jeffersonian Republican victory in the election of 1800, set the stage for a major reappraisal of the relationship of the courts to the national government. On one level the ensuing struggle over the judiciary was simply a continuation of the decade-long battle between Federalists and Republicans; but on another, more important level, it represented a struggle within the Republican party. For the most striking fact about the Republican party after 1800 is the rapidity with which it began to divide into factions. Until their victory in 1800 the Republicans had been an opposition party, united not by a common ideal but by a common enmity to Federalist policies. With victory secure, the problem of developing positive policies soon made it clear that the party was composed of different groups holding conflicting and irreconcilable attitudes toward the way the government should be administered.

I

When Jefferson's first administration began, the Republican party was made up of several roughly defined and sometimes shifting groups. Of these the most militant were the Old Republicans, whose philosophy of government had much in common with the states' rights and agrarian ideals of the Anti-Federalists. They wanted a weak central government whose powers were explicitly defined, and, believing that there were moral and social dangers inherent in the expansion of commerce and manufacturing, they held suspect any legislation which aided that kind of economic development. Because Old Republicanism's most prominent leaders, John Taylor and John Randolph, came from Virginia, it was often considered by contemporaries to represent the Old Dominion's own special brand of Republicanism. Actually there were a great many Virginians who were not Old Republicans, while there were many to be found in many other parts of the South and West, and in certain rural areas of the North. In addition, during the years 1801–5, the Old Republicans somewhat paradoxically received the support of a number of urban radicals who, while not agrarians, were political purists. The most important members of this group were Benjamin Austin, the aggressive and uncompromising leader of Boston's artisans; William Duane, the editor of the influential Philadelphia *Aurora;* and Michael Leib, the representative from Philadelphia county.

Although their ideology was essentially conservative, dating back in many ways to the Articles of Confederation, the measures which the Old Republicans advocated in the first decade of the nineteenth century were truly radical. They believed that the principles of the American Revolution had been so perverted that a thorough overhaul of the national government was needed. "In this quarter," wrote John Randolph shortly after Jefferson's election, "we think that the great work is only begun: and that without *substantial reform,* we shall have little reason to congratulate ourselves on the mere change of *men.*" [1] The Old Republicans viewed the revolution of 1800 in moral terms, as a triumph of good over evil. With the Federalists, who were tories and monarchists dedicated to the subversion of the principles of 1776, there could be no compromise.

Their attitude toward the judiciary was best expressed by **William Branch Giles:**

> What concerns us most is the situation of the Judiciary as now organized. It is constantly asserted that the Revolution is incomplete, as long as that strong fortress is in possession of the

> enemy; and it is surely a most singular circumstance that the public sentiment should have forced itself into the Legislative and Executive Department, and that the Judiciary should not only not acknowledge its influence, but should pride itself in resisting its will, under the misapplied idea of "independence." . . . No remedy is competent to redress the evil system, but an absolute repeal of the whole Judiciary and terminating the present offices and creating a new system, defining the common law doctrine and restraining to the proper Constitutional extent the jurisdiction of the Courts.[2]

The Old Republicans were driven by a sense of urgency that could be satisfied only by immediate action, and as soon as Jefferson's victory became evident, they were busy formulating the needed amendments to the Constitution.[3] Of all the various proposals none attracted more attention than Edmund Pendleton's article, *The Danger Not Over,* published in the fall of 1801 and endorsed by the Virginia legislature a short time later. The article began by praising the significance of the Republican victory in the recent election, but added that proper use should be made of the opportunity to prevent forever the abuse of the government's power if it should again fall into the wrong hands. The article then went on to suggest a number of needed amendments. The President was to be made ineligible to succeed himself, the term of office for senators reduced, special checks established to prevent the abuse of public credit, and the wording of the Constitution made more precise to prevent sophisticated interpretations. The suggestions in respect to the judiciary were of special importance in light of the growing attention being paid to that branch of the government. Appointments to the courts were to be made by the legislature and not by the President, the judges were to be subject to removal by a joint vote of Congress, and the use of the English common law was to be prohibited in all criminal cases.[4]

A second group, the moderate Republicans, represented a position diametrically opposed to that of the Old Republicans and urban radicals. Most moderate leaders, although there were some important exceptions, were men who had originally favored the adoption of the Constitution, only to be alienated from the

> It is so important for the permanent establishment of those republican principles for which we have successfully contended, that they should rest on the broad basis of the people, and not on a fluctuating majority, that it would be better to displease many of our political friends than to give an opportunity to the irreconcilable enemies of a free government of inducing the mass of the Federal citizens to make a common cause with them.[7]

Another important source of the moderates' desire to conciliate the Federalists was the concern and uneasiness that many of them shared about the large numbers of radicals and professional malcontents who had joined the Republican party during its years of opposition. This point of view was expressed with great clarity by James Sullivan, who was soon to become the Republican Governor of Massachusetts:

> To overthrow this party [the Federalists] which were subverting the Constitution, a number of men have been brought into influence, whose principles, or rather their feelings, are in opposition to all regular well established governments. There is a confidence in these men which is the occasional result of a frenzy. Should the present administration refuse to gratify their wishes, they immediately join the other party, and become as violent on their side as they have been against them. Having no idea of a solid rational government, they cannot be safely trusted with power. . . . In order to maintain the influence of the present government, I am of opinion that every exertion ought to be made to destroy the lines of party distinctions; and I am gratified when I see members sometimes voting with one side and sometimes with the other.[8]

Wilson Cary Nicholas, Republican senator from Virginia, felt the same way and used language remarkably similar to Sullivan's. He wrote:

> " . . . in every society there are a considerable proportion of people who are justly considered as a mere makeweight—without disparagement to our friends we have our full proportion of that sort of people. They are only held by their passions being properly excited and diverted, the bias of that descrip-

tion of men is strongly against those who rule, . . . the first
unfortunate or unpopular step may disgust them, and if we
have to contend with a powerful well disciplined party—
always on the watch, a direction may be given to the public
opinion before we are aware of the danger that may reinstate
the Federalists in the full possession of the Govt." [9]

Although not as explicit as Sullivan and Nicholas, most moderates shared their belief that the real danger to American society
and to continued Jeffersonian hegemony now came from Republicans bent on sweeping reforms, and not from the defeated
Federalists, and that it was a political necessity for the moderates
of both parties to unite.

The coming struggle over the judiciary posed a dilemma for
the moderate Republicans. Although unhappy over Federalist
control of the courts, they were not critical of the increased
power of the federal courts under the Judiciary Act of 1801 and
they were unwilling either to initiate or support any policy that
might lead to changes in the Constitution or affect the tenure or
power of the judges.

It is, of course, not possible to claim that all or even most
Jeffersonians belonged to either the moderate or Old Republican
wings of the party. Some, generally men from states where the
Federalist party was still a threat or even dominant, looked
primarily to the mass removal of their opponents from office.
Sharing this point of view were DeWitt Clinton, Elbridge Gerry,
Pierpont Edwards, Thomas Leiper, Joseph Hooper Nicholson,
and Caesar A. Rodney. Militant, but less committed to constitutional reform and agrarian values than the Old Republicans,
they were angered not so much by the increase in the power and
number of the federal courts under the Judiciary Act of 1801 as
by John Adams's exclusive appointment of Federalists to the
newly created positions. They did not want to see the national
judiciary destroyed, but they also did not want to see it remain
under the control of the Federalist party.[10]

There was also an amorphous group of Republicans, perhaps
even a majority of the party, who were simply followers. Lacking
a positive program, of their own, these Republicans looked to
the administration and to other strong leaders in the party for

guidance and explanation of what the "revolution of 1800" signified. Although they did not formulate policy, these followers could determine the outcome on many issues. Still others were probably indifferent to the whole question of what the recent Republican victory meant.

Although alignments of the factions within the Republican party were by no means hard and fixed in the spring of 1801, two things were clear. First, with victory secure, the differences between the Old and moderate Republicans were coming out into the open, and both sides believed that these differences were so great that they could not be compromised. Second, those Republicans who did not belong to either of these wings of the party were so disparate in point of view and so disorganized that they were incapable of becoming an effective third force. As a consequence, on almost all important issues they ultimately had to choose between the Old and moderate Republican points of view instead of creating their own alternatives.

II

With such divergent attitudes toward the meaning of the "revolution of 1800," party unity was at best a difficult problem. In this situation, the real balance of power lay in the hands of the party's leader, Thomas Jefferson, and in order to understand the many nuances, inconsistencies, and reversals that comprise the so-called Jeffersonian attack upon the judiciary it is necessary to describe the various factors that influenced Jefferson's position in the struggle.

Coming to terms with Jefferson is no easy matter. Federalist propaganda and late-nineteenth-century industrial-minded historians have pictured him as an agrarian-worshipping, wild-eyed revolutionary. More sympathetic historians in the twentieth century have overstated the case in the other direction, viewing him as a great apostle of liberty, having unbounded faith in man's ability to govern himself, and allowing no opportunity to pass that would further man's freedom.[11] It is only in recent years that scholars have been able to arrive at a balanced picture of Jefferson that does justice to the facts. The Jefferson who emerges is a man marked by moderation, not enthusiasm. He is best understood not as a great visionary who broke down the values of eighteenth-century America, but as a man who personified those values. During the period 1776–89, when radical democrats were advocating the supremacy of a unicameral legislature and denouncing the strong central government created by the Constitution, Jefferson's draft of the Virginia constitution provided for the traditional strict separation of powers, and with only minor reservations he supported the adoption of the Constitution. During the late 1790's, as some Americans were beginning to espouse a certain libertarian attitude toward freedom of the press, Jefferson continued to advocate the old common law doctrine of seditious libel. Even the reforms he advocated in the areas of religion, education, slavery, and criminal law were liberal and humanitarian rather than radical and democratic.[12]

Nor did Jefferson have an undying enmity toward the concept of a strong and independent judiciary. His various drafts of constitutions for the state of Virginia all contained provisions for judges to be appointed and to hold their positions for life tenure during good behavior. He had no objection to the establishment of a national judiciary under the federal Constitution in 1789. And even during the late 1790's, when he complained bitterly about Federalist control of the courts, his hostility was mainly directed toward particular decisions and particular judges rather than toward the idea of a strong and active and independent national judiciary.[13] He made clear his respect for the independence of the federal courts when, shortly after receiving word about Federalist intentions to pass the Judiciary Act of 1801, he wrote to Madison, "I dread this above all the measures meditated, because appointments in the nature of freehold render it difficult to undo what is done." [14]

The more perceptive of Jefferson's contemporaries recognized that he was neither an extremist nor a moralist unwilling to compromise with his own and his party's principles. In preferring him to Burr in the disputed election of 1800, Hamilton argued, "To my mind a true estimate of Mr. Jefferson's character warrants the expectation of a temporizing rather than a violent system." [15] John Marshall was in substantial agreement, although he put it less generously: "The democrats are divided into speculative theorists & absolute terrorists. With the latter I am not disposed to class Mr. Jefferson." [16] Members of Jefferson's own party expressed similar opinions. George Clinton reportedly accused Jefferson of being "an accommodating trimmer, who would change with the times and bend to circumstances for the purposes of personal promotion." [17] Even before his inauguration, many Republicans said that "the president intends to adopt the system of accommodation, and to endeavor by factors to draw over those who have been heretofore his opponents." [18] Though these observers may have confused Jefferson's inherent tendency toward moderation with political opportunism, there is very little indication, aside from bitter personal feelings and the rhetoric of campaign literature, that very many people seriously considered Jefferson an uncompromising radical.

Jefferson himself verified his inclination to moderation when, with his election secure, he began to minimize existing differences between the parties. In making these statements he always distinguished between the Federalist leaders, whom he dismissed as incurable monarchists, and the bulk of their supporters, whom he considered to be well-intentioned people who shared the same fundamental principles as the Republicans. To John Dickinson he wrote: "The greatest good we can do our country is to heal its party divisions & make them one people. I consider the pure federalist as a republican who would prefer a somewhat stronger executive; and the republican as one willing to trust the legislature as a broader representation of the people, and a safer deposit of power for many reasons. But both sects are republican, entitled to the confidence of their fellow citizens." [19] To another correspondent he maintained "that it was only to our foreign relations there was ever any division. These I hope can be so managed as to cease to be a subject of division." [20] In yet another letter, in response to a demand that the Federalists be removed from all the offices they held, he replied:

> I am endeavoring to proceed in this struggle with a view to justice, conciliation, and the best interests of the nation taken as a whole. Our most important object is to consolidate the nation once more into a single mass, in sentiment & in object.

. . . As to the mass of citizens not engaged in public offices, this division was an honest one, produced merely by the measures of France and England, and from a difference in their views of these measures. These being now settled the subjects of division have passed away and reunion will take place if we pursue a just, moderate proper line of conduct.[21]

In addition to Jefferson's own inclinations toward moderation and compromise, other factors reinforced his initial predilections toward conciliating the Federalists. Like most of his countrymen, he viewed America as a great experiment in republicanism which he hoped would convert the rest of the world by example. "We feel," he wrote to his close friend Joseph Priestly, "that we are acting under obligations not confined to the limits of our own society. It is impossible not to be sensible that we are acting for all mankind; that *circumstances denied to others, but indulged to us,* have imposed on us the duty of proving what is the degree of freedom and self-government in which a society may venture to leave its individual members." [22]

The great fear of Jefferson and other early advocates of republicanism, however, was that their experiment in liberty would prove a failure, a victim of the internal disorder and anarchy that its critics claimed was the inevitable result of a government whose authority rested in the people it governed. The election of 1800 seemed to be the beginning of the fulfillment of that fear. The campaign had been an exceptionally bitter one, marked by considerable vilification on both sides, and the polarization of parties. Jefferson's victory over Adams, by a mere eight electoral votes, had not been overwhelming; in seven of the sixteen states he did not poll a single electoral vote, a fact which greatly disturbed him, for he had predicted that "should the whole body of New England continue in opposition to these principles of government . . . our government will be a very uneasy one." [23] Tension had increased even more during the anxious weeks that passed before the tie between Burr and Jefferson was finally broken. During this time plots and counterplots, with both sides seriously considering the use of force, embroiled the country.[24] Jefferson fully appreciated that his inauguration represented the first peaceful change of government under the Constitution.

With no precedents to emulate, he realized that the course he chose to follow would influence the success and nature of future peaceful changes in administrations. Jefferson was concerned, in particular, that Federalist fears of Republican excesses would lead to disastrous results. Desirous of "effecting all the reformation which reason would suggest, and experience approve," he nevertheless added, "we see the wisdom of Solon's remark, that no more good must be attempted than the nation can bear." [25]

But if Jefferson inclined toward moderation on the basis of what was reasonable, he also had a tendency toward verbal extremism. Much of what he wrote sounded radical, though hardly any of his actions would place him in that category. Madison, many years later, tried to defend this side of Jefferson: "allowances ought to be made for a habit in Mr. Jefferson as in others of great genius of expressing in strong and round terms, impressions of the moment." [26] John Quincy Adams was a bit more harsh, but he described Jefferson in similar terms: "He was a mixture of profound and sagacious observation, with strong prejudices and irritated passions." [27] Jefferson's impulsiveness was compounded during his presidency by the scathing criticism he received from Federalist newspapers and the Federalist-controlled judiciary. Not especially thick-skinned, he was infuriated by some of these remarks. They sometimes irritated him so much that he found himself in complete sympathy with the radical and other militant Republicans who argued that it was impossible to conciliate the Federalists, and that, therefore, they should all be removed from office. There existed in Jefferson a certain tension between a moderation based on intellect and a tendency toward extremism based on temperament.

There was also another factor which qualified Jefferson's commitment to the moderate Republicans. Many of the moderates were experienced politicians who realized that the party was composed of groups with irreconcilable ideas, and they waited only for the proper moment to safely disassociate themselves from the radical and other militant members of their party. This same realism cannot be attributed to Jefferson, who never shared the distaste and fear that most moderates held for the extremists in their party, and who never was prepared to purge them. When it came to the make-up of the Republican party, Jefferson, as President, was a visionary: unwilling either to accede to radical and militant demands or to disengage himself from them, he wished to convert them. "The only cordial I wish to carry into my retirement," he wrote in 1805, when the intraparty struggle reached its most intense phase, "is the undivided good will of all with whom I have acted." [28] Although this course of action was admirable in many ways, it also had its limitations. While Jefferson maintained a semblance of party unity as no one else could have, he paid heavily for it in the lack of clarity with which the administration's objects were defined and the inconsistent manner in which they were pursued.

III

Official indication of what the course of the victorious Republican party would be came in the President's inaugural address. Jefferson had written the speech with care, for he wanted to correct any wrong ideas that existed about the aims of the new administration. The government was to have two leading objects: adherence to sound principle and conciliation.

Jefferson defined "sound principle" as peace, justice, economy, majority rule, states' rights, and the supremacy of the civil government over the military. But these were vague terms, open to many interpretations, and perhaps the most significant aspect of this part of the address was the President's failure to mention which specific acts of the previous administration had deviated from these principles. Even more important were the sections dealing with conciliation—the most eloquent of the entire speech. Jefferson went out of his way to quiet Federalist fears on such sensitive points as minority rights, property rights, commerce, religion, and entangling alliances with France; and, he went on to minimize existing disagreements between the two parties. "Every difference of opinion is not a difference of principle. We have called by different names brethren of the same principle. We are all Republicans: we are all Federalists." [30]

In the weeks that followed all the important executive appointments belied Federalist claims that Jefferson's election would mean the country's rule by radical agrarians from Virginia. Madison, who was hardly an agrarian, and whom Federalists viewed as the least objectionable of the Virginia Republicans, was made Secretary of State. The appointments of Levi Lincoln of Massachusetts as Attorney General, Henry Dearborn of Maine as Secretary of War, and Gideon Granger of Connecticut as Postmaster General reflected the President's concern over the sectional aspect of party alignment. Robert Smith, a Baltimore merchant, was finally prevailed upon to accept as Secretary of the Navy after a number of others with commercial connections had turned the position down. Rufus King, a Federalist, was retained in the key diplomatic post of Minister to England, while Robert R. Livingston and Charles Pinckney, both ex-Federalists, were appointed to similar positions in France and Spain. Albert Gallatin as head of the Treasury Department was Jefferson's most controversial appointment. Gallatin had long been a critic of Hamilton's fiscal policies, and the Federalists feared he would repudiate them. Rather than risk becoming involved in a direct confrontation with the opposition, Jefferson postponed placing Gallatin's name in nomination until the next session of Congress. Meanwhile, a campaign was waged in the Republican press stressing the reasonable and temperate nature of Gallatin's economic theories.[31]

The moderates also obtained control of the party press. Since the capital had just been removed to the District of Columbia, it was natural that an administration newspaper would be established. William Duane, articulate and vigorous editor of the Philadelphia *Aurora,* had been the leader of the Jeffersonian press during the recent campaign and seemed the most likely choice. In fact Duane showed up in Washington expecting to be given the job, which would have given him valuable government contracts for printing as well as the honor of becoming the first semi-official reporter of the debates of Congress. Unfortunately for Duane too many members of the administration held him suspect: his journalism was too belligerent, his Republicanism too uncompromising. Jefferson also doubted Duane's ability to follow a moderate course, later describing him as "honest & well intentioned, but over zealous."[32] The position went instead to

Samuel Harrison Smith, whose *National Intelligencer,* more than any other paper, came to represent the moderate Republican viewpoint. Almost immediately it pointed out to Republicans that with victory the times had changed, and that methods such as mass protest meetings, which they had used so effectively and which had so concerned Federalists as a threat to the stability of society, were "not only incorrect but dangerous organs of expressing National feeling." [33]

Formulating a policy toward incumbent officeholders proved to be the President's most difficult problem in the months immediately following his inauguration. Many Republicans demanded a general removal of the opposition, while the moderates advised against a policy of sweeping removals in order to further reconciliation. Jefferson knew the problem did not afford an easy solution. Although he had no intention of jeopardizing his chances for conciliating moderate Federalists by making arbitrary removals, he also felt that many of the arguments of those Republicans demanding removals were well taken. Republicans had been excluded from office during the Washington and Adams administrations, and it was unreasonable not to allow them their share of appointments now that victory had been achieved. Moreover, many Federalist officeholders had been guilty of using their offices for partisan political purposes. Many also had obtained their positions under dubious circumstances. This was particularly true of the "midnight appointments," which were defined as those made between 12 December 1800, when the Republican victory was first known in Washington, and midnight of 3 March 1801, when Adams left the presidency. Jefferson fully shared the irritation and anger of those members of his party who believed that what Adams had done was a deliberate attempt to obstruct the demonstrated will of the majority of the American people. He wrote a few years later to his old friend Abigail Adams,

> I can say with truth that one act of Mr. Adams' life, and one only, ever gave me a moment's displeasure. I did consider his last appointments to office as personally unkind. They were from among my most ardent political enemies, from whom no faithful cooperation could ever be expected, and laid me under

the embarrassment of acting thro' men whose views were to defeat mine; or to encounter the odium of putting others in their places. It seemed but common justice to leave a successor free to act by instruments of his own Choice.[34]

The patronage policy initiated by Jefferson reflected not only his anger over Adams's final appointments and his sensitiveness to Republican demands for a share of the spoils of victory, but also his reluctance to remove Federalists from office. All midnight appointees who held their positions at the President's pleasure were to be removed. These included surveyors, collectors, port officers, supervisors, commissioners of loans, marshals, and attorneys. Also to be removed were all officials guilty of misconduct and abuses in the administration of their offices. This, however, was to be the extent of the removals, and none were to be made simply for a difference of political principle. But if only a small number of Federalists were to lose their positions, very few were to be appointed to new ones. The political faithful had to be rewarded, and all future appointments were to come only from the Republican ranks.[35]

The exclusive control which the Federalist party had obtained over the national judiciary still remained a problem, however. The partisan use to which this branch of the government could be put had been amply demonstrated during the past decade, and had become a major Jeffersonian grievance. Something had to be done to protect the rights of Republicans in the federal courts. As the judges were irremovable, it became necessary to make sure that the other officers of the court were Republicans. After the judge, the two most important offices were those of the attorneys who prosecuted the government cases and the marshals who selected the juries and executed the courts' sentences. These positions were overwhelmingly held by Federalists, many of whom had committed various forms of legal oppression upon their political opponents. Consequently Jefferson decided that all Federalist attorneys and marshals, regardless of how legitimately they had obtained their appointments, or how impartially and efficiently they had administered their offices, were to be dismissed and replaced by Republicans.[36]

Aside from appointing a new set of attorneys and marshals,

there was little else Jefferson could do to counterbalance Federalist control of the courts without engaging in radical measures. A number of the commissions of Adams's last-minute appointments to the judiciary had been inaccurately filled out, or had not been delivered, and these Jefferson considered null and void. But while this action was to have far-reaching consequences, the number of offices involved was small, and it did not seriously weaken Federalist influence over the courts.

Any direct assault on the existing judicial establishment required at a minimum an act of Congress, and possibly even an amendment to the Constitution. The existing evidence as to whether Jefferson, in the spring of 1801, was seriously considering such measures is contradictory. There is one letter in which he does express his intention to ask Congress, when it meets, to repeal the Judiciary Act of 1801, but it is an isolated remark, and many of the President's actions appear to belie the conclusion that his mind was made up on the subject at this time. Any attempt to repeal the recent law was sure to meet with vigorous opposition, and Jefferson, during the early months of his administration, was determined not to give the Federalists any issue around which they could mobilize their supporters. In addition, many of Adams's final appointments to the courts were made so late that there had not been enough time to verify their acceptance. A number of these appointees, reluctant to accept positions that might have uncertain futures, returned their commissions. In every case, Jefferson quickly appointed a Republican successor, and at no time did he mention to any of these men that his position might only be temporary.[37]

Perhaps Jefferson hoped that a combination of Federalist resignations and Republican appointments would lead to a proportionate share of the courts being headed by members of his own party. Perhaps he was adopting a wait-and-see attitude toward the courts, hoping that Federalist judges would accept his overtures for conciliation and exercise restraint in the partisan uses to which they put their offices. At any rate, the evidence would seem to indicate that he had not really made up his mind as to what he wanted to do about the national judiciary. Consequently he vacillated, first appearing to favor one course, then another, so that he had no fixed or definite policy. Indeed, throughout the attack upon the judiciary that took place during Jefferson's first administration, this uncertainty was evident in all of his actions. The only thing he clearly never seemed to have favored was the total destruction of the independence of the national judiciary.

III

The Repeal of the Judiciary Act of 1801

Jefferson soon found that it was one thing to conceive and initiate a policy of conciliation and another to implement it successfully. From the beginning it was in trouble. His inaugural address was not enthusiastically received by the more militant members of the party, and although the speech was not openly criticized, praise for it was remarkably restrained. One Federalist newspaper, noting that the expectations of many Republicans had not been fulfilled, came right to the point: "The thoroughgoing Jacobins are much disappointed in the President's Speech. It is directly the reverse of what they wished it to be. . . . They make a show of approving it; but anyone acquainted with them can see that grief sits heavy at their hearts; and that their joy is only teeth outwards." [1]

I

Militant Republicans did not hesitate to make known to the President their unhappiness over his patronage policy. They claimed that the party's continued political success on the local level depended on the political faithful being rewarded. One local politician from western Pennsylvania warned Jefferson that "favors conferred on your enemies will be attended by no good consequences. . . . I can assure you the continuance of such characters tends to alienate the minds of your friends." [2] And

John Randolph wrote ominously to his friend Joseph Hooper Nicholson: "Does my memory deceive me, or did we indeed predict that the dissolution of the Republican party would commence with its elevation to power? What a powerful cement is adversity!" [3]

What made matters still worse for the President was that his policy of conciliation was not even being well-received by the Federalists at whom it was directed. The initial response to the principles expressed in the inaugural address had been favorable, but disenchantment came about almost immediately because many chose to interpret the speech as a promise of no removals. Jefferson's nullification of the undelivered commissions and his indiscriminate removal of marshals, attorneys, and all midnight appointees came under scathing criticism.[4]

The President, his equilibrium already disturbed by criticism from members of his own party, had little patience or sympathy for Federalist complaints. He felt it imperative, in fact, to dispel the mistaken impression that the conciliatory tones of his inaugural had meant that all Federalists would be secure in their offices. An opportunity arose when a group of New Haven Merchants drafted a remonstrance protesting the removal of Elizur Goodrich, Federalist collector of the Port of New Haven, and his replacement by a Republican, Samuel Bishop. Jefferson had no qualms about removing Goodrich. Not only was he a midnight appointee, but he had also been one of the Federalists who conspired, illegally, Jefferson believed, to raise Burr to the presidency. The President's reply began simply enough with a defense of his appointment of Bishop, but it soon became involved in the general problem of what principles were to govern removals. Jefferson pointed out that under previous administrations Republicans had been excluded from every office, and now that they were a majority they had a right to a proportionate share. "If a due participation of office is a matter of right, how are vacancies to be obtained?" he asked. "Those by deaths are few; by resignation none. Can any other mode than that of removal be proposed?" He concluded by asserting that only after a just proportion was obtained would it be possible to ignore party affiliations when making removals.[5]

Jefferson's answer to the New Haven Remonstrance represented a distinct change from his earlier thoughts on removals. In March, he had claimed that with few exceptions, no removals were to be made simply for a difference of political opinion, but by July he was asserting that, if necessary, in order to give Republicans their share of the political spoils, Federalists were to be dismissed on political grounds. This modification appears to have been a victory for those Republicans who were demanding sweeping removals, and it was objected to by the moderate Republicans. Strong opposition to the new policy developed in the cabinet. Madison, according to one apocryphal report, even threatened to resign. Lincoln also questioned it, and Gallatin cautioned that it would only worsen the situation: "The Republicans hope for a greater number of Removals; the Federalists also expect it." [6] The moderate position was best expressed by Wilson Cary Nicholas, to whom Jefferson had earlier complained of the difficulty of following a middle course. Nicholas was against any change in policy. He argued that Federalist criticism was not to be taken seriously, it was simply the last gasp of a dying party, and best ignored. As to criticism from radicals and office seekers, that was to be expected and nothing could be done to prevent a schism. He then added significantly, "I trust our loss cannot be great, I hope it will be confined to the interested and disappointed, and that the virtuous among the Republicans and Federalists will rally round you and form a phalanx that will awe into submission all those who would sacrifice everything to their own interest." [7]

Jefferson's response to the recommendations of caution from the moderate Republicans revealed that while he still remained convinced that moderation was the best course, he was becoming increasingly concerned about the practicality of pursuing it if it meant splitting the party. In a letter to Gallatin he indicated that his commitment to a policy of conciliation had definite limits. "While we push the patience of our friends to the utmost it will bear, in order that we may gather into the same fold all the Republican Federalists possible, we must not even for this object, absolutely revolt our tried friends. It would be a poor manoeuvre to exchange them for new converts." [8]

All this might not be worth relating had the Federalist reaction to Jefferson's change in policy not taken the form it did. The President's reply to the New Haven Remonstrance, just as Gallatin had predicted, had gone far to confirm the Federalists worst fears. "Jefferson is not the first chieftain of a party," wrote Harrison Gray Otis, "who has realized that the hour of success was also the hour of the decline of his personal influence among his own adherents. By proclaiming himself the head and champion of a party, he secures the continuance of their zeal and exertions." [9] To the Federalists, the President's reply was a signal for the beginning of a systematic course of persecution and revenge. Moreover, they were convinced that whatever moderation Jefferson had shown was the direct result of their intimidation, and therefore they were not hesitant to criticize him. Every removal, every new appointment, the Chief Executive's every action now became subject to the harshest possible treatment in the party's newspapers. So much so, in fact, that one of its leaders, George Cabot, had to caution, "The *language* of some of the Federal newspapers is perhaps a little too violent at this time." [10]

The Federalists discovered conspiratorial intentions in every contact that the President had with the courts. The other branches of the government, they believed, had already been corrupted, and a sustained effort would be required to prevent the same from happening to the judiciary. Executive influence in the operation of justice had to be prevented at all costs. Jefferson's refusal to recognize the appointment of four justices of the peace whose commissions had been approved but not delivered, and of a circuit court judge whose commission had been delivered but was inaccurately filled out, had already received widespread condemnation.

To this were now added charges that he had violated the Constitution by interfering with prosecutions that the Adams administration had begun under the Sedition Act against James T. Callender and William Duane. Actually in neither case was Jefferson so much interested in influencing the courts as he was in helping two luckless victims of what he believed was an unconstitutional law. In fact, he had taken pains to make sure he had not exceeded his authority before he remitted Callender's un-

expired sentence and discontinued the prosecutions against
Duane. Aside from this neither man received special benefits
from the administration. The Federalist press placed the worst
possible construction on these actions and some newspapers even
called for impeachment proceedings against the President.[11]

Federalist opposition was not limited simply to diatribes in
the press; it was also reflected in the actions of the courts. An
example of this occurred at the first session of the newly created
Circuit Court for the District of Columbia, when two judges
instituted a libel prosecution under the common law against
the editor of the moderate *National Intelligencer* for publishing
a letter signed "A Friend to Impartial Justice." The letter in
question had been written to defend Jefferson's removal of
Federalist marshals and attorneys and in so doing the author
had used some intemperate language to describe the partisanship
of the courts. The case immediately assumed political overtones
because the two judges who initiated the proceedings, William
Cranch and James M. Marshall, were Federalists, while a third
judge, William Kilty, a Republican, refused to support the
action. Because of the unwillingness of the District Attorney to
prosecute and of the Grand Jury to indict, the matter was eventually dropped, but not before it had become something of a *cause
celèbre*.[12]

This episode reflected not only the uncompromising attitude
of most Federalists, but also their determination to maintain
their old objectionable policies. It served to further excite those
Republicans who were demanding an assault on the judiciary. "It
would seem," wrote a correspondent from Virginia, "that the
friends of order being beaten out of the executive and legislative
posts, are about to mount their cannon *en barbette* and play
upon all the Republicans from the Gibraltar of the Judiciary
Department—Surely some amendments to the constitution of the
United States will be brought forward next session." [13] And the
Aurora pointed out, "these things are not without their use, as
they may tend to correct the *abuse of justice* in the end." [14]

The events of the summer and fall of 1801 posed a difficult
problem for Jefferson. Since his inauguration he had avoided
making any definite statements on the judiciary, but this policy

of evasion could not be carried on indefinitely. The partisan manner in which the Act of 1801 had been passed, and the continued arrogance of some Federalist judges, combined with the demands of many Republicans for an all-out attack on the national court system, had made the federal judiciary the foremost issue facing the administration.[15]

II

Congress, where any assault against the courts would have to be launched, was scheduled to meet in December. Jefferson's dilemma was that while he favored the removal of Federalist judges who had been midnight appointments, he also seriously doubted both the legality and expediency of initiating any legislation that might compromise the independence of the national judiciary or involve changing the Constitution. The views that the President finally expressed in his first annual address to Congress in December 1801 represented an attempt to resolve this dilemma. "The judiciary system . . . and especially that portion of it recently erected," he declared, "will of course present itself to the contemplation of Congress." To assist the Congress in its determination of the necessity of the recent expansion, Jefferson laid before it a highly inaccurate and hastily prepared statement of the number of cases decided by the courts since their first establishment and the number of cases pending when the Judiciary Act of 1801 was passed.[16]

Much of the significance of this message, like that of the inaugural address, lies more in what it did not request than in what it did. Nothing in it could be construed to support the demand of the party's radical wing. Most important, it did not suggest an amendment to the Constitution making the judges more dependent upon popular influence by changing the method of their appointment and tenure of office. All that Jefferson suggested was that the national court system might be too large for the amount of business it had to perform; and this was to be remedied in such a way as to prevent Republicans from making appointments to the judiciary a part of the spoils of victory. The President's reasoning on this latter point was made clear in a letter to the Governor of New Jersey three days before he sent his message to Congress:

> I am in hopes that public offices being reduced to so small a number, will no longer hold up the prospect of being a resource for those who find themselves under difficulties, but that they will at once turn themselves, for relief, to those private pursuits which derived from services rendered to others. Our duty is not to impede those pursuits by heavy taxes and useless officers to consume their gainings.[17]

There is another aspect of the annual message which also indicates that Jefferson still remained partial to the moderate Republicans' course of conciliation in its broader sense if not in all its particulars. In November he sent copies of his message to Madison and Gallatin, requesting suggestions for changes. On their advice he dropped a strongly worded passage defending his earlier actions in dismissing cases arising under the Sedition Act and rejecting the right of any department of the government to determine the constitutionality of another department's acts. On the margin of the draft he noted that: "This whole paragraph was omitted as capable of being chicaned, and furnishing something to the opposition to make a handle of. It was thought better that the message should be clear of anything which the public might be made to misunderstand." [18]

Jefferson's reluctance to tamper with the Constitution may have been the main reason for his cautious attitude toward the federal court system, but he also had others. Even if he had requested that the tenure of the judges be changed from life to a limited number of years it is doubtful that he could have gotten the needed support for such an amendment. For although on strict party lines the Republicans dominated both houses of Congress, their majority was more apparent than real. The Federalists in Congress were a well-organized and cohesive minority, while the Republicans were a loosely knit coalition of different points of view. Partly this was because some Northern Republicans feared domination by the Southern wing of the party; and partly it was because of personal rivalries among certain important Republicans for the party's leadership; but mainly it was caused by a fundamental difference of opinion on how to go about limiting the Federalist party's influence in the judiciary. Roger Griswold, a Connecticut congressman, described the situation:

> The attack upon the Judiciary which had been so fully decided on before the Session commenced has not been moved nor can the faction agree upon the extent to which they will proceed —Giles & Company are decidedly of opinion that the Supreme Court should be swept away together with those created at the last Session, and this opinion they have openly declared in all companies but the violence of the project has alarmed many of their party, and excited suspicions which are not favourable to the repeal of the Law of the last Session—Although I cannot promise myself that these suspicions will be sufficiently strong to prevent the blow against that law, yet I am persuaded from the delay and other circumstances that they find the task more difficult than they expected—And I am not without hopes that if the business is suffered to rest a little longer that it will be defeated altogether in this or the other branch of the Legislature.[19]

With Republican congressmen so at odds among themselves the repeal of the Judiciary Act of 1801 might never have been initiated, were it not for an episode in the December term of the Supreme Court. Four justices of the peace of the District of Columbia whose commissions Jefferson had refused to deliver— William Marbury, Dennis Ramsay, Robert R. Hooe, and William Harper—decided to test the legality of the administration's decision by initiating an original suit by petition before the Supreme Court for writs of mandamus requiring Secretary of State James Madison to deliver the commissions. On December 17, Charles Lee, counsel for the appointees and the former Attorney General, presented a preliminary motion to the court for a ruling to require Madison to show cause why such writs should not be issued against him. Madison had been informed the preceding day that such a motion would be made, but had declined to appear, and Attorney General Levi Lincoln, who was in the court, replied that he had no instructions on the subject, thus leaving the proceedings to the discretion of the justices. After considering the request for a day, Chief Justice Marshall declared the opinion of the Court, which granted the motion and then assigned the fourth day of the next term for hearing the arguments on the question of whether the petitioners were entitled at law to the issue of a writ of mandamus.[20]

Why the Federalists chose this particular moment to try to force the administration to deliver the justices' commissions is to be understood only on the ground that they hoped a show of determination would deter the Republicans on the court issue before they could unite themselves. This attempt to intimidate the Republicans failed; in fact, it had the opposite effect. Most Republicans, not only the militant ones but also many moderates, viewed it as a bold usurpation of power on the part of the Supreme Court and an attempt to embarrass the President. The Federalists' action went a long way toward uniting their opponents' disparate congressional majority. "The conduct of the Judges on this occasion," wrote the Virginia Senator Stevens Thomas Mason, "has excited a very general indignation and will secure the repeal of the Judiciary Law of the last session about the propriety of which some of our Republican friends were hesitating." [21]

The Supreme Court's action had another equally important effect. It brought to the fore Jefferson himself, the only person capable of exerting enough pressure to form a workable coalition out of the jarring opinion groups that made up the Republican party. Up to this point the President had only reluctantly committed himself on judicial reform in his annual message, and he had remained silent as Republicans bickered among themselves about how to proceed against the national court system. But the mandamus case convinced him that there existed a real and immediate danger of judicial control over the acts of the executive. In fact on the very day that the Supreme Court delivered its ruling in the *Marbury* v. *Madison* case Jefferson angrily wrote that the Federalists "have retired into the Judiciary as a stronghold . . . and from that battery all the works of Republicanism are to be beaten down and erased." [22]

Jefferson's commitment to repeal of the Judiciary Act of 1801 was now total. He occupied himself with the duties and difficul-

ties of uniting his party's majority in Congress, and the movement for repeal became known as "the President's measure." It
was not long before many Federalists and even some Republicans
began to complain of executive influence in the legislative
branch. "There is no doubt in my mind," wrote one Federalist,
"that . . . at this moment, the Executive as completely rules
both Houses of Congress as Bonaparte rules the people of
France." [23]

III

The effect of Jefferson's efforts became apparent on January 4,
1802, when John Breckinridge of Kentucky announced in the
Senate that he planned to raise the question of the Judiciary Act
of 1801. Two days later, he moved for its repeal. Breckinridge
began his supporting speech by questioning whether there had
been a need for an increase in the size of the federal judiciary.
He maintained that suits in the federal courts were decreasing,
not increasing; that a rise in the number of judges was a needless
expense; and, in a veiled reference to the enlargement of the
jurisdiction of the federal courts in land suits under the act, he
argued that such subjects of litigation were more properly left to
the state courts. He next addressed himself to the constitutionality of the repeal. This was necessary because the Federalist press
in recent weeks had maintained that the Constitution guaranteed
to federal judges tenure of office during "good behaviour," and,
therefore, the office once established could not be abolished; for
if the legislature had the power to abolish a judge's office, it could
destroy the independence of the judiciary. Breckinridge pointed
out that according to the Constitution, Congress had a right to
establish inferior courts and so by extension had a right to
abolish them. He ended by pointing out, with delicate irony, that
if his construction was wrong, then the Judiciary Act of 1801
which abolished the former circuit courts was also unconstitutional and therefore especially repealable.[24]

This latter point, the arguments for which had been prepared
for Breckinridge by John Taylor of Caroline, indicated that
Federalist protests about the unconstitutionality of a repeal act

had been so effective that they had to be answered. Jefferson complained that "some Republican members generally sound, will have some questions on this subject, because they are afraid to distinguish between a fraudulent use of the Constitution, and a substantially honest adherence to it." [25] John Randolph described the congressional alignment in more specific terms. "Parties here," he wrote bitterly, "consist of the old Federalists courting popularity—they are a small minority. The same kind of characters republicanized and luke warm republicans, who added to the former will perhaps constitute a bare majority of the house—and republicans who hold the same principles now that they professed under adverse fortunes." [26]

From January 8 through January 19 the Senate, sitting as a committee of the whole, debated Breckinridge's motion. Over half the Senators present spoke, some twice. The debate revealed that both sides were vying for support from moderate Republicans. Occasionally the radical sentiments of the more militant Republicans burst forth, but for the most part they restrained themselves and limited their discussions to the technical question of whether the repeal was constitutional. The Federalist's strategy was to emphasize that the repeal act was an attack on the independence of the judiciary and to describe it as merely the first step in a plan to dismantle the Constitution. "If we can rein in the sensibilities of our folks, and persevere in the course we have taken," noted Rutledge, " 'twill be difficult for them to preserve union among themselves. . . . The fight over repeal is not now a contest between Federalists & Republicans, *as they call themselves,* but between the *'Virginia Party,'* & the friends of the Constitution." [27]

According to party labels the Republicans held an 18 to 14 edge in the Senate. Two members of the majority, Stephen R. Bradley of Vermont and John Armstrong of New York, had failed to appear, however. The former had been detained by his wife's illness, while the latter had resigned unexpectedly and his successor had not yet been chosen. This was temporarily offset by the fact that two Federalist senators, Aaron Ogden of New Jersey and James Ross of Pennsylvania, also had not arrived. But they were expected at any moment. Then if only one moderate were to bolt the Senate would be evenly divided, leaving the deciding vote in the hands of the Vice President, Aaron Burr.

The precariousness of the Republican majority became evident on 19 January, when Jonathan Dayton, Federalist senator from New Jersey and a good friend of Burr, attempted to amend Breckinridge's resolution by striking out the word "repealed" and adding the words "revised and amended." Just what kind of changes in the Judiciary Act of 1801 Dayton had in mind is not clear, but it is obvious that his motion was a bid for moderate support. This effort to derail the repeal measure was barely defeated, by a 15 to 13 vote; and then only after John E. Colhoun of South Carolina, a moderate Republican who had commercial connections in Charleston, and supposedly "had been tampered with," switched to the Federalist side.[28]

Alarmed by Colhoun's apostasy and the imminent arrival of Ogden and Ross, Breckinridge immediately moved for and obtained the appointment of a committee to bring in a bill for repeal. The bill which the committee reported rescinded the Judiciary Act of 1801 and restored the old one of 1789. Before the bill could be passed it had to be read and considered three times. Things went well enough during the first two readings, but by the time the bill came up for the third reading the two missing Federalists had arrived. Dayton then renewed his motion to return the bill to a committee to work out a compromise. When the Senate tied 15 to 15, Burr voted for recommittal, and the bill was returned to a select committee which the Federalists, with Colhoun's and Burr's support, dominated.[29]

The ostensible reason for Burr's vote was that he wished simply to give the proponents of compromise a fair hearing; but there was more to it than that. His vote had not come as a surprise to some Federalists. In fact several days before Dayton's first motion for recommitment Burr had discreetly informed Gouverneur Morris that he would support a compromise measure. The real cause for the Vice President's defection is to be found in his growing estrangement from the administration. Suspected by Jefferson of being personally involved in the intrigues surrounding the recent election, Burr had not only been excluded from all policy-making decisions but had seen his patronage recommendations rejected while those of his rivals were solicited.[30]

The months following the inauguration had been difficult ones for Burr. Because of his close connections with many Federalists he had little to offer the militant wing of the Republican party; and as long as the President followed a course of moderation, he was denied room for political maneuvering with the moderates, the wing of the party he had the most in common with. But Jefferson's support for the repeal act gave Burr his chance. If he could bring in an acceptable compromise measure, it would enhance his stature not only with moderates of his own party but also with Federalists, and perhaps even pave the way for the eventual formation of a third party under his leadership.

Burr's ambitions were based on a realistic appraisal of the political situation, for many Republicans had strong doubts about the constitutionality of the repeal. Describing the situation in Congress, one newspaper correspondent observed, "here the repeal is considered very generally amongst the best of the democrats as a direct violation of the Constitution, and indeed the thoughtful amongst them tremble at the excesses to which party rage is hurrying us." [31]

There were many Republicans, moreover, who, if they did not doubt the constitutionality of the repeal act, did doubt its efficacy. This became evident when Senator Ross of Pennsylvania presented a petition from the Philadelphia bar praising the circuit court system created in the Judiciary Act of 1801 as a valuable institution which could be abolished only to the public's detriment. Although members of both parties signed the memorial, the leadership for it came mainly from Republicans. Its sponsors included Sampson and Moses Levy, Peter Stephen Deponceau, all prominent lawyers, and Alexander J. Dallas, the federal District Attorney for eastern Pennsylvania, who had received his appointment from Jefferson and who sent a strongly worded letter supporting the petition. They also included Thomas McKean, Jr., state Attorney General, whose father, the Governor, was also reputed to have given his tacit support to those Republicans opposing repeal.[32]

Just what motivated these Republicans is made clear in a letter from Dallas to Burr. Dallas claimed to share with other Republicans their indignation both over the manner in which the Judiciary Act of 1801 had been passed, and over the partisan way appointments had been made under it. While he himself did not have any doubts about the constitutionality of the repeal, he did think it "impolitic and inexpedient." It was impolitic, he argued, because the people had strong feelings on judicial independence, and if they ascribed the repeal act to party animosity, "the hazzard or loss in public opinion is greater than the hope of gain." It was inexpedient because it would resurrect an inefficient federal court system which would deprive some states, and Pennsylvania in particular, of "tribunals which have been found highly advantageous to the dispatch of business. . . . In this state justice, as far as respects our state courts, is in a state of dissolution, from the excess of business and the parsimony of the legislature." [33]

Pennsylvania was not the only state where Republicans opposed or had doubts about repeal. Memorials similar to the one submitted by the Philadelphia bar were later received from New York and New Jersey. Many Republicans in South Carolina, especially those in Charleston, expressed concern about the constitutionality and expediency of abolishing the new circuit courts. In Tennessee, the governor brooded over the dilemma of the moderates in these terms:

> Divesting the question of all party considerations it appears to me a very difficult and disturbing question. To deny the power of destroying the office by repealing the law seems to encroach on the proper power of the Legislature, and the contrary opinion if frequently reduced to practice would seem to destroy the independence of the judges and cause them to depend for the tenure of their offices on the will (or caprice) of the Legislature.[34]

It is impossible to tell what would have happened to a compromise measure had it been introduced in the Senate, because, much to Jefferson's relief, Senator Bradley came down from Vermont before the committee reported. Immediately Breckinridge moved to have his bill released from the special committee, and although the Federalists vigorously opposed the motion, there was nothing they could do against what had now become a well-disciplined Republican majority. "I have not the smallest expectation of hope," wrote James Hillhouse, one of the Federalist Representatives from Connecticut, "that the vote of a single member will be changed by the most impressive eloquence, or arguments the most conclusive. All questions are settled in private meetings and every member composing the majority of both houses comes pledged to suport the measures so agreed on." [35]

On 13 February, after the third reading, the bill for the repeal of the Judiciary Act of 1801 passed the Senate, 16 to 15. Without delay the bill was sent to the House, where a select committee had already been appointed and awaited only the outcome in the Senate. The Republicans held a majority of nearly thirty members in the lower chamber, and in short order they disposed of a series of Federalist attempts to postpone consideration of the bill. On 15 February it was brought before the House, meeting as a committee of the whole. The debate, which one member described as "tedious and in many instances very desultory," lasted through the first of March. The highlight came during an impassioned and vindictive exchange between Giles and James Bayard, in which each summarized, in his own partisan way, the twelve years of Federalist rule. Actually, they added very little to the constitutional arguments already developed in the Senate.[36]

The House finally passed the Senate bill unamended on March 3, with three Republicans, William Eustis, Joseph Varnum, and Joseph Smith, all of Massachusetts, bolting in an unsuccessful attempt to recommit the bill. But the Administration's victory was not as easy as the 59 to 32 vote would suggest. Once again there had been considerable talk of a compromise measure, and though it came to nothing, its supporters were influential enough to cause the President to denounce them as "wayward freaks which now and then disturb operations." [37]

Moreover, there is abundant evidence that many moderate Republicans unwillingly supported the repeal bill. Over and over again the Federalists complained of executive management and private caucuses during which their potential converts were kept in line. "They [the moderate Republicans] openly cursed the measure," noted Bayard, "and if it had been possible for them to recede, they would have joyfully relinquished the project. But they had gone too far, and were obliged to go through." [38] And Gouverneur Morris told of a Republican member who wrote home "that if the question on the repeal were taken by Ballot, they would certainly lose it but by calling for the Yeas and Nays they could hold every man to the Point." [39]

IV

The repeal of the Judiciary Act of 1801 probably really satisfied no one in the Republican party. The radicals had wanted a more extreme measure, and they only supported the repeal act because it was the best they could get. For those Republicans who wanted to see more members of their party on the federal bench it also was second best, but they, too, supported the repeal act, although some of them may have had doubts about its constitutionality, because it was what the President wanted. They had no intention of alienating themselves from the main source of federal patronage. Besides even if they did not personally benefit from the repeal act, it did deprive their opponents of valuable and influential offices. As for the moderate Republicans, the repeal act had put them in a very difficult position. Most of them were against repeal, but they too did not want to desert the President on his first major piece of legislation. A few of them, Colhoun in the Senate and Eustis, Varnum, and Smith in the House, defected; a few did not vote; and some declined to speak in support of the measure, but voted for it.

But it was the President's experience which was the most painful. His actions toward the federal judiciary had been motivated more by defensive than aggressive considerations. At first he tried to avoid a major clash, and, when the mandamus case made this no longer possible, he supported the repeal act mainly because he felt it imperative to establish Congress's constitutional right to legislate the establishment and abolition of inferior courts. It is clear that Jefferson did not consider or intend the repeal of the Judiciary Act of 1801 to be the first step in an assault on the federal judicial establishment. What Congress had done, Jefferson wrote to a friend, was only to "restore our judiciary to what it was while justice & not federalism was its object." [40]

The politicking involved in the passage of the repeal act also speeded up the process of fragmentation which became inevitable when the Republican party achieved victory. Although these disruptive eddies started when the President announced his policy of conciliation, they did not become apparent until the judiciary debate forced them to the surface. "The ruling party begin to dislike each other," noted Gouverneur Morris, who also predicted that many Republicans would turn to the Federalist party.[41] This, of course, did not occur, but there was growing talk of forming a third party. "Cannot good moderate men," asked one disenchanted Republican, "form a party of Constitutionalists composed of true patriots who will avoid extremes—That alone is wanting to make all men contented as far as they can be. . . ." [42]

IV
Judicial Review

The Federalists, like the Republicans, emerged from the election of 1800 a deeply divided party. A schism had taken place during the final year of John Adams's administration, and this breach persisted into the nineteenth century, determining both the nature and direction of Federalist reaction to the Jeffersonian attack upon the judiciary.[1]

I

The High Federalists, the more uncompromising of the two wings which made up the party, had been followers of Alexander Hamilton during the 1790's. They represented the party's ultra-commercial and pro-British interests. Their understanding of society was drawn mainly from the elitist values of those who had governed colonial America. Committed to the belief that the men who owned the country should rule the country, they totally rejected the concept of equality and its political implications. George Cabot, for example, "held democracy in its natural operation to be *the government of the worst.*" [2]

The High Federalists, never really party men, were a coalition of strong-minded individuals with similar points of view. They abhorred the idea of appealing to the popular will. While they did not deny that government should be founded on the suffrage and consent of the people, they believed the influence of the majority was to be felt only at election time. After the votes were counted, the successful candidate was responsible only to his own conscience. "Why are we here?" Gouverneur Morris had asked during the debate on the repeal act, "To save the people from their most dangerous enemy, to save them from themselves." [3]

Moral absolutists, the High Federalists were the temperamental counterparts of the radical wing of the Republican party. They were unable to accept the fact that anyone who differed with their opinions could be motivated by anything but the basest of desires. There was nothing complex about the High Federalists' attitude toward Jefferson and his party: Republicans were the very incarnation of all that was evil, atheists and anarchists who were insanely in love with the French Revolution. The High Federalists refused any kind of accommodation with the Jefferson administration. "Public opinion must be addressed," wrote Fisher Ames,

> must be purified from the dangerous errors with which it is infected; and above all, must be roused from the prevailing apathy, the still more absurd and perilous trust in the moderation of the violent, and the tendency of revolution itself to liberty.[4]

It was part of the High Federalists' tragedy that they neither realized that their own view of Jefferson was merely a caricature of his true intentions nor understood the significance of the deep division that existed within the Republican party over the formulation of policy. Unwilling to pander to the masses, and out of touch with reality, they were doomed to extinction. Following Jefferson's election many of them quietly accepted their fate and retired from public life. But others, like Timothy Pickering, Uriah Tracy, Roger Griswold, and, most important of all, Samuel Chase, were determined to do what they could to obstruct the implementation of Republican policy.

More numerous and less extreme were the followers of John Adams. They blamed the uncompromising attitude of the High Federalists for the party's defeat in 1800. "We must have a new sort of leaders," wrote one, "They [the High Federalists] have had their day. They cannot be sufficiently accommodating. . . . Let us have men who can relax their principles of morality as occasion may require and adapt themselves to circumstances." [5]

The Adams Federalists were more realistic than the High Federalists in their attitude toward the Republican party. Adams and Jefferson had always liked each other, and for a short time in 1797 there had occurred a temporary union between them. This alliance had not worked out, but now that the election of 1800 was over, and animosity toward the High Federalists for withdrawing their support in the recent political contest persisted, some Adams Federalists began to indicate their willingness to support Jefferson if he followed a moderate course.[6]

The most important advocates of John Adams's brand of Federalism were John Quincy Adams, Caleb Strong, William Pinkney, and James Bayard. But it was to none of these that the ex-President's mantle of leadership fell. Rather, it went to John Marshall, the newly appointed Chief Justice of the Supreme Court.

Marshall was born in 1755 on a small farm in western Virginia, and throughout his life he retained the coarse earthiness of his pioneer upbringing. When independence was declared he enlisted in the army. Of the various influences in his formative years this was the most important, for it was then that he became the ardent nationalist he would always remain.[7] He commented on his Revolutionary War experiences in an autobiographical sketch many years later:

> I am disposed to ascribe my devotion to the union, and to a government competent to its preservation, at least as much to casual circumstances as to judgment. I had grown up at a time when love of union and resistance to the claims of Great Britain were the inseparable inmates of the same bosom;— when patriotism and a strong fellow feeling with our suffering fellow citizens of Boston were identical;—when the maxim united we stand, divided we fall was the maxim of every orthodox American; and I had imbibed these sentiments so thoroughly that they Constituted a part of my being. I carried them with me into the army where I found myself associated with brave men from different states who were risking life and

everything valuable in a common cause believed by all to be most precious; and where I was confirmed in the habit of considering America as my country, and congress as my government.[8]

After leaving the army Marshall studied law. Before long he had hung out his shingle in the rapidly growing city of Richmond, and quickly established himself as an important member of the Virginia bar. He then entered politics, and from 1782 to 1788 he was a member of the state legislature. Here he fell in with the group which, under the leadership of Madison, helped bring about the ratification of the Constitution by the Old Dominion. Thus far, Marshall's career was not unlike any other rising young lawyer and politician in Virginia, but, during the 1790's, as nearly all of the Virginia nationalists went into the Republican party, Marshall resolutely remained a Federalist. And being a successful Federalist in the Old Dominion during the 1790's was no easy matter. It was at this time that Marshall developed and refined the technique of vigorously leading and espousing a minority viewpoint without becoming an extremist or alienating the majority. The High Federalist Theodore Sedgwick wrote a penetrating appraisal that does justice not only to Marshall's skill as a politician, but also to his influence over others:

> He has a strong attachment to popularity but indisposed to sacrifice to it his integrity; hence it is that he is disposed on all popular subjects to feel the public pulse and hence results indecision and an expression of doubts. Doubts suggested by him create in more feeble minds those which are irremovable.[9]

Marshall's ability to feel the public pulse served him well in the spring of 1799, when he became a successful candidate for Congress. During the campaign he was openly critical of Timothy Pickering's pro-British foreign policy and condemned the Alien and Sedition Acts. As a member of the sixth Congress he continued to act cautiously, defending Adams's decision to send a second peace mission to France and joining the Republicans to kill James Ross's controversial election bill.[10] These actions did not endear him to the High Federalists. "False Federalists, or such as act wrong from false fears, should be dealt hardly by," wrote

Fisher Ames. "The moderates are the meanest of cowards, the falsest of hypocrites." [11]

Adams's designation of Marshall to the Chief Justiceship in January 1801 was bitterly resented by the Hamiltonians, who wanted the position to go to William Paterson.[12] In fact the opposition of the High Federalists in the Senate was so strong that they seriously considered refusing to confirm his nomination. Only when they realized they could not induce Adams to change his mind, and that the only alternative to confirming Marshall was allowing Jefferson to fill the vacant position with a Republican, did they grudgingly accept his appointment.[13]

Although there was some mild criticism of Marshall's appointment in the press, the Republicans were, for the most part, indifferent to his promotion. Marshall was a respected Virginia lawyer, but he was not considered a major political figure or a dangerous political thinker. He had his enemies, and among them was Thomas Jefferson, but all that is known about the cause of their mutual dislike is apocryphal and their differences appear to have been based more on temperament and personality than on principles. The more radical Republicans did not like Marshall, but he shared many of the values of Madison's brand of national republicanism. Certainly he had little use for the self-righteousness which so distinguished the High Federalists.[14]

II

The repeal of the Judiciary Act of 1801 had been given a grim reception by the Federalist press. "The fatal bill has passed. Our Constitution is no more," announced one paper in a widely republished editorial; while another termed it "the death wound of our glorious Constitution." [15] Support for such an exaggerated view came from the most important High Federalists in and out of Congress. Typical was Roger Griswold's warning that repeal was merely the first step of a "faction determined at all events to destroy the Independence of the Judiciary & bring all the powers of Govn't into the House of Representatives . . . & a scene of administration must follow similar to the most violent under the French Revolution." [16]

Convinced that the Republicans planned to overturn the

Constitution, the High Federalists, during the debate over the repeal of the Judiciary Act of 1801, had frequently warned that the Supreme Court would declare such an act unconstitutional. The pending case of *Marbury* v. *Madison* was on the mind of every representative and senator, and it was frequently dragged into the discussion. For while the mandamus question had initially appeared simply as a contest between the judiciary and the executive, it had now taken on larger significance.[17]

Again and again in the course of the debate the Federalists insisted upon the power of the Supreme Court to declare acts of Congress unconstitutional. They argued that only this power vested in an independent judiciary could secure the country from a tyrannical legislature. Else, what was to prevent that body from passing laws contrary to the Constitution? Usually they argued the case for judicial review in abstract or historical terms, but sometimes it became concrete and immediate, as when Samuel Dana of Connecticut threatened that if the Republicans should pass the repeal act, the Supreme Court would annul it.[18]

The Republicans responded that if the judges of the Supreme Court possessed this power they could interfere with the machinery of the government whenever they wished, and they could become complete despots, oppressing the country at will. Judges, the Republicans argued, were not men whose characters were elevated beyond that of the rest of mankind, for in too many instances in the preceding decade judges had been motivated by party interest. The true check upon the acts of Congress was not the judiciary, but the state legislatures and the people themselves. These arguments usually concluded with the warning that if the repeal act were declared unconstitutional, impeachment of the justices of the Supreme Court was sure to follow.[19]

Controversy over the passage of the repeal act further increased the tension between extremists in the two parties. Several Republicans urged an immediate showdown with the Supreme Court in order to settle the question once and for all. Caesar Rodney, for example, assured the President that "there is no terror in their [Federalist] threats. Let them marshall themselves under the judges when they please; we are prepared to meet them." Republican threats were answered by counter-threats, with a number of Federalists going so far as to predict that if the Republican assault on the judiciary succeeded, secession and armed resistance would be the only recourse.[20]

Circumstances also appeared to reinforce the collision course of the two parties. The repeal act was not to take effect until the first of July, while the Judiciary Act of 1801 had changed the terms of the Supreme Court from February and August to December and June. This meant that the June meeting of the Supreme Court would be held while the atmosphere in the capitol was still hyper-tense; and the judges would not only be given a chance to proceed further with the mandamus question, but would also have the opportunity to consider the constitutionality of the repeal act before it became operative.

This was just the kind of explosive situation that Jefferson desperately wanted to avoid. On 18 March 1802 a special Senate commitee was appointed to re-examine the federal court system and recommend any necessary changes. Within a week it reported a bill whose singular feature was the abolition of the new June and December terms, and the immediate restoration of the old February term, but not the August one. The effect of this was that the Supreme Court would be adjourned from December 1801 to February 1803.[21]

This legislation, which passed the Senate on 8 April, was a skillful maneuver to deny the Supreme Court an opportunity to overturn the repeal act before it went into effect. It was recognized as such by the Federalists. "I fear now," wrote William Cranch, "that the judges . . . will act weakly." In the House, Bayard warned that the bill would establish a dangerous precedent. The effect of the bill, he pointed out, would be to suspend any meeting of the Supreme Court for fourteen months, and if this were possible what was to prevent a further suspension, with the ultimate result that the Court would be virtually abolished. He then concluded with a taunt, asking the Republicans if they were afraid that the Court would pronounce the repealing law void.[22]

Radical Republicans were also critical of the law. In a long letter to Jefferson, Monroe expressed his concern that postponement of the Supreme Court's meeting would be interpreted to mean that the administration was afraid of a direct confrontation on the repeal act. If repeal was right, and Monroe had no doubt that it was, what was there to be afraid of? Besides, he added, it probably was impossible to avoid a collision with the Supreme Court; and anyway, he suggested, "the best way to prevent one is to take a bold attitude and apparently invite it." This strategy, he continued, would have the additional benefit of bringing the moderate Republicans into line:

> The mild republican course of your administration has tended to put at repose the republicans, and relieve from further apprehension the federalists. In such a state of things the former have little motive for exertion. Having overthrown their adversaries they think it beneath their character to pursue them further. Many from the habit of activity they had acquired, from independence of spirit, rivalry or other cause, begin to separate from each other and even criticize the measures of reform that are proposed. But should the federalists rally under the judiciary and threaten anything serious it is presumable that republicans will revive from their lethargy and resume their former tone.[23]

But Jefferson, it is clear, had had enough of party warfare, and despite radical pressure and Federalist denunciation the bill passed the House on April 23 and became law three days later when he signed it.[24]

III

Denied the possibility of having the repeal law declared unconstitutional by the Supreme Court at its June term, the High Federalists decided upon a more immediate form of opposition. At a secret caucus of congressmen in Washington, they decided to ask the justices of the Supreme Court to refuse to perform the duty of circuit judges which the repeal act reimposed on them. If the Justices were to agree to this, the High Federalists would have the circuit judges created under the Judiciary Act of 1801 hold the circuit court sessions. Thus they would completely vitiate the repeal act.[25]

All that was required was the co-operation of the Supreme

Court justices. Both Samuel Chase and Marshall were approached with the plan, and they communicated it to the other justices. Chase suggested the desirability of a group conference in Washington, but also indicated his willingness to go along with the scheme. "I believe a Day of severe trial is fast approaching for the friends of the Constitution, and we I fear must be principal actors and may be sufferers therein. . . ." [26] Two weeks later, in a second letter, he supported the plan even more vigorously. He argued that the repeal act was unconstitutional and that only by impeachment could the already appointed circuit judges be deprived of their positions; therefore the Supreme Court justices ought to refuse to act as circuit judges. He conceded, however, that this was a decision to be made not by a single justice but by the Court as a whole. "The burthen of deciding so momentous a question, and under the present circumstances of our country, would be very great on all the Judges assembled, but an individual judge declining to take a circuit must sink under it." [27]

Marshall was more circumspect and less sympathetic to the plan. He pointed out that if the question were new, he would be unwilling to act in the character of a circuit judge, but since the justices had acquiesced in such duties under the Judiciary Act of 1789, he felt himself bound by the legislature's decision.[28] In another letter, while agreeing to abide by the decision of the other justices, he emphasized the gravity of the decision to be made. "This is [a] subject not to be lightly resolved on. The consequences of refusing to carry the law into effect may be very serious." [29] Then, a short time later, he expressed an even stronger opposition to the proposal when he took the position that the question respecting the constitutional right of the justices to sit as circuit judges had been settled and should not be introduced. "I have no doubt myself but that policy dictates this decision to us all. . . . I owe I shall be privately gratified if such should be the opinion of the majority & I shall with much pleasure acquiesce in it." [30]

As three of the other justices, William Paterson, Bushrod Washington, and William Cushing, accepted Marshall's recommendation, it was agreed to hold the circuit courts as scheduled.[31] The High Federalists were furious, but they apparently expected as much, for they correctly laid the blame on the Chief Justice. "I am neither surprised nor disappointed for it accords with my idea of the Judge," commented Gouverneur Morris.[32]

The High Federalists, however, were determined to get their way, and at a special meeting, attended by Morris, Griswold and Ogden, it was agreed "that the business must not stop there." [33] With the aid of the dispossessed circuit judges they planned to make a major political issue out of the constitutionality of the repeal act and eventually maneuver the Supreme Court Justices into the embarrassing position of having, in their official capacity, either to acknowledge or to denounce Congress' right to tamper with the federal judiciary.

Their plan consisted of three parts. The first was the publication of a widely reprinted pamphlet entitled *The Solemn Protest of the Honorable Judge Bassett*. The author, one of Adams's midnight appointees and the father-in-law of James A. Bayard, the House minority leader, claimed to be speaking not only for himself but for many of the other circuit judges as well. In a long, tedious, and often convoluted rehashing of the old arguments against the repeal act, the pamphlet called upon the Chief Justice and his associates to refuse to perform their circuit duties and to declare the repeal act unconstitutional. The second part of the High Federalists' plan was to have the circuit judges, under the leadership of Oliver Wolcott, petition Congress for a redress of grievances. This, the High Federalists believed, would serve to give them another opportunity to exploit Republican divisions on the subject. Finally, preparations were made to introduce a number of test cases into the circuit courts so that they could be carried up to the Supreme Court in time for its February meeting.[34]

The High Federalists were in for a rude shock, however, for Marshall and the other justices had no intention of backing down from their privately expressed opinions on the constitutionality of the repeal act. Because of this, a number of brief but intense encounters occurred between some of the justices and the High Federalists during the fall circuit term.

The first incident took place on September 18 in Hartford, Connecticut, after Bushrod Washington and Richard Law, the district judge, arrived to open the circuit court. Almost immediately, Roger Griswold, in two actions continued from the April term, entered a plea on behalf of the defendants denying the authority of the court to try the two cases. The substance of Griswold's argument was that the suits had been instituted in the circuit courts created by the Judiciary Act of 1801, and since the commissions of those judges had not been constitutionally vacated, that court still existed, and it was only there that the two continued cases were legally cognizable. The judges immediately denied the plea and ordered the docket to be called, but, finding no business ready for trial, adjourned.[35]

A similar incident took place a short time later when the first circuit court, presided over by William Cushing and John Davis, met in Boston. In this case it was Theophilus Parsons who raised the question of the constitutionality of the court, whereupon the judges temporarily suspended the pending actions and referred the question to the next day. During the intervening twenty-four hours, the judges apparently made it clear how they planned to rule on the matter, for when the court reconvened, Parsons, "very much mortified," abandoned his plea and business was carried on as usual.[36]

An even more determined effort was made on 2 December 1802, when the fifth circuit court, under the direction of Marshall himself, met in Richmond. This time Charles Lee, representing the defendant in a case known as *Stuart* v. *Laird,* denied the legitimacy of the court. In addition to repeating the same arguments as Griswold and Parsons had used in objecting to Congress' prerogative to transfer a cause from one inferior tribunal to another, he also questioned its authority to impose circuit court duties upon the Supreme Court justices. Marshall dismissed both these arguments as being insufficient and found for the plaintiff. Lee then appealed the decision to the Supreme Court on a writ of error.[37] It is doubtful that he had any real hopes for a reversal. A full six weeks before the scheduled meeting of the high tribunal, William Plumer reported that it was common knowledge that the Court would confirm the Chief Justice's ruling.[38]

These setbacks in the courtroom left the High Federalists completely demoralized, "It shows," wrote George Cabot, "how little dependence there is, even on good men to support our system of policy and government." [39] The High Federalists' situation was going from bad to worse. In Vermont, for example, an attempt to obtain support from the leading members of the bar to plead against the jurisdiction of the circuit court held by the Supreme Court justices was coldly rebuffed.[40] And when the High Federalists tried to lessen the political effects of the justices' intransigence by having the Federalist press ignore the circuit courts' activities, the effort only brought jeers from the Republican press. The Boston *Independent Chronicle,* for example, asked: "How has it happened that no *federal* paper has noticed the Circuit Court sitting in this town . . . which in happier times the *Centinel* [the leading Federalist newspaper in Boston] was so flippant with to enliven the spirits of its followers? . . . —Federalism must be ashamed of its own impostures, and shame is one sign of repentance." [41]

The hopelessness of the High Federalists' cause became still more apparent when, after Congress convened in December 1802, two more of their attempts to make political capital out of the judiciary issue were defeated. The first took the form of a memorial from the circuit judges, requesting that Congress assign their case to a judicial tribunal in order to determine whether their rights had been violated. The second was in connection with the pending case of *Marbury* v. *Madison.* Under the necessity of proving indisputably that their appointments had actually been made, Marbury, Hooe, and Ramsay petitioned Congress for an official transcript of the dates on which President Adams had nominated them and when the Senate consented. Republicans in Congress denounced both of these motions, the former as an attack on Congress and the latter as an infringement of the executive's rights. The main significance of the debate was that not only did the Republicans easily defeat these motions, but that they did so without the internal bickering that had marked the debate on the repeal act.[42]

Nor was there any sympathy among Republicans for the High Federalists' effort to have the repeal act declared unconstitutional. The moderate Republican position was clearly put by "True Federalist" in the *National Intelligencer:*

What have the republican administration done? They have restored the old and long established mode of administering justice. . . . The restoration of the old system has been pronounced unconstitutional. . . . But the charge would never have been made but from party animosity, from the hope of gaining party advantage by working on the prejudices of the people. . . . The majority have spoken in the audible language of a law, and the minority must obey. Such is the nature of our government. It is the only despotic feature it contains. The important subject then stands thus. The republicans have restored with but little variation, what the federalists formed. . . . *They might have done much more.* Had their object been to frustrate the administration of justice, they might have repealed many, nay, most of the material provisions of the judicial code. *They have not repealed one.*[43]

The final blow to the High Federalists' hopes was delivered by the Supreme Court itself when it met for its February 1803 term. The two most important cases then pending directly affected the judiciary struggle, and they were both decided in a manner favorable to the Republicans. The Court's decision in *Stuart* v. *Laird* was predictable, for it simply confirmed the justices' earlier views. Marshall, who excused himself from the case because he had ruled upon it in the lower court, could only have been pleased with Paterson's opinion, which upheld his decision and concluded with a stern warning that "the question is at rest and ought not now to be disturbed." [44]

The meaning of the Supreme Court's ruling in *Marbury* v. *Madison* is less easily understood. Because of the singular impact which the concept of judicial review has had on the development of American institutions, the significance of its origins has been misinterpreted and overdramatized.[45]

The main reason for the Republicans' opposition to the case when first initiated was that they viewed it as an attack on the executive's prerogative by the Supreme Court. Therefore, even though Marshall, in his opinion, delivered an extended lecture on the rights of Marbury and the other justices to their commissions, the Republicans were relieved when he admitted that it was not in the Court's jurisdiction to issue a writ of mandamus. This explains why the decision, when viewed in the context of the judiciary struggle during Jefferson's first administration, is best understood primarily as another defeat for the High Federalist cause.[46]

When Marshall's opinion was announced, it received very little criticism from even the most partisan of the Republican newspapers. The little hostility that did exist, moreover, was directed not at the Court's right to decide on the constitutionality of a law, but at the Chief Justice's stigmatization of the President as a violator of the laws he was sworn to uphold. The indications are that few Republicans were prepared to deny the right of the Supreme Court to review for itself an act of Congress.[47]

Certainly Jefferson in 1803 had no wish to deny it. In the passage deleted from his first message to Congress in December, 1801, Jefferson made it clear that he believed each branch of the government had the right to decide for itself the constitutionality of matters before it. What he would have objected to, and what Marshall did not assert, was a claim that the power of review was solely within the Supreme Court's province, or that the Court's judgment was superior to that of the other branches.[48] This is not to say that Jefferson was entirely pleased with the outcome of the case or that he did not eventually change his mind about the meaning of the decision. But in the spring of 1803 his irritation was directed at the Chief Justice's *obiter dictum* on the rights of federal appointees, and he neither challenged nor condemned the Court's exercise of judicial review. Only after Marshall tried to subpoena him during the Burr trial did Jefferson's hostility to the Court as an institution become overt, and it was not until long after he had given up the responsibilities of the presidency that he made his most extreme statements on the judiciary.[49]

The Court's decision also received little attention from the Federalist press. Praise for it was markedly restrained, and what little there was did not make an issue of Marshall's view of the right of the Court to declare an act of Congress unconstitutional but centered rather on the Chief Justice's rebuke of the President's handling of the undelivered commissions. Most of the papers, as a matter of fact, simply ignored the outcome of the case.[50]

As for Marshall, there are some indications that he had serious doubts about the political expediency of hearing the motion in the first place, and it is clear that his main concern when he delivered the opinion in *Marbury* v. *Madison* was to avoid a direct confrontation with the executive department. The surprising thing is that he went as far as he did in accusing the President of dereliction of duty. But the Chief Justice was an experienced politician, and he probably realized that Jefferson, preoccupied as he was with the diplomatic intricacies of the Louisiana Purchase and with the clashing interests within the Republican party, was not likely to get into a fight over a lecture that had no practical meaning. Besides, it must be remembered that the decision was on the whole conciliatory, demonstrating that the Supreme Court would not allow itself to be a tool for partisan purposes. The *Washington Federalist,* which was sometimes referred to as Marshall's paper, editorialized:

> There has not been wanting men even on the floor of Congress, base enough to make the most unwarranted insinuations against the Justices of the Supreme Court. They have called this application for a mandamus, *their* measure—instigated and supported by them as an hostile attack upon the Executive, to gratify party spirit, and increase their own power. Let such men read this opinion and blush, if the power of blushing still remains with them. It will remain as a monument of the wisdom, impartiality and independence of the Supreme Court, long after the name of its petty revilers shall have sunk into oblivion.[51]

Not only was the Chief Justice's decision consistent with his own disposition toward moderation, but it also made good political sense. There can be little doubt that if Marshall had ordered the mandamus delivered it would have precipitated a political crisis. Six weeks earlier the House had appointed a special committee to consider changes in the judicial system, and while *Marbury* v. *Madison* was being argued the following warning was prepared for publication in an important Republican paper: "The efforts of Federalism to exalt the Judiciary over the Executive and Legislature and to give that favorite department a political character & influence . . . will probably terminate in the degradation and disgrace of the judiciary." [52]

The High Federalists, of course, believed that the Republicans were so divided on the judiciary issue that they would not be able to take a united stand. As usual, their estimation of the situation was wrong. Although most moderate Republicans had expressed serious doubts about the wisdom of tampering with the court system, they also viewed the repeal act as a *fait accompli* and had no intention of deserting the President. For example, one representative, who had only reluctantly voted for the repeal act, warned that should it be declared unconstitutional it would be repassed as an amendment to the Constitution.[53]

V

Impeachments

Aside from the administration's resolve to stand firm on the repeal act there are no indications, in the winter of 1802–03, that it had any intention of further assaulting the judicial establishment, despite continued pressure from radical Republicans. As long as the Federalists accepted the repeal act and refrained from using the court for partisan purposes, the administration was willing to allow the issue of Federalist control of the national judiciary to remain dormant. The two Supreme Court decisions—*Stuart v. Laird* and *Marbury* v. *Madison*—prepared the way for such a *modus vivendi;* and it might well have come to pass were it not for certain events in New Hampshire which revived the issue and gave radical Republicans and High Federalists an opportunity to confront one another.

I

John Pickering had been one of the most distinguished members of New Hampshire's revolutionary generation, and he was respected and admired throughout the state. He was the author of its elitist constitution, which was established in 1784. Few men in New Hampshire were more erudite in the ways of the law, and in 1791 Pickering was appointed Chief Justice of the state's always inefficient and often inequitable court system. It was hoped that he would bring about the needed reforms, but sickness and a nervous disorder forced him to ignore his duties, and the court situation grew worse. Consequently, only three years after his appointment there was widespread demand for his dismissal. An attempt to remove him became entangled in the party battles of the 1790's, and failed by one vote in the New Hampshire House of Representatives. At this juncture an opening occurred in the federal court system, and the state's leading Federalists, looking for an easy solution to a difficult problem, persuaded Washington to appoint Pickering judge of the federal district court of New Hampshire.[1]

For a while Pickering successfully carried out the duties of a district judge, but then his condition developed into insanity and he became an alcoholic. So incapable was he of performing his duties that the Federalists themselves had to take drastic action. They made use of a provision in the Judiciary Act of 1801 which allowed the circuit judges to appoint one of their own number to discharge the duties of an incapacitated district judge. Then, in one of the ironies of history, the Republicans, through the repeal act, inadvertently forced Pickering to resume his position.[2]

Pickering's antics during the case *U.S.* v. *Eliza* attracted the administration's attention. The ship *Eliza* had been seized for violation of revenue laws, and the owner appealed to the district court for its release. Because the owner and his attorney were prominent Federalists, and the arresting officer and the district attorney were Republicans, the case immediately took on a political complexion. Pickering found for the claimant, and, when the district attorney pointed out that the judge had not yet heard the witnesses for the government side, Pickering is said to have jeered, "You may bring forty thousand & they will not alter the decree." According to witnesses this occurred while the intoxicated judge ranted, raved, and shouted profanities.[3]

The only provision in the Constitution for a judge's removal is "impeachment for, and Conviction of, Treason, Bribery or other high Crimes and Misdemeanors."[4] Pickering, although hopelessly insane, fit into none of those categories, and the Constitution does not provide for removal of a federal judge whose disabilities, while not warranting impeachment, nevertheless rendered him unfit to perform his duties. It probably would have been best for all had Pickering resigned, but unfortunately neither the demented judge nor his family would agree to this. The administration, in the person of Albert Gallatin, then approached William Plumer, one of New Hampshire's Federalist senators, and suggested that, unless Pickering resigned, it would be forced to take stern measures.[5]

Plumer had both political and personal reasons for his refusal to co-operate with the administration to pressure Pickering into resigning. For one thing, Plumer had just arrived in Washington as a freshman senator, and he shared the High Federalists' belief that the administration was plotting to overturn the Constitution. He believed they had already started by repealing the Judiciary Act of 1801, and to allow them to force a judge to give up his office would weaken the independence of the judiciary still further. Also, if Pickering resigned, his successor in all likelihood would be District Attorney John Samuel Sherburne, who was not only a Republican but also Plumer's personal enemy. Finally, Pickering was an old friend whom he was unwilling to desert in his time of need.[6]

On 4 February 1803 Jefferson sent the evidence against Pickering, along with a message, "to the House of Representatives, to whom the Constitution has confided a power of instituting proceedings of redress if they shall be of opinion that the case calls for them." This was what the radical wing of the Republican party had been waiting for, and less than a month later the House voted to impeach Pickering. The trial before the Senate, which Pickering was expected to attend, was not scheduled until the following session.[7]

Although Jefferson was now determined to see Pickering removed, there is every indication that he had turned to impeachment reluctantly and only as a last resort. Only two months before he had written to his good friend Thomas Cooper that "the path we have to pursue is so quiet that we have nothing scarcely to propose to our Legislature. A noiseless course, not meddling with the affairs of others, unattractive of notice, is a mark that society is going on in happiness." [8] Moreover, shortly after Jefferson sent his message to Congress he complained to Plumer that "it will take two years to try this impeachment. The Constitution ought to be altered so that the President should be authorized to remove a Judge from office, on the address of the two Houses of Congress." [9] And again, just before the trial began, he confided that, "This business of removing Judges by impeachment is a bungling way." [10]

II

The trial itself, which took place during the first two weeks of March 1804, raised a knotty problem for the Republicans. Pickering's insanity was common knowledge, but if this were admitted as evidence, they would be put in the intolerable situation of arguing either that a lunatic was accountable for his actions, or that a man mentally incompetent was guilty of "high crimes and misdemeanors." Thus, the Republicans were forced into the difficult position of claiming that Pickering was in his right mind. This did not please the moderate Republicans, among whom there was considerable reluctance about convicting a mental incompetent. "Some of our democrats feel uneasy," wrote Plumer. "They do not wish to act either as the accuser or judges of a madman; but one of my brother Senators told me he was resolved *not* to believe Pickering insane; but if the facts alledged [sic] in the impeachments were proved to remove him from office. This is the case with several of them. But still they feel embarrassed [and] fear to meet the shaft of ridicule, should the accused attend, the trial would be farcical indeed!" [11]

Pickering did not attend the trial. Instead, his son requested Robert Goodloe Harper, a well-know Federalist lawyer and former congressman from South Carolina, to appear and establish the judge's insanity. Immediately, John Randolph, Joseph Hooper Nicholson, and Caesar A. Rodney, the House managers in charge of the prosecution, argued that the testimony should not be heard. The Senate then retired to discuss the question as a committee of the whole. The debate that followed lasted three days. Those Republicans who had already decided on Pickering's removal made "the most perservering and determined opposition . . .

against hearing evidence and counsel to prove the man insane." The Federalists, of course, were equally determined to have the evidence admitted, which they believed if proved, would prevent any further proceedings. Meanwhile the uneasiness of the moderate Republicans increased. "The dilemma is," observed John Quincy Adams, "between the determination to remove the man on IMPEACHMENT *for high crimes and misdemeanors,* though he be insane, and the fear that the evidence of this insanity, and the argument of counsel on its legal operation, will affect the popularity of the measure." [12] When the final vote was taken nine Republicans bolted, helping to form an eighteen-to-twelve majority in favor of hearing Harper's testimony.[13]

The House managers immediately denounced the decision, and even withdrew from the proceedings. But it was all to no avail, as Harper was permitted to present his evidence. This consisted of depositions and extracts of court records which attested to Pickering's demented condition. Harper concluded with a plea against regarding insanity as criminal and asked that the trial be indefinitely postponed.[14] Once again the moderate Republicans were faced with a choice between unsatisfactory alternatives. While reluctant to convict an insane man, they also were unwilling to leave him in his current position.

At this point it appears that considerable pressure was exerted upon them by the administration, for without debate they voted to continue the trial, and witnesses for the prosecution were called. Adams commented that it "had evidently been settled by the members of the ruling party out of Court." [15]

The trial now took on a strongly partisan character. All the witnesses for the prosecution were Republicans, most of them federal officeholders who had received their appointments from Jefferson, and two of them stood to benefit directly from Pickering's removal. With no defense attorney present to cross-examine, there was little to restrain their testimony. After the prosecution presented its case, Plumer and the other New Hampshire senator, Simon Olcott, also a Federalist, gave further evidence of Pickering's insanity and tried once again to obtain a postponement of the trial but failed in this when a motion to pronounce judgment passed by a vote of twenty to nine.[16]

A short debate ensued on the form in which the final vote on Pickering's guilt would be taken. The Federalists proposed that the question be asked: "Is John Pickering, district judge of the district of New Hampshire, guilty of high crimes and misdemeanors upon the charges contained in the ———— article of impeachment, or not guilty?" The Republicans rejected this and adopted a less specific form: "Is John Pickering, district judge of the district of New Hampshire, guilty as charged in the ———— article of impeachment exhibited against him by the House of Representatives?" The decision to put the question in this way undoubtedly was made to ameliorate evident disquietude about convicting an insane man.[17]

Only twenty-six of a possible thirty-four senators participated in the final vote. One of the missing eight, Pierce Butler (R-S.C.) had left Washington for personal reasons long before the vote was taken. Seven others, David Stone (R-N.C.), John Brown (R-Ky.), Stephen Bradley (R-Vt.), John Armstrong (R-N.Y.), John Condit (R-N.J.), Samuel White (F-Del.), and Jonathan Dayton (F-N.J.), were present for the entire session and appear to have absented themselves deliberately from the final vote on Pickering.[18] Of those who remained to pronounce judgment it is by no means clear how many did so according to their own consciences. "If several of the Senators," observed Timothy Pickering, "were left to decide the question individually, their conscience would give way; but when a number of consciences are *joined together* they will bear much rough usage without being rent." [19] And John Quincy Adams was "certain several voted with extreme reluctance, and by a sacrifice of their own judgments to the domineering dictates of the managers from the House." [20] There was no crossing of party lines on the vote: nineteen Republicans pronounced Pickering guilty on every charge; seven Federalists voted for his acquittal. Although two-thirds of the senators present found against him, their nineteen votes represented only the barest possible majority of the entire Senate.[21]

The partisan and contradictory manner in which the trial was conducted has prevented the Pickering impeachment from ever being considered a strong precedent for anything. Yet its short-term political consequences were quite significant. Pickering was the first federal judge to be successfully impeached and convicted. Because of the special circumstances under which Pickering had violated the trust of his office, because the Federalist would not co-operate in obtaining his resignation, and because neither the Constitution nor the existing laws provided an adequate remedy, the administration was forced into the uncomfortable position of giving a very liberal definition to the clause of the Constitution which defined impeachable offenses. Plumer wrote, "the process of impeachment is to be considered in effect as a *mode of removal*, and not as a charge and conviction of high crimes and misdedemeanors." [22] What this meant for the radicals had become evident even before Pickering's trial began, for as Timothy Pickering reported:

> John Randolph says that the provision in the Constitution, that the judges shall hold their offices *during good behavior* was intended to guard them against the *executive* alone, and not by any means to control the power of Congress, on whose representation against the judges the President should remove them.[23]

Remarks such as these only served to strengthen the conviction of the High Federalists that the Republicans were engaged in a well-organized and determined campaign to establish their control over the federal judiciary. Capable of seeing only the most insidious intentions behind the administration's dealings with the judiciary, the High Federalists were aroused even more by Pickering's impeachment than they had been by the repeal of the Judiciary Act of 1801.[24] "If a considerable majority of the House were to impeach any man in the United States he would by the Senate be found guilty; because there could be no doubt that these measures originate with the administration, are made questions of party, and therefore at all events to be carried into effect according to the prime mover," wrote one angry New England senator.[25]

III

This view was more than confirmed when, on the very same day that the Senate voted Pickering guilty, the House passed a resolution, introduced by John Randolph, for the impeachment of Samuel Chase.[26]

Few members of the revolutionary generation were more bitterly partisan or more controversial than Chase. A prominent and militant proponent of colonial rights in the Maryland legislature during the 1760's, he had signed the Declaration of Independence and served as an active member of the Continental Congress between 1775–78. His congressional career was suddenly cut short in 1778, when Alexander Hamilton denounced him for using privileged information to speculate in the flour market. Chase returned to Baltimore, where he continued to speculate in mercantile and land ventures, practiced law, rebuilt his political reputation, and became an influential Anti-Federalist leader.[27]

In 1788 Chase was made a judge of the Court of Oyer and Terminer, and in 1791 he became Chief Justice of the General Court as well. Chase was an overbearing man, little concerned with the rights and feelings of others, and he had a stormy career on the bench. In 1794 a Baltimore Grand Jury issued a presentment against Chase charging that he had abused his authority by censuring a sheriff and by not summoning a proper jury. It also accused him of violating the state's Bill of Rights by holding more than one judicial appointment. Although nothing came of these charges, they are indicative of the strong feelings which his personality engendered.[28]

After the ratification of the Constitution, for reasons that are obscure, Chase became an ardent Federalist. A hard worker, willing to fight uncompromisingly for his beliefs, his turbulent disposition made him an ally who often proved more of a liability than an asset. Perhaps it was for just this reason that James McHenry recommended Chase for a position on the federal bench in 1795. President Washington was at first wary about nominating him, but when he had trouble filling a vacancy on the Supreme Court he offered the position to Chase, who accepted. It was an unpopular choice, even with the Federalists, and the Senate, uneasy about Chase's cantankerous nature, only reluctantly confirmed his appointment.[29]

In the years immediately following Chase's promotion to the nation's highest tribunal, he conducted himself well and delivered several influential and learned decisions. But at the same time he was becoming increasingly aroused by vitriolic Republican attacks upon the Adams administration, until, finally, when he made his circuit ride in 1800, his partisan nature got the better of him.

The first trial was that of an English emigrant, Thomas Cooper, who was the editor of a rural Republican newspaper in Pennsylvania. Cooper had been indicted under the Sedition Act for publishing an article attacking Adams and his supporters. For the most part Chase conducted the trial fairly, but when the time came for him to charge the jury, he lost his self-control. He began by expressing complete agreement with the prosecution and then went on to bring out points that the district attorney had failed to develop in his attempt to prove Cooper's guilt. Chase's charge made it inevitable that the jury should find Cooper guilty. When it did Chase fined him the limit the law allowed and sentenced him to six months in prison.[30]

Chase's animosity toward the Republicans became even more apparent at the second trial of John Fries, a minor militia officer who had led a group of angry Pennsylvania Germans in a rebellion against the federal tax collector. Arrested and tried for treason, Fries had originally been convicted and sentenced to death; but it was discovered that one of the jury had expressed a bias before the hearing, which resulted in the new trial at which Chase presided. The political implications of the trial were clear, and the Republicans obtained for Fries's defense the services of William Lewis and Alexander J. Dallas, two leading members of the Philadelphia bar. Lewis and Dallas were willing to concede the facts of the case but planned to argue that the facts did not come under the legal definition of treason, which was the charge against Fries. Shortly after the jury was impaneled, however, Chase handed down a written ruling which confined the defense to the facts. Infuriated, Lewis and Dallas denounced the decision and withdrew from the trial. Apparently Chase had misgivings about the fairness of what he had done, for the next day he offered to rescind his ruling. But Lewis and Dallas refused to continue, arguing that the jury had already heard the judge's opinion. This left Fries without counsel and he was again convicted and sentenced to death.[31]

Even more spectacular were Chase's activities in the sedition trial of James Callender, who was perhaps the most scurrilous newspaperman America has ever known. The Judge, familiar with Callender's abusive harangues, had repeatedly expressed in public his desire to see him convicted. Moreover, Chase considered the trial a personal test of strength because it was being held in Richmond, where the leading members of the Virginia bar practiced, and the Virginia bar was openly critical of the Sedition Act. Three of these lawyers, Philip Norborne Nicholas, William Writ, and George Hay, had rallied to Callenders' defense, and Chase arrived in Richmond determined to teach them a lesson. The multitude who packed the courtroom to see the already famous partisan in action did not leave disappointed. Chase began by forcing an allegedly hostile juror to serve. He followed this by ordering the defense to reduce to writing the questions they planned to ask their key witness, John Taylor of Caroline. After the defense lawyers had complied with this order, Chase then refused to allow Taylor to testify. Finally, he interrupted, badgered, and insulted the defense counsel so often that they abandoned the case. Convicted, Callender was sentenced to pay a fine of two hundred dollars and to serve nine months in prison.[32]

From Richmond, Chase proceeded to Newcastle, Delaware, where he addressed a grand jury which had returned no indictments under the Sedition Act. The Judge declared that there was a treasonable paper being published at Wilmington and ordered the United States attorney to search the paper's files. The jurors, anxious to return to their work, asked to be discharged, but Chase refused their request. He was forced to release them the next day, however, when the federal prosecutor reported that his investigation had revealed nothing seditious. Following as it did his earlier activities, this episode did not go unobserved by the Judge's enemies.[33]

By 1801 Chase had made himself the most hated member of the federal judiciary. Republican newspapers throughout the country characterized his actions as those of a "hanging judge," an American Jeffreys. One newspaper described him as "a character notorious for his enmity to Republican government, a man whose hostility to the cause of liberty will ensure to him never ending hatred." [34] His activities were repudiated even by the moderate Federalists. Adams, running for re-election in 1800, considered Chase's vigorous attachment to the party a liability, and he underscored his feeling by pardoning Fries.[35]

Yet, despite the popular groundswell against Chase and the desire of radical Republicans for impeachment proceedings, Jefferson, after becoming President, adopted a cautious attitude toward the Judge. This was part of his larger policy to establish a live-and-let live arrangement with the judiciary, and it implied the administration's willingness to forget past excesses in return for good behavior in the future. In fact Jefferson almost said as much in the summer of 1802, when he congratulated Cyrus Griffin, the district judge who had served with Chase in the Callender trial, for no longer being among those who "have lent their influence to the promotion of a certain set of principles disapproved . . . by the great majority of our citizens." [36]

Chase, however, increasingly bitter, adopted the hard line policy of the High Federalists and totally rejected any kind of accommodation with the administration. "There can be no union between the Heads of the two Parties," he wrote. "Confidence is destroyed; if attempted they will be branded as *Deserters*, and lose all Influence. Things must take their natural Course, from *bad* to *worse*." [37]

Less than two months later, on 2 May 1803, Chase delivered his charge to the federal grand jury in Baltimore, a charge that was soon to be famous. It was a tirade against Republican legislation on both the national and state levels.

> The late alteration of the Federal judiciary by the abolition of the office of the sixteen circuit judges, and the recent change in our state Constitution by the establishing of universal suffrage, and the further alteration that is contemplated in our State judiciary (if adopted) will in my judgment take away all

security for property and personal liberty. The independence
of the national judiciary is already shaken to its foundation,
and the virtue of the people alone can restore it. . . . Our
Republican Constitution will sink into a mobocracy,—the
worst of all possible government . . . the modern doctrines
by our late reformers, that all men in a state of society are
entitled to enjoy equal liberty and equal rights, have brought
this mighty mischief upon us; and I fear that it will rapidly
progress until peace and order, freedom and property, shall be
destroyed.[38]

Chase's charge was published in a Baltimore newspaper, and
an outraged Republican member of the Maryland legislature sent
a copy to Jefferson. The President might have ignored the charge
had it not followed Marshall's lecture in the Mandamus case and
Plumer's refusal to accept a reasonable solution to the Pickering
problem. As it was, Jefferson reacted immediately. He wrote to
Joseph Hooper Nicholson, asking, "Ought the seditious and
official attack on the principles of our Constitution and of a
State to go unpunished? And to whom so pointedly as yourself
will the public look for the necessary measures?" Because Republican conversations about Chase almost always turned to impeachment, and because Nicholson had definite Old Republican
sympathies and was one of the leading managers of the proceedings against Pickering, there can be no doubt that the President
was giving his consent to having Chase removed. It appears that
Jefferson expected the impeachment of Chase to be hazardous
politically, for he added, significantly, "for myself, it is better that
I should not interfere." [39]

Evidently Nicholson also had his doubts about the expediency
of attacking Chase, for he requested the opinion of the Speaker
of the House, Nathaniel Macon. Macon indicated his own dislike for the Judge, but pointed out that since Nicholson would
probably be appointed to the Supreme Court if Chase were convicted, it would be impolitic for him to prosecute. He then questioned the legitimacy of impeaching Chase for his political opinions. Thinking, undoubtedly, of the increasing number of
Republicans using the state benches for partisan purposes, he
warned, "it deserves the most serious consideration before a single

step be taken. Change the scene and suppose Chase had stretched as far on the other side, and had praised where no praise was deserving, would it be proper to impeach, because by such conduct he might lull the people to sleep while their interest was destroyed?" The tone of the letter suggests that Macon thought it might be well to ignore the episode.[40]

What followed is not entirely clear. Throughout the spring and summer of 1803, the Republican press, led by the *National Intelligencer*, assailed Chase, but no official action was taken. In the fall and early winter, the difficulties of the Louisiana legislation preoccupied the administration and Congress. Then, suddenly, on 5 January 1804, John Randolph rose in the House and demanded an investigation of Chase's conduct. Only after three days of debate and the extension of the investigation of Chase to encompass the activities of Richard Peters, district judge of Pennsylvania, did the House pass the motion. The inclusion of Peters, made at the request of Pennsylvania's militant Republicans, was designed to discredit him, but no one seriously expected his impeachment. The committee, headed by Randolph, reported its findings on 6 March. It cleared Peters, but recommended impeachment proceedings against Chase. Five days later the report was approved by a vote of 73 to 32.[41]

This achieved, Randolph announced that the requisite articles of impeachment would be presented to the House before it adjourned. As one of the prosecuting managers in the Pickering trial, Randolph knew of the reluctance of many moderate Republicans to accept any theory of impeachment other than the narrow one defined in the Constitution. If the radicals had had this problem in the case of a lunatic district judge, who had only barely been convicted, what could be expected at the trial of a Supreme Court justice, who would not only be present to defend himself, but in all probability would do it very ably?

At this point, Randolph made a fateful decision: he would convict Chase as a criminal. On 26 March he placed before the House seven articles of impeachment which he himself had drawn up. The first two articles covered the Judge's rulings in the Fries case, the next three his rulings in the Callender case, the sixth his refusal to discharge the grand jury at Newcastle, and the seventh his charge to the grand jury at Baltimore. The House failed to act upon these articles, however, and so they were not submitted to the Senate.[42]

Meanwhile, Chase, though publicly silent, was busy. He appointed Robert Goodloe Harper his chief counsel, and between them they began to solicit the aid of the most distinguished Federalist lawyers in the country. "Fees, of course," wrote Harper, "are out of the question."

> If you concur with me in opinion, that this is a great public cause, in which the honour of the federal party, the independence of the judiciary, and even the personal safety of the judges are involved, you will require no further motives for uniting with those who place themselves in the breach, and endeavor to resist the terror which threatens us with ruin.

Those approached by Chase and Harper included Alexander Hamilton, James A. Bayard, Joseph Hopkinson, Philip Barton Key, Charles Lee, Philip Wickham, and Luther Martin. Together, it was expected, they would undertake the task of collecting evidence for the Judge's defense.[43]

Chase, never an easy opponent, was under these circumstances formidable. True, he had acted with partiality in the courtroom. Richard Peters, for example, admitted that he "never sat with him without pain, as he was forever getting into some intemperate and unnecessary squabble." [44] But it was one thing to accuse a Supreme Court justice of excessive partisanship, and another to convict him of criminal behavior. A difficult task in itself, there were other circumstances that rendered it an impossible one.

VI
Republican Divisions

For four years Jefferson had skillfully prevented a deep, factional division in the Republican party. But the Chase impeachment, which brought to a culmination the Jeffersonian attack upon the judiciary, also helped to bring into the open the breach in the Republican party. Surprisingly, however, the man who was most responsible for this was not Chase or even Jefferson, but a Republican congressman from Virginia, John Randolph of Roanoke.

I

Randolph had entered politics at the age of twenty-five. Elected as a representative to the Sixth Congress, no one was more committed to the Jeffersonian ideals of agrarianism, economy, and states' rights, or more opposed to the Federalists' preoccupation with military preparedness and the alliance between government and the mercantile community that they had fostered during the 1790's. Randolph supported Jefferson in the election of 1800. He did so, however, not out of any personal attachment, but because he saw in Jefferson a means to substantial reform. "I am not," he wrote, "like some of our party who are as much devoted to him as the feds were to Gen'l Washington. I am not a monarchist in any sense. If our salvation depends on a single man 'tis not worth our attention—If he is unqualifiedly necessary to our political existence what is to be done when he is dead?" [1]

Even before Jefferson's inauguration, Randolph had expressed doubts about the President's ability to effect meaningful reforms. He was particularly concerned because Jefferson had received the support of many "whose Republicanism has not been the most unequivocal. There are men who do right from wrong motives, if indeed it can be morally right to act with evil views." [2] Along with other advocates of radical change Randolph watched with growing consternation as Jefferson implemented his policy of conciliation. They were especially disturbed at the President's unwillingness to sweep Federalists from office. Other administration measures, like the repeal of the Judiciary Act of 1801, the abolition of internal taxes, and the slashing of the military budget, while real enough, scarcely penetrated the periphery of the Federalist system. Most of Hamilton's financial measures remained intact, and nothing substantial had been done to initiate constitutional reform. By 1803 Randolph was bemoaning the influence of moderate Republicans and stressing the need for a return to principle. The following year he wrote to James Monroe:

> our political adversaries have dropped all open opposition, expecting (nor is the hope by any means desperate) that we shall dissolve in our weakness. In truth after deducting from our number those who are influenced by local or *personal* views we cease to be a majority at least I fear so.[3]

Despite his hostility to administration policies, Randolph's influence in Congress grew between 1801 and 1804. Though he was a skilled parliamentarian, he also owed much of his rise to circumstance. During the 1790's, first Madison and then Gallatin had led the party in the House, but now both were members of the cabinet. Their departure left a power vacuum in the Seventh Congress, and Randolph, William Branch Giles, and Samuel Smith competed for the position of majority leader. Randolph had a strong ally in Nathaniel Macon, who, as Speaker of the House, selected him to head the powerful Ways and Means Committee. His influence increased even further when his chief opponents, Smith and Giles, were elected to the Senate in 1803.[4]

Jefferson, however, showed little confidence in Randolph. In the spring of 1802 he called on Giles to defend the repeal act, and in December of that year he urged Caesar A. Rodney to run for Congress, stressing the need for capable leadership. When irritated by Chase's charge to the Baltimore grand jury, the President turned to Nicholson, not Randolph, with his clandestine request for action.[5]

Randolph was temperamentally unfit for the give and take required of a majority leader. His fanatical commitment to the twin doctrines of states' rights and agrarianism caused him to show contempt for all who disagreed with him. "His insolent haughty overbearing disposition know no bounds," commented one observer.[6] His first open break with the administration took place on the kind of government to be established in the Louisiana territory.[7] According to William Plumer,

> Several of the leading Democrats differed from him in opinion, & considered his opposition as imprudent—& the debate was by many of the party considered as a mere question respecting his personal influence—& they with great spirit resolved to show their independence & voted against him—. . . . Some of the democrats in the hearing of federalists said that *Randolph was assuming & very arrogant & that they hated him.* His manners are far from conciliating. Many of the party dislike him —& on trifling measures they quarrel with him, but on all measures that are really important to the party they unite with him. He is *necessary* to them—they know it—he knows it—& they dare not discard him. These frequent quarrels may eventually sour their minds against him, & prevent a reunion—A few of them consider themselves as *personally* injured by him, they will probably never *cordially* unite with him—but at present, with the majority of them its like the bickerings of lovers who contend but afterwards unite with greater zeal.[8]

The President watched Randolph's behavior with growing concern. To DeWitt Clinton, Jefferson confided the fear that "our leading friends are not yet sufficiently aware of the necessity of accommodation and mutual sacrifice of opinion for conducting a numerous assembly." [9] When the first session of the Eighth Congress met in October of 1803, the President's sons-in-law, John W. Eppes and Thomas Mann Randolph, were present as new members. Both quickly became active spokesmen for the administration, and by the end of November John Randolph was becoming concerned about his own influence in Congress. Either unwilling to compromise or incapable of it, he found himself estranged from the Republican majority on several issues. He wrote to the President explaining his position. Jefferson's reply was neither candid nor reassuring. Disclaiming control over the actions of his sons-in-law, and denying any desire to influence Congress, he concluded with a statement that experience had taught him "the reasonableness of mutual sacrifices of opinion among those who are to act together for any common object, and the expediency of doing what good we can when we cannot do all we would wish." [10]

There is every indication that Randolph's loss of prestige spurred his decision to move an inquiry into Chase's conduct. One congressman, Samuel Taggart of Massachusetts, suggested that Randolph, "apprehensive his influence was in the decline," may have tried to increase his leverage in Congress and at the same time force the administration into a more radical course by taking the initiative against the Judge. When the motion was made there was some opposition in the House by Republicans who argued that a committee of inquiry should not be appointed until the charges against Chase were made public. These dissenting Republicans, Samuel Mitchill and John Smith of New York, James Mott of New Jersey, and James Elliott of Vermont, voted against the motion. In the Senate, John Armstrong and Stephen Bradley spoke openly against it.[11]

There is no evidence to indicate that Randolph made his motion either at the request or with the consent of the President. Jefferson may still have wanted Chase removed, but it is doubtful that he would have wished Randolph to have the credit for it. Seven of Randolph's eight articles of impeachment concerned complicated legal questions, and only one referred to Jefferson's original reason for suggesting action against Chase: his charge to the grand jury at Baltimore. Still, in January 1804 the antagonism of most Republicans toward Chase was greater than it was toward Randolph, and the Republicans, albeit reluctantly, passed the motion.

II

Even though Jefferson received the enthusiastic and unqualified backing of his entire party in his bid for a second term, Republican divisions nevertheless became more pronounced in 1804. In Virginia the radicals began a movement aimed at preventing the arch-moderate, James Madison, from succeeding Jefferson as President in 1808, and the moderates in Congress made an unsuccessful attempt to replace Nathaniel Macon with Joseph B. Varnum as Speaker of the House.[12]

The issue that divided the party most deeply, however, was the Yazoo compromise. This problem dated back to 1795, when a corrupt Georgia legislature had been bribed by land speculators to sell to them, for a penny and a half an acre, over 35 million acres of Indian land in the Yazoo territory (what is today Alabama and Mississippi). The following year a reform-minded legislature, elected by an irate citizenry, rescinded the act authorizing the sale. Unfortunately, in the intervening time much of the land had been resold to Northern speculators, most of whom had no knowledge of the fraud involved and many of whom had resold the land to parties even further removed from the original contract. The federal government became involved in 1798 when it disputed Georgia's jurisdiction over the Yazoo territory. This dispute ended in 1802 when the state relinquished all claim to the western land. Georgia's cession, however, provided that the national government assume the responsibility of satisfying the claims of innocent second, third, and fourth party purchasers of Yazoo land. To accomplish this, Jefferson appointed a special commission, which included among its members Madison, Gallatin, and Levi Lincoln. The commission found against the claimants, but for reasons of "tranquility," and because of "equitable considerations," strongly recommended "a compromise on reasonable terms." It suggested that the federal government set aside five million acres of land to be used to satisfy the claimants and to bring the matter to a satisfactory solution.[13]

When the commission presented its report to the House in February 1804, Randolph immediately rose to oppose it. He attacked the committee's recommendations with a combination of states rights' and moral arguments, and, in a series of eight resolutions, affirmed the right of the Georgia legislature to repeal the corrupt bargain of 1795. He denounced the proposed settlement, arguing that the original act was so evil that any compromise with it was out of the question. Although not adopted, his resolutions garnered considerable support, and Randolph succeeded in preventing the House from legislating. Further action was postponed until the following session.[14]

Randolph's opposition to the Yazoo compromise was a frontal attack upon the administration. He argued openly that honoring a fraudulent contract was no different from trading upon government influence, which Republicans claimed had taken place under Hamilton's financial plan. As the commission was headed by three cabinet members, he was in effect accusing the administration of repudiating the principles upon which it had been elected. Randolph was also determined that those Republican congressmen who had failed to support his resolutions should not go unscathed. He publicly denounced them, and almost precipitated a duel with one of them, Joseph Alston of North Carolina, when he threw a glass of wine in his face during a private argument over the issue.[15]

The political implications of Randolph's opposition were great. New England speculators benefited most from the compromise, and the representatives and senators from that section supported the commission's recommendations almost to a man. The administration's ardent support for a compromise measure reflected the growing importance of the New England interest in the Republican party. The party's rapid growth in the area east of the Hudson river since 1800 was to a certain extent a consequence of the division that developed within the Federalist party, but to an even larger extent it was a result of the administration's deliberate cultivation of the New England interest in order to achieve national unity.

In the spring of 1804 there still remained considerable cause for concern about New England's political future. Rumor had it that disunionist sentiment was rife throughout the section. This proved to be more apparent than real, however, and some Federalist leaders, realizing that they could not get sufficient popular support for secession, attempted to enter in to an alliance with Aaron Burr. The Vice President, who was neither trusted nor well liked by Federalist politicians, was popular with the voters, and even more important, he appeared to be receptive to the Federalists' plans. Burr had not been renominated for the vice presidency, and his only hope for a political comeback was to win the New York gubernatorial election. For this he needed both Republican and Federalist support. Burr never committed himself to separation, but he did privately guarantee that if elected he would administer the state in a manner satisfactory to the Federalists. A shrewd politician, Burr had realized for some years that an open break in the Republican party was pending, and this was yet another attempt on his part to create a third force of Federalists and moderate Republicans which he hoped would follow his leadership.[16]

In this fluid political situation, those Republicans associated with the administration were in great danger. Failure to deliver on the Yazoo compromise could cost them dearly. If the radicals should become strong enough to control policy, their actions would increase Burr's chances by cutting the middle ground out from under the administration. From neither side could the administration expect much succor. Somehow, it had to eliminate both Burr and Randolph from positions of political leadership. This, of course, would be a difficult task, yet behind all the maneuvering that followed lay the deep conviction among administration moderates that an accommodation with New England was necessary—not only for national unity but also for their own future control of the Republican party. Postmaster Gideon Granger, one of the administration's top political strategists, expressed this clearly in a letter to DeWitt Clinton on the upcoming New York gubernatorial election:

> The political balance of your state is to be decided by western counties who are principally Yankees, and who if I mistake not

will go with New England whenever her citizens are agreed
among themselves. And if measures less violent & more congenial with the principles of the government than some which
have been proposed in Congress are not pursued I do not
hesitate to say three years will not pass away before the six
eastern states will be united and they will take with them New
Jersey. When this is done they will want but *four* in the Senate
& fourteen in the House to form a majority. Indeed there is no
doubt all things considered that the strength of the nation this
day is East of the Delaware. In addition to this we are to take
into consideration the new relations of things west of the
Mountains. Before the late treaty [Louisiana Purchase] the
great weight of the western people was safety, now it is prosperity.—When they look abroad to the various states in the
Union, they must perceive that they cannot derive any aid
from the Atlantic States South of the Susquehannah—Neither,
Merchants, Capital, Carriers, purchasers, artists, mechanicks,
nor indeed settlers (unless indeed some little in Baltimore)—
while with that whole Section they come into competition are
becoming rather rivals than friends. This sentiment will grow
and rest assured the period is not remote when a strong political union will be formed between the states east of the Delaware and west of the mountains. It is founded in nature. It
cannot be successfully resisted.—It is owing to these considerations that I have such extreme anxiety on the subject of a
junction.—between the Eastern people.—Nor do I hesitate
to say, tho I may be in an error when that Junction takes place
the foundation is laid to produce a new state of politics.[17]

As it turned out, the elimination of Burr proved to be a
relatively simple matter. Morgan Lewis, a moderate Republican,
was nominated to oppose him in the New York gubernatorial
election. This effectively split the Republican vote and, combined with Alexander Hamilton's opposition within the Federalist party, cost Burr the election.[18] But the problem of Randolph
still remained. By the summer of 1804 he had proven himself a
more dangerous enemy of the administration than Samuel Chase,
and his political future in large part rested upon the Judge's
conviction.

III

Because of Chase's impending trial, the second session of the Eighth Congress began a month early on 5 November. Randolph immediately secured a select committee, which he himself headed, to prepare a final draft of the articles of impeachment. The committee reported on 4 December, with eight articles in place of Randolph's original seven. In addition to some consolidation, two new articles significantly altered the nature of the proceedings. The original articles had been exclusively directed at Chase's alleged criminal behavior. The new ones, articles six and seven, accused him of mistakes in procedure during Callender's trial. If a conviction could be obtained on this ground, it would serve as a precedent for the removal of any judge who made an error in the courtroom.[19]

We can only speculate as to why Randolph abandoned his earlier decision to convict Chase solely as a criminal. In effect, he was returning to his initial claim that impeachment did not necessarily have to mean criminal behavior, a claim strongly supported by Giles in the Senate. Perhaps Randolph realized, after examining the evidence, that the case against the Judge was not as strong as he had supposed. Perhaps, since he was determined to break with the administration, he hoped to use the trial as a springboard from which to attack the other Supreme Court justices. Apparently enough Republicans were willing to give him the rope to hang himself, for the House accepted the articles and selected seven managers to prosecute the impeachment. These were John Randolph, Joseph H. Nicholson, Caesar A. Rodney, George Washington Campbell, Peter Early, John Boyle, and Christopher Clark. It also determined upon 2 January, 1805 as the day for Chase to answer the charges against him.[20]

Meanwhile Randolph continued to go his own way. On a number of minor bills brought before the House, he returned to first principles and broke with the administration. In each case the Republican majority politely listened to Randolph's arguments, which were similar to those used by the Jeffersonians against the Federalists during the previous decade, and then quietly passed the pending legislation over his objections.[21]

The moderate Republicans were also active, though more secretively. Now that Burr was no longer a political threat he could be a useful ally in the difficult task of eliminating Randolph. As Vice President, he would preside at the trial, determining procedure and ruling on questionable points. He also had a small personal following in the Senate. Of the thirty-four senators, there were twenty-five Republicans. Twenty-three votes were needed to convict Chase. It was a foregone conclusion that all nine Federalists would vote not guilty as a bloc, making only three Republican defections necessary to bring about an acquittal. Such a verdict would seriously weaken Randolph's position. Of course this meant that Chase would remain on the bench, but he was getting old, and, with Marshall as Chief Justice, it was clear that Chase's influence on the Court was not what it once was.

Shortly before the trial the administration began to cultivate the Vice President. One Federalist noted: "Mr. Jefferson has shown more attention & invited Mr. Burr oftener to his house within this three weeks than ever he did in the course of the same time before. Mr. Gallatin, the Secretary of the Treasury, has waited upon him often at his [Burr's] lodgings—& on one day was closeted with him more than two hours. The Secretary of State, Mr. Madison, formerly the intimate friend of General Hamilton, has taken his murderer into his carriage and rode with him. . . . The Democrats of both Houses are remarkably attentive to Burr." [22]

Those Republicans who were determined to see Chase convicted knew what was happening, and they too attempted to secure the Vice President's favor. A petition was circulated among the senators, requesting that Governor Bloomfield of New Jersey enter a *nolle prosequi* on the indictment found against Burr by the Bergen County grand jury for killing Hamilton. Duane took up Burr's defense in the *Aurora*. Pressure was put on Burr's supporters. Giles, for example, cornered Israel Smith and spent a long time elaborating on Chase's guilt. But the radicals were at a disadvantage, for they did not have as much to offer Burr as the administration, which controlled patronage, did.[23]

Throughout all this Chase quietly continued to prepare his defense. He realized that the increasing internal tension within

the Republican party was working in his favor. "I gain everything by Delay and can only lose by haste," he wrote.[24] In
accordance with this strategy, when Chase appeared before the
Senate on 2 January 1805, to answer the charges against him, he
requested a postponement until the following session. Burr, a
skillful lawyer himself, took this occasion to use his position as
President of the Senate to badger and embarrass the Judge. The
Vice President was apparently making it known that his influence
could be decisive. The Senate agreed to give Chase an extra
month, until 4 February, to finish preparing his defense.[25]

A month was all Chase needed, for on 29 January 1805 the
Yazoo issue came up again in the House. The claimants had
retained Postmaster General Gideon Granger to act as their
agent. Randolph, who had an enormous capacity for indignation,
could not be contained. He ferociously denounced Granger and
demanded his resignation. He imputed to the administration all
kinds of corrupt motives and private deals behind the compromise. "It is the spirit of Federalism," he shrieked. "He lashed
demos & feds indiscriminately," one observer noted. "He treated
no man that was opposed to him with either respect or decency." [26]

With this last tirade, the master of Roanoke crossed the Rubi-
con. Up to this point most Republican members of the House,
while privately expressing their dislike for Randolph, had swal-
lowed their pride and had generally accepted his leadership, but
this was no longer to be so. One Federalist Representative wrote
to a friend that Randolph had "resigned his office of ruling the
majority in Congress, for the substantial reason that he finds they
will no longer be ruled by him. . . . One thing is certain the
party at present seem broken and divided, and do not act with
their usual concert." [27] Randolph was denounced in the House
by James Jackson of Virginia, Erastus Root of New York, Matthew Lyon, now of Kentucky, and James Elliot, who had won
re-election in Vermont as a Republican on an anti-Randolph
platform. "I never witnessed so much rage & indignation in a
deliberative assembly before," commented Plumer.[28]

The significance of all this was clearly recognized by Samuel
Taggart, who wrote:

The unanimity of the majority is broken. They do not act with their former unanimity. Their leaders have lost their overbearing influence. The Samson Randolph is shorn of his locks, and as to any overbearing influence in the House is become as weak as another man. Indeed, I believe for him to be very zealous in support of a question, would be a very ready way to loose it if the decision was confined exclusively to the Democratic party. Such is the derangement of the party that I believe no man in it could introduce a subject into the House and make any certain calculations of carrying it merely as a party question. . . . I believe for six or seven weeks, the Federalists have been in the majority on more questions than in the minority.[29]

Despite all this Randolph remained a formidable opponent. Given his determination to attack the administration, his decision to make an issue of the Yazoo compromise was a wise one. There may have been resentment over the intemperate and arrogant manner in which he castigated his opponents, but a majority of Republicans thought his opposition was essentially right. His motion to repudiate the compromise was only barely defeated: 63 to 58. Since the motion was unanimously opposed by the Federalists, this meant that more Republicans voted for it than against it. In fact Randolph's stand was so popular in Virginia that ten out of twelve of the Old Dominion's Representatives, including the President's two sons-in-law, broke with the administration and supported the motion rather than risk the chance of not being re-elected.[30]

On the Chase impeachment, however, Randolph was more vulnerable. Those of the Judge's friends who were away from Washington and unaware of the significance of Randolph's split with the administration despaired for his future, but those closer to the scene were more sanguine. They realized that a number of Republicans, motivated in varying proportions by a genuine fear for the independence of the judiciary and by a desire to embarrass Randolph, were inclined to vote for acquittal. In addition to the Burrites, there were two new senators from New York, John Smith and Samuel Mitchill, both of whom as members of the House had opposed Randolph's original motion for an inquiry into Chase's conduct. Also mentioned were Robert Wright and Samuel Smith of Maryland, William Cocke and Joseph Anderson of Tennessee, and David Stone of North Carolina.[31] Wright's attitude, in particular, was an indication of what the final outcome would be, for, as John Quincy Adams wrote in connection with another issue, his opinions "answer the purpose of the vane on a steeple; they show which way the wind blows."[32]

VII
Chase's Acquittal

The trial began on 4 February, a cold and dreary day. Aaron Burr had been given exclusive power to make the necessary preparations. Like most Americans he looked to England for precedents, and was especially influenced by the recent proceedings against Warren Hastings. As a result the Senate Chamber looked more like a theater than a court room. Burr had his own chair placed in the center and against a wall. At each side benches, covered by bright red cloths, were extended to seat the senators. Directly in front of them were two enclosed areas. The House managers occupied one, Chase and his battery of lawyers the other. Behind the senators, in three rows of tiered benches, draped with green cloth, sat the representatives. Above, in specially built semicircular galleries, also covered with green cloth, sat the rest of officialdom. Further back, and open to the public, was the permanent gallery. Over a thousand spectators were present. The Senate, commented Uriah Tracy, was "now fitted up in a style beyond anything which has ever appeared in this country." [1]

I

The first day was devoted solely to the presentation of the Judge's answer to the charges against him. It consisted of a long and detailed analysis of each article of impeachment. In less capable hands the reply could have been a protracted bore, but as it had been prepared by some of the best lawyers in the country, it was not. Morover the audience was receptive. Many of the senators were themselves lawyers, and almost all were capable of appreciating the technical legal arguments involved.

Chase's answer at once revealed the defense's strategy—to deny that any of his actions were indictable offenses under either statute or common law. He questioned the merit and legal fitness of the articles of impeachment which accused him of misconduct in the trials of Fries and Callender by raising a number of complicated, very subtle, and even moot legal questions, such as the binding quality of local customs, the reciprocal rights and duties of the judge, jury, and defense counsel, the legality of bad manners in a court room, the rules of submitting evidence, and the problems of criminal intent. He denied outright that the procedural mistakes he had made at the Callender trial were impeachable offenses as defined by the Constitution. To the articles which accused him of misconduct in charging a grand jury and in refusing to release it at Newcastle, Delaware in June 1800, Chase replied that he only did his duty by directing it to investigate an alleged offense, and that he dismissed its members when they refused to make any presentments or indictments. Finally, to the article which accused him of misconduct in charging a grand jury at Baltimore in May 1803, he denied making any seditious statements, and gave a brief history of jury charges to demonstrate that he acted according to custom. He concluded by defending his right as a citizen to speak on political topics.[2]

Chase may have been nobody's favorite, but he also was nobody's fool. It was an impressive performance. At his best, as on the articles accusing him of procedural mistakes in the Callender trial, the judge demolished the charges against him. At his worst, as on the articles accusing him of misconduct in the Fries and especially the Callender trial and for delivering a partisan charge to the grand jury at Baltimore, Chase's defense was at least as good as the case the prosecution made against him. Throughout the trial, Chase effectively referred to the failure of the prosecution also to impeach the district judges, Richard Peters, Cyrus

Griffin, and Gunning Bedford, who had presided with him at the different trials, and who had concurred with his actions. Although he never said it directly, he implied that he was being tried for his political convictions.

II

Several days of adjournment followed, during which the House submitted a replication to Chase's answer, and the expected witnesses for both sides began appearing. When the court reconvened on 9 February, all the managers and the full complement of Chase's defense counsel were present. It included Robert Goodloe Harper, Joseph Hopkinson, Philip Barton Key, Luther Martin, and Charles Lee.[3]

The trial began in earnest when Randolph rose to speak. Since he had written the articles of impeachment, it was natural to expect him to refute the arguments made against them. Under the right conditions Randolph could be a moving and persuasive speaker. But against the cold legal logic of Chase's reply his primarily emotional appeal fell flat and his legal naïveté became all too apparent. "This speech is the most feeble—the most incorrect that I ever heard him make," commented one senator.[4]

From this point on, the case for the prosecution continued to deteriorate. An attempt to discredit Chase's explanation of what had happened at the trial of John Fries proved unsuccessful. Lewis and Dallas, while defending their own actions at the trial, proved unwilling to support the charges against Chase. Other witnesses also failed to substantiate Randolph's claims. In fact, the defense forced Edward Tilghman, an established Philadelphia lawyer, to admit that while Chase may have been precipitous in submitting a written opinion when he did, his doing so broke no law.[5]

A detailed examination of the Callender trial followed next. George May's testimony substantiated the charges against Chase, but his unwillingness to answer the defense's questions, and his undisguised hostility to the Judge, destroyed much of its value. His testimony was followed by that of John Taylor, Philip N. Nicholas, John Thompson Mason, and John Heath. They all substantiated what everybody already knew: Chase was capable of hasty judgment. But they contributed no proof of willful criminal behavior on his part. An additional witness, John Tripplett, testified that before the trial began Chase had expressed a desire to see Callender convicted. He refused to recant under a gruelling cross-examination by Harper, and this proved to be the only bright spot in the prosecution's otherwise unsuccessful attempt to document its case.[6]

Randolph also failed to establish the other charges against Chase. Eyewitnesses to the incident at Newcastle said nothing to contradict the Judge's interpretation of what had occurred. John Montgomery described the charge to the grand jury at Baltimore in a manner unfavorable to the Judge, but he was not convincing; other witnesses added little that was new to the proceedings.[7]

On 15 February Harper delivered the opening speech for the defense. A simple and direct statement, it focused on the Callender trial, and the charge to the grand jury at Baltimore. Many witnesses were called, all of whom undermined Randolph's assertion that Chase deliberately and willfully violated the law. The most effective witness, by far, was William Marshall, the Chief Justice's younger brother, who served as clerk of the court where Callender had been tried. His testimony corroborated Chase's on every point, and the skillful manner in which he handled Randolph's cross-examination further strengthened the favorable impression he made.[8]

Only once did Randolph make any telling points with his cross-examination. The High Federalists could hardly have been surprised when the witness turned out to be John Marshall. Even when he was examined by the defense, his answers had not helped Chase. They were vague and evasive, and he seemed to question Chase's conduct in a number of instances. Under Randolph's prodding, Marshall's lack of sympathy for the Judge became even more apparent. Plumer noted that Marshall appeared frightened, "and there was in his manner an evident disposition to accommodate the managers." [9]

Harper next channeled his energies toward defending Chase from the charges brought against him for delivering his charge to the grand jury in Baltimore. Harper recalled John Montgomery to the stand, and after asking him to identify and read aloud an article he had written in the Baltimore *American* describing the charge, Harper announced his intention to prove it a gross distortion of what Chase actually had said. Randolph protested on the ground that Harper was implying that Montgomery had lied, but in one of the key rulings of the trial, Burr upheld the defense. The testimony of all the witnesses that followed indicated that the accuracy of Montgomery's account left much to be desired.[10]

By this time it was clear to everyone that the articles of impeachment had been poorly constructed and that the Judge would probably be acquitted. Even Timothy Pickering, never optimistic about anything in which he had to depend upon Republican decency, conceded, "I am now disposed to believe after hearing the testimony of the witnesses for the prosecution, and some of those produced by the Judge that they will not find 23 Senators hardy enough to condemn him." [11]

Joseph Hopkinson defended Chase from the charges in article one. In his speech he repeated the defense's basic assertion that an indictable offense was the only basis for impeachment; and then he carefully demonstrated how the witnesses' testimony supported Chase's interpretation of what had happened at the trial of John Fries and cited legal precedents for the Judge's actions. He was followed by Philip Barton Key and Charles Lee, who did the same thing for Chase's rulings in the Callender trial.[12]

The high point of the defense came on 23 February, when Luther Martin spoke. He was a known alcoholic with crude manners, who often used ungrammatical English, but he was considered by many of his contemporaries to be the best trial lawyer in the country. He lucidly expounded the relevant legal points involved in the case; he declared Chase innocent of any indictable offense; he disparaged and ridiculed the opposition's lack of legal knowledge. And, most important of all, he raised embarrassing questions: Why had it taken five years to initiate impeachment proceedings against Chase? What were the implications of the trial for an independent national judiciary? Had not the defense counsels in the Fries and Callender cases acted irresponsibly by withdrawing their services during the trials? [13] It was a fine summation, and it finished the destruction of the prosecution. Plumer noted, "Mr. Early said today he was weary of the cause and intimated his regret that the impeachment was ever brought forward. . . . and I believe he spoke the language of the majority of the House." [14]

Randolph concluded for the prosecution on 27 February. He began by announcing he had lost his notes. Then, instead of refuting the defense's interpretation of impeachment, he denounced it. Instead of using logic, he damned his opponents. It was an unforgettable performance, and an admission that the prosecution really had no case against Chase. John Quincy Adams described it in these terms:

> he began a speech of about two hours and a half, with as little relation to the subject matter as possible—without order, connections, or argument; consisting altogether of the most hackneyed commonplaces of popular declamation, mingled up with panegyrics and invectives upon persons, with a few well-expressed ideas, a few striking figures, much distortion of face and contortion of body, tears, groans, and sobs, with occasional pauses for recollection, and continual complaints of having lost his notes.[15]

After some minor remarks by Harper questioning the validity of Randolph's histronics, the court adjourned.

The Senate reconvened shortly after noon on 1 March to vote on the articles of impeachment. Each article was read in its entirety, and the question was put to each senator whether Chase was guilty or not guilty of a high crime or misdemeanor as charged. This took two hours to complete, and throughout, the chamber, filled with spectators, remained hushed. After the last senator voted and the votes were tabulated, Burr announced that there had not been a constitutional majority against Chase on any count, and therefore he was acquitted. Burr then permanently adjourned the Court.[16]

As was expected, the nine Federalists voted not guilty on every article. Six Republicans joined them: Bradley, Mitchill, Israel Smith, the two John Smiths, and John Gaillard. The highest vote for conviction was nineteen, on the article accusing Chase of misconduct for delivering a partisan charge to the grand jury at

Baltimore. Not a single vote was cast against Chase on one of the articles accusing him of procedural mistakes at the Callender trial, and only four votes were cast against him on the other article. This was a clear repudiation of Randolph's attempt to broaden the interpretation of what the Constitution indicated were impeachable offences. Less than half the senators voted guilty more than four times. Even the meaning of these votes is not altogether obvious. For example, William Cocke, who cast his vote against Chase seven times, privately admitted that he was glad the Judge had been acquitted because it "would have a tendency to mitigate the irritation of party spirit." [17] Republicans as well as Federalists were responsible for Chase's acquittal.

III

There is no simple explanation as to why so many Republicans voted for Chase's acquittal. Some sincerely believed he was being treated unfairly. While disapproving of what he had done, they believed the punishment did not fit the crime. George Clinton wrote:

> I will only observe that several of the members who voted for his acquittal had no doubt but the charges against him were substantiated and of course that his conduct was unproper and reprehensible, but considering that many parts of it were sanctioned by the practice of the other Judges ever since the commencement of the present Judiciary systems and that the act with which he was charged was not prohibited by any express and positive law they could not consistently with their ideas of justice find him guilty of high crimes and misdemeanours. It was to such refined reasoning of some honest men that he owes his acquittal.[18]

Many of these same Republicans were also unwilling to weaken further the independence of the judiciary. Their grievances against the courts before 1800 were real enough, but Marshall had initiated a period of judicial self-restraint, and there existed in 1805 little evidence to substantiate the radicals' claim of judicial tyranny. Moreover, the Pickering impeachment had been a sobering experience. Many moderate Republicans had been bullied into condemning the New Hampshire district judge, and they now realized that if they condemned Chase it would only lead to a further and more serious attack on the Supreme Court. They were unwilling to allow this to happen.[19] "All parties appear to wish it had never been commenced," wrote Plumer. "I believe we shall not hear of another very soon." [20]

The most important explanation for Chase's exoneration, however, is to be found in the struggle between moderate and radical Republicans for domination of the party. The differences between the two wings were fundamental, and they left little room for compromise. Throughout most of his first administration, Jefferson, though partial to the moderates, was able to control though not eliminate the tension between the two groups. But in 1804, when the administration sponsored the Yazoo compromise, the radicals led by John Randolph bolted. It would be hard to overemphasize the disruptive effect this had upon the party. The ensuing struggle began in earnest after Chase was impeached but before the trial began. As a consequence many Republicans who at first favored the Judge's removal later changed their minds because they did not want to increase Randolph's prestige and influence. The master of Roanoke recognized this when he complained, "the *Whimsicals*' advocated the leading measures of their party until they were nearly ripe for execution, when they hung back; condemned the step *after* it was taken, and, on most occasions, affected a *glorious neutrality*." [21]

Thomas Jefferson was the most important member of the group who changed his mind. The trial, it is clear, forced him to choose between the radical and moderate Republicans. It was not a choice he made willingly. For while he rarely followed the radical Republicans' counsel, he was never prepared to purge them from the party. But Randolph's uncompromising opposition forced him to make a choice. He could either surrender to the radicals or continue to push forward with his policy of conciliation. Jefferson described the tensions and difficulties involved in making the choice in the following manner:

> I did believe my station in March 1801 as painful as could be undertaken, having to meet in front all the terrible passions of federalism in the first moment of its defeat & mortification,

and to grapple with it until completely subdued. But I consider that as less painful than to be placed between conflicting
friends. There my way was clear & my mind made up.
I never for a moment had to balance between two opinions.
In the new divisions which are to arise the case will be very
different. . . . However under difficulties of this kind I have
ever found one, & only one rule, *to do what is right,* & generally we shall disentangle ourselves without almost perceiving
how it happens.[22]

If Jefferson had any doubts about which way to turn they must
have been eliminated by the presidential election of 1804, which
proved the moderates' desire for a realignment of political parties
to be realistic. In his successful bid for re-election, Jefferson carried every state which had supported him in 1800, and also won
impressive victories in Vermont, Rhode Island, New Hampshire,
Massachusetts, Pennsylvania, Maryland and North Carolina.
Only Connecticut and Delaware still eluded him. Because of
this, and despite his desire to see Chase removed, Jefferson never
did anything to aid Randolph. In the year preceding the trial
he neither commented upon the impeachment proceedings nor
discussed them in his private letters. When the subject was raised
at the numerous dinner parties to which he invited congressmen,
he merely hung his head in silence. Without Jefferson's influence
the attempt to repeal the Judiciary Act of 1801 would have failed.
Had he not officially recommended Pickering's impeachment, the
insane judge probably would have been acquitted. Therefore the
President's unwillingness to become involved, even behind the
scenes, with the Chase impeachment must be included as a
decisive factor contributing to the final verdict.[23]

To a very large extent Chase's acquittal was a direct result of
Randolph's opposition to a number of important Republican
measures. Randolph had begun to realize this when he noted a
few days before the trial began that "the Yazoo claim—Louisiana
—& the impeachment are all at this time on my shoulders, &
crush me to earth." [24] In fact, the final vote was probably more
against Randolph than for Chase. During the trial Rufus King
reported from New York that "we have heard of a rude and dis-
orderly debate in the House of Representatives concerning the

Georgia Claim; and some persons have conjectured that a serious division would arise among the Democrats—nay, that it already exists, and that Judge Chase's best hope of acquittal proceeds from it." [25] After the trial John Quincy Adams observed that Madison "appeared much diverted at the petulance of the managers at their disappointment." [26] Randolph also claimed there was a connection between the two events, and several months later he wrote that Richard Cutts from Massachusetts told him "he was glad" of Chase's acquittal, "since the Yazoo question had failed." [27]

The trial had a number of important consequences. Its result signficantly affected the careers of some of the most important political figures of the period. To begin with it led to a marked change in Chase's behavior. He believed he had a fair trial, was pleased with the verdict, and considered it a justification of his official conduct; but he never again actively participated in politics. Though he continued to serve as an associate justice of the Supreme Court until his death in 1811, the final years of his career were neither distinguished nor controversial. They were typified by the following comment which appeared in the *National Intelligencer* shortly after his acquittal: "Judge Chase delivered a short and pertinent charge to the grand jury—his remarks were pointed, modest and well applied." [28]

Aaron Burr made use of the trial to salvage something from four disappointing and unpleasant years as Vice President. The administration's desire to see Chase acquitted made things easy for him. Burr's supporters were probably inclined to vote not guilty on their own. Israel Smith, for example, had absented himself from the crucial votes on the repeal of the Judiciary Act of 1801 and from the resolution calling for Pickering's impeachment. If a conviction had been required, Burr might not have wanted or been able to deliver the necessary votes. He was also fortunate in another way. The rough manner in which he treated Chase when he first appeared before the Senate had not done his waning reputation any good. But Randolph's bungling of the prosecution allowed Burr to preside over the trial in a dignified and impartial manner. This even won him the respect of some of the Federalists, despite their bitterness over his slaying of

Hamilton. Always quick to take advantage of a good opportunity, Burr made use of his farewell address to praise the Senate's decision and to congratulate it on a job well done. "This body," he observed, "is growing in importance. It is here if anywhere, that our country must ultimately find the anchor of her safety, and if the Constitution is to perish, which may God avert, and which I do not believe, its dying agonies will be seen on this floor." [29]

There were also material benefits. The evidence is such that it is impossible to say with certainty what the *quid pro quo* between Burr and the moderates was, or even that a deal was made, but this much is clear: until this point the Vice President's supporters had not received many of the administration's favors. Now Burr's advice was solicited upon a number of important appointments. His stepson, J. P. Prevost, was made Judge of the Superior Court at New Orleans; his brother-in-law, James Brown, was appointed Secretary of the Louisiana Territory; and James Wilkinson was given the governorship of that territory. Since Wilkinson, who was "the most intimate friend, or rather the most devoted creature of Colonel Burr," was in town during the trial, it should not have come as much of a surprise to the administration when Burr next turned his attentions to the Southwest.[30]

Chase's acquittal delivered so serious a blow to Randolph's prestige and influence within the Republican party that he never recovered from it. His lack of preparation and inept handling of the trial put him in an especially bad light, because for the preceding year he "had boasted with great exaltation that this was *his* impeachment—that every article was drawn by *his* hand, and that *he* was to have the whole merit of it." Even his friends were disgusted with him.[31] Quick to realize what had happened, the Federalists showed him no mercy. One widely republished editorial gleefully proclaimed that "the malignant *monkey* who led the prosecution is not likely to do much mischief hereafter." [32]

Randolph's loss of influence became apparent the same day Chase was acquitted. Enraged by the verdict, the master of Roanoke, that afternoon, delivered "a violent phillipic" in the House, denouncing both Chase and the Senate. He concluded by moving an amendment to the Constitution proposing that the President, at the request of a majority of both Houses of Congress, be given the right to remove any federal judge. Under different circumstances Randolph's amendment might have received considerable support and serious attention. Precedents for it existed in several of the state constitutions, and Jefferson himself in early 1803 suggested such a change. But coming as it did at the culmination of the struggle between radical and moderate Republicans over the judiciary and other issues, it simply served to give Randolph's enemies another opportunity to embarrass him. "Administration," observed Plumer, "disapproved of this violent measure." [33] By a large majority the House referred the resolution to a committee and postponed its consideration until the next session. Observing these proceedings, Chase reminded Hopkinson, "I have always said that my enemies are as great fools as knaves." [34]

PART TWO

The Struggle over Judicial Reform in the States

VIII

Post-Revolutionary Attitudes Toward the Legal Profession

The struggle on the national level was only one phase of the Jeffersonian attack upon the judiciary. On the state level there took place a series of bitter fights which in many ways involved issues even more fundamental than those in the nation at large; for in addition to patronage considerations, personal animosities, and the threat of constitutional upheaval, there were also demands for root-and-branch legal reform.

I

It took almost the entire colonial period for a legal profession to develop in America. During the seventeenth century, when the requirements of justice were few and simple, there was no need for people specifically trained in the law, and in some colonies lawyers were actually prohibited. Not until the eighteenth century, as the growth of population and commerce created a more complex society, did a legal profession begin to appear. Then it grew very rapidly, and by the eve of the Revolution there existed a large number of lawyers and judges skilled in the intricacies of the common law and a legal system modeled closely on that of England.[1]

The Revolution wrought havoc upon the American legal profession. There were a number of separate but converging reasons for this. First, while the great majority of lawyers supported independence, the most prominent members of the profession remained loyal to the mother country. With the withdrawal of the British army, these Tory lawyers either left America or were forced into retirement. Second, the widespread social dislocation which accompanied independence increased the demand for legal services beyond what the legal establishment could provide. As a result much of the legal work fell into the hands of the inadequately trained lawyer or the unscrupulous pettifogger. Finally, the Revolution engendered widespread hostility toward everything English, especially the common law. What made this so disastrous was that there was nothing with which it could be replaced. The lack of indigenous law reports and law books made it difficult and at times impossible to know what the law was on many points. Consequently justice was often administered inconsistently and arbitrarily in different parts of the same state or even in the same county.[2]

Intensifying the antagonism toward the legal profession was the depression that followed the end of the war. As popular demands for relief legislation either went unheard or, when implemented, proved ineffectual, the economic hardship that ensued brought bankruptcies, foreclosures, insolvencies, innumerable cases of personal hardship, and a rapidly expanding debtor population. Frustrated, angry, and worried about their future well-being, people desperately searched for the cause of their difficulties. A villain was needed. Lawyers prospered while others suffered. Many lawyers were wealthy, most were comfortable, and, in small communities, they usually owned the best houses in town. Many people took the prosperity of lawyers as proof that the legal profession not only benefited from litigation, but actually created and needlessly prolonged it. The small farmer who found himself spending more time in the courtroom than in his fields was not inclined to look very far for his villain. Whenever trouble appeared it came in the guise of a lawyer. This description of lawyers by J. Hector St. John de Crèvecoeur is typical:

> They are plants that will grow in any soil that is cultivated by the hands of others; and when once they have taken root they will extinguish every other vegetable that grows around

them. The fortunes of their fellow citizens, are surprising! The most ignorant, the most bungling member of that profession, will if placed in the most obscure parts of the country, promote its litigiousness and amass more wealth without labour, than the most opulent farmer, with all his toils.[3]

Hostility toward lawyers was exploited by emerging democratic groups who complained of established orders. The man who stated this deep hostility most clearly was Benjamin Austin, a radical Boston artisan dedicated to a literal application of the philosophy of the Declaration of Independence. Between March and June of 1786, under the pseudonym "Honestus," Austin published a series of articles in the Boston *Independent Chronicle*. These essays, later republished as a pamphlet entitled *Observations on the Pernicious Practice of the Law by Honestus,* condemned lawyers as sophists who needlessly confused, extended, manipulated and complicated court cases in order to charge high fees. For this Austin had a radical solution: "It has . . . become necessary for the welfare and security of the Commonwealth, that this 'order' of men should be ANNIHILATED." [4]

Austin argued that lawyers were dangerous on three counts: politically, because they were the class of men most often elected to the legislature; economically, because once in power they deliberately made the laws complicated so as to ensure their future services; and socially, because the moneyed aristocracy, by paying high fees, used the legal profession to make simple cases intricate, thus preventing the poorer classes from obtaining justice.

Austin proposed a number of changes in the administration of justice in order "that the laws may be executed upon the strictest principles of *equity*. That the *rich* and *poor* may ever be on an equality while they are appealing to the justice of their country." In criminal cases he advocated the state's appointing, as a counterpart to the Attorney General, a special defense attorney with a fixed salary to appear for all prisoners. For the pleading of civil cases, he urged the appointment of intelligent friends instead of paid professionals who distorted the truth for higher fees. It would be even better, Austin argued, if the judges received the evidence directly from the parties involved, and then personally delivered it to the jury with an opinion on any controversial points of law. "Laws and evidence, without the false glosses and subterfuges too often practiced by lawyers," were all that were needed for a jury to reach a fair decision.

To lessen the time lost and trouble and expense incurred in the trial of court cases, Austin urged the frequent use of referees to settle disputes. After agreeing to arbitrate their differences, both parties would submit the relevant evidence to three prudent men. Having no interest in the contest, these men could provide an amicable and equitable solution. For example, a dispute involving mercantile concerns could best be arbitrated by three merchants familiar with the problems involved. Controversies between tradesmen or farmers could be settled in a similar manner, thus eliminating court costs and lawyers' fees.

Austin also advocated simplification of the law. He believed that the legal profession's power lay in the mysterious and ambiguous character of the common law. Lawyers purposely brought in numerous precedents from old English authorities to confuse the issues and to make the bar indispensable. What was wrong, Austin asked, with a legal code "dictated by the genuine principles of Republicanism, and made easy to be understood by every individual in the community?"

Austin's views were widely shared. After Shays's Rebellion, John Quincy Adams complained that "the popular odium which has been excited against the practitioners in this Commonwealth prevails to so great a degree that the most innocent and irreproachable life cannot guard a lawyer against the hatred of his fellow citizens. The very despicable writings of Honestus were just calculated to kindle a flame which will subsist long after they are forgotten." [5]

Popular hostility to lawyers was not limited to Massachusetts. The legislatures of most states received petitions demanding that the powers of the courts to interpret the law be reduced and that the legal profession be suppressed. At times force was used. Lawyers were beaten and judges harassed; courthouses were burned down or their doors nailed up. Although these tactics achieved few permanent successes, popularly controlled legislatures throughout the country did deprofessionalize judiciaries by appointing ordinary citizens to the bench and by simplifying legal procedure. In Georgia, New Hampshire, New Jersey, New York, North Carolina, Pennsylvania, Rhode Island, and Vermont, ministers, would-be theologians, physicians, shoemakers, tailors, and farmers became judges. In some states only those English precedents specifically authorized by legislative enactment or by declarations of the courts were allowed to have effect. Other states passed acts prohibiting members of the bar from referring to, or citing, the common law.[6] John Dudley, a farmer who had become an associate justice of the New Hampshire Supreme Court, clearly and simply expressed the underlying philosophy of the movement. Concluding his charge to a jury, he reminded them:

> You've heard what has been said by the lawyers, the rescals; but no I wont abuse 'em. 'Tis their business to make out a good case—they're paid for it, and they've done well enough in this case. But you and I, gentlemen, have sumthin' else to think of. They talk about law—why, gentlemen, it is not law we want, but justice. They want to govern us by the common law of England; trust me for it, common sense is a much safer guide for us. . . . A clear head and an honest heart are wuth more than all the law of the lawyers. There was one good thing said by 'em though; 't was from one Shakespeare, an English stage-player, I believe. No matter for that 't was e'ven most good enough to be in the Bible—'Be just and fear not.' That's the law in this case, gentlemen, and law enough in any case in this court. It's our business to do justice between the parties; not by any quirks of the law out of Coke of Blackstone—books that I never read and never will—but by common sense and common honesty between man and men. That's our business, and the curse of God is upon us if we neglect or turn aside from that. And now, Mr. Sheriff, take out the jury; and you Mr. Foreman, don's keep us waiting with idle talk—too much o' that a'ready, about matters that have nothin' to do with the merits of this 'ere case. Give us an honest verdict that common sense men needn't be ashamed on.[7]

Popular hostility toward the legal profession continued unabated throughout the last quarter of the eighteenth century. In 1793 "A Susquehanna Farmer," pleading for relief from professional men, asserted that he would be happy to see judges and lawyers "honorably employed at the plough. I expect they would make skillful farmers and useful members of society when they would have more of a common interest therewith, for they themselves will acknowledge that in the arts of delay, the chicane, bargains, etc. in use with these gentlemen and upon which much of their profits depend . . . they have not a common interest with the community. . . ." [8] In 1801 a candidate for the Virginia General Assembly noted, "the being a lawyer was with some a fatal objection, their taking it for granted that a lawyer was interested in multiplying the laws and making them more complex." [9] And that same year, in New Jersey, the Republican Committee of Essex County warned the voters that the Federalist ticket had been selected by lawyers and judges, men "who wish to fatten themselves on the hard earnings of the industrious farmer and mechanic." [10]

II

Conscious of their profession's limitations, many judges and lawyers realized that, to a large extent, the demands for reform were justified. "The Courts must be altered;" wrote one member of the legal establishment in North Carolina.

> . . . Against the present system the cries of the people are loud; they must be heard. But what affects me most is, that the censure is pointed at the Bar, when the occasion is seated much higher. It is a melancholy consideration that we have not proper materials in this country to form the officers which the constitution makes necessary. We must do the best we can with such stuff as we have, until our academies and colleges supply us with something that may be more equal to the purpose.[11]

The problem facing the legal establishment, therefore, was twofold: the attack upon it had to be repelled, and its causes had to be eliminated. Responsible members of the bench and bar searched for the necessary remedies.

Efforts were made to improve the quality of the judiciary. The difficulties of riding circuit, combined with the unwillingness of economy-minded legislatures to pay high salaries and the reluctance of successful lawyers to give up lucrative practices, created a situation where appointments to the bench had to come from the legal profession's less qualified members. One foreign traveler noted, a bit harshly: "It's quite a farce to go to their courts. One of the judges will perhaps get up, scratch his head like a country clown, and ask the most nonsensical questions upon the face of the earth. In general, they are very ignorant men. . . ." [12] While adequate remuneration and better working conditions for judges were constantly demanded by those who hoped to bring about a reformation in the administration of justice, complete success was rarely achieved in this area.

Also of concern was the ease with which unsuitable applicants could enter the legal profession. People hoping to improve the quality of the legal profession worked through local bar associations in New England and the courts in other sections, rather than through state legislatures, to establish professional standards of admission. By 1800, most states had formal rules prescribing lengthy periods of preparation for would-be lawyers. Many states, especially the New England ones, encouraged applicants with college degrees by requiring less preparation of them than of those without degrees. Several states also required two or three years' experience in the lower courts before permitting lawyers to practice in the higher ones.[13]

Attention was given the quality of legal training. For what good would it do to establish higher standards if only a few could meet them? The traditional apprenticeship system of legal education was scrutinized and found wanting. At best it only provided the aspiring lawyer with practical skills, and rarely with a comprehensive understanding of the nature of jurisprudence. Moreover, as Jefferson pointed out, most of the time "the services expected in return have been more than the instruction have been worth." [14] To correct this, colleges were encouraged to offer courses in law to their undergraduates.

In 1777 the state of Connecticut proposed to establish a professorship of law at Yale. The school balked, however, when the legislature attempted to retain control over faculty appointments. Success was achieved two years later in Virginia, when Jefferson, then governor, helped establish a "Professorship of Law and Police" at the College of William and Mary. By the end of the century law courses had been added to the curricula of many colleges.[15]

An equally significant advance toward quality in legal training was made when, in the closing years of the eighteenth century, several law offices became private law schools. The first, and by far the most important of these was the Litchfield Law School, founded by Judge Tapping Reeve in 1784. Distinguished by a systematic course of lectures delivered daily and never published, the school attracted students from throughout the country.[16] Peter Van Schaack's school, established at Kinderhook, New York in 1786, also acquired a national reputation, as did George Wythe's, established at Richmond in 1791.

Another matter of concern was the widespread uncertainty, and even chaos, that came with the rejection of the English common law. "When I came to the Bench," wrote James Kent of his appointment to the New York Supreme Court, "there were no reports or state precedents. . . . We had no law of our own, and nobody knew what it was." [17] And in South Carolina a prominent jurist observed, "the laws of this country, on which depend the lives and property of the people, now lie concealed from their eyes, mingled in a confused chaos, under a stupendous pile of old and new law rubbish." [18]

To meet this challenge there arose a body of law reporters, and what followed was, perhaps, the most significant achievement of the legal profession in the post-Revolutionary period: the beginning of the establishment of an American code of law. It began when Connecticut, in 1784, passed a statute requiring the judges of the state's supreme and superior courts to file written opinions in order to establish "a more perfect and permanent system of common law in the state." Five years later, Ephraim Kirby published the first fully developed volume of law reports in the United States. In 1790, Alexander Dallas issued the first volume of his reports for Pennsylvania; and in 1795 George Wythe published the decisions of the Virginia High Court of Chancery. North Carolina began publishing its reports in 1797, Kentucky in 1803, New York in 1804, Massachusetts in 1805, New Jersey in 1808, and Maryland and South Carolina in 1809.[19]

Many Americans worked to bring about these kinds of reforms. James Kent, James Wilson, Theophilus Parsons, Joseph Story and Alexander Dallas played important roles, but, in the years immediately following independence, no one did more than George Wythe. Born in 1726, the son of an established Virginia planter who held a seat in the House of Burgesses, Wythe was given every opportunity for advancement which his time and place afforded. He was carefully tutored in Latin and Greek by his mother; he attended the College of William and Mary; he studied law in the office of an uncle; and he was admitted to practice before the Virginia General Court at the age of twenty-one.[20] As a lawyer, Wythe was respected both for the depth of his learning and for his uncompromising adherence to principle. It was generally acknowledged that no one in the Old Dominion knew more about the law, and, according to one contemporary, he "would never engage in a cause he thought wrong, and would often abandon his cases when he found they had not been fully represented to him."[21] Other attorneys, like Edmund Pendelton, may have been more successful because they were more effective in the courtroom, but Wythe became the acknowledged leader of the legal profession in Virginia. Jefferson, in 1788, believed him to be "one of the greatest men of the age, having held without competition the first place at the bar of our general court for twenty-five years, and always distinguished by the most spotless virtue."[22]

After independence, Wythe's legal talents were called upon to help smooth Virginia's transition from colony to state. In 1777, along with Jefferson and Pendelton, he was appointed to the committee in charge of revising the Old Dominion's laws. The three lawyers spent over two years examining the myriad of precedents that made up the common law, relevant English laws, and all Virginia statutes in order to create a workable system. They dropped acts and precedents deemed inappropriate for a republican experiment, rewrote others, and proposed several new ones. Altogether, the complete work consisted of 126 bills, most of which eventually became law. In 1785, Wythe also joined forces with Pendleton and John Blair to collect and publish, in a single volume, all acts passed by the Assembly prior to 1779 as well as the various and still operative ordinances of the convention of 1776.[23]

In 1776 Wythe had been appointed one of three judges to sit on the newly established Virginia High Court of Chancery. In 1788 when the number of judges was reduced to one, Wythe became sole Chancellor of the state. Called the American Aristides, he distinguished himself by his strong sense of justice. In 1792, in the face of an overwhelming public opinion, Wythe ruled that the pre-Revolutionary war debts owed by Virginians to British merchants had to be paid. He defended his decision in these terms: " a judge should not be susceptible of national antipathy, more than of malice toward individuals;—whilst executing his office, he should not be more affected by patriotic considerations. . . . What is just in this Hall is just in Westminster Hall, and in every other practorium upon earth." [24]

Wythe was convinced, as were most members of his profession, that the judiciary should be kept independent of popular control. In 1782, while delivering his opinion in the controversial case *Commonwealth* v. *Caton,* he warned the legislature against trying to arrogate too much power. Otherwise, "in administering the public justice of the country [they] will meet the united powers at my seat in the tribunal, and pointing to the Constitution, I will say to them, 'here is the limit of your authority, and hither shall you go, but no further.' " [25]

Wythe made his greatest contribution to the legal profession through his work in education. Before the Revolution Jefferson had served a brief apprenticeship under Wythe, and as the experience had been a happy one, he appointed his distinguished preceptor to the newly established chair in law at The College of William and Mary. Wythe proved to be a very fortunate choice. He worked hard to make a success of his new position, discharging his duties "with wonderful ability both as to theory and practice." He delivered a series of lectures which contrasted and elaborated upon the intricacies of English and Virginia law, and he established a system of moot courts and legislatures by which he trained students in the actualities of judicial and parliamentary procedure.[26]

Wythe taught at William and Mary until 1791, when he moved to Richmond. From that year until his death in 1806, he kept a private school for a select group of young men. As a teacher he tried to pass his own virtues on to his students, and for the most part he succeeded. The result was that during the early national period there developed in Virginia one of the most respected and least criticized legal establishments in the country. And almost all of its most distinguished members, who included such diverse luminaries as John Marshall, Spencer Roane, St. George Tucker, Littleton Waller Tazewell, Archibald Stuart, Benjamin Watkins Leigh, and James Monroe, were educated and influenced by Wythe.

III

Both Austin and Wythe were Republicans, and they are indicative of the heterogeneous composition of Jefferson's following. Both men agreed that some kind of legal reform was necessary, but they differed sharply over the kinds of changes to make. The difference was that between a radical and a moderate; between one who demanded changes conceived as a total alternative to the existing legal establishment and one who hoped to work within the established system by modifying and improving it. What Austin and other radicals like him wanted was a cheap, simple, easily available and speedy system of administering justice, one that would ensure equality and provide security with only a minimum of contact with the legal profession. What Wythe and other moderates like him wanted was a technical legal system capable of maintaining order and providing stability, harmony, and uniformity, and which would require a well-trained and highly specialized legal establishment.

But to set up two individuals as prototypes of the struggle over judicial reform is to oversimplify. Local circumstances, the quality of available leadership, and the politics of a given situation often made compromises necessary. It is to illustrate these complexities that three case studies have been made of states where the struggle over judicial reform was particularly intense: Kentucky, where one of the earliest fights between radical and moderate Jeffersonians over judicial reform occurred, and where the Republicans were almost completely dominant politically; Pennsylvania, where there was one of the bitterest and most intensely fought struggles over judicial reform on the local level, and where the Republicans were clearly in the majority but the Federalists were still strong enough to exert an influence when Jeffersonians began to battle each other; and Massachusetts, where one of the most articulate debates over judicial reform took place, and where the Federalists still continued to dominate politics after 1800.

IX
Radicals vs. Moderates in Kentucky, 1791-1796

In Kentucky the struggle between radical and moderate Jeffersonians over judicial reform began when the state secured its independence from Virginia. Before then the citizens had been engrossed with the difficulties of separation and of opening the Mississippi to naviagtion, but with a constitutional convention called for April 1792, the public turned its attention to the problems involved in establishing a government.[1]

I

Campaigning for the election of delegates to the convention began in the summer of 1791. By this time it was also evident that there was considerable popular support for radical ideas. As one worried member of the legal establishment described it:

> The people of Kentucky are all turned politicians from the highest in office to the Peasant. The Peasantry are perfectly mad. Extraordinary prejudices and without foundation have arisen against the present officers of Government, the lawyers and the Men of Fortune. They say plan honest Farmers are the only men who ought to be elected to form our Constitution. What will be the end of these prejudices it is difficult to say, they have given a very serious alarm to every thinking man, who is determined to watch and court the temper of the people.[2]

The differences between radicals and moderates were openly debated during the fall and winter of 1791–92. This was possible because John Bradford, the printer and editor of the state's lone newspaper, the *Kentucky Gazette,* opened its pages to all points of view and published a series of essays on the nature and purpose of the new government.[3]

The radicals argued that, at best, government was a necessary evil. To support this position they quoted from the works of Tom Paine, whom they much admired, and from James Burgh's *Political Disquisitions.*[4] Some, like "Will Wisp" believed that government was more evil than necessary. "I have long been of opinion," he asserted, "that the business of government is a cheat. . . . For what do you think men are to understand by governing a country? Is it not to get good salaries and to keep the common people in subjection? . . . government is nothing but playing rogue by authority of law." [5]

What the radicals feared most was power, and its potential for misuse by a ruling class, which included lawyers. "Salamandar," believing "the fewer lawyers and Pick-pockets there are in a country the better chance honest people have to keep their own," recommended that a provision be included in the constitution prohibiting lawyers from serving in the government.[6] "H.S.B.M." agreed, and warned that if lawyers ever got into the assembly they would make the laws intricate and entangled to ensure their own employment, with the result "that he who has the heaviest purse will generally gain the cause," and "the labouring man's property will become a prey to the few monied men that may be amongst us." [7]

Radicals believed that government and laws were dangerous commodities and the less people had to do with them the better. Realizing, however, that some kind of government was necessary, they desired one that would be directly and continually responsive to the needs of its citizens. They advocated a unicameral legislature, annual elections, manhood suffrage, and the election of most local and state officials. As for the laws, they demanded "that the statutes, or other laws of England, or any other nation, or state, be not adopted as such; but that a simple and concise code of laws be framed, adapted to the weakest capacity; which we humbly concede will happily supercede the necessity of attornies pleading in our state." [8]

The moderates, for their part, believed government should be republican in form, but not responsive to the whims and caprices of its citizens. "X.Y.Z." denigrated direct democracy and described representative government as "one of the greatest improvements which has been made in the science of civil government." [9] "A.B.C." asserted, "all just power is derived from the community over which it is to be exercised. Yet no act of power ought to be exercised by the community at large except the election of such trustees as may be necessary to originate and keep the Government in motion." [10] Above all else, the moderates feared the tyranny of the majority. They favored a bicameral legislature, a system of checks and balances, a Bill of Rights, and an independent judiciary.[11]

According to the moderates, the purpose of government was to maintain peace and harmony, and to protect the people against those who were of "turbulent and restless disposition." [12] They believed government should be directed not by the people who had neither the leisure, information, nor natural talents for self-government, "but by general laws equally binding." [13] In direct opposition to the proponents of unrestrained democracy and simple government, they argued that is was the presence and not the absence of government that created liberty. They further argued that a complicated system of jurisprudence was actually a positive good.

> The laws of a free government will unavoidably be numerous and intricate, because they must regulate all the variety of affairs which are transacted in a country; for whatever is not regulated by law must depend on the arbitrary will of the rulers, which would put an end to civil society.[14]

In addition to competing on the ideological level, radicals and moderates both made strenuous efforts to elect "right thinking" delegates to the constitutional convention. The moderates urged the voters to elect only men of education, experience, wisdom, and integrity; men whose superior characters were attested to by their accomplishments and their high standing in the community.

In particular, they stressed the need to elect lawyers, whose skills would be useful in the complicated and difficult task of drafting a new constitution. And they warned the people that "to avoid knaves it would be a mistake to elect fools." "Novices . . . will only be able to establish under the name of a constitution, a collection of absurdities expressed in unintelligible languages, which will produce misery at home and disgrace abroad." [15]

Radicals denounced the suggestion that only "great and wise men" should be elected to the convention as an attempt to put the people "off their guard, that they may become an easy prey to the swarms of Rapacious locusts that are now hovering about our country, waiting for the opportunity to sap the vitals and suck the blood of the unwary." [16] "Philip Philips" informed his readers, "I never was a friend to larned men for I see it is those sort of fokes who know how to butter thare own bred and care not for others. I always thot it was not rite they should go to convention or to the legislater." [17] Calling great men dangerous, "Will Wisp" urged "everyone who is for the good of the country [to] keep up the cry against Judges, Lawyers, Generals, Colonels and all other designing men." [18]

But to revile "great men" in the press was one thing, to defeat them at the polls another, for they were usually rich men, who knew how to wheedle poor people "out of just rights, by flattery, grog or the way of ruffled hand." [19] To prevent this from occurring, radicals sought to organize a system of county committees similar to those used during the Revolution. They proposed that in every county the local militia company choose a committee to meet at the county seat with other local committees, and together nominate representatives for the convention. The ticket agreed upon would then be sent back to the local committees, which would either give their approval or make the necessary changes before returning it to the county committee.[20]

The purpose of the committee system was twofold: to obtain the will of the people, and to prevent "designing men" from taking over. Elected delegates would be instructed on matters of the greatest importance. The hope was even held by some radicals that the committee system would be made permanent and be given the power of veto over bills passed by the assembly.[21] But this was for the future. What mattered at the moment, and what the future depended upon, was how effectively popular support could be marshalled in support of the plan.

Moderates were quick to perceive the dangerous implications of the committee system, and they launched a fierce attack upon it. They questioned the motives of its organizers; they used threats of force to prevent people from attending meetings; they ridiculed the peoples' desire to write instructions; and they asked pointed questions. Could not the elections at which committeemen were selected be as easily corrupted as regular elections? Why, if the committee system was meant to encourage democracy, were its meetings to be held behind closed doors? What would happen if the different county committees gave contradictory but binding instructions? [22]

The attack was successful. While efforts were made to organize committees in every county, only in Bourbon County was any kind of popular enthusiasm generated, and even there the committee was not to be an important force. The ensuing election put the moderates in firm control of the convention.[23]

II

The convention was dominated by George Nicholas, a man who represented the antithesis of everything the radicals believed in. He was the son of Robert Carter Nicholas, Old Dominion nabob and lawyer. He was a graduate of The College of William and Mary, he had been a colonel in the army, and was related by marriage to the wealthy Smiths of Baltimore. He had studied law under George Wythe, and, during the 1780's he was an important force in Virginia politics, having worked with Madison and Marshall to bring about ratification of the federal Constitution. When he emigrated to Kentucky, in late 1789, he was a land speculator, a nascent industrialist, and a leading member of the bar.[24] Although Nicholas was only a recent arrival, his impressive abilities as a public speaker, his extensive knowledge of the law, and his political experience in Virginia immediately singled him out as an important figure. His election to the convention was considered a matter of the "utmost importance" to the moderates.[25]

Nicholas won, and he did not disappoint his supporters. He

prepared assiduously for the convention, and, when it met, immediately obtained control of it by introducing a series of twenty-one resolutions which he urged be used as a basis for drafting the constitution. In his address to the convention Nicholas spoke at length of the importance of creating a government with sufficient and proper powers:

> There is less danger in giving them at first. Tyranny is oftener produced by making it necessary to assume power, than by giving large powers in the first instance. The government must have the power necessary to accomplish its objects and fulfill its trusts. . . . Each man gains more by others being restrained from injuring others. This is the substance of the whole argument in favor of all government. Liberty consists not in being restrained by no law, but in being subject only to such as are equal and properly made. Extreme liberty is near to and generally produces slavery. Government must be strong enough to compel confidence and respect in the people, or they will resort to expedients that will destroy it.[26]

Nicholas knew that a powerful government could also be a dangerous government, but he believed that history had provided the remedy. "Experience has proven the only effectual mode to be to make ambition restrain ambition, and power check power by setting a *few* to watch and control the *few*." [27] He then went on to warn that under no circumstances should all the powers of government be given to an omnipotent unicameral legislature checked only by the passions of the people. He urged instead that the executive, legislative, and judicial departments be carefully separated; that the legislature be bicameral with both houses popularly elected; that the governor also be chosen by the people, and given a long term of office, a fixed salary, a qualified veto, and wide powers of appointment; that the suffrage be extended to all free men over twenty-one; that a Bill of Rights be attached to the constitution; and that a provision be included guaranteeing the institution of slavery.[28]

The judiciary was the subject of Nicholas's most important speech.[29] It was clearly an attempt to answer, point by point, most of the arguments of the radicals. He began by elaborating on the importance of the courts. They were the guardian of the constitution, and the only protection against the encroachment of the executive and legislature upon the Bill of Rights. They also enforced the laws, for "laws are necessary to unite duties with privileges, and confine justice to its proper objects; but laws are a dead letter without courts to expound and define their true meaning and operation . . . without courts there can be no government."

Yet another purpose of the courts, according to Nicholas, was to "establish a speedy, uniform, and equal administration of justice throughout the state." Such a system of justice, Nicholas argued, would have immense material benefits. It would force men to be honest and punctual in meeting their obligations; it would help make the state prosperous because people would be required to live within their incomes; and it would aid in the establishment of a credit system throughout the state which, in turn, would help borrowers obtain credit in other states at lower interest rates.

As for the judges, they were to be appointed by the governor and to hold their offices during good behavior. Their salaries were to be fixed, and competent enough to allow them to live in comfort. This was necessary because "Courts will never be truly respectable, nor fully answer the purpose of a just and uniform administration of justice until the judges are superior in legal knowledge to the bar; this cannot be the case until it is an object with the best lawyers to be judges."

At this point, Nicholas returned once more to the urgent question of the day: whether the laws were to be few and simple or many and complex. He argued that the purpose of the law was to prohibit wrongs and protect rights,

> and wherever there is a *right* which is not *protected,* or a wrong which is not *prohibited* there is one law too few . . . that government is a miserable servitude . . . where the law is uncertain and unknown; and it only is under the security of certain and known laws, that a country can be prosperous and happy.

Nicholas urged the Kentucky convention to adopt all the laws of Virginia, leaving it up to the legislature to revise or repeal the unnecessary ones. This, of course, also meant the adoption of the English common law, that "perfection of reason."

Nicholas also urged the establishment of a supreme tribunal, or Court of Appeals, as it was eventually called. This court would prevent injustices from being perpetrated by the lower courts, and correct unintentional errors. Most important of all, it would ensure "having one law of the land in every part of the state."

Turning his attention to the large number of disputed land claims filling up court dockets throughout the state, Nicholas pointed out that they had already turned Kentucky into a pettifogger's paradise, and that they had created a situation where the great majority of the people could not be sure of their land titles. Worst of all, uncertain land titles retarded the state's economic development by preventing people from improving or selling their land, and by hindering immigration.

Concluding his speech on the role of the courts, Nicholas asserted that the future well-being of Kentucky depended on the speedy resolution of these land disputes. To this end, he proposed that the Court of Appeals be given both original and final jurisdiction in all land cases. Admitting that his proposal denied to suitors the right to appeal, Nicholas pointed out precedents for this in both the Virginia and federal Constitutions. In addition, he argued that it was a small price to pay for the establishment of a general land law by judicial decision.

After Nicholas presented his proposals, it took the convention only sixteen days to complete its work. The final document as drafted by a committee which Nicholas headed conformed to his resolutions in almost every particular. The only important difference was that where Nicholas had recommended that the governor and members of the Senate be popularly elected, the constitution provided that they be chosen by a college of electors. There appears to have been considerable opposition to giving the Court of Appeals original jurisdiction in all land disputes, however. In the end, a compromise was effected wherein the constitution gave to the court the powers which Nicholas demanded for it but with the proviso that the legislature had the right, at any time, "to pass an act or acts to regulate the mode of pro-

ceedings in such cases or to take away entirely the original jurisdiction hereby given to the said court in such cases." [30]

The constitution was the expected result of a convention dominated by moderate Republicans. It was also a great personal
triumph for George Nicholas.

III

Nicholas immediately consolidated the position of influence he
had gained through his role at the convention by forming an
alliance with Isaac Shelby, a popular Revolutionary War hero
and Indian fighter, who was elected the state's first governor.
Among Shelby's earliest acts were his appointment of Nicholas
as attorney general and his endorsement of his views on the
importance of an efficient judiciary. In his opening address to
the legislature, the governor defined the chief goal of his administration as the creation of prosperity:

> Amongst the means which ought to be used for that purpose
> none will be found more efficacious than the establishing
> public and private credit on the most solid basis. The first will
> be obtained by a scrupulous adherence to all public engage-
> ments—the last by a speedy and uniform administration of
> justice.
>
> The happiness and welfare of the country depends so much
> on the speedy settlement of our land disputes, that I cannot
> forbear expressing my hope, that you will adopt every
> necessary measure to give full operation to the mode pointed
> out by the Constitution for that purpose.[31]

The General Assembly immediately passed an omnibus bill
drafted by Nicholas for the establishment of a system of lower
courts. The act provided nothing new or strange: it merely copied
the Virginia county court system, making only the changes necessary to accommodate the original jurisdiction in land disputes
now vested in the Court of Appeals. Justices of the peace were
given jurisdiction in all cases of less value that £5, or 1000
pounds of tobacco. If a justice's judgment amounted to less than
one-half the value of either, it was final; if more, an appeal to

the court of quarter sessions was allowed. A quorum of any three of four specially designated justices of the peace made up a county court in each county. These courts had jurisdiction in all cases involving wills, letters of administration, mills, roads, and the affairs of orphans, as well as broad powers of administration and taxation in local matters. Each county also had a court of quarter sessions which met on fixed days at fixed places four times a year for six-day terms. In addition to hearing appeals from the decisions of local justices of the peace, this court had cognizance of all cases at common law and chancery, and criminal cases involving fines and imprisonment. More serious cases, treason, murder, and certain felonies and misdemeanors, were tried by a jury in a Court of Oyer and Terminer which met twice a year at Frankfort, and from which neither writ of error nor appeal were allowed.[32]

After the omnibus court bill was passed, Shelby refused to sign it. In his veto message, however, the governor made it clear that he was opposed only to its wording, not to its substance. He pointed out that under the separation of powers clause of the constitution, justices of peace, but not judges, were allowed to sit in the General Assembly. He noted that, in the returned piece of legislation, members of the court of quarter sessions were called judges, and he recommended that they be called justices. Both House willingly made the change in wording, after which the Governor signed the measure into law. Thus Shelby put himself into a position to make use of his patronage powers to reward faithful members of the legislature.[33]

The next administration bill called for the establishment of a Court of Appeals with all the powers given to it by the constitution. Members of the legislature who believed that the Court would have too much power introduced a counterresolution in both Houses to take away the high court's original jurisdiction in land cases. This new measure was passed by the Senate but killed by the House, and its final defeat came when the Senate voted to withdraw its support after the two Houses conferred to accommodate their differences. Once again, the governor got his legislation passed.[34]

The Nicholas-Shelby program suffered a temporary setback

when economy-minded members of the legislature prevented passage of an act fixing the salaries of the judges of the Court of Appeals at $150. The House reduced the amount to $75, but the Senate would not agree; and when the two branches failed to resolve their differences, the matter was laid over until the next session. This caused some embarrassment to the governor, as the men he appointed to the high court refused to accept their positions until their salaries were established. But Shelby prevailed at the next meeting of the legislature, and the judges' salaries were fixed at $300.[35]

The first year under the new constitution had begun and ended with the Nicholas-Shelby men in firm control of the government. They retained control for the next two years, during which the moderates in the legislature increased the fees of justices of the peace, raised the salaries of judges, streamlined divorce proceedings, provided for the keeping of court records, and modernized the legal code.[36]

Nicholas and Shelby maintained their influence by making effective use of their control of the patronage and by staying on the right side of public opinion on national issues. During 1793 and 1794, the Kentucky political scene was dominated not by local issues, but by such national issues as the federal excise tax, the Mississippi question, the French alliance, and British control over the Indians in the northwest territory. On all these issues, the moderates vigorously supported the emerging Republican party centered around Jefferson and Madison, and this won for them considerable popular support.[37]

During these same years, the radicals were ineffective as an opposition force. Although they were determined, they lacked able leadership. There were also a small number of dissident moderates who had broken away from the larger group because of patronage differences, personal enmities, and assorted local considerations. A few of the dissidents, men like Benjamin Logan, Alexander Bullitt, and John Adair, had some sympathy for the radicals' demands, but most of them simply wanted power and offered no real alternatives in policy. Also in opposition to the moderates were the Federalists, the hard core of whom had opposed separation from Virginia. Their point of view had few adherents, and, according to their leader, "no matter what the service to be performed or the question to be decided was, to establish upon a candidate that he was a Federalist was the equivalent of his exclusion from office." [38]

IV

The superficial calm which characterized Kentucky politics came to an end in December 1794. The immediate cause was a decision by the Court of Appeals which threatened to overturn thousands of land titles. On no other issue would it have been possible to arouse as many people. Land was what Kentucky was all about. It was in search of land that the speculator, the planter, and the farmer had dared to venture across the mountains in the first place. And in no other state of the union was there as much confusion over land titles as in Kentucky. The origins of the situation lay in the unsystematic manner by which Virginia had distributed its western lands. The Old Dominion had parceled out its Kentucky lands first as a bonus to soldiers for fighting in the French and Indian War, then as a grant to the Transylvania Company, and finally as an inducement to obtain enlistments during the War for Independence. Moreover, many had made purchase through the land office, while thousands of small farmers had simply settled on what appeared to be unclaimed land.[39]

As little was known about the geography of Kentucky, the locations of the various grants were only vaguely described. Efforts made to survey the area merely complicated the problem. Because the surveyors were constantly harrassed by hostile Indians, their work tended to be inaccurate. In addition, over a period of several years, the same terrain of land was often marked off several different times, so that what might be designated as an individual lot by one surveyor would be included as different parts of several contiguous lots by another. As a result of these overlappings, the state became "shingled over" with land claims to which two, three, and sometimes even four and five persons held conflicting titles.[40]

The Virginia General Assembly had tried to correct this situation in 1779 when it passed an act to regulate the manner by which land titles were to be acquired and verified. Among other things, the act established a special commission to adjust conflicting land claims. In general, the law contained too many loopholes and was not sweeping enough to bring about a permanent solution to all of Kentucky's land problems, but the special commission managed to adjudicate over 3200 disputes. Because the commission's decisions had been upheld by the Virginia Supreme Court for the District of Kentucky, they were generally considered to be final. This, of course, made those land claims decided upon by the commission especially valuable, for they appeared to represent the only certainty in a state where almost all other real estate holdings were shrouded in uncertainty.[41]

This is the way matters stood until the fall of 1794. Then the Court of Appeals ruled, by a two to one vote, in the case of *Kenton* v. *McConnell,* that the commission's findings were reversible.[42] The decision caused an immediate uproar and was denounced as the work of speculators and their lawyer henchmen. A memorial to the legislature described the decision as a deliberate attempt "to reverse justice, encounter common sense, encourage [legal] strife and set at naught the peace of thousands." [43] Because Benjamin Sebastian and George Muter, the judges who had delivered the decision, were part of the ruling group, and because the winning lawyer was none other than George Nicholas, who had only recently resigned his position as attorney general in order to devote his full energies to private practice, opposition to the court's decision became synonymous with opposition to the Nicholas-Shelby faction.

A direct consequence of the unpopular decision was the formation of a temporary alliance between the Federalists, radicals, and some dissident moderates. Although the political views represented were basically irreconcilable, there was one way in which they complemented each other nicely: the Federalists and dissident moderates provided experienced political leadership, while the radicals provided considerable popular support. An early indication of the strength of this coalition came when Humphrey Marshall introduced a resolution into the House of Representatives declaring that the two judges who had delivered the decision were "destitute of integrity" and had been influenced by "corrupt motives." When the House ordered Judge Muter and Judge Sebastian to appear before it to defend themselves against the charges, they refused on the ground that it would compromise the independence of the judiciary if the legislature were allowed to review their decisions. An attempt to remove them by address followed, but it failed to obtain the necessary two-thirds majority, and, in the end, a much milder resolution simply censuring the two judges was agreed to by both Houses.[44]

But the resentment aroused by the controversy persisted and it expressed itself in other ways. The coalition of radicals, Federalists, and dissident moderates elected Humphrey Marshall to the United States Senate and further increased its strength in the legislature during the spring elections in 1795. When the legislature convened at Frankfort in November, over half of its number were new members. But there was no need to resume the attack on the judges, for as soon as the election results became known, the court met and reversed its earlier decision.

The legislature, however, was unwilling to allow the matter to rest there, and it promptly passed several important acts relating to the judiciary. It revoked the original jurisdiction of the Court of Appeals in land disputes and abolished the Court of Oyer and Terminer. The powers taken away from these courts were vested in six district courts, which were also given concurrent jurisdiction with the court of quarter sessions in all cases involving the common law and chancery. Finally, the legislature passed an act prohibiting sheriffs and justices of the peace from sitting in the General Assembly.[45]

V

Measured against the antagonisms uncovered during the debate over the constitution four years earlier, the reorganization of the judiciary in 1795 was a relatively conservative movement. Though supported by radicals, the leadership of the movement for reorganization came from Federalists and dissident moderates, many of whom were themselves lawyers, and it was they, not the radicals, who benefited most from the changes made in the court system. Under the judiciary system established in 1792, almost all cases of any importance had been pleaded in either the Court of Appeals or the Court of Oyer and Terminer. As these courts met just twice a year, and then only at Frankfort, practice in them, which could be lucrative, was monopolized by a few of the most eminent members of the profession, most notably those who supported the Nicholas-Shelby ruling clique. What the judiciary act of 1795 did by establishing district courts at different points throughout the state (Washington, Paris, Lexington, Franklin, Danville, and Bardstown, but, significantly, not at Frankfort, where the Court of Appeals continued to meet), was to open the way for a much larger number of lawyers to obtain high fees by pleading important cases.

The legislature of 1795 enacted only one measure that could be considered genuinely radical: an arbitration act which allowed for the settlement of disputes outside of court. The law provided that when both parties to a dispute agreed, they could nominate arbiters and prepare written statements of their cases, to be filed at any court of record. After recording the statements, the court's clerk was to pass them on to the agreed upon arbiters. The arbiters, who did not have to be lawyers, could subpoena witnesses. They were pledged to decide matters submitted to them according to law and equity and were required to provide a written copy of their decision to each of the parties in the controversy and to the court which had commissioned them. Settlement by arbitration was to be final, and appeals were to be allowed only upon receipt of proof that the decision had been obtained through partiality or corruption. If no appeal was made within thirty days of a ruling, the court was instructed to execute the judgment in the same manner as if a regular suit had been heard.[46]

Because no roll call vote was taken on the arbitration act, it is impossible to tell how many Federalists and dissident moderates, if any, supported the measure. Probably they were not very happy about the act, as it was based on radical principles, not requiring the use of lawyers and reducing the court from a decision-making body to an administrative agency. Commenting upon its passage a number of years later, Humphrey Marshall noted, "Thus by a side wind and under the specious pretence of expediting and cheapening the administration of justice, was the trial by jury dispensed with; and the door thrown open by law, for every species of irregularity." [47]

But other radical measures were not forthcoming. For shortly after the passage of the arbitration act in late 1795, the ever tenuous alliance between radicals, Federalists, and dissident moderates was dissolved, and during the next eighteen months an uneasy calm once again prevailed in the politics of the state. Yet, during this same period, most Kentuckians found themselves slowly but surely being forced into the same ideological division which had split them during the winter of 1791–92, and by the same issue: the calling of a constitutional convention.

X

Judicial Reform in Kentucky, 1796-1802

The Kentucky Constitution of 1792 contained no provision for amendment and provided only two methods by which a special convention for its revision could be called. First, it provided that the legislature could call a convention any time two-thirds of the members of both Houses believed it to be in the public interest. Second, it stipulated that a referendum should be held after five years, in 1797, to determine whether or not the people believed the constitution needed revision. If a majority of the voters favored revision, another referendum was to be held the following year. If the response was affirmative, the General Assembly was to call a convention for 1799.[1]

I

The radicals, as one would expect, had begun campaigning for a new constitution almost as soon as the government went into operation in 1792.[2] But it was not until after 1796, when the movement for another convention attracted the support of a large number of dissident moderates, whose objectives were different and more limited than those of the radicals, that it really started to gain momentum. Many of these dissident moderates merely wanted to tighten up the wording of the existing constitution. Others were interested only in providing for the popular election of the governor and the senate, or in a provision for the abolition of slavery.[3]

The chief opposition to constitutional reform came from the moderates entrenched in the Senate. They had successfully blocked all previous attempts to call a convention, but they could do nothing to prevent the referendum in 1797, and grudgingly agreed that it should take place during the May elections for representatives. Opponents of constitutional reform did their best, however, to see that the referendum got as little publicity as possible, and many of the voters remained unaware that anything special was happening in the election.[4]

Poor preparation, inefficiency, and perhaps even a touch of chicanery turned the referendum into a farce. Five of the state's twenty-one counties submitted no returns on the convention issue. But the sheriffs had a good excuse, as "the acts of 1797 never were transmitted . . . [until] some months after the election."[5] A preliminary count indicated that of a total of 9804 voting in the election, 5446 favored a convention, 440 opposed it, and 3928 failed to express an opinion. By the use of a little political arithmetic, the moderates managed to have the number of ballots cast recorded as 11,970, of which only 5576 favored a convention. When the legislature met in January 1798, the moderates immediately proposed that all "silent votes" be counted as negative ballots, which, of course, would mean that there would be no convention. The House, however, turned down their proposals, passing, instead, a bill put forward by the pro-convention coalition, authorizing a second referendum. But the Senate added so many unacceptable amendments, that the assembly, after a long struggle, adjourned with the matter unresolved.[6]

It was not George Nicholas, but John Breckinridge, a relative newcomer to Kentucky politics, who took the lead in the moderate campaign against the constitutional convention. Declining health and preoccupation with his duties as the first Professor of Law at Transylvania University in Lexington had forced Nicholas to retire from active politics. Breckinridge, another upper class Virginian, was fully prepared for political leadership. Born in 1760, the son of well-to-do parents, Breckinridge entered The

College of William and Mary at the age of twenty. He studied law with George Wythe for a short time, but dropped out of school to take a seat in the House of Delegates. After several years of political tutelage he returned to college, and he was finally admitted to the Virginia Bar in 1785. Eight years later he declined a seat in Congress in order to move to Kentucky, where greater opportunities beckoned.[7]

Breckinridge did well for himself. At first he remained outside the dominant Nicholas-Shelby clique, but he quickly won acceptance. His abilities and his legal training under Wythe combined to make him one of the most important lawyers in the state. Within one year of his arrival he was pleading important cases in the Court of Appeals, and along with Nicholas and James Brown, both of whom had also studied under Wythe, dominated the Lexington bar. The trio established a debating society and held moot courts in which young lawyers discussed the intricacies of the law and received instruction in Coke and Blackstone.[8]

Politically, Breckinridge was closely allied with Madison and Jefferson on the national level and with the moderates on the local level. When Nicholas resigned as Attorney General in 1793, Breckinridge succeeded him, and four years later he won a seat in the Kentucky House of Representatives. As a member of the House, Breckinridge led the fight to liberalize the state's penal code, and tried, unsuccessfully, to revive the Court of Oyer and Terminer. But he mostly concentrated his efforts on opposing the movement for the calling of a constitutional convention. Breckinridge claimed that most people were happy under the existing constitution and that the agitation for a new one was the work of a "restless minority." His main concern, however, was with the dangerous implications of the movement for the convention.

> I have for sometime been uneasy at that spirit for innovation and change, which has been so predominant in the councils of this country. So long as they were confined to cases, which could only produce temporary inconveniences or mischief and might be corrected by the same hand which produced them there was nothing very serious to apprehend . . . But more serious mischiefs are now underfoot and if not timely checked

or prevented by the good of this country will be the fore-
runner of measures which will ultimately bring down upon
us anarchy and wretchedness.[9]

Breckinridge, however, was too shrewd a politician not to have
realized that the legislature's refusal to provide for a second
referendum was only a temporary victory for the moderates. Nor
could he have been unaware that convention proponents, especially radicals, were urging the public to write in their prefer-
ences for a convention when they went to vote during the May
1798 elections for members of the Assembly. Because the convention issue had been before the public for almost a year, and since,
as one writer put it, "it was the one method left by which the
people can (in a peaceful way) introduce a convention," it appeared that a majority of the voters might follow the instructions of the radicals.[10]

Recognizing this peril, Breckinridge led the moderates in a
vigorous campaign to educate the public about the dangers inherent in a convention. His strategy was to divide and conquer, to
somehow convince dissident moderates and other non-radicals
"that there are some restless spirits amongst us both in and out
of the legislature who cannot conceive they enjoy the rights and
privileges of freemen unless they are authorized to involve themselves and fellow citizens in ruin." [11]

Under Breckinridge's leadership, the moderates undertook a
campaign to deliberately exaggerate the extent of radical support
for slave emancipation and to equate it with an all out attack on
property rights. It was a very effective maneuver in a state where
a large proportion of the people were slaveholders and an overwhelming majority owned land. One writer, for example, warned
the people that "the advocates of total change" intended "an
abolition of all laws for the recovery of debts, and an immediate
and total emancipation of your slaves, without regards to the
rights of property." [12]

These accusations were strenuously denied by convention advocates, who denounced them as "nothing more than an aristo-
cratical bugbear calculated to frighten the people from exercising
their rights." [13] "A voter" cleverly and effectively turned the
attack back on the moderates:

The man of landed property is told that *agrarian laws* will be passed; and the slaveholder is alarmed by the fear of *immediate emancipation.*

And can you, my countrymen, be frightened out of your rights by such artful, but visionary alarms? To the meaning of an agrarian law many of you may be strangers as no laws of that kind have passed for many centuries. With *agrarian practice* every lawyer of America who takes *one half* of your land to advocate your claim to the other, will render you perfectly acquainted. And is not this latter species of *agrarian* distribution of property a serious evil and the only kind of *agrarian* policy from which we have anything to apprehend? And do these men who enjoy the benefits of this mode of dividing property dare to insinuate, that the honest citizens of this commonwealth feel the same rapacious dispositions to seize upon the fruits of the industry of their neighbours? Believe them not. The seeds of virtue are implanted in your hearts.—You will respect the property of your fellow citizens, that your own may be respected.[14]

To be sure, anti-slavery sentiment existed in Kentucky, but it was not nearly as extensive as the moderates claimed. Throughout the state, many Baptist, Methodist, and Presbyterian ministers believed slavery corrupted the country's morals and that it was against the will of God, and in the towns, anti-slavery societies argued that the institution was inconsistent with the Declaration of Independence and bad economically for both the owner and the state, but neither group advocated immediate abolition. In fact, the most important anti-slavery spokesman was young Henry Clay, and he merely expressed a desire to see gradual and compensated emancipation.[15]

The radicals advocated neither immediate emancipation nor the confiscation of any kind of property. Rather, they emphasized the necessity of freeing the state from aristocratic control, of finding some way of settling the numerous land disputes whose "perplexity and expense of law proceedings loudly call for some constitutional provisions," and of doing something about the senate, which "will throw every obstruction in way of reform however salutary, [and] forever prevent any improvement of our judiciary system." [16]

Despite all their efforts to distort the issues, the moderates did badly in the spring elections. Breckinridge himself barely retained his seat in the legislature, while a preliminary count of votes throughout the state indicated that the radicals and their allies had a popular mandate for calling a convention.[17] The legislature did not meet until November, however, and so nothing could be done until then. In the meantime, something was happening on the national level which would eventually aid the moderates' cause.

II

The Alien and Sedition Acts, signed into law in July 1798, touched off widespread popular resentment throughout the country. In Kentucky, opposition to the Acts found expression at special meetings held at local court houses. In the beginning, at least, these meetings were unplanned expressions of hostility to the federal government on the part of the people. The overwhelming majority of Kentuckians had been hostile to the national government ever since its inception, and they viewed the Alien and Sedition Acts as part of an insidious plan devised by the Federalists to increase the powers of the central government and to rob the people of their liberties.[18]

Jefferson and Madison had also been enraged by the passage of the Alien and Sedition Acts. Believing them to be oppressive and unconstitutional, they decided to have resolutions of protest introduced into the Virginia and North Carolina legislatures. The Virginia resolutions were written by Madison; the North Carolina ones by Jefferson. Their activities were shrouded in secrecy, and only Wilson Cary Nicholas, a younger brother of George Nicholas, was taken into their confidence. To him fell the responsibility for having the resolutions introduced in the Virginia and North Carolina state legislatures.[19]

It was at this juncture, during the late summer of 1798, that Breckinridge took a brief trip to Virginia. Because the trip involved considerable risk, putting him out of touch with affairs in Kentucky, the question naturally arises as to why he chose this particular time to travel to Virginia. It may, of course, simply have been made for reasons of health, or to visit relatives, or to make some kind of business arrangement. Yet it seems significant that even before he left Kentucky, there was widespread talk of resistance to the Alien and Sedition Acts. An example was the recommendation of "Philo-Aegis" which was published in the *Kentucky Gazette:*

> My plan is this, let the legislature of Kentucky be convened by the governor, let them pass resolutions praying for a repeal of every obnoxious and unconstitutional act of Congress.[20]

There is no evidence that Breckinridge had any foreknowledge of what Jefferson and Madison were planning. He may have journeyed to Virginia to recommend a plan of action similar to the one they had already decided upon, but with one difference. Breckinridge wanted the resolutions to be introduced in the Kentucky legislature; and doubtless he also hoped that he would be given the honor of introducing them. That he would travel to Virginia to consult with Jefferson and Madison on the matter would not be surprising, for they were the party's leaders, and he would have wanted to make sure of their support before taking such a drastic step.

At any rate, whatever his reasons for traveling to Virginia, once he arrived Breckinridge visited Wilson Cary Nicholas. When Nicholas took him into his confidence and told him what Jefferson and Madison were planning, Breckinridge requested that he be allowed to meet with Jefferson. This request was denied, probably to minimize the danger to Jefferson, who was then Vice President, of being accused of plotting against the government. But Breckinridge was able to persuade Nicholas that it was safer to have him introduce Jefferson's resolutions in the Kentucky legislature, where they were assured of adoption, than to risk having someone else introduce them in the North Carolina legislature, where there was a good chance they might be rejected. Before leaving, Breckinridge gave Nicholas his most "solemn assurance" that Jefferson's name would be kept out of the matter.[21]

When the Kentucky legislature convened on November 7,

Governor James Garrard issued a call for action by declaring that under the federal system a state had the right to censure the national government and, specifically, to condemn the Alien and Sedition Acts as unconstitutional. Breckinridge introduced Jefferson's nine resolutions, slightly revised, the next day. They were passed, almost unanimously, by both Houses of the legislature two days later.[22]

The moderate-led opposition to the Alien and Sedition Acts had two immediate and important effects on Kentucky politics. First, much to the relief of the moderates, it pushed the convention issue into the background. Second, it gave to the moderates, especially Breckinridge, who kept his word about not involving Jefferson and who thus received all the credit for sponsoring the resolutions, and George Nicholas, who came out of retirement long enough to denounce the Alien and Sedition Acts, an opportunity to pass themselves off as the protectors of the peoples' liberties. One moderate, writing from a radical stronghold, noted to Breckinridge that "the people through the country . . . have given an almost universal plaudit to your resolutions respecting Congressional tyranny." [23]

The moderates next turned their attentions to finding some way of using their new-found popularity to prevent the radicals from making major changes in the constitution. They realized that they could not prevent the convention from meeting, and so they agreed to an act providing for the election of delegates. Their plan, however, was to make sure that the right kind of people were elected as delegates and the call immediately went out for "the most independent and principled men amongst us to step forward and prevent mischief." [24] At a special meeting held at Bryant's Station in Fayette County, a series of resolutions, written by Breckinridge and George Nicholas, were adopted, providing that no candidate should be supported unless he publicly declared himself to be opposed to legislative interference with slavery and in favor of a bicameral legislature, the protection of property, and an independent judiciary.[25]

The radicals, in the mean time, were not inactive. They chose their own slate of candidates, repeatedly denied any intention of confiscating private property, and denounced the meeting at

Bryant's Station as aristocratically inspired by "the same minority which at first resisted . . . [and who] have now assumed the mask of acquiesence, and are attempting by strategy to accomplish the objects which they have despaired of securing by manly opposition." [26] But it was the Breckinridge-Nicholas men who triumphed in the election. Only one anti-slavery delegate was elected, and, while the radical delegation was considerably larger, it was still a definite minority.

Breckinridge dominated the convention which met at Frankfort on 22 July 1799, in much the same manner as Nicholas had dominated the earlier one. He made some minor concessions, but he had his way on the major issues. The governor and Senate, along with the lieutenant governor (a newly created office), were made responsible to the people every four years. The governor was also made ineligible to succeed himself for seven years after the expiration of his term in office. But not all of the changes in the 1799 constitution were in a democratic direction. Sheriffs and coroners, who had previously been elected, were now to be appointed by the Governor. The secret ballot established by the constitution of 1792 was replaced by a *viva voce* system of voting. And the constitution was made even more difficult to revise. The new document required as a first step in calling a convention that a majority of each House of the legislature enact a law during the first twenty days of a session for taking the sense of the people on the expediency of changing the constitution. Only after a majority of all those in the state who were eligible to vote, not simply a majority of those who actually voted, favored the calling of a convention for two years running, could one be called. At a time when a 60 per cent turnout of eligible voters was considered high, this made it virtually impossible to change the constitution.[27]

The only attempt the radicals made to change the Constitution of 1792 fundamentally was their proposal to alter the judiciary. Under the leadership of Felix Grundy, the radicals sought to establish a system of county circuit courts which they believed would help make the administration of justice cheap, convenient, and locally oriented. The convention defeated the measure 30 to 23.[28] The moderates opposed the circuit court measure in part, as some radicals claimed, because it represented a threat to their control over the existing court system. An even more important reason for their opposition was their belief that it would be unwise for the constitution to provide specifically for a lower court system, for this would mean that every time the people decided they wanted to change the judiciary, they would have to call another convention to amend the constitution. On this point Breckinridge was in agreement with Ninian Edawrds, who opposed the measure because he believed "that too frequent changes in the constitution of a state is among the greatest of evils, for it unhinges government, relaxes the springs, begets incertitude in its operations, and creates a political chaos in society." [29]

The convention's work was aptly described by Edwards as "alterations and not amendments" to the constitution.[30] The new constitution differed from the old on some small points, but it could hardly be considered a radical departure, especially when the changes made are compared with those that had been desired by the radicals. The legislature remained bicameral, the slavery provisions of the previous constitution remained intact, and the independence of the judiciary continued to be secure.

III

The radicals, while disappointed by the results of the convention, were not discouraged. After the adoption of the constitution, they shifted their campaign back to the legislature, where they continued to advocate the establishment of a system of county circuit courts. In their pursuit of this end, the radical's benefited from two important developments.

The first was the growing political importance of the Green River Country. Sometimes referred to as the "south country" or the "southside," it was the section of the state Breckinridge described as being "filled with nothing but hunters, horse thieves and savages. And a country where wretchedness, poverty and sickness will always reign." Its emergence as a political force in Kentucky politics began in 1795, when the legislature, hoping to encourage settlement, passed an act putting the lands in that part of the state on the market for the low price of thirty dollars per hundred acres. Additional acts, passed in 1797 and 1798, extended credit for lands to be purchased and delayed the due date for payment on lands which had already been purchased. At first the moderates supported these measures, believing that they would contribute to the economic development of the state. But as they watched the rapid growth of population in the south country, they became concerned. Moderate strength was centered in the Blue Grass area in the northern part of the state, and after it became clear that the Green River region was turning into a radical stronghold, they began to oppose the passage of further relief measures. But their opposition came too late, for, in addition to the southside delegation in the legislature, there were too many representatives from other sections of the state who also favored cheap land and easy credit, so that "Green River debt legislation" continued to be passed. The phenomenal growth of the southside is shown by the fact that more than two thirds of the new counties created between 1792 and 1800 were in that section of the state.[31]

The second development that benefited the radicals after the failure of constitutional reform was the emergence of Felix Grundy as a leader capable of energetically championing their cause. Born in 1777, the son of middle class English emigrants, Grundy grew up in Washington county, which was part of the Green River area. He was his mother's "last and favorite son," and she did her best to see that he was well educated. He attended the Bardstown Academy, which at that time was under the direction of Dr. James Priestly, and he studied law for two years under George Nicholas. He began practicing law in 1795 and became a state's attorney the following year. Grundy entered politics in 1799 when he was elected Washington County's delegate to the constitutional convention. His performance at the convention clearly indicated that Grundy had no intention of joining the moderate establishment, and that his sympathies lay not with the legal profession or the large plantation owners but with the small farmer. His constituents were so pleased that they elected him to the legislature in 1800. Almost immediately he became the acknowledged leader of the Green River delegation, a position which made him one of the most powerful men in the legislature.[32]

Grundy wasted no time in introducing a bill to abolish the District Courts and the Courts of Quarter Sessions and to establish instead circuit courts which were to meet three times a year in each county for six-day terms. Each circuit court was to have jurisdiction in all cases of chancery and common law arising in the respective counties, and was empowered to hear and determine cases of treason, murder, felonies, and other crimes and misdemeanors in the county in which the crime was committed. The measure passed the House but was killed in the Senate when the speaker cast the deciding vote against it. "Our Assembly," wrote Henry Clay, a firm moderate on the judiciary issue, "they have indeed attempted much and done little; but I have heard it remarked, perhaps not improperly that this is the best evidence of their superior wisdom." [33]

Undaunted, Grundy tried again when the legislature met the following year. This time he offered an even more radical proposal: it provided that each court be presided over by one judge riding circuit and by two assistants residing in the county where the court was held. As these assistants were to be paid only two dollars a day, which was much less than any lawyer could make pleading cases, the assistant judges invariably would be men not learned in the law.[34] Grundy's proposals precipitated a debate that lasted four days.

Grundy began his defense of the proposed change in the judicial system by defining "the great object of government . . . to be to make the people contented and happy," and by asserting "that this could be done only by an equal and impartial distribution of advantages and privileges." He pointed out that under the district court system established in 1795, suitors and witnesses were forced to travel great distances to the courts. Since this took both time and money, neither of which small farmers could spare, the existing system of administering justice, he argued, worked to the benefit of the rich and to the detriment of the poor.[35]

The remedy, Grundy maintained, was for every case to be tried in the county of the defendant's residence. This meant that the judges must ride circuit and hold court in each county. This would help distribute justice more equally since under it suitors and their witnesses would no longer be required to travel to attend court. Benjamin Logan, a dissident moderate with gubernatorial aspirations, who warmly supported Grundy's circuit court measure, argued that the key question was "whether it be better to establish a system which will make it the interest of the lawyers to follow the business, or to be so complaisant to them as to make the business follow the lawyers." [36]

Both Logan and Grundy admitted that the circuit court measure was a radical innovation, but insisted upon its necessity. Logan took the position that "the inconvenience, perfidity, the oppression and the danger to public tranquility, accompanying the present system were so great, that the change was absolutely necessary to the stability of the government and to the happiness of the people." [37] And Grundy warned, "Let us decide that nothing shall be done, unless the same thing has been done heretofore; and we at once put a stop to every kind of improvement." [38]

The radicals and their allies denounced those who opposed the measure as interested parties: established lawyers who controlled the business of the existing court system; judges who did not want the inconvenience of riding circuit; land speculators who owned property in different parts of the state and who did not wish to have the legality of their land titles decided upon by local juries; and selfish citizens whose property values were enhanced because they resided in areas adjacent to where a district court met.[39] There was, of course, considerable truth to all these charges, but many of those who were opposed to the adoption of the circuit court system were motivated by more than self-interest. In support of their position, the opponents were able to marshall strong arguments that the circuit court system would bring about a change for the worse in the administration of justice.

The opponents of the circuit court system warned that there simply were not enough capable and honest lawyers to handle the business which a multiplication of the number of courts would produce, and that as a consequence sharpers and pettifoggers would be given an increased opportunity to prey on the unsuspecting. They argued also that the proposed change would lower the quality of the judiciary, as good judges facing the grueling ordeal of riding circuit would return to private practice "to employ in behalf of individuals, those talents, which in the service of the state had been rewarded with poverty and disgrace." [40] And they flatly denied that under the circuit court system justice would be cheaper or that it would be administered more equally. What would happen was graphically described by "A Poor Farmer":

> Will not a want of confidence in circuit courts together with the ignorance of many of the lawyers who will attend them, occasion appeals from the greater number of their most important decisions? Consequently will not the court of appeals be deluged with business; and in that way, to say nothing of the costs to the litigants, the community be subjected to the intolerable evil, of a delay of justice in its supreme judicial tribunal?
>
> Will not the dispersed situations of the circuit courts, as well as a contemptible opinion of the greater number of their judges and lawyers, drive a multitude of suitors into the federal court: where the fees are excessively high, and where there is no security, that the decision will be in conformity with the decisions of our court of appeals! [41]

Yet another argument against the proposed change in the judiciary system was that its enactment would endanger that unformity of decision which was so vital to the economic development of the state. Under the district court system the judges often got together to agree upon a definite set of rules for settling disputes, but the new system allowed so little opportunity for communication between the judges, and gave so much power to assistants who were not learned in the law, that it was inevitable that justice would be administered differently in one part of the state than in another. The effect of this would be to shatter the confidence of the people, especially those who belonged to the business community, in the judicial system. As one member of the legislature put it:

> The judiciary is a component part of the government, and perhaps the most important part. To change it unnecessarily

would impair public credit, which in young countries particularly it is indispensable to cherish. The man who lends,—the man who forms a contract, has no confidence in the mode which the [proposed] law has provided for him to recover his property.[42]

Beneath all these arguments, however, was the fear on the part of the moderates that a frequent reorganization of the courts would damage the efficiency of the judiciary, and the belief that what was at stake was less a question of whether the administration of justice should be convenient and equal and more one of whether or not the independence of the judiciary should be sacrificed to the whims and caprices of the people. Sometimes this anxiety appeared above the surface. "Brutus and Cassius" wrote in *The Palladium,*

> It is indeed in the highest degree absurd that multitudes are incessantly perplexing themselves about forms of government and law making, who would be perfectly contented with the mere shadow of a judiciary regardless of the substance: whereas, without honest, wise and independent courts, the best devised constitutions are no more than paper walls, and the most wholesome laws dead letters: without such courts, there is no security, for life, liberty or property.[43]

Hoping to avoid a direct confrontation with the radicals on the circuit court issue, the moderates offered to compromise by increasing the number of district courts and by abolishing the quarter sessions courts. But Grundy, who was determined to have his own way, rejected it.[44] His measure was defeated during the 1801 session of the legislature, and he immediately reintroduced it when the assembly reconvened the following year. And again it was defeated. Many of the moderates now became so confident that they were no longer willing to compromise, and they defeated a proposal to extend the district court system. This proved to be a mistake, for there were many members of both Houses who favored changing the existing judiciary system to make the administration of justice more convenient for the people, and yet were reluctant to support so radical a measure as the circuit court system. But after the defeat of their measure to increase the number of district courts they decided they had no alternative but to throw their support behind Grundy's circuit court system. Realizing this, the "cunning and intriguing" Grundy reintroduced his measure, which this time passed by a substantial majority.[45]

The moderates were incensed by what had happened. "Our Assembly," wrote one of them, "have played the devil with our judiciary system." [46] Governor Garrard, a firm moderate, vetoed the bill, citing the "radical and extensive" changes it provided. Two days later, however, both Houses of the legislature, for the first time in the history of the state, repassed the measure by the two-thirds majority necessary to override the governor's veto, and it became law.[47]

IV

While the Circuit Court Act proved to be a popular measure, its effect was, in fact, what the moderates had predicted it would be: to impede rather than improve the administration of justice. By far the greatest difficulty arose from the antagonism that developed almost immediately between the circuit judges and their various assistants. The judges resented being forced to share the decision-making process with men who were not trained in the law. Reportedly, one of them, after listening to a case, would contemptuously turn from one assistant to the other and ask, "What do you guess?" [48]

For their part, the assistants had plenty of opportunity to retaliate. According to Humphrey Marshall:

> . . . when the assistants concerted they knew as much, or more than their president [the circuit court judge], they were commonly refractory, and kept him in check. He being in general a resident in town, or an itinerant on his circuit, or a lodger in town where the court was held, could attend early; or late; while his brother judges [the assistants], residing in most cases in the country, remained at home for breakfast; then came to town, put up their horses at the tavern, took a round of smoking or chattering; then to court; and if anything had been

done, were ready to rehear, and confirm, or reverse it. For it is to be remembered, that the presiding or circuit judge, could hold court in the absence of his assistants; subject, nevertheless, to have everything he did undone by them: And which soon taught him to do nothing when they were away, unless he had previously obtained the control over one of them at least.[49]

Also, as the moderates had predicted, the hardships involved in riding circuit and the general inadequacy of judicial salaries combined to discourage the more capable members of the bar from accepting positions on the bench. In the early years of statehood the Kentucky legislature generally turned a deaf ear toward pleas from the legal profession for the establishment of high salaries for judges, and it became widely recognized that in almost every county of the state the lawyers were more able than the judges. In 1804, a foreign traveler described Kentucky's court as being noisy and crowded with

> judges sitting as silent spectators, attornies wrangling and disputing among themselves within the bar, parties often clamorous, witnesses pertinacious and contemptuous, and what may be called the people, some sober and others drunk— laughing, talking sometimes shouting, and not unfrequently brawling and fighting.

This observer placed the responsibility for the "confusion and tumult" squarely on the shoulders of the judges, who he described as "men not generally selected from the most respectable and best informed citizens . . . many of them them are very ignorant, some of them are not respected in the neighborhood, and others whose moral characters will not bear scrutiny or investigation." [50]

Kentucky moderates did their best to mitigate what they believed were the unfortunate effects of the circuit court system. Under the leadership of William Littell, they made progress in the simplification, codification, and publication of the law, which helped bring a semblance of uniformity to the administration of justice. They also worked for, and finally obtained, in 1816, a repeal of those sections of the Circuit Court Act providing for assistants. But these changes were long in coming, and by the time they were made, most people outside the state and even many people inside the state had come to believe that only the federal courts offered an adequate system of jurisprudence which could protect their rights and interests in Kentucky.

XI

Courts and Politics in Pennsylvania, 1799-1805

The struggle over judicial reform in Pennsylvania was an especially bitter one. In 1799 the court system hardly met the state's needs: dockets were overcrowded, the administration of justice was slow and inefficient, and people in the western part of the state were constantly complaining about the inconvenience and expense of traveling east to plead cases before a Supreme Court which met only in Philadelphia. Moreover, most of the judges, protected in their office by life tenure, belonged to the defeated Federalist party; while the leadership of the dominant Republican party, which had to cope with the problems of the administration of justice, was made up of a number of strong personalities who were in fundamental disagreement over the nature and meaning of judicial reform.[1]

I

Thomas McKean was the ostensible leader of the Pennsylvania Republicans. He was sixty-five years old when elected governor in 1799, and no other member of the state's revolutionary generation had so adroitly and successfully weathered the political storms following independence. A radical on home rule but a conservative about who should rule at home, McKean had little sympathy for the state's 1776 Constitution. Yet the following year he accepted appointment as Chief Justice of the Supreme Court, a position he held for twenty-two years. He favored the adoption of the federal constitution and was an active member of the convention that drafted the Pennsylvania Constitution of 1790, but he early switched his allegiance to the Republican party. It is no wonder that one angry Federalist described him as a "weathercock." [2]

Arrogant and tactless, McKean was not a popular public figure and probably would not have been nominated for governor had he not had the backing of Alexander J. Dallas, the most skillful Republican politician in the state. An émigré from the British West Indies, Dallas had arrived in Philadelphia in 1783 at the age of twenty-four. He rapidly established himself as an energetic young man learned in the law and eager to enter public service, and in 1791 he was appointed secretary of the Commonwealth. The governor at the time was Thomas Mifflin, a genial old military hero with little administrative ability, who throughout his nine years in office relied heavily on his secretary's talents. By taking advantage of the governor's dependence, and by liberally interpreting the duties of his office, Dallas accumulated a great deal of power. When Mifflin retired, Dallas had little trouble bringing about the election of McKean, whose political views coincided with his own.[3]

McKean and Dallas joined the Republican party partly because they disagreed with Federalist policies and partly because it offered good opportunities for political advancement, but not because they were inclined to any kind of radicalism, especially in legal matters. McKean's concern for judicial independence and his hostility to legislative supremacy were well known; while Dallas, one of the most prominent members of the Philadelphia bar, was a leading advocate of a moderate kind of judicial reform. Both supported Jefferson for the presidency in 1800 and denounced the Adams administration, yet they were always less inclined than many other members of their party to engage in the more extreme measures of opposition. After Jefferson's election they warmly endorsed the moderate Republican position on federal patronage, and they opposed the repeal of the Judiciary Act of 1801.[4]

Gathered around McKean and Dallas were a number of like-minded individuals with whom they shared part of their power: Peter Muhlenberg, a Revolutionary War general and Episcopalian minister with a large German following, who hoped to be McKean's successor; Tench Coxe, secretary of the land office and co-author of Hamilton's *Report on Manufactures*, about whose conversion to the Republican party there were many mysterious rumors, and who some suspected had once been a loyalist; Senator George Logan, a well-known physician and gentleman farmer, who was a member of an important Quaker family; and Albert Gallatin, Dallas's close personal friend, who represented the group's interest in Jefferson's cabinet.

The Republican party in Pennsylvania in 1801 also included a large and vigorous group of radicals, although none of them was a member of the ruling inner circle. The most articulate and most important member of this group was William Duane, a professional agitator who in the course of his lifetime was involved in disputes on three continents. An American by birth, he was reared in Ireland and trained to be a printer. In 1787 he went to India, where he published several newspapers and served in the Bengal government. He had a stormy career which culminated in his arrest and the confiscation of his property in 1794, after he got into a dispute with leading members of the East India Company. Deported, he sailed for England, where he failed to obtain the restitution of his property but did manage to preside at a large public meeting protesting alleged parliamentary violations of the British Constitution. Shortly afterwards, he left for America. He joined Benjamin Franklin Bache on the Philadelphia *Aurora*, and when Bache died in 1798, Duane became editor. He turned the *Aurora* into the leading Jeffersonian newspaper in the country. In 1799 he was arrested under the Sedition Act, and, until the case was dismissed by Jefferson two years later, he was continually in court defending himself.[5]

Duane had an indefatigable ally in Michael Leib, the congressional representative from Philadelphia county. Born of German immigrant parents, Leib had studied medicine under Benjamin Rush, but he preferred the excitement of politics. Leib first became known for his work in the German and Democratic societies of 1793 and soon became a leader of the Philadelphia Tammany Society, from which, he later wrote, "Judges and Common Law do not receive much hommage [sic]." He was an ambitious man whose dandified appearance belied his political shrewdness. The *Aurora*'s backing made him a powerful force in Philadelphia politics.[6]

On the national level Duane and Leib favored the wholesale removal of Federalists from office and major changes in the national court system. They also disliked the moderation of "McKean, Dallas and Company," and had in fact opposed McKean's nomination for governor in 1799, although they supported him in the ensuing election.[7] For their part, the moderates had few illusions about either Duane or Leib. They willingly admitted that Duane had proved himself an ally of inestimable worth in bringing about the defeat of the Federalists, but they still did not like or trust him. Dallas came right to the point in 1805, when he expressed the belief that as long as Duane had power "the State [and] the United States will never enjoy quiet."[8]

McKean was elected in 1799 by less than 5000 votes; three years later he won by over six times that many, losing only three of the state's thirty-three counties. The intervening years saw not only Jefferson's election to the presidency but also the virtual disappearance of the Federalist party as an effective opposition in Pennsylvania politics. All this, McKean believed, made a schism inevitable. "Whenever any party are notoriously predominant they will split; this is in nature, it has been the case time immemorial, and it will be so until mankind becomes wiser and better."[9]

II

During McKean's first administration the divisions in the Republican party arose mainly from factional quarrels involving personal animosities and differences over dispensing patronage.[10] Following his overwhelming re-election in 1802, however, a more serious and more divisive issue, one that involved basic principles as well as interest, arouse: judicial reform. As in most states at the beginning of the nineteenth century, the Republican administration of Pennsylvania was saddled with a court system which, in the words of the governor, "the extension of Commerce and Agriculture, the increase of population, and the multiplication of counties" have made "no longer adequate to the regular and efficient administration of justice." [11]

There was no question but that some kind of judicial reform was necessary. All Republicans agreed on this; they disagreed, however, about what kinds of changes were to be made. McKean favored reform along moderate lines. In his annual addresses to the legislature in 1800 and again in 1801 he recommended increasing the number of Supreme Court justices and revising the lower court system "upon a plan more adequate to the state of population and commerce." Bills to this end were introduced into both Houses of the legislature by the Governor's supporters but were killed by Republicans desiring more radical judicial reform.[12]

What these radicals wanted was the creation of a code of laws free of Latin phrases and technical terms, which they believed would be more consistent with "the plain and simple nature of a Republican form of government"; the simplification of court procedure and the establishment of a system of arbitration to reduce the "sophistication and pretensions" of the legal establishment and allow laymen to plead their own cases; and a judiciary less under the control of the Federalist party and more responsive to the wishes of the people.[13]

In the legislature the leadership for the radical program of judicial reform came from a pair of rising politicians whose constituencies were to be found in the state's rural interior. Simon Snyder of Northumberland county, forty-three years old in 1803, was a former justice of the peace who took great pride in the fact that none of his decisions had ever been appealed to the regular courts. He represented his county at the state's constitutional convention in 1790, and in 1797 he was elected to the lower house of the legislature, a position he held until he became governor in 1808.[14] Snyders' most important ally was Nathaniel Boileau of Montgomery County, who had been born in 1763 and had graduated from Princeton. He also was first elected to the legislature in 1797.[15] Together Synder and Boileau persistently denounced the legal profession, the common law, and the idea of an independent judiciary. They strongly favored extending the jurisdiction of the justices of the peace, who almost always were laymen, and the establishment of a permanent system of arbitration as part of the state's judicial procedure. Their ideas received vigorous and articulate support from the Northumberland *Republican Argus,* which had been founded in December 1802 by John Binns, a radical Irish revolutionary and former member of the London Corresponding Society who had emigrated to America after being imprisoned several times in England.[16]

In 1799 the legislature passed a three-year temporary act extending the jurisdiction of the justices of the peace to all actions involving less than twenty dollars. When the act expired in 1802, the radicals succeeded in raising the limit to one hundred dollars. The measure, popularly known as the Hundred Dollar Act, was presented to the governor on 3 April, the day before adjournment. This meant, as stipulated in the constitution, that unless McKean vetoed it the act would become law within three days after the legislature reconvened in early December. It also meant that McKean had almost eight months to consider the matter.

Although the Hundred Dollar Act would have alleviated the problem of overcrowded dockets in the regular courts, McKean vetoed it. In his message to the legislature on December 9 the governor emphasized the radical implications of the measure, warning that "it would be unwise further to indulge the spirit of innovation." McKean went on to argue that it would be a mistake to leave the administration of justice to such a large extent in the hands of men who were untrained in the law and upon whom there were few restraints; that the act circumscribed if it did not violate the state constitution's guarantee of trial by jury; that the prohibition of arguments by counsel would place at a disadvantage those litigants who lacked the talents to plead effectively for themselves; and finally, that though the intention of the act was to decrease the cost of litigation, its effect really would be to increase it, because the decisions rendered by non-professional justices of the peace would be so unsatisfactory as to necessitate more appeals than ever.[17]

An attempt to override the veto failed in the Senate, but the radicals managed, after much jockeying between the House and the Senate, to pass a bill establishing a system of arbitration. They also attached a provision to a general act for the erecting of private dams on public streams, which gave to justices of the peace jurisdiction in cases of values up to fifty dollars where damages had been caused by such dams.[18]

McKean vetoed both measures. In his message on the arbitration bill he warned against "crude theories, fanciful alterations, new projects, and pleasing visions." He also made clear his belief that "innovations, especially in the administration of justice are dangerous. It is always safer, to borrow from former establishments, than to introduce plans entirely new, to travel on a beaten road, than one before untrodden." In both veto messages he repeated most of the arguments he had used against the Hundred Dollar Act. The radicals tried to override McKean's veto of the arbitration bill, but they could obtain only a simple majority, not the necessary two-thirds. They did, however, manage to repass the general dam act, a sure sign of their growing strength.[19]

McKean's vetoes thrust into the foreground the basic issue separating moderate and radical Republicans on judicial reform. According to one account, when a radical delegation from the legislature asked the governor to reconsider his vetoes, "he deliberately took out his watch and, handing it to the chairman, said, 'Pray, Sir, look at my watch; she has been out of order for some time; will you be pleased to put her to rights.' 'Sir,' replied the chairman with some surprise, 'I am no watchmaker; I am a carpenter.' The watch was then handed to the other members of the committee, both of whom declined, one being a currier, the other a bricklayer. 'Well,' said the Governor, 'this is truly strange! Any watchmaker's apprentice can repair that watch; it is a simple piece of mechanism, and yet you can't do it! The law, gentlemen, is a science of great difficulty and endless complications; it requires a lifetime to understand it. I have bestowed a quarter of a century upon it; yet *you,* who can't mend this little watch, become *lawyers all at once,* and presume to instruct me in my duty!' " The delegation reportedly beat a hasty retreat.[20]

III

At the same time that the moderate and radical Republicans of Pennsylvania were quarreling over judicial reform they were also turning their attention to the separate but closely related problem of what to do about Federalist judges who were using their positions on the bench for partisan purposes.

The immediate object of their scorn was Alexander Addison, "the transmontane Goliath of federalism" in Pennsylvania.[21] A native of Scotland, born in 1759, Addison had been educated for the ministry at Aberdeen University. He emigrated to America and in 1785 settled in Washington County, where he began to study law. Six years later he was appointed president judge of the fifth judicial district. An uncompromising Federalist, he opposed the Whisky Rebellion and helped to suppress it. He also violently denounced, in a widely published charge to a grand jury, the principles set forth in the Kentucky and Virginia Resolutions.[22]

The incident which proved to be the beginning of Addison's undoing occurred in December 1800, when, in an address to a grand jury on the "Rise and Progress of Revolution," he spoke critically of McKean's recent election. One of the associate judges, a Republican by the name of John B. C. Lucas, tried to reply, but he was ruled out of order by Addison and the other associate judge, John McDowell, also a Federalist. The cry immediately went up for Addison's impeachment, but Lucas preferred to appeal the ruling to the state Supreme Court. The Court declared that associate judges had equal rights with president judges to address grand juries, but declined to take any action against Addison on the grounds there was no proof of criminal intent.[23]

Two months later, Addison, with the aid of McDowell, once again prevented Lucas from addressing a grand jury. At the next meeting of the legislature the Republicans of western Pennsylvania presented a petition with 384 names to the house demanding Addison's impeachment. It was referred to a special committee which, after investigating the charges, recommended that articles of impeachment be drawn up. They were, and the House approved them by a 65 to 8 vote. The Senate then scheduled the trial to take place at the next meeting of the legislature in December.[24]

Addison's trial began on 17 January 1803. Dallas conducted the prosecution for the House, and Addison acted as his own defense counsel, evincing, as one newspaper put it, "the most insolent, arrogant and overbearing conduct." After a trial of nine days the Senate convicted him by a vote of 20 to 4. The next day Addison was removed from office and disqualified from ever again holding a judicial office in Pennsylvania.[25]

There had been substantial agreement among Pennsylvania Republicans about the need to impeach Addison, and even the Federalists did not protest very strenuously. But almost immediately radical and moderate Republicans divided over what should happen next. The radicals, viewing Addison's removal as merely the first step in a general housecleaning operation that was long overdue, began to file complaints against other judges and justices they objected to. The moderates, on the other hand, were opposed to a wholesale assault on the judiciary. The real danger, McKean believed, did not come from the Federalists, who were "not only humbled but subdued," but from members of his own party against whom "no small share of vigilance must be kept for a few years more to prevent their running riot." [26]

The episode which brought these differences out in the open and made a major issue of removing Federalists from the judiciary began with the presentation to the legislature of a memorial from a Philadelphia merchant, Thomas Passmore. In the memorial Passmore protested the activities of three members of the state Supreme Court, Chief Justice Edward Shippen and Associate Justices Thomas Smith and Jasper Yeates, whom he charged with arbitrary conduct that was "pregnant with so many alarming consequences to the rights and liberties of the people."

Passmore's difficulties had begun in 1801 when he insured one of his vessels with the Philadelphia underwriting firm of Andrew Bayard and Andrew Petit. When the vessel sprang a leak and had to be abandoned, Passmore filed a claim. The case, upon the consent of both parties, was referred to arbitrators, who found for Passmore and made him a substantial award. Believing the judgment to be excessive, Bayard and Petit hired Dallas to challenge it, and he filed a bill of exceptions with the Supreme Court. Angered at not having received immediate payment, Passmore posted a notice in a coffee house denouncing Bayard as "a liar a rascal and a coward." Dallas, instead of instituting a separate libel suit, chose to associate this event with the original suit by asking the Supreme Court to hold Passmore in contempt. The Court ruled that Passmore had not been deliberately disrespectful, but ordered him to apologize to Bayard. When Passmore refused to apologize the Court fined him and sentenced him to thirty days in prison.

Passmore submitted his memorial to the legislature just a few days after Addison's conviction, and the House responded by appointing a committee to investigate his charges against the three judges. When the committee reported a short time later, it expressed its disapproval of what the Supreme Court justices had done but did not recommend any action to be taken against them. It recommended instead that a bill be drafted to define more carefully the powers of the judges in questions of contempt. But this did not satisfy the radicals. They had the matter recommitted to a special committee which not only reported in favor of a bill to define contempts of court, but also urged that an inquiry be made into the conduct of the judges in question. Although the overwhelmingly Republican House accepted the special committee's report, it failed by a 36 to 36 vote to pass "An Act concerning Contempts of Court." [27]

Up to this point Duane and the *Aurora* had not played a very important role in the struggle over judicial reform. To be sure, Duane, like most Republicans, believed that some kind of judicial reform was necessary, but he was not especially partisan to Snyder and Boileau's measures. Passmore's plight, however, which was very similar to his own experience under the Sedition Act, attracted his immediate attention. He bitterly denounced the legislature's failure to pass a bill restricting the power of the courts in contempt cases, and he predicted:

The frequent abuse of power by judges of the courts and justices of the peace will one day render a total revision of the received maxims concerning the tenure of judicial office necessary. It will one day be a subject of enquiry, why judges and justices of the peace should be more independent of the control of a free people, than those who have the formation and the execution of the laws entrusted to them. It will become a subject of enquiry, whether there is any analogy between what is called the *independence of the judges* in England, and the independence of the judges in America—and whether making the former independent of the *king* justified the making of the latter independent of the people.[28]

The great significance of the Passmore affair was that it served to forge a working, if somewhat uneasy, alliance between country and urban radicals. Starting in the spring of 1803, the push for judicial reform and Duane's determination to have the justices of the Pennsylvania Supreme Court impeached and convicted became inseparably entwined.[29]

IV

With the approach of the fall elections, the divisions in the Republican ranks widened. Determined to present their case to the public and to rally popular support for their cause, the radicals began publishing in the newspapers a series of essays defending the innovations in the Arbitration and Hundred Dollar bills, and excoriating those who tried to justify the governor's vetoes. They also circulated petitions throughout the state endorsing their program of judicial reform.[30] Meanwhile the moderates were also busy. In Philadelphia they made an attempt to wrest control of the city's politics from Duane and Leib, and from Lancaster there was increasing talk among those calling themselves "moderates" of forming a third party to bring "into the legislature, the *virtue* and *talents* of both parties." [31]

The elections, however, were generally favorable to the radicals. In part this was because the moderates did not make a concerted effort, but the main reason was that the Federalists, while in agreement with McKean's position of judicial reform, were as yet unwilling to rally to his defense. In fact the Federalist attitude between 1802 and 1804 was one of detached amusement at the governor's difficulties. One Federalist newspaper, commenting on events in Pennsylvania and Maryland, where McKean's counterpart, John Mercer, was having similar problems, noted that they

> have both by this time discovered the impossibility of ruling a mob without indulging them in every whim, however mischievous or extravagant. These two gentlemen have in no small degree contributed to put in motion the waves of democracy; and now that they have each gained a snug harbor, they vainly attempt to command a calm. The event is such as was expected; they have both been pretty decently *splashed*.[32]

When the legislature convened in December, McKean immediately found himself in serious trouble. One of the last measures of the previous legislature had revived the act of 1799 extending temporarily the powers of the justices of the peace. McKean now chose to veto it. Less than two weeks later the House repassed the bill with a resounding 75-4 vote, and the Senate overrode the veto by an equally decisive 20-2 vote. This was followed a month later by the passage of the Hundred Dollar Bill, which included provisions for voluntary arbitration if both parties agreed. Judgment was to be final in all cases involving values less than fifty-three dollars. Realizing that it would be futile to veto the measure, McKean allowed it to become law without his signature.[33]

Then on March 20 the House impeached Shippen, Yeates, and Smith by a vote of 57-24, with nineteen Republicans joining five Federalists in opposition. The judges requested that the trial be held immediately, but the Senate voted to postpone it until the next session. Four days later, Hugh Henry Brackenridge, the lone Republican judge on the Supreme Court who had been excepted from impeachment, because he had not been present when the court had made its ruling on Passmore's contempt, sent a letter to Snyder, now Speaker of the House, declaring his support for his fellow justices and requesting that he be removed along with them. Snyder and the House viewed the letter as a "premeditated insult," but refused to impeach him; instead with the concurrence of the Senate they voted to address the governor for his removal. McKean, however, to the disgust but hardly to the surprise of the radicals, declined to take any action.[34]

Brackenridge's insolence, combined with McKean's known sympathy for the impeached judges, served only further to convince Snyder, Duane, and other radicals that a conspiracy existed on the part of the state's legal establishment to thwart the will of the people. And this conviction was reinforced when Dallas, who had so successfully prosecuted Addison, declined a request from the House that he conduct the prosecution of Shippen, Yeates, and Smith, and then accepted, along with Jared Ingersoll, the position of chief counsel for the defense. Every other lawyer of any prominence or ability in the state also refused to aid the prosecution in any way.[35]

The fall elections saw the moderates make a more determined effort to regain control of the legislature. The battle in Philadelphia was especially hard fought, for the moderates had established their own newspaper, *The Freeman's Journal*, to defend McKean and the existing judicial system, and almost immediately it engaged in a vicious exchange with the *Aurora*. Similar battles were fought in other parts of the state. The moderates, or *Quids*, as the *Aurora* termed them, made a determined effort to elect third party men in Delaware, Chester, Lancaster, Bucks and Washington counties. But again, many Federalists, despite the pleas and assurances of the moderate Republicans that "the time is now come that political intolerance should cease," continued to withhold their support, and these efforts were generally unsuccessful.[36] Nonetheless, it was clear after the legislature met that radical domination was not as great as it had been the previous session.

As scheduled, the Senate convened on 7 January 1805, as a court of impeachment. Boileau headed the House committee in charge of the proceedings; while Caesar A. Rodney, a lawyer and congressman from Delaware, who was to be one of the managers in the approaching trial against Chase before the United States Senate, had been engaged as chief prosecutor. The trial lasted three weeks. The essence of the prosecution's case was that the judges had no legal right to try to force Passmore to apologize to

Bayard, and that, therefore, their ruling was arbitrary and constituted a "high misdemeanor" for which they should be removed from office. Dallas's defense revolved around two main points. The first was that the judges under the English common law of contempts, which he argued was applicable in Pennsylvania because never explicitly prohibited, had every right to punish Passmore. The other was that even if the judges were wrong in what they had done, in order to convict them it was incumbent upon the prosecution to prove that they had willfully, not merely mistakenly, committed the error.[37]

The Senate voted thirteen to eleven to convict, but, since a two-thirds vote was necessary, the three judges were acquitted. The moderates, of course, were jubilant. "All is well," wrote one, "Law (nay, even the *Common Law*), with common sense (tho' not Tom Payne's), and common Honesty, have triumphed over Anarchy, Folly and Rascality." [38] The radicals, and Duane in particular, were enraged. In fact, even before it knew of the Senate's decision the *Aurora* warned that "an acquittal (if it were possible) would involve this state in dangers and afflictions not inferior in their consequences to those which produced the revolution of 1776." [39] In the ensuing months Duane was to do his best to fulfill this prophecy.

XII

Constitutional and Judicial Reform in Pennsylvania, 1805-1808

The acquittal of the Supreme Court justices created a permanent division between radical and moderate Jeffersonians in the Pennsylvania Republican party. Even Dallas, who, despite his dislike and distrust of the radicals, had hoped to avoid an open break because he feared it would threaten continued Jeffersonian hegemony in Pennsylvania, had now come to realize that "perhaps the crisis is arrived when some attempt should be made to rally the genuine Republicans round the standard of reason, order and law. At present we are slaves of men whose passions are the origin, and whose interests are the object of all their actions." [1]

I

Throughout February 1805, the *Aurora* denounced the Senate's verdict in the impeachment trial of Shippen, Smith, and Yeates; demanded that the judiciary be made more amenable to popular control; and reiterated its belief that the liberties of the people were being undermined by a "monkist priesthood" of lawyers. Then, on the last day of the month, it published a draft of a memorial urging that a convention be called to amend the state's constitution. Probably written by Boileau, the memorial argued that all three branches of the government needed to be drastically altered. Senators should be elected annually instead of for four-year terms. The executive's veto and extensive patronage powers had to be curtailed, because they allowed the governor "to control the acts of the legislature, to the utter subversion of the principle that the majority shall govern." It was the judiciary, however, which needed the most revision: the laws under which it operated had to be made less obscure and complex, the administration of justice less expensive, and the judges themselves more dependent upon the people by being periodically brought "to the tribunal of an election, or reappointment." [2]

The moderate Republican response to the idea of a constitutional convention was immediate and predictable. Denouncing the proposal, they defended the existing state constitution, which had been framed in 1790 and modeled after the Federal Constitution. And they exhorted "the firm and decided friends of the constitution and laws, and not anarchy—of liberty not licentiousness— . . . [to] give an effectual opposition to this wild . . . mad scheme." [3]

Realizing that they would have to formalize their opposition to the calling of a convention, the moderates, under the leadership of Dallas, established "The Society of Constitutional Republicans." The main purpose of the new organization was to defend the existing state and federal constitutions, which were "the noblest invention of human wisdom for the self government of man." At its first meeting, the Society issued a memorial of its own protesting the calling of a convention and made arrangements for its publication in German and English and its distribution throughout the state. [4]

McKean, meanwhile, continued to battle with the legislature. The particular incident which received the most publicity was the governor's refusal to honor the request of a radical delegation, made up of Speaker of the House Simon Snyder and Representative Abraham McKinney, that one Henry Latscha be appointed justice of the peace for the Mahoney district in their home county of Northumberland, which was a radical stronghold. In justifying his refusal McKean argued that the only thing to recommend Latscha was his membership in the Republican party and that he had already appointed too many justices of the peace because "of their being good republicans, without their possessing . . . other proper qualifications." He also expressed his determination to appoint someone better qualified to the position, even if he were a Federalist.

Not content to let the matter rest there, McKean launched into a diatribe against a retiring congressmen who, in his farewell address, assured his constituents that even though "I am now returned to my plough . . . I shall do my utmost at election to prevent all men of talents, lawyers, rich men from being elected." The governor had been enraged by this comment, and he had observed that if a constitutional convention were held it would probably be "clodpoles (or, if they please, clodhoppers) of the same pernicious sentiments," who would be chosen as delegates to a convention. He denounced the advocates of a convention as "weak, mischievous, and wicked," described the present constitution as "the production of as patriotic learned and enlightened men, as, perhaps, ever assembled for a similar purpose," and defended the need for lawyers to sit in the legislature.

> Why are not lawyers and rich men to be as well trusted, in the administration of legal affairs, as any others; Can any man vote for a new law, who is utterly ignorant of the old? What kind of interpretation can he give, who is stranger to the text, on which he comments! The lawyers are in the perpetual study of morals, and their duties to society; . . . and surely those who thoroughly understand and are governed by the laws ought to be esteemed among the wisest and best of men.[5]

McKean also continued to make liberal use of his veto power. He declined to consent to a bill by which he believed the legislature arrogated to itself, at the expense of the executive branch, the power to appoint the Comptroller and Registrar Generals. "A large public body," he argued, "is not so well qualified to select the best characters for subordinate officers, as a single person, responsible, unfettered and independent." Following this he refused to sign an act that signficantly extended the powers of the justices of the peace and made it mandatory for claimants to submit their cases to referees for settlement before they could go to court. Referring the legislature to his veto messages over the past three years, McKean reasserted his belief that arbitration denied to citizens their constitutional right to a trial by jury and mockingly asserted that rather than have to bear the "time, trouble, delay & expense" of arbitration the suitors would be better off if they simply paid "a certain stipulated sum of money to the State, for an allowance to have a trial by Jury in the first instance." [6]

By the spring of 1805 it was clear that neither group—moderates or radicals—had achieved political dominance or had attracted overwhelming popular support to their side. An attempt to repass the legislation over the governor's vetoes failed, and the radicals suffered still another defeat when the House voted not to call a convention. But the radicals took their fight into the approaching gubernatorial campaign, winning a major victory and gaining some revenge when the party caucus voted not to renominate McKean. Instead Simon Snyder was chosen, on the stated ground that the party's candidate "should not be a lawyer, and that a clodhopper should be preferred." [7] McKean and his supporters were not to be outdone, however, and a few days later thirty-four moderate Republicans and Federalists openly endorsed his re-election on a coalition ticket. The governor, determined to make a fight of it, wrote to his son that the struggle with the radicals had revived "the spirit & exertions of my prime of life—[one] who has not been affected by the roaring of the British lion, cannot possibly be frightened by the braying of Asses." [8]

II

The election of 1805 proved to be one of the bitterest in the history of the state. It would determine not only the next governor but also whether the Constitution was to be revised; for it was generally agreed, by both sides, that the outcome would be used as a measure of public feeling on the need for a convention.

As the campaign developed it became clear that two sets of fundamental principles were involved. Defending their decision to drop McKean and run Snyder, the radicals argued that the governor had been insolent, arrogant and generally disrespectful of the wishes of the people. Specific charges against him included his numerous vetoes of the legislature's (and therefore the people's) attempts at judicial reform; his refusal to heed the legislature's (and therefore the people's) request to remove Brackenridge; his repeated defenses of the legal fraternity, of which he was part; his use of patronage powers to create an interest loyal to himself as opposed to the people, while at the same time denying appointments to Republicans who represented the people's point of view but who differed with McKean in opinion; and his willingness to co-operate with the Federalists. Similar charges were also leveled against Dallas, whom the radicals viewed as the evil genius controlling the state government from behind the scenes.[9]

The radicals' main issue was the need to overhaul the state constitution and make the government more directly and immediately responsible to the electorate. The essence of their argument was that the Pennsylvania Constitution of 1776, with its provisions for a judiciary to be elected and appointed for specific terms, an annually elected legislature, and a weak executive dominated by the legislature, had most fully expressed the democratic implications of the Revolution. On the other hand, the Constitution of 1790, with its independent judiciary, strong and independent executive, and senators who held their offices for four-year terms, had made the government less democratic. No one could make this case more ably than Tom Paine, that arch radical, who more than any other individual had helped bring about the adoption of the Constitution of 1776, and who had recently returned to America. He endorsed the radical position in 1805:

> At the time this Constitution [of 1790] was formed, there was a great departure from the principles of the Revolution, among those who then assumed the lead, and the country was grossly imposed upon. This accounts for some inconsistencies that are to be found in the present Constitution, among which is the negativing power inconsistently copied from England. While the exercise of the power over the state remained dormant it remained unnoticed; but the instant it began to be active it began to alarm; and the exercise of it against the

rights of the people to settle their private pecuniary differences by the peaceable mode of arbitration, without the interference of lawyers, and the expense of tediousness of courts of law, has brought its existence to a crisis. . . .

Much yet remains to be done in the improvements of constitutions. The Pennsylvania Convention, when it meets, will be possessed of advantages which those that preceded it were not. The ensuing Convention will have two constitutions before them; that of 1776, and that of 1790, each of which continued about fourteen years. I know no material objection against the Constitution of 1776, except that in practice it might be subject to precipitancy; but this can be easily and effectually remedied. . . . But there have been many and great objections and complaints against the present Constitution and the practice upon it arising from the improper and unequal distribution it makes of power.[10]

There was much criticism of the executive and legislative branches of the government as they existed under the Constitution of 1790, but the main thrust of the radical argument was against the judiciary and the existing legal system. Judges had to be brought under the direct control of the people. Lawyers as a group were innately depraved and dishonest, and had an unnatural and exaggerated influence in the running of the government. And the common law, that product of aristocratic deviousness, was incompatible with the plain republicanism of the American people. In arguing this latter point the radicals distinguished between what they called *"lawyers law,* and *legislative law."*

Legislative law is the law of the land, enacted by our own legislators, chosen by the people for that purpose. Lawyers law is a mass of opinions and decisions, many of them contradictory to each other, which courts and lawyers have instituted themselves, and is chiefly made up of law reports of cases taken from English law books. The case of every man ought to be tried by the laws of his own country, which he knows, and not by opinions and authorities from other countries, of which he may know nothing. A lawyer, in pleading, will talk several hours about law, but it is *lawyers law,* and not *legislative law* that he means.[11]

Although the radicals had made these arguments repeatedly since 1802, they found their fullest expression in 1805 in a series of essays by Jesse Higgins, a Delaware Republican, which were first published in the *Aurora* and then republished in the same year as a pamphlet entitled *Sampson Against the Philistines*. Written for the "common reader" and "honest ignorant," the pamphlet represented the most important reiteration of the radical position on judicial reform to appear since Benjamin Austin had attacked the legal profession in 1786.[12]

The main purpose of the pamphlet was "to expose to full view the prodigious evil of our jurisprudence, to show the absurdity of common law, and to suggest a competent remedy for that evil by a reform." The chief villain of the piece, predictably, was the legal profession, which

> has become truly a subject of the most serious concern; the loose principles of persons of that profession: their practice of defending right and wrong indifferently, for reward; their open enmity to the principles of free government, because free government is irreconcilable to the abuses upon which they thrive; the tyranny which they display in the courts; and in too many cases the too obvious understanding and collusion which prevails among the members of the *bench,* the *bar,* and the *officers* of the court, demand the most serious interference of the legislature, and the jealousy of the people.[13]

As a remedy for existing evils in the state's legal system, the author of *Sampson Against the Philistines* proposed a series of radical reforms which he believed would make the administration of justice "speedy, convenient and cheap." Lawyers, he urged, were to be excluded as much as possible from all trials, as the only way to avoid "those absurd *rules of evidence, pleadings,* and everything which has changed simple justice into a *professional mystery,* which has contributed to the oppression and plunder, rather than the happiness and security of the people." [14] Where their participation was absolutely necessary, lawyers were to be paid a fixed sum by the state, so that "we should have the learning and wisdom of such men to assist the jury, as their talents and integrity should recommend, instead of the ingenuity and artifice of the profession." [15] All cases were to be heard before local tribunals, with appeals, which "are not only useless but highly injurious to society and even justice itself," allowable only under the most serious circumstances.[16] And finally, and most importantly, arbitration was to be made mandatory if either party desired it, because it "will soon reduce the business of the courts of justice within due bounds; and in some time, even render reference itself seldom necessary, as people will settle their own business without putting it on the docket, when they find neither *injustice* nor delay can be effected by it." [17]

The moderates fully appreciated the fundamental nature of the radical attack and its dangerous implications. They believed, in fact, that "the Revolutionary faction in Pennsylvania intend to overturn the government of the United States, if they can accomplish the destruction of our state Government." [18]

Replying to radical arguments, the moderates warned the people about the danger of their being "wheedled out of liberty" by demagogues and reformers who painted "an imaginary Elisium" and urged a return to "pristine imbecility." They opposed radical demands for fundamental change in the institutional structure of the government, and defended the need for a balanced constitution with an independent judiciary and strong executive, as opposed to one with an all powerful legislature, by arguing that "pure democracy cannot exist in a populous country." In particular, they stressed the importance of the government's being strong and active, for if the people wanted to be protected in their "persons and properties," they had to be subject to "laws and . . . the strong arm of publick justice." Or as another writer put it: "you cannot . . . be in the possession of more liberty than you now are, unless you abolish government entirely, and revert to a state of nature and barbarism." [19]

Most of these arguments of the moderates had appeared in one form or another during the past three years, especially in McKean's various veto messages. But they received their most important and fullest expression in a lengthy address issued by the Society of Constitutional Republicans. "Unanimously approved" at a meeting on 9 June and signed by seven members of the correspondence committee, it was mainly the work of Dallas. Originally published in the *Freeman's Journal,* the address was reprinted by other newspapers throughout the state, and over 25,000 copies were distributed in pamphlet form, in both English and German.[20]

This address began by expressing surprise over the "cry of social discontent" and apprehension about the "spirit of political innovation." It went on to urge the people to be careful of those who offered "the glitter of impracticable theories for the steady light of experience." And it contained an abusive attack upon the activities of "a small but active *combination* of malcontents" who "have exposed the form and substance of our government, the code of our laws, the system of our jurisprudence, and the administration of justice, . . . to the scorn of the world."[21]

Conceding that the present constitution was not perfect, the address denied that its defects were "such as demand the corrective of a convention." Rejecting the radical claim that the existing government was undemocratic and so strong as to be dangerous to the liberties of the people, it argued that the government was responsible to the wishes of the people and that "the use of power is essential to the order and peace of society." It also contained a strong defense of the common law as "consistent with true liberty and genuine republicanism" and as absolutely necessary for the state's continued well being.

> The common law of Pennsylvania is the common law of England as stripped of its feudal trappings; as originally suited to a colonial condition; as modified by acts of the General Assembly, and as purified by the principles of the constitution. For the varying exigencies of social life, for the complicated interests of an enterprising nation, the positive acts of the legislature can provided little; and independent of the common law, rights would remain forever without remedies and wrongs without redress. The law of nations, the law of merchants, the customs and usages of trade, and even the law of every foreign country in relation to transitory contracts originating there but prosecuted here, are parts of the common law of Pennsylvania. It is the common law, generally speaking, not an act of Assembly, that assures the title and possession of your farms and your horses, and protects your persons, your liberty, your reputation from violence; that defines and punishes offences; that regulates the trial by jury; and (in a word comprehending all its

attributes) that gives efficacy to the fundamental principles of the constitution. If such are the nature and uses of the common law, is it politic, or would it be practicable, to abandon it? Simply because it originated in Europe cannot afford a better reason to abandon it than to renounce the English and German languages, or to abolish the institutions of property and marriage, of education and religion, since they, too, were derived from the more ancient civilized nations of the world.[22]

The address concluded with a trenchant statement of the purposes of the Society of Constitutional Republicans and of what the moderate Republicans stood for in the gubernatorial campaign of 1805:

It is an effort to preserve institutions and men we know and approve against projects which we cannot comprehend, proposed by men whom we cannot trust, whose object cannot be good. . . . It is a cause of principle independent of party. . . . For ourselves we think that it is time to evince to the world that a democratic republic can enjoy energy without tyranny, and liberty without anarchy.[23]

III

The election was contested in almost every township of every county in the state. The radicals generally retained control of the regular party machinery, while the moderates developed their own organization. The latter's strength came mainly from the state's major urban areas, Philadelphia, Lancaster, Harrisburg and Pittsburgh, and from the older, more established commercial farming communitites in Berks, Chester, Delaware, York, Montgomery, and Lancaster counties. The radicals, on the other hand, drew most of their support from the less commercialized but heavily populated agricultural counties of Northumberland, Dauphin and Mifflin; from the recently settled far northwestern part of the state, where many of the inhabitants were squatters who favored increasing the powers of local courts and justices of the peace as a way of protecting their holdings from absentee proprietors; and from Philadelphia county, which the Leib-Duane machine controlled.[24]

The German vote in populous Berks and Northampton counties was one of the keys to the election. Because Snyder was of German extraction the radicals might have had a big edge here, but the moderates skillfully offset this by getting Joseph Heister and Peter Muhlenberg, two of the most prominent Germans in the state, to endorse McKean. Muhlenberg in particular was important, for as one moderate noted, "the weight" of his "opinion among our Germans is immense." His support of McKean, moreover, was unqualified. In an open letter he warned the thrifty and hardworking German farmers that a change in the state's constitution would be disastrous to their interests, and described Snyder as an "honest good man," who, if elected, would not be able to bring "honor to himself and the Germans," but "would bring ridicule on them as well as himself." [25] Both counties voted for McKean.

Also of great signficance in determining the outcome of the election was the growing support among Federalists for McKean. At first an open alliance between the two groups was opposed by some moderate Republicans who feared their cause would be irrevocably damaged by radical charges of apostasy, and by a number of extreme Federalists who believed that it would be in the long range interest of their party to remain neutral during the election. But there were enough members of both groups who realized that only through "an union of honest men," however uneasy such an alliance might be, in support of McKean would it be possible to save the state's constitution. Consequently, as the election approached, co-operation between moderates and Federalists in the form of joint meetings and official support for each other's candidates increased.[26]

The election was very close. McKean won by less than 5000 votes, carrying the city of Philadelphia and seventeen counties, while Snyder carried the other seventeen counties. The moderate Republican-Federalist coalition also captured control of both Houses of the Legislature. McKean had won, but a majority of the Republicans supported Snyder; the Governor, as Gallatin noted, owed "his re-election to the Federalists." [27]

IV

Realizing that "a check had been given to dangerous projects, but no decisive victory had been obtained over the body of the Revolutionists," the uneasy but triumphant *Quid* coalition turned its attention to the "actual healing of the distresses caused by delay and expenses in the administration of justice," and rushed to implement their moderate program of judicial reform.[28]

As soon as the legislature convened in December 1805, McKean vetoed a radical inspired judiciary bill which had been passed in the closing days of the previous session. He then requested the legislature to undertake the "establishment of a pure, able and efficient administration of justice," by increasing the number of both judges and local courts.[29] The resulting judiciary act, passed in February 1806, created four additional judicial districts with courts of quarter sessions and common pleas. It also reduced the original jurisdiction of the Supreme Court in civil suits, allowing the lower courts to handle more cases. It divided the state into two districts and required the Supreme Court to meet once annually in Pittsburgh and twice in Philadelphia. It was expected that this would ensure greater uniformity of decisions among the lower courts and eliminate the necessity of westerners having to travel across the state to try appeals. As a sop to the radicals, a tame arbitration act was passed, allowing the use of referees in cases where it was requested by all parties, and making the decision binding only when no one objected.[30]

McKean also turned his attention to finding an energetic and knowledgeable Chief Justice to replace Edward Shippen, who had been forced by old age and ill health to retire. The governor had a hard time, however, for the recent bitter struggle over constitutional and judicial reform had made qualified men reluctant to accept the position. It was first turned down by Dallas, because he was unwilling to subject himself to "the influence of desperate and violent men upon our popular and legislative movements in the State business." [31] McKean, at this point, apparently decided that the position would "have to be conferred on one not deemed a Republican," for it was next offered to and turned down by Edward Tilghman, a Federalist, who had studied law at the Middle Temple in London and who generally was considered to "have the most accurate legal judgement of any man of his day" at the Philadelphia bar.[32] The position was finally accepted by another Tilghman, William, who also was a Federalist, and who was "well aware of the difficulties and danger of my situation." [33]

Actually William Tilghman did very well. He served as Chief Justice of the Pennsylvania Supreme Court until his death in 1827, and during this period he managed to remain aloof from the bitter partisan struggles that continued to rack the Keystone state's politics. He was a hard worker, and this, combined with an enormous competence in the technical aspects of the law, allowed him to have a lasting influence on the development of Pennsylvania jurisprudence, his greatest contribution being the successful incorporation of equity principles into the regular legal system.[34]

In the fall of 1806 the radicals regained control of the legislature, and they retained it for several years. They failed, however, to implement their program of judicial reform. McKean was mainly responsible for this. Appreciating the value of the Hundred Dollar Act, he allowed it to become permanent and even consented to increasing the number of cases to which it was applicable; but he continued to use his veto power to prevent the legislature from weakening the independence of the judiciary, from drastically revising and oversimplifying legal procedure, from abolishing the common law, and from making arbitration mandatory or binding in any way.[35]

In 1808 Snyder was elected governor. But by this time he had broken with the urban radicals, and the need for judicial reform was no longer very great, as the state's legal system, operating under Tilghman's leadership and under the reforms instituted in 1806, was becoming efficient and reasonably equitable. Even more important, by 1808 Pennsylvania politics had come to be dominated by the issues which were to lead the country to war in 1812, and those issues were producing new political alignments. In Pennsylvania the moderates had won, at least on judicial reform.[36]

XIII

The Debate over Judicial Reform in Massachusetts, 1799-1806

In Kentucky and Pennsylvania the judiciary struggle was primarily between radicals and moderates within the Republican party, and only secondarily a contest with the Federalists. In Massachusetts the reverse was the case. There, until 1806, the Federalists dominated politics, and they initiated the movement for a moderate kind of judicial reform.

I

The Massachusetts judiciary had more than its share of imperfections, and in the generation following independence it was a constant source of controversy.[1] The main problem was the inefficient court system adopted in 1782. For what the legislature had done was to adopt the time-worn and tradition bound court system of the colonial period—cumbersome, expensive, and overly complicated—which was no longer adequate to serve a rapidly expanding commercial state with an increasing population.

The Inferior Courts of Common Pleas, found in every county, were especially inefficient. These courts had appellate jurisdiction in most civil cases heard before justices of the peace, and original jurisdiction in cases involving land titles. Most of their work, however, dealt with suits against debtors, in which trials were by jury if requested. The trouble with these courts was that their decisions were not final, since most of them were appealed as a matter of course to the Supreme Court. For example, a litigous-minded member of society, and Massachusetts had its share, might bring an action involving as little as fifty cents before a justice of the peace, to which he could summon dozens of witnesses. If the decision went against him he could appeal it to the Court of Common Pleas, where, after numerous continuances, with all the witnesses attending, he could be granted a trial by jury. If the judges in the Court of Common Pleas ruled on points of law during this trial, he could then file a bill of exceptions and request a new trial before the Supreme Court. Consequently, as one writer complained, "the public are saddled with the expense of juries and officers of law in every county who sit days innumerable" and accomplish nothing. "While the parties and what is more distressing and cruel the witnesses also are carried from court to court, and often to a great distance from their families; to dispose in suits before the Supreme Court, the whole value of which suits, would not bear their expenses." [2]

The situation in the Supreme Court was even worse. The highest court in the state, consisting of a Chief Justice and four associate justices, heard appeals from the lower courts and had original jurisdiction in criminal cases of the most serious sort and concurrent and original jurisdiction in most land cases. Here it was rare for a case to be heard in less than two years. In large part this was because of the grueling system of circuit riding required of the justices. To perform their duties, the justices traveled on circuit, visiting every county in the state at least once a year, and the more populous counties, like Essex, Suffolk, Middlesex, and Worcester, twice a year. Although most of the cases were tried before juries, the full court was expected to attend every session; and rarely, if ever, was the docket cleared before the court found it necessary to adjourn in order to move on to the next county. Very often, especially in the winter, bad weather and poor traveling conditions would interrupt the circuit. Sometimes the delay involved would necessitate skipping some of the scheduled sessions.[3]

Also contributing to the Supreme Court's inefficiency was a

long-established tradition which allowed the loser in a case before it to appeal, almost automatically, not only on points of law but also on fact. Any losing party, provided there were not already two jury decisions against him, could request a new trial. All this, of course, took time, causing inconveniences and additional expense to the parties and witnesses involved.[4]

Many lawyers took advantage of this situation because a system of costs had developed which made delay profitable for them. According to the prevailing fee table, a lawyer was allowed 33 cents a day per case for his attendance in court. This would not have amounted to much if confined to actual time taken to plead a case, but since one could never be sure if and when the court would get around to hearing a particular case, this, in practice, became the rate of pay for the lawyer's attendance at the entire session of the court. Thus, an attorney who had a practice of fifty cases would get $16.50 for every day the court sat. It was clearly in his interest to keep his cases in court as long as possible.[5]

Still another cause of the state's legal problems was its inability to get capable men to sit on the bench. The arduous circuit riding duties, the dangers of holding the August term in Boston during the height of the fever season, the short vacations, and the low salaries made the position of Supreme Court justice unattractive to the more able members of the bar who were making more money, and living an easier life, by practicing law. In 1800 the justices on the bench were old revolutionary patriots who at one time might have been good jurists but who now were too feeble and deaf to control the court. The result often was chaos, as opposing lawyers interrupted and badgered each other and showed disrepect for the admonitions of the justices. To make his point, Fisher Ames observed, a lawyer had to "go into court with a bludgeon in one hand and a speaking trumpet in the other." [6]

In 1798 the legislature appointed a special committee to look into the matter of judicial reform. This committee, headed by John Lowell, expressed "a strong conviction of the real necessity of some effectual reform in the Judicial Department of this Commonwealth," and made a number of detailed recommendations.[7] The following year the legislature passed an act increasing the number of Supreme Court Justices to seven, dividing the state into eastern and western circuits, and reducing to three the number of judges necessary to preside at circuit sessions in every county except Suffolk, where the full court was still expected to attend. The purpose of the new system was to double the number of terms, enabling the court to clear the docket. To this end another act was passed in 1800, providing that in stated types of cases, if the third justice could not attend, two could constitute a quorum.[8]

The new system was more efficient than the old one, but not efficient enough. The justices heard more cases than they ever had before, but they still could not clear the docket or even keep pace with the increase in business. "Everything," wrote one judge, "has been done which the system would permit to do the business of the court, and everywhere the business is accumulating." [9] In 1804 it was reported that in most parts of the state it took at least two years for a cause to come to trial and that in some counties the delay was even greater.[10]

II

By 1803 the situation had become so serious that the governor, Caleb Strong, appealed to the legislature to act. Harrison Gray Otis, the powerful Speaker of the House of Representatives, also agreed that something had to be done.[11] But the man who did the most to articulate and begin to implement sweeping change was Theodore Sedgwick.

A graduate of Yale and a lawyer by training, Sedgwick had impressive political credentials. He had served several terms in the Continental Congress and had been a member of the convention which drafted the state's constitution in 1780; he had actively participated in the crushing of Shays's Rebellion; and he had played a prominent role in the state convention which adopted the Federal Constitution in 1788. During the 1790's he became a High Federalist, acting as one of Hamilton's leading lieutenants in the House of Representatives during Washington's administration, and serving first as a senator and then as Speaker of the House during John Adams's presidency.[12] Fiercely partisan, Sedgwick retired from active politics when Jefferson was elected in 1801. He returned to Stockbridge to become a gentleman farmer, but found this life dull. Hearing that there was going to be an opening on the state Supreme Court, he successfully solicited the position, for he undoubtedly agreed with Fisher Ames that "we may need the state tribunals as sanctuaries when Jacobinism comes to rob and slay." [13]

Sedgwick immediately made his influence felt inside the courtroom by demanding that members of the bar maintain professional standards. Lawyers who spoke out of turn or who otherwise disrupted the court were severely rebuked. Those who did not speak to the point were cut off. He refused to grant requests for delays which he deemed unnecessary and he did not hesitate to lecture unprepared advocates on the responsibilities which they had to their clients, nor did he ever tolerate disrespect for the court.[14]

Outside the courtroom, in a series of letters both public and private, Sedgwick advocated reforms in the organization and administration of the courts which he wished to see made. These letters are especially important because they contain almost the entire program of judicial reform which moderates wished to see implemented in Massachusetts.[15]

He often began by urging that something be done to guarantee a proper income to the Justices of the Supreme Court. He advised fixing their number at five, since it probably would not be possible to get the legislature to budget adequately for more. In addition to substantial raises, he also wanted the justices, whom he expected would be honorable men, to be allowed to divide among themselves all the fees received by the court. The point of a competent income was crucial for Sedgwick:

> The salary ought to be such as that the office may be accepted without much pecuniary sacrifice by any man in successful practice. Such as will induce men of middle age to go on to the bench. Such as will enable all the judges to reside in the capital, from which immense benefits would be derived. And not such as will oblige the Governor to supply vacancies from the old, the lazy, the worn out, or what is worse those who have never been worn at all.

Sedgwick also recommended, as very important, the adoption of a system of *nisi prius* terms for the Supreme Court on circuit. By this arrangement a single judge would preside over all jury trials (trials of fact) except those involving capital crimes and divorce and alimony, which would be heard in conjunction with the Courts of Common Pleas at specially arranged sessions. This would substantially increase the number of jury cases and help alleviate costly delays in civil cases.

In addition to *nisi prius* terms, special law terms would be held each year in Boston and two other towns at which the entire court was expected to attend. At these meetings, questions which had arisen during the circuit sessions on difficult points of law involving writs of error, certiorari, special verdicts, Demurrers, Bills of Exceptions, motions for new trials, and causes continued for advisement could be treated at length. This, Sedgwick believed, would be an improvement over the old system because many books of law, sometimes even an extensive library, were needed to decide complicated law questions. In many counties these books were not available, and where they were, the "hurry and fatigue" involved under the old arrangement made it impossible to use them. "Half the evils of the present system," he wrote, "are imputable to the press and variety of business, in the midst of which law questions have been discussed, as far as they have been discussed at all."

The number of time-consuming appeals and reviews had to be limited:

> If the system be, as at present complex, awkward and perplexing every effort will, by the best part of the community, be made to avoid being entangled by it, but if on the contrary it be wise, simple, and as expeditious as is consistent with security, it will command confidence and be considered as the most certain means of obtaining justice and will of course be resorted to by all men who wish to obtain it. . . . At present a man who is compelled to resort to law, to obtain redress of an injury must make up his mind to endure several years vexation before he obtains the object of his pursuit. Will he not practice every expedient before he will submit to the alternative? On the contrary had he a moral assurance that a few months would terminate his vexation would he feel the same reluctance?

Prolonged litigation also led to corruption of character:

> There is nothing which tends to render animosity more ardent than long continued legal controversy; and when the passions are roused, men are too apt to consider all means as justified by the end. Hence, every exertion, there is reason to apprehend, will, under such circumstances, too frequently be made to give a wrong coloring to facts; and there exists a facility in doing it, by the admission of evidence in the form of deposition. It, therefore happens, too often, as all gentlemen conversant in our courts of justice can testify, that on the trials of appeals, actions depending altogether upon oral testimony, assume a very different complexion from what they first exhibited, and further vexation on their trial by review.

One way of preventing unnecessary delays was to expand the jurisdiction of the Court of Common Pleas and to make its decision final in certain low value cases. Another was to have the circuit judge enter judgment and award execution despite exceptions to his rulings, while still another was to charge double costs for appeals based on frivolous grounds. Of course, the success of this kind of arrangement depended upon having responsible, learned, and able judges, whose rulings and decisions would be based on careful deliberation.

Sedgwick also counseled that under no circumstances should juries be permitted to interpret the law. Allowing juries, as was sometimes done in post-revolutionary Massachusetts, to mingle law with fact in arriving at their decisions, he believed, had contributed greatly to the disastrous inefficiency of the state's legal system. "In all instances where trial by jury has been practiced, and a separation of the law from the fact has taken place, there have been expedition, certainty, system and their consequences, general approbation. Where this has not been the case, neither expedition, certainty nor system have prevailed."

He also argued that the quality of juries had to be improved. Under an existing act justices of the peace, "men of the first consideration and weight of character in their counties," were exempted from jury duty. He advised that the act be repealed, otherwise the community would be denied the services of educated men upon whose "intelligence, integrity and independence," a successful administration of justice was so dependent.

Finally, something had to be done to end the "mischievous uncertainty" that existed as to what the law was. Sedgwick granted that it was generally understood to be made up of the common law as modified by statute and custom, but "of the whole, as a connected and consistent system, there exists at present, no written exposition, to which a citizen, a student, or a lawyer can have recourse. Hence the perplexities of doubt and the evils of uncertainty." As a partial remedy to this and to produce "a correct uniformity of decision," Sedgwick advised the state to undertake the publication of the Supreme Court's decisions.

The legislature acted upon many of Sedgwick's recommendations. In 1803 it passed an act which enlarged the jurisdiction of the Courts of Common Pleas and gave them the power to regulate appeals.[16] In 1804 it passed an experimental act reducing the number of Supreme Court Justices to five and providing for *nisi prius* sessions at one of the two terms held by the court in each county.[17] The system proved to be such a success that the following year it was made permanent. This latter act provided that in causes where exceptions had been made which the presiding judge considered "frivolous, immaterial, or intended for delay," he could enter judgment immediately.[18] And that same year, in 1805, the legislature passed an act making provision for the appointment of a recorder of the decisions of the Supreme Court.[19]

But these measures were only part of the overall-scheme of judicial reform Sedgwick had proposed. They did not become partisan issues. There were, however, other parts—increasing the judge's salaries and circumscribing the powers of juries to interpret the law—which were more controversial and which were vehemently opposed.

III

Some opposition to the reforms proposed by Sedgwick came from lawyers who had built large and profitable practices based on the complexity and inefficiency of the existing legal system, and who wished, therefore, to maintain the status quo. But they never consolidated their influence because too many other members of their profession, including the most important members of the Massachusetts bench and bar, favored the proposed changes. Nor were they able to channel their opposition effectively, since the Federalist party, to which almost all of them belonged, was also committed to reform.[20]

More serious was the Republican opposition to Sedgwick's proposals. They did not oppose judicial reform *per se,* for most Jeffersonians fervently wished to make the administration of justice more equitable and convenient. They objected rather to specific changes which increased the power of the courts. "Many will doubtless be the plans suggested," wrote one writer who signed his name "Decius," "and many the plausible arguments prompted by interest, pride and party views, to increase the power and influence of an order of men, already too powerful, and too dangerous." [21]

The Republicans had a number of political grievances against the Massachusetts judiciary. High on their list was the general exclusion of all members of their party from positions on the bench. Not a single Republican sat on the Supreme Court, and very few served in the lower courts. For instance, in Berkshire County, one of the most decidedly Jeffersonian areas in the state, seventeen attornies were allowed to practice before the Supreme Court. Eleven were Federalists, of whom ten had been commissioned as justices of the peace. Of the six Republicans, only one had been commissioned. The county sent twenty members to the General Court. Of these, six were Federalists, four of whom were called on to serve as justices of the peace, while fourteen were Republicans, and only two were so appointed. The Republicans' situation was even worse in other parts of the state.[22]

The fact that this situation was in large part the result of the Federalists' unwillingness to recognize the legitimacy of the Republicans as loyal Americans only served to aggravate the situation further. For it meant that the Federalists usually appointed to the bench "characters the most obnoxious to Republicans, and the most bitter in their opposition to the existing [national] administration." [23] The conclusion which the Jeffersonians drew from this was that their opponents were using the state court system to arrogate for themselves "a steady permanent political influence." [24]

The activities of some of the judges more than justified this charge. In post-revolutionary Massachusetts, as in other parts of the country, the four- or five-day court session was a signal for the surrounding countryside to gather together, and the chance to make political converts was great. Farmers came to the court towns to meet old friends and to make business deals, peddlers to restock and sell their wares, wives to shop and gossip, children to meet their friends and play, and everyone to be generally entertained by attending the legal proceedings. This meant large crowds, and the judges, or "travelling lecturers" as their opponents sometimes called them, took advantage of the opportunity by using their charges to juries not only to instruct in the law but also "to inflame passions or excite prejudices on controverted political topics." [25]

The partisanship of the courts in libel cases of a political nature was especially infuriating to the Republicans. The conviction in 1803 of Carlton Carleton, editor of the *Salem Register,* for an attack on Timothy Pickering's character brought out their wrath, for "in the same town a Federal paper is suffered with impunity to vent columns of the most atrocious slanders and malicious libels against the President and other public officers and private citizens whose *shoe latchets Mr. Pickering is not worthy to unloose.* What a picture do these thing present of *federal* power and *federal* justice." [26]

An article in the *Independent Chronicle,* signed by "Amicus Curiae," expressed the anger, bitterness, and vengeful feelings of Republicans toward Federalist partisanship on the bench. Addressing the Justices of the Supreme Court, he wrote:

> The people are divided into two great political parties, from one of which you are all selected. No *Republican* has a seat on your bench, or is admitted to a participation in your judicial consultations. Being exclusively Federalists, you are in danger of being, and appearing to be, partial in cases of a party nature. Notwithstanding the boasted independence of our judiciary you are not exalted above responsibility, but are

answerable, at least at the tribunal of public opinion. If, under your administration, writers and printers of your own politics are suffered to libel their and your political opponents, with impunity; while those of the opposite party are prosecuted and punished what pretensions will you have to the reputation of IMPARTIALITY, that first of judicial values? And what confidence will, or can be reposed in your administration, by one half the community? [27]

The belief that a Federalist-controlled court system could not or would not administer justice fairly was of fundamental importance in determining the attitude of Jeffersonians toward judicial reform. For when the reforms proposed by the Federalists served simply to make the administration of justice more prompt, equitable, and easily available, the Republicans generally did not object to their being implemented. But when they materially benefited the judges or increased their powers or could lead to a further increase of Federalist control of the courts, the Republican opposition became firm and uncompromising.[28]

The differences in the attitudes of the two parties toward judicial reform came to the surface in early 1803, when the Federalists undertook to remove one of the justices of the Supreme Court who was no longer capable of performing his duties. The object of the controversey was Thomas Bradbury, "a learned, independent and upright judge," whose "talents, services and integrity were questioned by no one," but who had suffered a palsy stroke and showed no signs of recovering. Bradbury expressed his willingness to resign, but, because he considered the office his property ("an estate in the office I hold during good behaviour as by law an estate for life to be forfeited only by misbehaviour"), and because he had no other source of income, he asked the legislature to give him a pension. The Federalists agreed to this and immediately proposed a general bill to provide half pay for life to retiring justices of the Supreme Court. They did this partly because they accepted Bradbury's argument that the office was his private property and partly because they wanted to take care of him as a loyal party member, but they also believed the idea of an old-age pension might make the position of Supreme Court Justice more attractive to future nominees and perhaps even encourage the other old men of the court, Robert Treat Paine and Francis Dana, to resign and make way for the appointment of more energetic and reform-minded younger men like Sedgwick.[29]

The Republicans expressed enthusiasm for getting Bradbury off the bench, but they denounced the pension bill as part of a plot of an "intriguing faction" which for twenty years had been trying to do the people out of their rights. "Pensions and Sinecure Places," they argued would lead to the establishment of an army of placemen and were irreconcilable with the idea of a free government. They "are a part of the machinery of monarchy. They are closely allied to a standing army, an unextinguishable debt, and a system of oppressive taxation." The Republicans also completely rejected the claim that the office was Bradbury's property.

> Republican principles will suffer no man to feed upon the *public* bounty, without an equivalent service to the *Public*. . . . If a *Judge* accepts of an honorable office; which endangers neither his life nor his limbs, with an honorable and equivalent salary during his continuance in office, he has no claim upon his Country, because he may chance to grow old and become incapable any longer of earning his compensation. He knows the condition upon which he accepts. He knows the tenure by which he ought to hold his office; that he shall be able to perform its duties, and render to the public a service equivalent to his salary. No man ever accepted the appointment of a judge, unless he considered the honor and emoluments of his office, taken together, as a full satisfaction for the private business he might surrender, and the labor and fatigue of his official duty. He receives, then, his *quid pro quo,* while he is capable of rendering the services of a judge. When he is no longer capable he can no longer earn his salary and it is his duty to resign.[30]

But what if he were unwilling to resign? The Jeffersonian reply was that "the people are not to suffer . . . to pay men for going out of office," when the State constitution provided that the governor upon the address of both Houses of the legislature and with the consent of his Council could remove them. Their position was simply that, "when a judge is no longer competent to do his duties and refuses to resign [he] should be removed—not bribed with a pension." [31]

The lower House defeated the pension bill 43 to 78.[32] This put the Federalists, friends of an improved but still independent judiciary, in an embarrassing position, for they were publicly committed to getting Bradbury off the bench and now had to support a motion for his removal by address. Most of them did this, but only very reluctantly, because they feared it would further inflame the controversy and lead to additional Republican demands for action against the other judges. They were right. A short time after the legislature passed the motion for Bradbury's removal, Francis Dana delivered a series of charges to the Grand Juries of Suffolk, Hampshire, and Worcester counties, denouncing the legislature's action as unconstitutional because Bradbury had not committed any indiscretions or crimes but had been incapacitated by an act of God. The Republicans responded immediately, defending the legislature's actions, accusing Dana of trying to raise the judiciary above the will of the people, and demanding that he be indicted for libeling the government. The matter, however, was allowed to rest there when Dana, because of old age, resigned a short time later.[33]

Closely related to the pension issue was the question of salary increases for justices of the Supreme Court. According to the State's constitution they were to have "honorable salaries, ascertained and established by standing laws." In compliance with this provision the legislature had, in 1782, passed an act allowing the Chief Justice $1,066.66 and the other justices $1,000 salary annually. At the time it was a satisfactory though not generous provision, but inflation soon made it inadequate. An act in 1790 allowed the Chief Justice $1,233.33 and the other justices $1,166.66 annually, but even these increases did not prove sufficient. Therefore, in 1794, the legislature started granting the judges supplementary sums of money annually. This went on until 1803 when, as part of their over-all program of judicial reform, the Federalists introduced a bill to have the judges' salaries raised to $2,000.[34]

Traditionally the party of economy, the Republicans would

have opposed the measure under any circumstances, but they were especially concerned because it was generally conceded by everyone that once raises were granted it would be unconstitutional to take them away. Since Republicans held the judges responsible in large part for the state's legal problems, they argued that they did not deserve salary increases. "The people," wrote one, "suffer more in their rights and property, by the neglect and misconduct of the judges, than by any other set of men in office; and yet we are continually beset by them for more salary . . . the judges instead of having one dollar added to their salary ought to have a quarter's pay deducted from their annual grant." [35] Republican writers also expressed the fear that a salary increase would be interpreted by the judges as an indication of approval for their partisan excesses and spur them on to commit more. As a "Friend to the People," put it: "It should also be remembered that men are wrought upon by their hopes as well as their fears . . . there is a very extreme evil which may follow the making of profuse grants to the judges." [36] Between 1803 and 1806 the Republicans managed to defeat all attempts to raise the Supreme Court Justices' salaries permanently, although in 1803 an act was passed allowing them for the next three years $800 annually in addition to their established salaries.[37]

The Republicans also considered sinister the attempts made by Federalist judges to limit the power of juries to the determination of facts. This issue was brought before the public in a slander case, *Howland* v. *Colegrave*, tried before the Supreme Court at Lenox in Berkshire county. After they had heard the testimony, Judges Theodore Sedgwick and Samuel Sewall asserted in their address to the jury that the plaintiff's testimony had not proved the defendant guilty of slander, instructed it to bring in a verdict of not guilty, and "intimated" that if it did not the verdict would be set aside. The jury, however, declared the defendant guilty, bringing the wrath of the Federalists down upon them. "Justice," for example, argued that it was the jury's responsibility "to receive the law from the court, and to determine the mixed question of law and fact according as the law is given them by the Court. The form of the Juror's Oath obliges him to give his verdict according to law and the evidence given him; not according to his own opinion of the law but as it shall be stated to him by the court." [38]

Republican writers, on the other hand, defended the jury's right to interpret the law and to bring in a decision contrary to that ordered by the court. "Camden" admitted that on points of law the greatest attention should be given the opinion of the court, but went on to argue that the question still remained: "suppose a difference in sentiment between the judges and the jury, with regard to the law . . . what is to be done?—The jury must do their duty, and their whole duty; they must decide upon the law as well as upon the fact." [39] To do otherwise would be to ask a man "to judge against his own judgment; in other words to sacrifice his honor and conscience—who would willingly be a juror upon these degrading terms?" [40]

But at the heart of the Republicans' opposition to attempts to limit the jurisdiction of juries was the fear that it would make the courts more dangerous than ever.

> It may seem at full view, to be somewhat extraordinary, that twelve men, untutored in the study of jurisprudence; should be the ultimate interpreters of the law, with a power to over-rule the directions of the judges, who have made it the subject of their long and elaborate researches and have been raised to the seat of judgment for their professional abilities and skill. But a deeper examination of the subject will reconcile us to what, at first may appear incongruous.
>
> Juries undoubtedly may make mistakes; they may commit errors; they may commit gross ones; but changed as they constantly are, the errors and mistakes can never grow into a dangerous system. The native uprightness of their sentiments will not be put under the weight of precedent or authority etc.[41]

IV

The radical program of judicial reform in Massachusetts consisted of more than simple opposition to pension bills, salary increases, and attempts to limit the rights of juries, or demands for vengeance against partisan judges; it also included the presentation of an alternative policy of legal reform. The main inspiration for this reform program came from the extreme democratic ideas of the Revolution, which had their emphasis upon the distrust of all governmental power. Consequently, just as fear of increasing the power of judges tied together the different strands of Republican opposition to Federalist proposals for judicial reform, so too did it determine the essential characteristics of the changes which the radicals advocated.

Radical Republicans found the idea of an independent judiciary whose officers held their positions for life tenure on the basis of good behavior especially disturbing. Judges, after all, were men, "the offspring of humanity and have weakness, folly, passions and prejudice for their lot, in common with the rest of mankind." As such they were, like any other office-holder, corrupt or corruptible. "What security," asked one Republican writer, "can we have for the integrity of men, who possess their offices for life, and without control, when we are taught to distrust the bodies annually elected by the people themselves?" [42]

For a radical Jeffersonian there could be but one answer: an elective judiciary. "It appears very evident to me," argued John Leland, an itinerant Calvinist minister and a political power in the western part of the state, "that the election of all officers, to fill all parts of the government, is the natural genius that presides over the United States and if my conviction is just, there will be spasms and commotions in the states, until such amendment takes place." Rejecting the argument that the people were not capable of selecting the men best qualified to be judges, he replied, "for if men have not wisdom enough to choose judges, they have not enough to choose Presidents, Governors, or legislatures; which notion saps the foundation of all representative governments, and supports the monarchical. If men are incompetent to elect their judges, they are equally incompetent to appoint others to do it for them." Leland acknowledged the need for courts to declare acts of the legislature unconstitutional, but asked, "though the people have this judiciary check against the usurpation of the legislature, what check have they against the usurpation of the judiciary?" The solution, he repeated, lay in "the leading doctrine of the American Revolution . . . 'that responsibility was the best expedient to keep men honest.' Why this maxim should be inverted in the judiciary establishment alone, I can never see." [43] There were many Republicans, throughout the state, who agreed with him.[44]

But the main thrust of the radical argument was against the legal system itself. "Decius," who addressed an open letter to the legislature at a time when it was considering various moderate proposals for changes in the organization of the courts, complained, "everyone is silenced by the melifluent sound of a set of men, who artfully persuade us, that without this ruinous and vexatious mode of ending legal controversies, we can have no true liberty; preposterous idea!" [45] The crux of the problem, wrote another Republican, was that as long as "we are . . . led by professional altercation and depend wholly on those who live by rendering our appeals to the law vague and uncertain, we can never expect to remedy the evils attending our judiciary, and if we had fifty judges with 10,000 dollars salaries, we should be under the same calamity we now experience." [46]

Radical Republicans argued that the real cause of the state's legal problems lay in the existence of a large and dangerous undemocratic legal profession whose interests were "not congenial with the general welfare of the community." [47] They denounced lawyers as "swindlers," "speculators," "sharpers," "plunderers," "bloodsuckers," and "leeches." They believed there were too many lawyers in the legislature; that too many benefited economically when adversity struck the community; and that too many were rich and had houses which "are generally the most showy in the parish, and their wives and daughters the most flashy in the congregation." [48] Worst of all, money made lawyers immoral men:

> Who would make out, as clear as light
> That white was black, and black was white
> And with like arguments well strung
> That wrong was right, and right was wrong.[49]

As for the solution, radicals advocated limiting the use of lawyers in settling disputes. They praised the kinds of reforms being contemplated in Pennsylvania and urged that similar measures be implemented in Massachusetts. In particular they wanted all cases involving "trifling demands to come under the exclusive jurisdiction of justices of the peace and not be subject to trial by jury since "such trials are attended with more evils than benefits." They also wanted, and here they were in essential agreement with the moderates, the Courts of Common Pleas to have final jurisdiction in cases involving less than one hundred dollars. This they believed would permit such cases to be settled at less expense than they presently were and prevent needless delays which "are chiefly all the works of attornies; from motives of interest." [50]

But most important of all, the radicals wanted to see the creation of a system of reference which could be used as a substitute for the lower courts. This was necessary, according to one writer, because the people were in the process of discovering "the absurdity and inconsistency of those who are ever urging the *necessity* and *importance* of courts of law, while at the same time they are destroying that *confidence* among the people which alone must substantiate their sanctity and respectability." [51] Another writer suggested that the creation in each town of arbitration boards would make the administration of justice more prompt.

> By delay and management, or common cause, which might be settled by three men in one hour, the men "learned in the law" have had the address to hang up in court for two or three years. Two farmers, instead of spending their money in a court of law, could have their dispute settled with more satisfaction to both parties by submitting their business to three of their neighbors. It is probable seven eighths of the actions now pending are of this description. . . . This cordial arbitration would prevent numberless disquietudes among neighbors, and would tend to relieve the bench of judges from a multiplicity of cases which now come before them and increase their labor.[52]

Radicals also believed that even in the more important and complicated cases which required the presence of men "learned in the law" it was necessary for juries to play an active and dominant role because they represented the only democratic element in what was otherwise a profoundly undemocratic system of settling disputes. Thus, in opposing a Federalist-sponsored bill to declare the incompetency of juries in questions of law, they argued:

> The doctrine now attempted to be promulgated, to render the jury incompetent to law, is to depreciate the character of every other man in society but practitioners of it. It is similar to the declaration, that the people are their own "worst enemies"— that they are ignorant as to every particular on which is founded either the political or legal principles of the constitution and of the laws. Should this once become the prevailing sentiment, in a few years no man would be considered of any weight in society but those connected in the judiciary department. This doctrine would pervade the legislative branch and none would be eligible to make laws but those in the practice of them.[53]

The radicals did more than simply defend the rights of juries to interpret the law; they demanded that safeguards be set up to ensure that jury members be democratically selected, rotated more often, and protected from intimidation. They suggested that juries should have the right to cross-examine witnesses and lawyers, and should be allowed to bring in any decision they wished. As one radical writer put it, "the jury, being of the neighborhood, may, and ofttimes do know something of their own knowledge, as to the matter itself, the credit of the evidence etc. which may justly sway them in delivering their verdict . . . as when a man is indicted, and no evidence comes against him, the direction of the court is, *you* are to acquit him, unless of your own knowledge you know him guilty." [54]

To the argument that most juries were incapable of interpreting the law, the radicals entered this caveat:

> We say that the error lies not with the jury, but within the complex system of English laws adopted as authorities. On this comprehensive system, founded on cases no way analagous either to our constitution or customs, the judges themselves get confounded, and the lawyers sport with their client with a parade of wonderful learning and investigation. It is laughable to hear men talk seriously about the certainty of that which has become proverbial for uncertainty.—"The glorious

uncertainty of the law," is an observation as familiar as the expences of it.—Not that it is uncertain as it relates to the verdict of a jury, but its uncertainty consists in the explanation of those who profess exclusively to be its expounders. After we have heard a cause, attended with all the variety of opinions given on the subject, the mind of the audience is generally more satisfied by the decision of the jury than from all the comments on the law, however elaborately delivered. The fact is, the jury hear the variety of opinions, and are able on mature deliberation, to judge accurately on the precise point of controversy.[55]

Radicals condemned what they called "the ridiculous parade of law knowledge" as "mere farce for both the *attornies* have *authorities* to prove their respective positions—if one asserts that *white* is *black*, he gravely comes forward with his *authority*, and if his antagonists says that *black* is *white*, he produces with like gravity an authority equally as 'learned in the law.' " [56] To correct this, radicals argued it was necessary to eliminate the common law, streamline court procedure, and generally simplify the law. The question the legislature had to decide was whether it was going to

further the cause of equity, reason and justice; and the interest of nine tenths of the society; or . . . advance the interest of the battalions of law characters, law officers, and all their humble adherents and litiguous suitors? Shall we be directed by reason, equity and a few simple and plain laws promptly executed, or shall we be ruled by volumes of statutes and cases decided by the ignorance and intolerance of former times? [57]

V

The radicals believed essentially that government at best was a necessary evil, that while it served some useful purposes it was always a potential danger to the rights and liberties of the people because it could easily become oppressive and arbitrary, and, therefore, that it was important for government and the laws which it enforced to be made as simple, as weak, and as directly responsible to the will of the people as possible.

The moderates, on the other hand, argued that the real cause of the Commonwealth's legal problems lay in the inability of an archaic court system to keep pace with the state's commercial development and expanding population. They were horrified by the proposals of the "radicals who," they claimed, were "more gifted at complaining than reforming, and more zealous to pull down than to put up." [58] The moderates viewed the proposals of the radicals as the work of "lunatics," "fanaticks," and "visionaries" bent on overturning a constitution and legal system "which ought to be as immutable as possible," and of designing demagogues who, in order to get elected, "tell a profligate rabble that they are sovereigns" and appeal "to the prejudices and passions of the multitude." [59] In like manner, Thomas Dwight predicted that if the Republicans ever got into power, they would "probably innundate and sweep away liberty, property and Law." [60]

To be sure, the moderates were as fully committed as the radicals to a republican form of government, but they wished "to restrain it from licentious excess and to guard it from profanation. The Democrats think on the contrary, that without excess there is no liberty; if anything is restrained or denied nothing is granted. . . ." Those critical of radical proposals abhorred the idea of an uncomplicated government, directly and immediately responsible to the people. "It is the simplicity and singleness of democracy that ought to be dreaded," wrote one. "All simple governments are despotisms." [61] Fearing majority rule, the moderates advocated a government which provided for a bicameral legislature, a strong executive, and an independent judiciary.

In particular, the moderates condemned the radicals' "hypochondriack terror of power," and argued that only a strong and active government could make liberty possible. "Such is the natural propensity of man to usurpation and domination," argued one, "that it may be truly said that where there is no law there is no liberty." [62] And Theophilus Parsons believed that "a due administration of the law is the only security of our social and civil rights and it is a source of consolation if our political rights should ever be abused." [63]

What the moderates wanted was a "Government of laws not of men," for they believed freedom without law meant freedom to do wrong as well as right. Laws and their enforcement protected the people from their own worst instincts and made true liberty possible.[64]

> Real liberty is not the power of doing what we please, but is a system of RESTRAINT, by which we are PREVENTED from injuring another in property or person, and are in like manner ourselves protected from his violence and injustice. Real liberty is a code of laws, containing COMMANDS, PROHIBITIONS, and MENACES, in which the will of individuals is so far from being CONSULTED, that it is directly CONTROLLED. Real liberty has for her officiating minister, judges, sheriffs and constables, whilst her residence is surrounded by gaols, pillories, and gibbets.[65]

Because they believed the government and governed were two separate and distinct estates, the advocates of moderate judicial reform opposed radical proposals for increasing the power of juries and making the judiciary elective. "Acirema" described as absurd the idea "of attempting to support a republic which is a 'Government of Law'—and not of the capricious *will* of the rulers of the day,—without an independent *judiciary,* who should be the sole *interpreters of the Laws*—when the same body of rulers make the laws, and interpret them there is no liberty." [66] "Rational Freedom," argued another Federalist, "has everything to hope from the judiciary; it can have nothing to fear." [67] And in the same vein another writer warned, "It is often the case when 'men feel power they forget right'; and a firm and enlightened judiciary rears the only barrier against the usurpation and tyranny of ambitious Democrats, and the criminal designs and fraudful machinations of rogues." [68]

In addition to the anti-authoritarian and extreme democratic implications of the radicals' proposals, the moderates also feared their anti-intellectual implications. "What a glorious system," wrote Theodore Sedgwick, "—so simple and so intelligent—the trade of lawmaking requires less study and less talent than to make the head of a pin! Nor is all this learning and genius not only not necessary but by our own masters the sovereign people are absolutely reprobated and denounced as disqualifications of the character of legislator." [69] For their part, the Federalists believed that most people were not capable of being public servants because of "the extensive nature of the science of government." They stressed "that its acquisition demands vast exertions of the mind, perservering exercise of the intellectual powers, and that a faithful discharge of official trust is an arduous undertaking, for which all are not equally qualified." [70]

The Federalists were particularly effusive in their praise of the common law. "The body of the English Common Law," wrote one, is, "the only body for right and liberty that ever had an intelligent soul to inform it . . . and we hope for liberty's sake [it is] immoveably established in the states." [71] Another Federalist described it "as the pride of the human intellect, which, with all its defects, redundancies, and errours [sic], is the collected wisdom of the ages, combining the principles of original justice with the infinite variety of human concerns." [72] The very fact that the Republicans attacked the common law, the Federalists believed, was proof of how far their opponents had let themselves be led astray by their anti-intellectual attitude toward judicial reform. "Vain are the clamors against it. None revile it who know what it is. The common law is the immutable principle of justice, as practiced upon, and sanctioned by the experience of ages. By this law, we enjoy in society, our estates, our good name, our liberty and our lives." [73]

XIV

The Politics of Judicial Reform in Massachusetts, 1803-1808

Although the Federalist party dominated Massachusetts politics during the years 1797–1806, the Commonwealth was never a one-party state. The Republicans were always able to maintain a strong minority in the legislature, and they had leadership, organization, and a knowledge of politics which allowed them, especially after 1800, to make it steadily more difficult for their opponents to stay in power. The stronger the Jeffersonians became, however, the harder they found it to maintain unity in a party which drew its support from a diverse coalition of doctrinaire democrats, religious radicals, professional politicians, and ambitious businessmen who had been denied social and political acceptance by the ruling group.[1] They were especially divided on the issue of judicial reform.

I

The titular head of the Republicans in Massachusetts was Elbridge Gerry, the party's gubernatorial candidate between 1800 and 1803. A Marblehead merchant, revolutionary patriot, and delegate to the Philadelphia Convention of 1787, where he had refused to sign the Constitution, Gerry had been on good terms with both Jefferson and John Adams during the 1790's. In 1797 he tried, unsuccessfully, to effect a reconciliation between Jefferson and Adams. He did not belong to the radical wing of the Republican party. The underlying strategy behind his gubernatorial campaigns was to convince the Federalists of his moderation and of the advantage to the state of a chief executive on good terms with the national administration.[2]

Sharing this view, and having no sympathy with the radical program of judicial reform, were several other important Republicans: William Eustis, a socially prominent physician who maintained good relations with the Federalists and who was elected Boston's representative to Congress in 1800 and 1802; Perez Morton, a member of the state legislature and one of the wealthiest men in the Commonwealth; Charles Jarvis, the party's leading orator in the General Court; Aaron Hill, Postmaster of Boston and state senator from Middlesex county; and Richard Cutts, a large landowner, merchant, and representative to Congress from York county, Maine.[3]

The Republican Party in Massachusetts also had an active and influential radical wing. John Leland, an itinerant Baptist preacher, and Thomas Allen, a New Light Calvinist minister, were two important members of this group. These leading religious figures of Berkshire county, used the pulpit and the pages of the *Pittsfield Sun* to demand changes in the state's legal system and to preach an aggressive and uncompromising brand of Jeffersonianism.[4] John Bacon, Berkshire's representative to Congress and an implacable foe of an independent judiciary, also expressed this point of view.[5]

But it was Benjamin Austin who did the most to keep alive the revolutionary fervor of republicanism, to espouse the radical program of judicial reform, and to fight against an alliance with the Federalists. A forty-eight-year-old resident of Boston in 1800, Austin had been taught the dynamics of radicalism and revolution by Sam Adams in the decade preceeding independence. In 1786 he acquired a national reputation as the author of *Observations on the Pernicious Practice of the Law,* and from that time on he was generally referred to as "Honestus.' He also opposed the adoption of the Federal Constitution, served several times in the Massachusetts Senate during the early 1790's, and, according to John Quincy Adams, would often show up at the Boston town meeting with a large group of men "who looked as if they had been collected from all the Jails on the Continent, with Ben. Austin like another Jack Cade at their head." [6]

Among the Federalists, there was no one "more universally and more deeply despised than Austin." [7] Although he possessed little formal education, Austin was a gifted writer—probably the ablest polemicist in the state. A close friend and advisor of Abijah Adams, editor of the most widely read Jeffersonian newspaper in New England, the *Independent Chronicle*, Austin frequently used its columns to express his hostilities to the legal profession. He interpreted Jefferson's election as a God-sent opportunity to revive the principles of 1776 in their uncontaminated form, and was unalterably opposed to any policy of accommodating the Federalists. In 1802, in an attack upon Republican moderates, he expressed his feelings in this way:

> An union of republicans and monarchists can never be expected; an union with those who advocate unnecessary taxes, and those who are opposed to them, is chimerical; an union of those, who use scurrility and defamation, with those who substantiate their measures by reason and sound policy, is reversing every logical decision; an union of friends of order and the revilers of an administration which inculcates peace abroad and harmony at home is as impossible as a cordiality between God and mammon.[8]

Levi Lincoln, the Attorney General of the United States, while not strictly a radical, shared many radical attributes. Born in 1749, he was a Harvard graduate who had entered politics in the early 1770's, and had served on committees of correspondence and safety and as a member of the provincial congress. Although a lawyer by training, he never won the respect of his profession. His meager legal talents were a source of humor to his political enemies. One Federalist newspaper described him as such a bad lawyer "that Judges cannot hear his name pronounced without a smile." [9]

When he first arrived in Washington as Jefferson's Attorney General, Lincoln was a moderate, favoring a policy of conciliation toward the Federalists.[10] But after he spent the summer of 1802 surveying the political situation in Massachusetts he changed his mind. "The Republicans in general," he complained to Jefferson, "have hitherto in my opinion been too inattentive. They have been too timid and accommodating to their enemies. To those who will never accommodate, but on terms of an unconditional surrender. There can be no reconciliation consistent with the present measures, with the preservation of the existing system of government—I once thought otherwise." [11]

Of those Republicans who did not fit into either the moderate or radical camp, the most important was James Sullivan, the leading Jeffersonian lawyer in the state. During the 1780's, Sullivan had worked to reorganize the state's laws and to defend his profession against the attacks of "Honestus" in a series of articles written under the pseudonym "Zenas." He was one of the first members of the American Academy of Arts and Sciences. In 1801 his book, *The History of Land Titles in Massachusetts,* was published, and in the same year he began work on a history of the criminal law which he did not live to complete. His legal talents were so respected that the Federalists allowed him to serve as the state's Attorney General from 1790 to 1806.[12] He did not like the radicals and had no sympathy with their position on judicial reform. To a friend he privately expressed the opinion that "there are men, who have a seat in the front rank of republicanism, who constantly express sentiments which are not congenial to any form of government that can subsist among men." [13] But he also disliked co-operating with the Federalists and was sharply critical of the favorable attitude of many of the moderates toward speculative and commercial banking.[14]

For a while the moderate Republican strategy of conciliating the Federalists appeared to make sense. When Gerry first ran for governor, in 1800, he received the endorsement of President Adams, and he did surprisingly well, though he lost the election. He was again unsuccessful the following year, but he made further gains, and the Republicans, in a spectacular victory, captured the entire Boston delegation to the General Court. Moreover, following Jefferson's victory in 1800, several important Federalists, Henry Knox, Benjamin Waterhouse, John Lovell, and John Quincy Adams, seemed to indicate a willingness to be accommodated.[15]

Despite these hopeful signs, however, the politics of accommodation did not produce the desired results. There were too many Federalists who refused to be conciliated, and in ensuing elections they increased their share of the vote in the gubernatorial contest, regained control of the Boston delegation to the General Court, elected John Quincy Adams and Timothy Pickering to the United States Senate, and barely failed to defeat Eustis in his bid for re-election to Congress. This last contest caused one Jeffersonian politician to express the opinion that the Republicans' mistake had been to use a "needle where a knife was necessary & a smoothing plain [sic] where a broad axe was wanted." [16]

Following Gerry's poor showing in the election of 1802, an attempt was made to drop him as the party's gubernatorial candidate. The driving force behind this attempt came from a group of political careerists and dissident moderates who wished to share in the benefits of Republican control of the State House and who no longer felt that Gerry had any chance of winning. The radicals also supported the movement, however, and they tried to secure the nomination for Lincoln. But the moderates were opposed, arguing that the move would "play the devil with the cause in Boston," and work "generally against any and all elections where they [the moderates] may have placed any hopes of succeeding." [17] Some moderates even went so far as to argue that it would be a mistake on the part of the Republicans to put up any opposition to the incumbent Federalist governor, Caleb Strong, whom they described as a man "of a mild and moderate temper and . . . on that account entitled to great respect." [18] In the end, Gerry managed to retain the nomination, but he was swamped in the ensuing election because many of the moderates deserted him for Strong and a large percentage of the radicals did not vote at all. [19]

In 1804 the party agreed upon James Sullivan as a compromise candidate, for "there could not be a strong union of Republicanism in any other person." [20] In the election that followed, many moderates continued to vote Federalist, but the radicals, despite their unhappiness over Sullivan's ties to the legal profession, supported him. They did this partly because they believed in party regularity, but also because Sullivan was popular with the voters and stood some chance of eventually winning. They were not disappointed in this last hope, for not only did the party make considerable gains in the legislature, but also Sullivan, though defeated, polled 10,000 more votes than Gerry had received the previous year. The Jeffersonians were finally on the road to victory in Massachusetts.[21]

II

In December of 1804, Levi Lincoln, having just resigned his position in the cabinet, began the long trip back to his home in Worcester. On the way he stopped in New York, where he spent some time conferring with Tom Paine, whom he described as a man of "surprising intellect" and of "bold independent reflections." Arriving in Massachusetts in the early part of 1805, he wrote to Jefferson predicting that the party would make an all-out effort to gain control of the state and that "the struggle will be the warmest & most severe we have ever experienced." He also predicted there would be "some, *unmade, half-made, double-made,* verbal professional republicans, who give us trouble, and on whom no dependence can, or ought to be placed." [22]

Lincoln was right on both counts. Encouraged by Sullivan's success in the previous election, inspired by Jefferson's capture of the state's electoral votes in the presidential election of 1804, and aroused by the debate over judicial reform, the Republicans made the election one of the most bitter in the Commonwealth's history.[23] This in turn upset the moderates, causing Lincoln to complain:

> Boston acts awful in this business. Cold, divided & dissatisfied in the conduct of some of her Republican leaders. Our cause has often been more injured by its difficult or pretended friends than by its most active and avowed enemies. Such friends if they must be called friends, possess great attachment to the general object of pursuit; and yet disapprove every measure deemed necessary for its attainments & persons who are to lead in those measures, the time, & means & the mode of prosecuting them. With such characters everything which is, is wrong; wrong in time, in principle or in fact, and so far from being right, without a statement of what is right.[24]

Despite their internal differences, the Republicans did well in the 1805 election. Sullivan reduced Strong's majority to 4000 votes, and the party just missed capturing control of the General Court. Confident that victory was in their grasp, the radicals redoubled their efforts. Governor Strong was the biggest obstacle to the Republican party's success. An old, moderately inclined patriot, he was very popular with the voters and did not fit into the radical Jeffersonian stereotype of the Federalists as tories and monarchists. About the worst that they could say about him was that he was "a kind of half lawyer and half farmer, who is averse to any good, and has no great disposition to do mischief, and is only used by his party to cover their designs." [25]

Shrewdly recognizing that they stood little chance of capturing the governorship by attacking Strong personally, radical Republicans went out of their way to emphasize instead the deep ideological differences involved in the election. "No two parties," argued one, "ever existed in any Country, where their ultimate objects were more diametrically opposite to each other in principle." [26] The radical strategy was not so much to convert Federalists as it was to bring out those Republicans who had not voted in previous elections because they did not like the alternatives presented to them. It was no accident, the radicals knew, that the steady growth of Republican power in Massachusetts coincided with the most intense period of the debate over judicial reform. In the election of 1806 they stressed in particular that the Federalist party was controlled "by the Lawyers, a numerous host; the bloodsuckers of society; who from the nature of their vocation, must necessarily be in favor of an extensive and complicated system of government and laws." [27]

As the struggle for control of Massachusetts became more intense, the differences between radical and moderate Republicans became more pronounced. The moderates, many of whom were heavy investors in the New England Mississippi Land Company, actively lobbied for the Jefferson administration's position on the Yazoo issue, opposed the impeachment of Samuel Chase, and were heard to express themselves "as favoring a third party system of politics." The radicals, on the other hand, took advantage of the moderates' backsliding to strengthen their influence in the party. This was necessary because, in 1806, there were still many

Republicans who, while unhappy with the moderates' policy of accommodation, were also uneasy about the extremism of the radicals, but who now accepted them as legitimate allies. Levi Lincoln described his conversion in these terms:

> Benjamin Austin whom I have heretofore had my prejudices from an idea that he had availed himself of vulgar and popular errors in advocating principles inconsistent with a regulated & well ordered govt. has done & does more to support republicanism & hold its enemy in check, than a score of his countrymen equally capable of being useful, were they equally zealous.[28]

It was Sullivan who suffered the most from the crossfire between the moderate and radical factions of his party. Even though he stood a good chance of winning the election in 1806, neither group really wanted him, and attempts were made to drop him. The moderates, perhaps because they feared he would win and bring the radicals into power with him, tried to squeeze him out of Massachusetts politics by requesting Jefferson to make him Attorney General. The radicals, for their part, were embarrassed because he was a lawyer and unsympathetic to their attacks upon the legal profession. But neither faction could come up with an acceptable substitute. The radicals stayed with Sullivan, accepting Lincoln's advice that even with him, "firmness, independent spirit & perseverence can and certainly will revolutionize Massachusetts." [29]

As for the moderates, they remained unreconciled to either Sullivan or the growing influence of the radicals. Recognizing, as Josiah Dwight noted, that "the moderate Democrats" had been "staggered with recent events in Pennsylvania," the Federalists began to make a point of giving extensive press coverage of events in that state as an example of what could take place if the Republicans came to power with the radicals in control. For a while there was even some talk of forming a third party, but neither the moderate Federalists nor the moderate Republicans were prepared to leave their own parties.[30]

The Federalists, realizing that the Republicans would probably control the legislature after the spring elections, made a final attempt to reform the judiciary. Under the leadership of Edward S. Livermore they introduced one bill for increasing and making permanent the salaries of the justices of the Supreme Court, and another for giving the high court exclusive final jurisdiction in deciding points of law. The first bill was considered especially important because without it, as Livermore noted, "all . . . will prove abortive." [31] Both bills failed. The Federalist advocates of moderate judicial reform now hoped for some kind of miracle in the ensuing election or, more realistically, hoped for continuing moderate Republican influence to prevent a radical onslaught on the state's legal system.

They did not have to wait very long. As a result of the election of 1806 the Republicans gained control of the legislature, captured the lieutenant governor's office, and ran so close a second in the gubernatorial contest that it became a disputed election. The new, Republican-controlled General Court met in June to decide the matter, and for a while it appeared that it would be resolved along strictly partisan lines with Sullivan declared the winner. But a number of Republican moderates bolted at the last moment and gave the election to Strong.[32] This action was severely condemned by the radical press and brought forth a Federalist retort that the complaining was being done by those Republicans "decidedly bent on dissolving all the common ties of society and on pushing party spirit to its utmost extent . . . and betray[ing] their fears that moderate men of different parties unite." [33]

III

Following their party's victory in 1806, the moderate Republicans demonstrated an even greater willingness to co-operate with their Federalist counterparts than they had shown when they were out of power. Co-operation between the two groups on the issue of judicial reform began in the spring of 1806, when Francis Dana, because of sickness and old age, resigned as Chief Justice of the Supreme Court. Under normal circumstances the position would have gone to the ranking justice on the court, Theodore Sedgwick, but Samuel Sewall and Isaac Parker, in concert with the

Boston Bar Association and other high-ranking Federalists, urged Governor Strong to give the position to Theophilus Parsons, which he did at once.[34]

Sedgwick's feelings were hurt, and for a while he even considered resigning from the court. But despite Sedgwick's reaction, the appointment of Parsons was an intelligent move on the part of the Federalists. He was the undisputed leader of the Massachusetts bar, and many New Englanders, including Jeffersonians, would have argued that where the law was concerned he was the most learned man in the country. His acknowledged intellectual leadership brought a dignity and respect to the Massachusetts Supreme Court which Sedgwick, for all his ability and effort, could not have supplied.[35]

Moreover, and this was crucial, at the very height of the debate over judicial reform, Parsons was much less offensive to the Republicans than Sedgwick. Both had been elite-minded nationalists and hard-line social conservatives during the 1780's, but they went different ways after the adoption of the Constitution in 1787. Sedgwick enthusiastically embraced the High Federalist cause, while Parsons, for the most part, withdrew from politics and devoted most of his energies to studying and practicing law. When the Federalist party split in 1800, Sedgwick sided with Hamilton, while Parsons supported Adams. The moderate Republicans, almost to a man, detested Sedgwick, whereas they respected Parsons for both his abilities and his achievements.[36]

Parsons had not sought the appointment as Chief Justice; it had been solicited for him by his friends and admirers. And he accepted it at great personal sacrifice, for it was estimated that he had a private practice worth in excess of $10,000 a year. But he only accepted it on the understanding that his salary would be increased and made constitutionally permanent.[37]

Parsons's terms for acceptance of the appointment were communicated by the Federalists to the legislative leader of the moderate Republicans, Joseph Story. "Story's ambition is boundless, his mind active, but not strong," commented a Jeffersonian clergyman with radical leanings. "His flights are quick, but not high. He skims but does not rise." [38] Twenty-seven years old in 1806, Story was a Harvard graduate who had studied law under Samuel

Sewall and Samuel Putnam. In 1801 he moved to Salem and began practicing law. He immediately attached himself to the Crowninshield interest, and his political star rose quickly: in 1802 he was appointed to a committee to revise the town's ordinances; the following year he solicited, received, and then turned down an appointment as naval officer for the port of Salem; and he served in the state legislature between 1805 and 1808. As for his position on judicial reform during these years, he later noted: "I uniformly stood by the law and gave it all my support." [39] He described his political position during this period in the following terms:

> Though I was a decided member of what was called the republican party, and of course a supporter of the administration of Mr. Jefferson and Mr. Madison, you are not to imagine that I was a mere slave to the opinions of either, or that I did not exercise an independent judgment upon public affairs. The Republican party then and at all other times embraced men of very different views on many subjects. . . . I was at all times a firm believer in the doctrines of George Washington and an admirer of his conduct, measures and principles during his whole administration. . . . I look back to that period of my life with some honest pride in recollecting that I was not betrayed into any departure from a just moderation of conduct, though my party from being a minority, in the progress of events, obtained a triumphant possession of all the legislative and executive departments.[40]

At the June 1806 meeting of the legislature, the same session at which the gubernatorial contest was decided in Strong's favor, Story headed a special committee to consider increasing the salaries of the Supreme Court justices. The committee recommended that the judges be given an adequate "permanent compensation" and questioned "any measure which has the immediate tendency to place the judicial department at the footstool of the legislature." A long and arduous debate followed, and only after considerable crossing of party lines, which saw country Federalists and radical Republicans lined up against urban Federalists and moderate Republicans, did the legislature pass a bill fixing the associate justices' salaries at $2400 and the Chief Justice's at $2500 annually.[41] "This though by no means adequate to their merits or their claim," wrote a Federalist, "is so much better than what was formerly done that we can not but felicitate ourselves." [42]

The radical response was predictable: the compensation alloted to the judges was exorbitant, while "the act itself appears to be nothing short of a premeditated blow at the *root of Democratic Government,* and a *Chief Corner Stone* of the great *Fabric of Aristocracy.*" Launching a campaign for the repeal of the act, the radicals condemned those Republicans who helped it pass as "men who make high pretensions to Democratic principles, and who at the same time, are among the most forward and zealous advocates of compensations like these." [43]

Radical resentment toward the judiciary rose to a fever pitch during the late summer and fall of 1806. It began in early August when Austin's son was shot and killed by a partisan Federalist lawyer, Thomas O. Selfridge. Only a few days before the unfortunate event Austin had singled Selfridge out, in one of his many attacks upon the legal profession, as a troublemaker who deliberately instigated suits for profit. When Selfridge demanded a public apology and Austin refused, Selfridge posted an advertisement in the *Boston Gazette* calling Austin "a coward, a liar and a scoundrel." Following this, and unknown to Austin, his son Charles, then a senior at Harvard, armed himself with a club and set out to defend his father's honor. There were conflicting stories as to what happened when the two men met: according to those eyewitnesses partisan to Austin, Selfridge fired before he was struck or even threatened, while Selfridge's friends at the scene claimed he had been struck several times and even warned his assailant before firing. The event immediately became a political issue, with Austin and his friends describing it as a political murder. The Federalists quickly rallied behind Selfridge, and he had the services of four of the leading members of the Massachusetts bar, Samuel Dexter, Christopher Gore, Harrison Gray Otis, and Fisher Ames, to plead his case.[44]

The case was heard by the Grand Jury at the November meeting of the Supreme Court in Boston. As part of his charge, Parsons delivered a long and elaborate explanation of the common law principles involved in the law of murder, manslaughter, and justifiable homicide, whereupon the Grand Jury brought in an indictment for manslaughter only. "A performance," the *Independent Chronicle* called it, "calculated to disturb, rather than promote the peace of society." When the case came to trial on 23 December, the same paper observed, "we cannot but be struck with the number of lawyers who appear aiding and assisting in the cause. It is a melancholy reflection, that the death of an innocent young man should excite so much anxiety among individuals in the bar, to exculpate the offender." The trial lasted less than a week, with the defense successfully resolving the question of who attacked whom first in Selfridge's favor, and basing a large part of their case upon Austin's inflammatory character and the right of a libeled man to protect his honor. It took the jury only fifteen minutes to bring in a verdict of "not guilty." The radicals, needless to say, were enraged, and they took to the newspaper vowing revenge upon the courts and the legal profession.[45]

Still another Republican grievance against the judiciary, shared by the moderates as well as the radicals, was that the Supreme Court interfered politically on the side of the Federalists. In June of 1806 the Republican-controlled legislature passed an election bill expressly recognizing the right of unincorporated areas to vote. It clearly was an attempt on the part of the Republicans to legitimatize the increasing popular participation in statewide elections which was proving so beneficial to their cause. Strong received the bill on the last day of the session, but he did not sign it. After the legislature adjourned, he submitted the bill to the Supreme Court, and, in accordance with Section II, Chapter III, of the Massachusetts Constitution, requested the opinion of the Court on its constitutionality. Four of the judges, Parsons, Sewall, Parker, and Thatcher (Sedgwick not being able to attend) submitted a unanimous report advising that the proposed bill was unconstitutional. When the legislature reconvened in January of 1807, Strong vetoed the bill, submitting the Supreme Court report along with his own opinion. This brought forth a storm of Republican protest. "To be plain," wrote one, "I think Governor Strong had his doubts, and the Justices of the Supreme Court likewise, concerning his re-election the ensuing year." [46]

Despite the fulminations of the radicals about real and imagined grievances, the moderate coalition continued to push their program of judicial reform. When the legislature reconvened in January of 1807, Story was once again appointed head of the judiciary committee, this time with instructions to recommend whatever changes were needed to make the courts more efficient. Story had already conversed and corresponded with a number of the leading Federalists, most extensively with Sedgwick and Sewall. To both men he sent copies of a bill he planned to introduce for increasing the powers of the Supreme Court justices at *nisi prius* terms to rule on appeals and interpret the law. Although they had some minor criticisms, both men expressed substantial approval of the bill, Sewall going so far as to describe it as "the quintessence of all that has been fabricated on the subject." [47]

When the bill was introduced into the legislature, it immediately ran into radical opposition, and it was voted down by a large majority. Two days later Story asked for a reconsideration, but the bill was again defeated, 140 to 77. During this session, one Republican, according to a Federalist report, declared "his firm belief that Story was as much a *federalist* as any man in the house." Disgusted, Story moved, and the motion was immediately adopted, that his committee on the judiciary be discharged.[48]

The tensions generated by the apostasy of the moderate Republicans on the judiciary issue were carried over into the gubernatorial contest. The radicals, still distrustful of Sullivan but nevertheless unwilling to drop a likely winner, secured, over the objections of the moderates, Lincoln's nomination as the party's candidate for lieutenant governor. Hoping to salvage the election, the Federalists appealed to the moderate Republicans to vote for Strong because:

> Governor Strong has the confidence of the moderate men of all parties. Sullivan wants that of his own. Indeed it is said that Sullivan is the mere "cats-paw" of his party, and that if chosen he is to be superseded by Jacobin Lincoln—a man so little known, and so unpopular where known, that they dare not risk him as a candidate for the office he aspires to.[49]

Despite internal discord, total victory finally came to the Massachusetts Republicans in the election of 1807, when they captured the State House and further consolidated their control of both Houses of the legislature. Dominating all three elective branches of the government for the first time since 1797, Republicans naturally wanted the patronage benefits of power. But it was still not clear whether the party, despite the demands of some of its members, would go along with a radical overhauling of the State's legal system.

If the radicals had any hopes at all that Sullivan would tacitly consent to an attack on the courts, they were soon set straight. For in his inaugural address, the governor unequivocally endorsed the moderate position:

> The Judicial department will invariably claim the first regard of patriotism. Upon its wisdom and purity, freedom, property and all the valuable possessions in civil society depend. In all countries, the principles and feelings of the magistrates and judges ought to be in a coincidence with the nature of the government, since this is its principle [sic] source of energy. The judiciary necessarily is an expensive branch of administration; in a state where an inquiry by grand juries and trials by petit juries are fixed by the constitution as the strong barriers of the peoples rights, the modes of punishing crimes, and of obtaining justice on private demands, are more expensive still. A cheap, ready and plain manner of obtaining remedies from wrongs, and of compelling the execution of contracts, by fixed, established rules, forms the strongest lines of a good government. Under this impression, the people in forming the constitution, declared that all the judges should hold their offices as long as they should behave themselves well, and that the judges of the supreme judicial court should have permanent and honorable salaries, established by law. The office of jurors may be thought by some to be a burden; but if that institution should be abolished, there would no longer be freedom or property. It ought to be guarded by laws, not only against corruption, but against all undue influences and party prejudices. There is no doubt but that improvement may be effected in the jurisprudence of the commonwealth; and therefore the attention of the legislature will not be withdrawn from it. But in all altercations, a sacred regard will be had to the constitution; while the plans adopted shall have a degree of perfection as to render them respectable and permanent.[50]

The radical Republican press greeted the address with stony silence, while the Federalists praised it. "We feel happy in assuring the reader," observed the *Columbian Centinel,* "he will find in it much to applaud and but little to disapprove. . . . The remarks on the importance of the Judiciary, and the indispensable necessity of supporting its independence, are pre-eminently accurate, and the paragraph respecting jurors—though it must operate like wormwood upon some of his partizans—will be received by the wise and good as political gospel. . . . The speech enforces the necessity of treating Chief Magistrates and the civil authorities with respect; and of giving ready obedience to the laws." [51]

Bipartisan support again secured for Story the chairmanship of the judiciary committee, and he was instructed to report to the next session of the legislature the alterations in the existing court system necessary for the "interest and happiness of the Commonwealth." The Federalists were considerably less pleased, however, when Sullivan began commissioning a substantial number of Republicans as justices of the peace. With the aid of the Republican-dominated legislature he reorganized and appointed a new set of judges to the Courts of Sessions, and arrogated to himself, at the expense of the county courts, the right to specify attorneys for the Commonwealth. All this was done in the name of reform, but it also was a way to provide places for the party faithful. The act reconstituting the Courts of Sessions, for example, created about eighty positions which provided the justices three dollars per day for attendence and two dollars for every ten miles' travel. But none of the acts was radically oriented, for they in no way fundamentally effected the state's legal system.[52]

The radicals, in the interval between the June 1807 and January 1808 sessions of the legislature, continued to agitate for sweeping changes in the administration of justice. They attacked the common law, particularly its interpretation in the Selfridge case, denounced the recent increase of the salaries of the justices of the Supreme Court, and reiterated their demands for arbitration boards, an elective judiciary, and expanded powers for juries, and even spoke of removing the present judges.[53] At the same time they were also beginning to realize that, in the face of a veto and Story's control of the judiciary committee, they stood little chance of getting any of these measures through the legislature. "It appears at present," wrote John Bacon, a peren-

nial antagonist of the judiciary, "that we have in this Commonwealth, a decided, perhaps sufficient majority of professed Dem-
ocratical Republicans. . . . Had we equal evidence that our
information, talents, integrity & real patriotism were in proportion to our numbers, I should I confess fell a greater degree of
confidence & satisfaction in contemplating the projects before us,
than I now do." [54]

When the legislature reconvened for its winter session in January 1808, Story immediately presented the judiciary committee
report. It had been prepared in co-operation with the Federalists
and consisted of three bills for reorganizing the courts. For the
first bill, the committee "availed themselves of the learned labors
of their predecessors," and they recommended dividing the Supreme Court into three circuits. The second bill further enlarged
the jurisdiction of the Courts of Common Pleas. The third bill,
establishing a court of equity, was the most controversial, providing for a system of administering justice which was different from
but not opposed to the common law; the new jurisdiction would
be mostly in cases of fraud, trusts, accidents, and mistakes "where
natural justice gives a right, and the common law has provided
no means to enforce it," and where regular courts of law "can
not decide conformably with the principles of substantial justice." [55]

The main grievance of the radicals against equity jurisdiction
was that it provided for a system of administering justice which
was vague, and that it gave too much power to the presiding
judge, for it allowed jury trials only in certain cases. Led by
Bacon and other radicals, the legislature, by rejecting or permanently tabling the different bills, set aside the entire report.[56]

The radicals, it is clear, had begun to organize themselves.
They still lacked capable leadership in the legislature and so
could not take the initiative; yet they controlled enough votes to
prevent measures they disapproved from passing. Story in particular had become an object of their disdain. Almost gleefully William Bentley noted in his diary that Story was out of political
favor:

> He began with great fury, but as soon as he reached as far as
> the public fervour could carry him, as far as the House of
> Representatives, he was not content to lead his bretheren but

fell immediately into the hands of the opposition & dared to
come forward with a project of salaries for the judges which
the opposition could not in the days of their glory obtain. He
gained it by surprise & from the confidence of his friends. They
were alarmed. He could not open his eyes. He dared still to
venture & came with three bills of Judicature. They were rejected as far as they had his patronage, & as he confessed he
had lost all influence in the house. . . .[57]

The most able people belonged to the moderate Republican
and Federalist coalition, and they held the key government positions. But they were in a minority in the General Court and
could no longer implement the positive aspects of their program.
In the long run, however, this benefited the advocates of moderate judicial reform, for it prevented changes along radical lines.
The significance of this in practical terms can be seen by examining developments in the District of Maine.

IV

In Massachusetts' eastern frontier area, the struggle between radical Republicans on the one side and moderate Republicans and
Federalists on the other involved more than a conflict over abstract principles. It involved also the disposition of millions of
acres of land. The District of Maine, which was part of Massachusetts until 1820, had been a Federalist stronghold until 1803.
The area's conversion to Jeffersonian principles after that date
paralleled the debate over judicial reform and contributed significantly to the Republican victories in 1806 and 1807. "If that
part of the state could stand neuter," wrote Fisher Ames, "Massachusetts proper would be right some years longer." [58]

Squatters provided one of the most important sources of Republican support in the District. During the 1780's and 1790's,
when most other states were inaugurating a cheap land policy in
hopes of settling their frontiers, Massachusetts sought to pay off
its Revolutionary War debt as quickly as possible by selling its
public domain to the highest bidders. Unable to afford the high
prices charged for land, but still wanting farms of their own,
many would-be farmers migrated to the District and indiscrimi-

nately settled wherever they pleased, without bothering to determine whether or not the land had already been sold. Some made extensive improvements, clearing and cultivating the land and building homes, barns, fences, and wells. So long as no one bothered them, everything was all right, but often absentee proprietors would ask outrageous prices for title to the land or try to eject the occupants in order to obtain for themselves the value of the improvements.

Much of the land in Maine was owned by speculators who had close ties with the Federalist party and who used their influence to have the legislature pass the measures necessary to press their demands against trespassers. The Republicans, on the other hand, sided with the squatters. In 1805, the Republican delegation to the legislature from Maine, led by William King, a moderate, moved for and obtained an investigation into the origins and terms of the original land grants. They had discovered that many of the largest proprietors had failed to fulfill the terms of their original contracts with the state, usually by not having settled a fixed number of families to ensure development of the area. By demanding that the state institute suits of forfeiture, King and his associates consolidated their influence among their constituents. They also "artfully persuaded" them, as David Cobb, the Federalist president of the Senate, pointed out, that, if they got the Federalists out of office, the Republicans would make much of the land revert back to the Commonwealth, "and then whatever land they occupied the government would give them as settlers." [59]

This resulted in a political revolution in Maine that had definite radical overtones. Even as early as the summer of 1804 one Federalist had written:

> Our adversaries are vigilant and active. They dare to threaten an insurrection in the county if opposed in executing their projects. Such discontents exist which arise from circumstances and causes of a partial and local nature that we are seriously apprehensive that threats will be executed. It has been their favorite object to obtain the controul of militia. This they have completely effected. One or two desperate and unprincipled characters have lately been elected to the command of

regiments and reports are now circulating that an armed force
will be collecting for the purpose of preventing the county
courts transacting business at their session of the ensuing
week.[60]

In 1805, Harrison Gray Otis, a temperate man not usually
given to hyperbole, wrote to Charles Willing Hare, an executor
of the estate of William Bingham, one of the largest absentee
landlords in Maine, that "designing men" were encouraging "a
spirit of insubordination and enmity to the legitimate rights of
property . . . which was of consequence more violent and dangerous among the semi savages who steal land from non residents
and hide from justice in the recesses of the wilderness." [61]

Following the Republican triumph of 1806, Hare traveled to
Boston to inspect the situation for himself. He quickly perceived
that his Federalist friends could no longer protect his interests
and decided to make a deal with William King and several other
Maine Republicans. In return for a small interest in the speculation, consisting of three townships along the Kennebec River,
King and his associates agreed to assume the settlement duties,
and they advanced the state $80,000 in bonds against nonperfor-
mance. They then pushed through the legislature, with Federalist support, a resolve extending the settlement deadline by six
years and freeing the Bingham interest from all of its obligations
to the state. Reporting back to the other trustees of the Bingham
estate, Hare wrote: "All danger of forfeiture is removed. . . . We
have created a common bond of interest with some of the popular
leaders in Massachusetts who have promised to support us against
all future injustice." [62]

In King and his associates the absentee landlords had important and influential allies in the Republican camp, but they
lacked the strength to prevent the squatters from continuing to
agitate for legislation protecting them from ejection. During 1806
and 1807, tension between the representatives of the proprietors
and the settlers continued to mount. According to one delegate
to the General Court:

> the squatters are about to "manage their affairs in their own
> way" . . . who know amid the revolutions that are impending
> what may await us.

[A representative] presented yesterday something like a petition to alter or revise the laws respecting *murder*, & some of the members moved that it be printed!! So I heard. . . . It is expected that the next thing will be the impeachment of Parsons, & perhaps all the rest of the Judges.[63]

When King's arrangement with the proprietors was disclosed, he immediately found himself in deep political trouble. As part of his campaign to regain his lost popularity with his constituents, King secured the passage of the Betterment Act. Passed over the objections of the proprietors, this law prevented the ejection of settlers who had been on the land for over six years without compensation for improvements, as assessed by a local jury; and it provided that, if the titleholder chose to sell, then he would receive from the settler payment for the value of the land, which would also be assessed by a local jury.[64]

During the year between the introduction of the Betterment Bill in June 1807 and its passage in 1808, the large landholding companies made an all-out attempt to pressure the settlers into buying their lands at high prices. When the squatters refused to be intimidated, sheriffs and their deputies were sent to remove them, but they met armed resistance. The main scene of the disturbances was in Kennebec county, where the land was claimed both by the Plymouth Company and the Pejapscot proprietors. The farmers of the area were especially angry because some of them, hoping to make their holdings legitimate, had bought their land from one company only to find that the title was disputed by the other, thus necessitating their buying their land a second time in order to make it secure. Many settlers, therefore, refused to pay for the land unless they could be guaranteed a clear title, but the proprietors nevertheless continued to threaten them with ejection when they refused to buy.[65]

The sheriff of Kennebec county was Arthur Lithgow, a former Federalist recently turned Republican. He and his deputies were utterly corrupt, and they were thoroughly disliked by the community.[66] Moreover, they had close ties with William King and the other landlords. One day, when they were trying to eject some squatters, they were set upon and routed by a large number of settlers dressed as Indians. Enraged, Lithgow attempted to call out the militia, but Sullivan, after consulting with his council, recognized that the settlers were being unduly harassed by unjust demands for their lands, and refused to give his consent. Further investigation brought additional disclosures and revealed Lithgow in such a bad light that the governor removed him and appointed the more popular but still moderate John Chandler as his successor.[67]

Meanwhile the Betterment Law had gone into effect, but the squatters, who at first were jubilant, soon became disillusioned when they discovered that the law contained unrealistic provisions and many loopholes. For example, if a settler sued to buy the land he was on, he was required to pay what the jury decreed to be its value within one year, something few settlers were in a position to do. In addition, the law failed to protect the settler from defective titles. Finally, the landlords, with the aid of their legal advisers, found numerous ways to get around the act: they brought separate suits for pasture and woodlands and for mowing and tillage, and they broke up the lots in such a way as to allow them to keep for themselves the improved areas and to sell the unimproved parts to the settlers.[68]

The situation became so tense in 1809 that a surveyor of one of the land companies was murdered. Seven men were brought to trial, and after hearing the case the judge ordered the jury to convict them. But they were acquitted, for, as one member of the jury argued, it did not make sense to hang seven men for killing one. Having failed to force the governor into calling out the militia, and finding the new sheriff unresponsive to their wishes, the proprietors turned for help to the Supreme Court, which ordered the militia to quiet disorders and to protect surveyors who were trying to untangle disputed titles.[69]

The proprietors, by appealing to the common law and by raising complicated procedural questions, managed to keep the issue of legal ownership of much of the best land in the District of Maine tied up in the courts for years. But in the end, because both landlords and farmers were willing to compromise over what had turned into an embarrassing and expensive problem, most squatters who managed to endure the long legal battles— and there were probably many who did not—secured legitimate titles at fair prices. Even so, this only occurred because the Commonwealth, under both Federalist and Republican administrations, proved willing to recompense landlords for disputed tracts or to give them equivalent amounts of unsettled land in other parts of the state. If the radical program of judicial reform had gone through in 1807 or 1808, this compromise would probably not have taken place, because the courts could not have been used to stave off "the confiscating avarice of Democracy." [70]

V

Even before the political stalemate over the judiciary occurred in 1808, the issue of legal reform had been superseded as the most important political issue before the public by widespread concern over America's position as a neutral power in the Napoleonic Wars. This led to a political reaction which allowed the Federalists to recapture the Massachusetts House and legislature in 1809. Although the Federalist resurgence did not prove to be permanent, the Republicans regaining control of the government in 1811, it did serve to weaken permanently the radical assault.

The struggle over judicial reform in Massachusetts had been resolved in the moderates' favor. Under the leadership of Chief Justice Parsons, who served until his death in 1813, the Supreme Court brought to fruition most of the changes started by Sedgwick: it streamlined procedure, shortened trials, cleared the dockets, raised the professional level of the bar, maintained decorum in the courtroom, and in general made the administration of justice more prompt and less expensive than it had been. After 1805 the Court's opinion were reported, and the basis was laid for the establishment of a meaningful common law, one which could be used to good effect by a growing commercial community.[71]

PART THREE

Toward a Redefinition
of Jeffersonian Democracy

XV

The Jeffersonians and the Judiciary

The Jeffersonian Republicans were not a monolithic party and they did not share a single all-encompassing attitude toward the judiciary. What took place was not simply a struggle over the judiciary system, but a number of different struggles involving different judiciary systems on the state and national level.

There were many ways in which the different struggles were not interrelated. No formal organizational links existed between the various groups of radicals and moderates.[1] The leaders of the radical movement in particular did not appear to have had any sense of a common cause. There is no evidence to indicate that either Randolph or his followers, with the exception of Leib, had any sympathy with what Grundy, Duane, Snyder or Austin were trying to do, while the support Randolph received from these leaders of radical judicial reform on the state level was restrained and cautious. The issues on the state level and those on the national level were not the same. In part this was a consequence of the way powers had been distributed under the federal system of government created by the United States Constitution: the jurisdictions, the amount of business done (dockets were overcrowded on the state level, while there was a decline of business before the federal courts during Jefferson's administrations), and the needs for reform of the different judiciary systems varied. But it was also because radicals were proportionately stronger on the state level than on the national level—in Pennsylvania and Massachusetts they came to dominate the Republican party and were defeated only when the moderates went into alliance with the Federalists, while they proved victorious in Kentucky where the Federalists were not very strong—and so they were able to raise more fundamental questions.

All this, however, should not obscure the way in which the various movements were tied together. Despite the lack of organizational links, radicals on both the state and national level and within the different states expressed a common concern over the relationship of the judiciary to the legislature and the tendency of judges who held their offices during good behavior to be indifferent to popular sentiment. Radicals throughout the country also shared a common hostility to entrenched moderate influence. For their part, moderates in the various contests over the judiciary generally used similar arguments, indicating a shared ideological position on the need for a strong, active, and independent judiciary. And almost all key appointments on the federal level during Jefferson's administrations went to people who were aligned with the moderates in the different local battles, while the radicals were generally proscribed. But even more fundamental was the belief, shared by all sides, that what really was involved was the extent to which the republican, and, in its most extreme form, democratic, heritage of the American Revolution was to be fulfilled. "I had always expected," wrote Jefferson, "that when the Republicans should have put down all things under their feet, they would schismatize among themselves. I have always expected, too, that whatever names the parties might bear, the real division would be into moderate and ardent republicanism." [2]

I

On the national level, where victory clearly went to the moderates, the fight between the radicals and the moderates began immediately following Jefferson's election. Writing in 1810, John Taylor recalled the radical position in these terms:

> There were a number of people who soon thought and said to one another that Mr. Jefferson did many good things, but neglected some better things; and who now view his policy as very like a compromise with Mr. Hamilton's. . . . Federalism, indeed, having been defeated, has gained a new footing by being taken into partnership with republicanism. It was this project which divided the Republican party by changing its principles from real to nominal.[3]

In the sense that the attack upon the national judiciary during Jefferson's first administration did not bring about any extreme changes, Taylor was certainly right. All that was accomplished was the repeal of the judiciary act of 1801 and the removal of a lunatic district judge. In every other way the national judiciary remained much as it had been under twelve years of Federalist rule: judges held their positions for life tenure during good behavior, the Federal courts were organized in much the same way as they had been under the Judiciary Act of 1789, and the Supreme Court remained staffed almost exclusively with Federalists. If anything, the national court system had been strengthened by its ability to withstand the radicals' attack and by Marshall's decision not to engage in partisan activities.

Chase's acquittal proved to be the turning point of the struggle between the moderates and the radicals on the national level. For following the verdict, the radicals became hopelessly divided among themselves over how to proceed. Randolph went into permanent open opposition and, because he was obliged, as Jefferson noted, "to give to it other grounds than those which we know are to be the true one," he launched a series of attacks upon the administration's handling of foreign policy when the Ninth Congress convened during the winter of 1805–06.[4] Randolph took with him into open opposition a small and dedicated group of followers. The great majority of the radicals, however, did not follow Randolph's lead and break with the party. Although they continued to be sympathetic to the reasons for Randolph's opposition they could not accept his leadership, finding him too overbearing and difficult a person to work with. Moreover, they were embarrassed by the violence of his attacks on the President, for whom most radicals—Duane and Austin included—still retained considerable personal loyalty. The great majority of the radicals continued to prefer to reform the party from within. Neither group—that which broke with the party and that which tried to work within it—was very successful during Jefferson's second administration.[5]

It was the moderates who benefited most from Chase's acquittal. The leader of this group was James Madison, who, during the 1780's, had been an outspoken and effective critic of the weak central government created by the Articles of Confederation, and who had played a role of the most fundamental importance in the writing and the adoption of the United States Constitution. During the 1790's, partly because of the demands of his Virginia constituency and more importantly because of his opposition to Hamilton's pro-English foreign policy, Madison was often found in alliance with extreme proponents of a states' rights philosophy of government. Yet, in essentials, he always remained a nationalist. This was obvious both before and after 1800, as he consistently and successfully used his enormous influence to temporize Jefferson's extremist tendencies.[6] In fact, Madison was sometimes singled out for praise by the Federalists and more frequently condemned by the Old Republicans and other radicals for the administrations' failure to engage in root and branch reform.[7]

Chase's acquittal served to strengthen even futher Madison's already strong influence in the Republican party. "The President wants nerve," confided John Adair, a Kentucky congressman with radical leanings, ". . . for more than a year he has been in the habit of trusting almost implicitly in Mr. Madison. Madison has acquired a complete ascendancy over him." [8] The principles of the administration, according to Randolph, had become those of the Federalists, "christened over again and swaddled in the garb of moderation." [9]

Under Madison's leadership the moderates quickly isolated Randolph and made him politically ineffective. William Branch Giles was allowed to slip quietly back into the administration's favor. He showed his gratitude by trying, unsuccessfully, to prevent Randolph's re-election to Congress in 1806. Joseph Hooper

Nicholson took a position on the Maryland bench. It was a long way from the appointment to the Supreme Court that he had once hoped for, but it was a generous concession to a needy man with a large family who had only recently supported the losing side in an intense intraparty struggle. It also deprived Randolph of an important ally. During this same period, Jefferson, concerned for Monroe's political future, sternly warned him not to become too closely allied with the Old Republicans. The President also took pains to conciliate Nathaniel Macon and other important Republicans throughout the country. "There is no longer a doubt," wrote Randolph, "but that the principles of our administartion have been materially changed. . . . Suffice it to say that everything is made a business of bargain and traffic, the ultimate object of which is to raise Mr. M[adiso]n to the presidency." [10] Those who continued to oppose the administration were treated harshly. Several of Randolph's closest followers were defeated for re-election; others barely succeeded. Macon did not openly break with the party, but he remained attached to Randolph, and because of this he soon lost his position as Speaker of the House. Only Randolph's control of his own congressional district saved him from obscurity.[11]

The ability of the moderates to consolidate their control of the Republican Party on the national level assured the future of an independent national judiciary. It meant that for the first time since 1800 the justices of the Supreme Court were secure on the bench; and they remained secure throughout Jefferson's and Madison's administrations. There were further attempts to circumscribe the powers and independence of the federal judges, but they were easily disposed of through an alliance of moderate Republicans and Federalists.[12]

II

It has been argued that the Jeffersonians, having failed to destroy the Supreme Court by a frontal attack, next tried to transform it through the slow process of replacement, only to be thwarted once again as Marshall converted to his point of view all the Republican appointees. This interpretation is of dubious value.

For while there can be no doubt that Marshall, by the clarity of his thought and his general intellectual toughness, influenced his fellow judges, it is equally clear that he did not have to do very much converting. Actually all of the judges whom Jefferson and Madison appointed to the Supreme Court came from the moderate wing of the party and had already proven themselves to be able lawyers and friends of a strong, active, and independent judiciary.

Jefferson's first opportunity to make an appointment to the Supreme Court came at the height of the judiciary struggle, in February 1804, when the aged and dying Alfred Moore, who had been riding circuit in Georgia and South Carolina, resigned. "The importance of filling this vacancy with a Republican and a man of sufficient talents to be useful is obvious," wrote Albert Gallatin. Pointing out that "practice is as loose in Georgia as in New England and that a real lawyer could not be found there," the Secretary of the Treasury, who was a firm moderate on the judiciary issue, recommended that a choice be made from South Carolina, which "stands high in that respect at least in reputation." [13] The administration apparently had no specific person in mind, for it made a thorough canvass of available talent. The man finally agreed upon was William Johnson, "an excellent lawyer, prompt, eloquent, of irreproachable character," and a man who was acceptable to moderate Federalists.[14]

Johnson was thirty-two years old when he was appointed to the Supreme Court. Born in Charleston and named after his father, a minor leader in South Carolina during the Revolution, he was a graduate of Princeton, where he had studied under John Witherspoon; he had also read law in the office of C. C. Pinckney, a South Carolina Federalist who was his party's perennial candidate for President after 1800. Admitted to the bar in 1793, Johnson quickly gained a reputation for being one of the best lawyers in the state. Politically he was a moderate Republican, never espousing anything resembling a radical kind of Jeffersonianism. He shunned completely any attachment with the Charleston Republican Society and sided with Federalists on local issues involving equal representation for the back country, tax reform, and bank charters. In 1794 he was elected to the state legislature, where he joined in a movement to reform the judiciary along moderate lines by raising judges' salaries, revising the state's antiquated system of county courts, and establishing a system of circuit courts. In 1799 he was elected by the legislature to the Appellate Court of Common Pleas, or Constitutional Court, where he served until his appointment to the Supreme Court and where by his decisions he proved himself to be a friend of strong and active government on both the state and national level.[15]

Jefferson made his second appointment to the Supreme Court in September 1806, when William Paterson died. The President's choice this time was Henry Brockholst Livingston, who had been strongly recommended for the position by Albert Gallatin.[16] Born in 1757 to one of the most prominent landholding families in New York and New Jersey, he was the son of William Livingston, a former governor of New Jersey; a cousin of Robert R. Livingston, head of the family interest in New York; and a brother-in-law of John Jay. He attended Princeton, where he was a fellow student of James Madison, until the Revolution broke out. He served in the Continental army, entering with the rank of captain and leaving as colonel. Following his military service he studied law under Peter Yates of Albany, was admitted to practice in 1783, and quickly became one of the most prominent members of the New York bar.[17]

During the 1780's and 1790's Livington promoted state banking interests and speculated in confiscated lands and state and national securities. He favored the adoption of the Federal Constitution in 1788, but, like the rest of his family, denounced the Jay Treaty and became a Jeffersonian during the 1790's. For a while he appears to have flirted with the radical wing of the party, but he always defended their positions in a legalistic and not a revolutionary way. In 1802 he was appointed a judge of the Supreme Court of New York, where he became an admiring colleague of James Kent. He supported the victorious moderate Republicans in the New York gubernatorial contest of 1806, and when he was appointed to the United States Supreme Court a short time later, William Plumer noted that he "supports the reputation of an able lawyer and good judge. I believe his app't. will be generally approved." [18]

Jefferson's third opportunity to make an appointment to the

Supreme Court came in February 1807, when Congress passed an act increasing the number of justices from six to seven. The purpose of the law was to extend the Federal circuit court system to the western states of Kentucky, Tennessee, and Ohio, where an increasing population had overburdened the dockets of the district courts. Because most of the cases pending were involved in one way or another with the area's peculiarly complicated system of land laws, the act specifically required that the justice appointed be a resident of the newly created seventh circuit.[19]

Jefferson requested that each member of Congress from the interested states privately communicate to him their first and second choices for the position. George Washington Campbell, an undistinguished lawyer and congressman from Tennessee who had been a member of the House committee that tried Chase, was the group's first choice. But the administration was unenthusiastic about him, and he was declared ineligible for the position on the grounds that his appointment would violate Article I, section 6, of the Constitution, which prohibited the selection of any man for an office who had been a member of Congress when that office was created. The nomination went instead to Thomas Todd of Kentucky, who had been the second choice of the congressmen polled.[20]

Born in Virginia in 1763, Todd served in the army during the latter part of the Revolution, after which he migrated to Kentucky. He quickly became a partisan of the separation movement and served as secretary to the numerous conventions leading up to the state's independence. During this same period he studied law under his brother-in-law, Harry Innes, and clerked for him in the federal district court. Eventually he became first clerk, and then, in 1801, judge, on the Kentucky Court of Appeals, a position he held until his appointment to the Supreme Court. He had close ties to the George Nicholas—John Breckinridge wing of the party in both economics and politics, being involved in land speculation with them and being a moderate on both constitutional and judicial reform. Henry Clay, who succeeded Breckinridge as leader of the Kentucky moderates, was especially pleased when his good friend Todd was appointed to the high court.[21]

Not one of the judges that Jefferson appointed to the Supreme Court did anything to weaken the independence or influence of the national judiciary or to espouse a radical brand of Jeffersonianism. Livingston, whom Joseph Story described in 1803 as a "very able and independent judge," sat on the bench for seventeen years.[22] He was an expert on maritime and commercial law, but he wrote only a few opinions in these areas and in most cases simply concurred in the majority opinion handed down by Marshall. Todd served for twenty years and was an expert on land titles and other problems related to real property, but he also wrote few opinions and for the most part agreed with Marshall's handling of controversial questions. When Todd died in 1826, Story noted "that though bred in a different political school from that of the Chief Justice, he never failed to sustain those great principles of constitutional law on which the security of the Union depends. He never gave up to party what he thought belonged to the country."[23] Johnson, on the other hand, served on the court for nearly thirty years and had serious differences of opinion with the Chief Justice. But they were not over such fundamental questions as the need for a strong national government, an independent judiciary, the sanctity of contracts, or the protection of property rights; rather, they were on the less important issues of *seriatim* opinions and the relative powers of the Federal legislature and Federal judiciary.[24]

Madison had two opportunities to make appointments to the Supreme Court. The first came in September 1810, when Thomas Cushing died, an event which Jefferson in one of his more malicious moments described as a "circumstance of congratulation" because it meant that the high court was now evenly divided between three Federalists (Marshall, Chase, and Bushrod Washington) and the three recently appointed Republicans. Since Cushing had been the only member of the court from New England, it was generally understood that his successor would also come from that part of the country. What followed is not altogether clear from the available evidence. Madison first offered the position to Levi Lincoln, whom he knew would not accept it; then to Alexander Wolcott, an important Republican politician from Connecticut, who accepted the position but who had such poor qualifications that Madison must have known he would be rejected by the Senate; then John Quincy Adams, minister to Russia who also declined it; until, finally, it was accepted by Joseph Story. All this may have been necessary to get Story accepted, because the nomination went to him over the objections of many Massachusetts Republicans and of Jefferson, who considered him a "pseudo-Republican" for having deserted the party on the embargo. Story's role in the struggle over judicial reform in Massachusetts had also, of course, made it abundantly clear that he was a firm friend of a strong and independent judiciary.[25]

Even before Madison nominated Story a second vacancy occurred, for Samuel Chase died on June 17, 1811. Caesar Rodney of Delaware and Robert Smith of Maryland were spoken of as candidates, but the position went to Gabriel Duvall, a relatively obscure fifty-one-year-old resident of Maryland who was a former congressman, Comptroller of the Treasury since 1802, and reputedly "a competent lawyer." [26] Little is known about Duvall's political background except that he had helped successfully to organize his home state for the Republicans during the election of 1800 and often advised Jefferson and Madison on appointments there. Politically he appears to have been closely allied to Samuel Smith, the leader of the moderate wing of the party in Maryland.[27]

Story and Duvall took their seats when the Court met for the February session in 1812. Story worked very closely with the Chief Justice and went on to become one of the most important members of the Supreme Court, while Duvall appears to have been the least consequential member of the Marshall Court. No further changes were made in the Court's personnel until 1823. It was this court, made up of five moderate Republicans and two Federalists, that established American commercial and and constitutional jurisprudence along nationalist lines.[28]

III

On the state level, with the exception of Kentucky, victory also went to the moderates, and the results were as far-reaching as they had been on the national level. Moreover, the struggle between radicals and moderates over judicial reform on the local level was not limited simply to Kentucky, Pennsylvania, and Massachusetts, but took place, with variations caused by local conditions and with varying degrees of intensity, in a number of other states.

In Maryland, with the aid of the Federalists, the moderate Republicans won a stunning victory. The state's constitution of 1776, one of the most conservative in the country, had carried over, almost intact, the judiciary system of the colonial period. Under this system, most cases were tried either in county courts, which had jurisdiction over misdemeanors and civil cases involving small sums, or in the General Court, meeting at Annapolis on the western shore and Easton on the eastern shore, which heard appeals from the decisions of the county courts and had original jurisdiction in civil cases involving large sums of money or land titles, and in major criminal cases. During the last decade of the eighteenth century it had become clear that these courts were inadequate to meet the needs of a state with a rapidly expanding commercial community and a growing population. The fact that the General Court met only in two places required long trips from suitors, witnesses, and jurors, making justice expensive and inconvenient. It worked special hardships upon the rising business community of Baltimore, which supplied many of the leading advocates for judicial reform along moderate lines. Moreover, the low salaries granted to county judges made it very difficult to get able men to accept positions on the bench, thereby fracturing uniformity in the justice administered from county to county.[29]

In 1796 the Federalist-controlled legislature passed a judiciary act dividing the state into five districts with a chief justice for each district and two associate justices in each county. Under this act each chief justice was required to ride circuit and meet with the associate justices in each county several times a year to hear appeals from the county courts. The act served to bring a semblance of uniformity to county court decisions, but it was sharply criticized by Republicans for leaving too much power in the hands of the General Court and for increasing the number of judgeships to which only Federalists were appointed. When the Republicans came to power in 1801, they immediately repealed the judiciary act of 1796, an action which their opponents denounced as inimical "to the prosperity of Maryland, and to the purity of justice." A number of intractable Federalists attempted to have the repealing act of 1801 declared unconstitutional by the General Court on the ground that it deprived those judges who held their positions, during good behavior of their offices. But the General Court, desirous of avoiding a direct confrontation with the Republican controlled legislature, declared the law constitutional.[30]

In 1802 the Republicans passed a judiciary act of their own. It abolished the General Court and vested all original jurisdiction in the county courts, whose decisions were subject to review by a Court of Appeals. Before it could become law, however, the act had to be passed by two successive meetings of the legislature. When the bill came up for the second time in 1803 it was defeated by a coalition of moderate Republicans and Federalists, who complained that the act was so loosely written that it would endanger the independence of the judiciary and would allow the courts to come under the control of people untrained in the law. It was in opposition to the passage of this act that Chase delivered his famous charge to the Grand Jury of Baltimore for which he was impeached.[31]

Having thwarted the passage of a judiciary act which would have been amenable to radical innovations, moderate Republicans and Federalists proceeded to pass one of their own in 1804 and again in 1805 that was more in line with their concept of judicial reform. The act provided that all original jurisdiction be vested in the county courts, which were to be divided into six judicial districts, and that each county be presided over by two associate judges and each district by a chief judge, all of whom were required to have training in the law. It also provided for a Court of Appeals, made up of the chief judges of the six districts, which could revise the decisions of the county courts. The act allowed the administration of justice to be decentralized and made more efficient in such a way as to ensure uniformity and to keep the courts under the control of the legal profession.[32]

By the end of 1805, partly as a consequence of the fight over judicial reform and partly as a consequence of concurrent struggles over various kinds of electoral reform, there existed an open alliance between moderate Republicans and the more tractable and temperate members of the Federalist party. And despite the vituperation of the radicals, who denounced the moderates as "fawning, double-faced, designing dupes," the alliance fructified almost immediately. First, in December 1803, a Republican governor, with the consent of a Republican legislature, appointed as the state's Attorney General William Pinkney, a moderate Federalist who was considered by many to be the greatest trial lawyer in America during the first two decades of the nineteenth century. Then they appointed William Kilty, a moderate Republican, who was to compile and publish *The Laws of Maryland* (1798–1800), as Chancellor of the state in 1806. Finally, they provided for the reporting of the decisions of the Court of Appeals, thus allowing for the meaningful development of Maryland's common law.[33]

In North Carolina the moderate Republicans placed the blame for their state's legal difficulties upon the Court Act of 1777. Under this law justices of the peace, men who rarely had any kind of legal training, were authorized to hold magistrate's courts to try minor infractions of the law and to settle petty disputes. Appeals from the magistrate's court were heard by the county courts, which consisted of at least three justices of the peace who met at times fixed by the leglislature. This court had original jurisdiction in most civil cases, in criminal cases where conviction did not involve death or dismemberment, and broad administrative duties. Above the county courts was the Superior Court, consisting of three judges, elected by joint ballot of both Houses of the legislature who held office for life tenure during good behavior. In 1805 this court met twice a year in eight district towns: Wilmington, New Bern, Edenton, Halifax, Hillsboro, Salisbury, Morganton, and Fayetteville. It heard appeals from the county courts and had original jurisdiction in high value civil suits and in criminal cases of the most serious sort.[34]

Moderates opposed the established court system for two reasons. First, they objected to the county courts where justices of the peace, described as "insensible to cogent argument," "not in the habit of consulting legal accuracy," and indifferent to "precedent," "legal reasoning," or "what the law was," handed down unpredictable decisions.[35] Second, they were sharply critical of the fact that the Superior Courts only met in certain district towns, which, they believed, made going to court so expensive and inconvenient for most suitors, witnesses, and jurors as to make it "a system which is calculated to benefit the few to the injury and oppression of the many." [36]

What was needed, the moderates believed, was a complete change in the state's judiciary, a change which would meet the needs of an "improving people, whose minds are expanding, whose wants are increasing, and whose relative situations are daily changing." [37] To this end William Porter in 1805 introduced a bill in the Assembly to bring justice closer to the people by establishing in each of the state's sixty counties a Superior Court which would meet twice a year. To make this practicable, the law proposed to increase the number of Superior Court judges to six and to divide the state into six circuits of ten courts each. The measure passed the House, but the Senate voted to postpone consideration until the next session, thereby allowing the bill to be debated publicly.[38]

Opposition to the measure came from the Federalists, who, the moderates claimed, represented both established lawyers, who practiced in the district towns and feared that if the bill passed it would mean a reduction of business and consequently of fees, and the district towns themselves, which greatly benefited from the business brought in during the court sessions. There was considerable merit to this charge; but the evidence also indicates that the most responsible members of the legal profession in North Carolina, most of whom were Federalists, sincerely believed that the new system would increase the opportunities for "pettifoggers," "second rate lawyers," and "men, but of little reputation" to prey upon the people, and had grave doubts as to whether it would be possible to find able and learned judges to accept the rigorous duties involved in riding circuit under the new system.[39]

Radical Republicans also opposed the Porter Bill, though for reasons very different from those of the Federalists. The radicals viewed the measure as the beginning of an insidious attack upon the county court system and believed that if Superior Courts were established in every county the exclusive original jurisdiction of the county courts would soon be abolished. "Who will be gratified at this change?" asked one radical. "Not the great body of the community. . . . Who then? All those who draw fees or perquisites of office that are concerned in carrying on suits, for none of them labour for nothing." [40]

Radical spokesmen defended the "common sense" decisions handed down by justices of the peace in the county courts, and they took issue with the moderate argument that the proposed changes in the court system would make the administration of justice cheaper. The radicals granted that the new system would make it easier and less expensive for litigous-minded citizens to take their cases to the Superior Courts, but argued that the new system, by increasing the number of courts and court officers, would cost the public considerably more to maintain than the old system.[41] The radical case against the moderate proposal for judicial reform was put most clearly by "Country Squire," who wrote in a Federalist newspaper but who was clearly trying to attract radical support:

> Much has been said about the great expences at which witnesses are brought to Superior Courts. . . . However great this hardship may be one cannot be led to believe that to obviate the evil, the community should be saddled with a heavy tax entirely unnecessary, only for the advancement of a single benefit, which for the most part only serves the interests of litigous men. Of what consequence is it to my honest neighbor, whose "understanding extends no farther than a tolerable knowledge of plowing," and who never goes to law himself, whether those contentious men—whose names stand on the Superior Court docket are compelled to pay for witnesses fifty dollars, or whether they get clear by the payment of ten dollars only. These controversies respecting a horse race, which the farm yard notary has neither the time nor the inclination to visit, do not touch on his interest, but when an onerous tax is levied on his property to bring "law to every man's door" he would then only think of the change to curse it.[42]

If they had been able to unite, the combined forces of the radical Republicans and the Federalists might have prevented the Porter Bill from passing, but the differences between the two groups could not be overcome. The Federalists shared the dislike of the moderates for the simple kind of justice being administered by justices of the peace, while the radicals tended to be moral absolutists who were so committed to party regularity that they could not bring themselves to co-operate with an opposition party they considered to be evil. The moderates, of course, played upon this aspect of the radicals' feelings by stressing the importance of party unity and the great dangers involved in co-operating with the enemy. This tactic proved to be so effective that when the legislature convened in the late fall of 1806, the moderate Republicans were confident of victory.[43]

Realizing that some kind of judicial reform was inevitable, and, indeed, favoring it, the Federalists offered a compromise bill whereby the number of Superior Court districts would be increased to twenty. But the moderates, knowing that they had brought enough radicals into line, refused to compromise; and, anxious for the patronage benefits to be derived from the staffing of sixty new courts, they rejected the measure and proceeded to pass the Porter Bill in December 1806.[44]

That was not the end of judicial reform in North Carolina, however, for the following year, just as the radicals had feared, the moderates turned their attention to circumscribing the powers of the county courts. They proposed a bill giving the newly established Superior Courts concurrent jurisdiction with the county courts in all civil and criminal cases, which they expected would eventually render the county courts superfluous. The radicals fought the measure fiercely, warning of the dangers involved in a "proliferation of the courts," of being overwhelmed "by an army of judges," and of the threat to liberty of "an expensive and burthensome judiciary." But it was to no avail, as this time the Federalists sided with the moderates and helped pass the measure in 1808. The moderates had finally curtailed the prerogatives and powers of the county courts and justices of the peace and created a court system capable of administering justice uniformly.[45]

Judicial reform was an issue in still other states. Bitter battles were fought between radical and moderate Republicans, with the Federalists often holding the balance of power, in Ohio, New Jersey, and New Hampshire.[46] In South Carolina and New York it is possible to find examples of radical rhetoric, but in both states the moderates easily had their own way. Yet even here there was co-operation with the Federalists. For just as Theophilus Parsons of Massachusetts and William Tilghman of Pennsylvania, both of whom had been Federalists, had been appointed to important judicial posts by Republican governors and legislatures, so too was Henry William DeSaussure made Chancellor of South Carolina in 1808, and James Kent, in New York, appointed Chief Justice of the Supreme Court in 1804 and Chancellor in 1814 by the moderate Republicans.[47]

Coming as it did during the formative era of American law, the moderate triumph on the state level in the struggle over judicial reform had far-reaching consequences. It meant, just as it had on the national level, the establishment in many states of judiciaries which were both bipartisan and nonpartisan. It also meant a continuing awareness on the part of the legal profession of the need to regulate and improve itself, or, failing to do this, of suffering the consequences involved in having the public do it for them. Finally, it meant the creation of conditions which allowed for the eventual establishment of an efficient, dependable, and uniform system of justice which could adapt to the rapidly changing requirements of American life during the nineteenth century. The radicals, to be sure, continued to demand a more democratic kind of judicial reform, and, during the Jacksonian era, they scored a number of triumphs in the more recently established states. But in the older states, where the moderates had been victorious during the Jeffersonian era, the radicals were not able to attract the same kind of popular support they had had before 1806, for the simple reason that most of the public grievances against the courts and the legal profession had been remedied.

XVI
Law and Society in Jeffersonian America

An important question remains: why were some Republicans radicals and others moderates on judicial reform? In an attempt to answer this question, consideration must be given, first, to some of the basic political, religious, and socio-economic forces at work in America during the early national period; then, to showing how these forces affected people's attitudes toward the role of law and toward the Good Society; and, finally, to superimposing on these basic patterns of allegiance another division on the leadership level which was less fundamental but not less important.

I

One fundamental difference was between those Americans who wished to see the democratic tendencies of the Revolution fulfilled and those who wished to see them resisted. Here it is important to define carefully what is meant by eighteenth-century democracy, for it is something very different from democracy as we understand it in the twentieth century. Today when we use the word democracy it brings to mind many associated concepts: majority rule, minority rights, freedom of religion, desegregation, monopoly regulation, women's rights, old age security, equal opportunity for employment, open housing. In short, today the word democracy has not only a political meaning, but also a social and economic one. But twentieth-century democracy is not an idea that appeared fully developed; rather, it is a concept which has been growing since the seventeenth century. During the late eighteenth and early nineteenth centuries the issue of democracy was strictly a political one, limited simply to majority rule by white protestant males.[1]

Twentieth-century democrats also differ from those of the eighteenth century in their view of the nature of man. The former are generally optimistic and emphasize man's perfectability; whatever evils do exist, they believe, can, given enough time, be mitigated through widespread education. Twentieth-century democrats generally do not mind giving the government extensive powers if it is used to further what they believe are democratic ends. Eighteenth-century democrats were more pessimistic about man's nature; they stressed in particular that man tended to be corrupted by power. The central problem for the eighteenth-century democrats, therefore, was how to protect the rights of the governed from subversion by their rulers; and they believed the only way this could be done was to make the government as weak, as simple, and as immediately and directly responsible to the people as possible. It was for this reason that eighteenth- century democrats favored such devices as broad suffrage, annual elections, rotation of office, legislative supremacy, and the diffusion of political power through decentralization in order to prevent its consolidation in a few hands.[2]

A twentieth-century democrat would find many of the things an eighteenth-century democrat stood for repugnant. Today's democrat is also a liberal; he is willing to accept, and even encourages, a reasonable amount of diversity and pluralism. The eighteenth-century democrat was often actively anti-liberal, too concerned about the threat of minority rule to be worried about the dangers of an elective despotism to minority rights. Moreover an eighteenth-century democrat usually had more than his share of prejudices: he generally had no love for Negroes, or Catholics; his main interest in Indians was to kill them; and he was suspicious of men of learning.[3]

There were many people in eighteenth-century America who,

while favoring a republican form of government, opposed the movement toward democracy.[4] Where these elite-minded Americans differed from their democratic-minded counterparts was in the extent to which they believed government should be directly and immediately responsive to the wishes of the people. The elite-minded retained the pre-Revolutionary notion that the purpose of government in large part was to protect the people from themselves, and that the government therefore should not be directly susceptible to the wishes, whims, and caprices of the governed. They believed government should be strong and active, argued that the men who owned the country should rule the country, wanted representation in the legislature to be by interests as well as population, had a special bias toward an independent judiciary and a strong executive, and favored high property qualifications for voting and office holding, and a strong central government.[5]

The struggle between the democratic-minded and the elite-minded had begun even before America declared independence, but it manifested itself most clearly in the drafting of the first state constitutions and in the battles over the establishment of a central government. Many of the ideas of the democratic-minded were put into practice in the Pennsylvania, Georgia, and Vermont Constitutions, and to a certain extent in the Articles of Confederation. The Massachusetts Constitution of 1780 and, to a somewhat lesser extent, the United States Constitution of 1788 are good examples of the institutional implementation of the views of the elite-minded.[6] To support their position the elite-minded took their inspiration and many of their ideas from the political writings of John Adams and James Madison; whereas, if Kentucky, Pennsylvania and Massachusetts are any indication, the democratic-minded most often appealed to the writings of Tom Paine.[7] What is not generally recognized by historians, however, is that the conflict between these two points of view did not end with the so-called "Constitutional Settlement" of 1788 but continued into the 1790's and the first decade of the nineteenth century, finding expression in numerous attempts, sometimes successful, to rewrite the constitution of older states; in the conventions which framed the constitutions for the newer states of Kentucky, Tennessee and Ohio; and especially in the struggle over judicial reform in many of the states after 1800.[8]

To a large extent, therefore, it is possible to interpret the division between radicals and moderates over judicial and legal reform as part of a wider struggle taking place between Americans over how democratic their political institutions should be. For, all things being equal, those who were democratically inclined supported the radical position on judicial reform, which advocated an elective judiciary and a system of laws and the machinery for their enforcement which was directly and immediately responsible to the people and closely controlled by local interests. Conversely, those who were opposed to giving the people too much power supported the moderate position on judicial reform, which provided for judges to be appointed and to hold office for life tenure during good behavior and a legal system which was not subject to the immediate control of the public.

II

Pervasive as was the struggle over whether to fulfill or resist the democratic tendencies of the revolution, it, in itself, is not enough to explain fully the intense moral antipathy which radicals had for the legal profession. To understand this aspect of the fight over judicial reform, one has to turn to the religious dimension of the American Revolution, to the struggle between the advocates of a rational or liberal kind of Protestantism on the one hand and the advocates of an emotional or evangelical kind of Protestantism on the other.[9]

This division can be traced to the religious revivals known as the Great Awakening. Arrayed on one side in this struggle were the educated clergy of the formally organized and established churches: Old Light Congregationalists, Old Side Presbyterians, and Anglicans. These clergymen, the proponents of a rationalistic Christianity, stressed the importance of learning and intellect in the religious experience, and were opposed to all unnecessary displays of emotion at religious services. By the end of the eighteenth century, most of the supporters of this kind of Christianity came from urban areas and other commercial centers along the seaboard, where there was a heavy concentration of prosperous merchants, rich planters, well-to-do lawyers, and other members of society who were more concerned about the problems of living in this world than they were about the importance of God and salvation in the world to come.

On the other side were those who believed that emotion should play a vital and dominant role in the religious experience. They argued that spiritual authority lay not in the church but in the individual's heart and conscience. Led by revivalist preachers, some of whom were educated and ordained but many of whom were not, they criticized the ministers of the established churches for preaching erroneous doctrines and for not truly knowing Christ. They called for the country to undergo a spiritual reformation, and sometimes their fervent exhortations and dramatic flourishes brought forth extreme responses which included raving, ranting, shouting, weeping, howling, fainting, and "the jerks." This kind of religion was especially popular among the less well-to-do in rural and frontier areas. Beginning in the 1720's when large numbers of people began to undergo conversion experiences, the forces of revivalism and enthusiasm won several impressive victories, and the Protestant denominations which accommodated them—Baptists, Methodists, New Light Congregationalists, and New Side Presbyterians—grew rapidly in size and importance.

During the 1730's and 1740's the evangelical attack upon the established churches was a religious issue, but it began to take on a political dimension during the Revolutionary era. Viewing independence as a divinely ordained opportunity to purify and transform a corrupt society, and espousing an ideology with increasingly radical and democratic overtones, dissenting ministers played an important role in the politics of the post-Revolutionary era. In particular they led the fight to separate church and state and to make government more directly responsible to the people. By 1800 the dissenting clergy had become a vital and important part of the Republican coalition; and since Jefferson's victory coincided with the "Second Great Awakening" of 1800–1801, it was only natural for the evangelical clergy to hail it as God's way of giving them another chance to implement what they believed were the true principles of 1776.[10]

Anti-legalism was an especially important dimension of revivalist thought. Jonathan Edwards, one of the most important and least emotional leaders of the Great Awakening, often denigrated the rationalist approach to religion as a "legal scheme." [11] Most evangelical ministers had little use for lawyers, whom they considered to be an avaricious and depraved lot. George Whitefield, for example, writing in his journal at the height of the first Awakening in 1740, noted: "As for the *Business* of an *Attorney*, I think it *unlawful* for a christian, at least *exceeding dangerous: Avoid it* therefore, and glorify God in some *other station.*" [12] Sixty-five years later, in a sermon demanding an elective judiciary, John Leland, in similar terms, decried "the host of lawyers who infest our land . . . like the swarms of locusts in Egypt, and eat up every green thing." [13]

It was the legal system itself which evangelical preachers held most suspect. The law, they believed, was too rational, too complex, and too much under the control of designing intellectuals. From the beginning of the Great Awakening down through the political battles over judicial reform during the first decade of the nineteenth century, the revivalist ministers were among the leading proponents for appointing lay judges, for establishing courts of arbitration and other extrajudicial bodies which prohibited lawyers from practicing before them, and for generally simplifying legal procedure and the complicated science of jurisprudence.

Revivalist preachers, by providing a dynamic and vocal, if unlearned, leadership, played an important role in the radical attack upon the judiciary. For example, among the leaders of the radical delegation to the Kentucky Constitutional Convention of 1792 were David Rice, a New Side Presbyterian minister; James Garrard, George S. Smith, and John Bailey, Baptist clergymen; Benedict Swope, a German reformed minister; and Charles Kavanaugh, a Methodist preacher.[14] The areas of rural Pennsylvania where most of the political strength of the advocates of a radical kind of judicial reform lay had been criss-crossed numerous times by dissenting clergymen from the Presbyterian, Methodist, Baptist, and German churches.[15] In Massachusetts, the radicals were strongest in Berkshire County, where the Baptist preacher John Leland and the New Light Calvinist minister Thomas Allen were political powers. The radicals were also strong in the District of Maine, which had large Baptist and Methodist populations. In fact, one Federalist newspaper reported that the District had been converted to Jeffersonian principles largely because "a certain itinerant preacher is going about the country, and instead of preaching the gospel, is instilling poison and party spirit into the minds of such of the people as are without the means of information." [16]

III

Taken in conjunction with the struggle over the democratic tendencies of the Revolution, the division between the proponents of an evangelical and a rational Christianity helps to explain the radical postion on judicial reform. But it is not adequate to explain fully what motivated the moderates on this issue. To do this one has to turn to still another division in American society during the late eighteenth and early nineteenth centuries: that between the agrarian-minded and commercial-minded parts of the population.[17]

Commercial-minded people were found in cities, in farming areas along the coast, and in river valleys where cheap transportation facilities allowed them to raise profitable crops for market. These commercial-minded Americans—lawyers, market-oriented farmers, planters, merchants, bankers, and artisans—were all part of the market economy. Many were educated and cosmopolitan, but above all else they were businessmen. Indeed, some of them had, for the eighteenth-century, a sophisticated understanding of how economic growth took place, the role of banks and credit, and the importance of a system of jurisprudence in affording opportunity and security to a business community.

Agrarian-minded people were found in rural areas, far from cities and inexpensive transportation. The overwhelming majority of these people were small farmers, who at best had only a minimum of contact with the commercial nexus. Most of them were uneducated and lived in simple, isolated, and tradition-oriented communities. They invariably were ignorant of the complexities involved in economic development. They also tended to be provincial and superstitious, distrusting change, cities, impersonal economic organizations such as banks and corporations, and people who were cosmopolitan and educated.

Agrarian-minded people were the most important source of support for the radical attack upon the state judiciaries. In large part this was because the radical program of judicial reform spoke to the immediate needs and interests of people who were outside the market economy; for self-sufficing agricultural societies were simple, static, and primitive, and the people who lived in them did not perceive any use for, or for that matter were they able or willing to pay the high taxes necessary to support, a learned judiciary and an elaborate system of jurisprudence. What these people wanted was a cheap, simple, and easily accessible legal system for settling disputes; a system under the control of men who were locally known and trusted and who could easily be held accountable for their decisions.[18]

In like manner, commercial-minded people were the main source of support for the moderate program of judicial reform. Again, the main reason for this was that it spoke to the real needs and interests of the rapidly expanding business community to be found in America during the early national period. For what people engaged in commercial disputes needed and wanted was a highly rationalized legal system which would protect property by minimizing the innumerable risks involved in investing capital in a newly developing nation; a system which would ensure order and stability and guarantee to debtors and creditors that their rights and obligations would be constant in different parts of the same state despite local prejudice; and a system which would be flexible enough to allow for the development, as experience dictated, of the legal devices necessary for sustained economic growth.[19]

In Kentucky the radical stronghold was south of the Green River, an area populated by recent arrivals who for the most part were outside the market economy. Recalling what this part of the state was like during the 1790's, Peter Cartwright, an itinerant revivalist minister, described it in these terms:

> There was not a newspaper printed South of Green River,
> no mill short of forty miles, and no schools worth the name.

We killed our meat out of the woods, wild; and beat our meal, baked our bread. . . . We raised, or gathered out of the woods, our own tea. We had sage, bohea, cross vine, spice and sassafras tea, in abundance. As for coffee, I am not sure that I ever smelled it for ten years. We made our sugar out of the water of the maple tree, and our molasses too. These were great luxuries in those days.

We raised our own cotton and flax . . . our Mothers and sisters carded, spun, and wove it into cloth, and they cut and made our garments and bed clothes, etc.

Let it be remembered, these were days when we had no stores of dry good or groceries.[20]

The moderates, on the other hand, were to be found mainly among commercial farmers and planters in the bluegrass area and in Lexington, the state's rapidly developing urban center, and their leaders were primarily planters and lawyers who had emigrated from Virginia in search of greater economic opportunity.[21]

In Pennsylvania the moderates' strength came mainly from the state's major urban areas: Philadelphia, Lancaster, Harrisburg, and Pittsburgh; and from the older more established commercial farming communities in Berks, Chester, Northampton, Delaware, York, Montgomery, and Lancaster counties. The radicals drew most of their support from the less commercialized but heavily populated agrarian counties of Northumberland, Dauphin, and Mifflin; from the recently settled far northwestern part of the state, where many of the inhabitants were squatters; and from populous Philadelphia county, which the Leib-Duane machine controlled.[22]

Massachusetts was proportionately more commercialized than either Kentucky or Pennsylvania, and it is not surprising that it was here that the advocates of a radical kind of judicial reform were weakest. Support for moderate proposals of judicial reform came from the Federalist party, which drew its main strength from the populous coastal counties of Essex and Suffolk and from towns along the navigable Connecticut River in Hampshire county.[23] Republicans who supported the moderate position on judicial reform came primarily from Boston, Salem, and the business community in Maine. The radicals, on the other hand, drew their strongest support from the small farmers of Berkshire County, who were too far removed to enjoy the commercial benefits of the Connecticut River, and from the squatters of Maine.[24]

IV

The crucial question, of course, is: to what extent did the divisions between the democratic-minded and elite-minded, between the proponents of an evangelical and rational kind of religion, and between the agrarian and commercial segments of the community coincide with each other? The answer would seem to be that they did coincide, although somewhat imperfectly, and that while it is impossible to fit everyone in the age of Jefferson into two neat and fixed categories, those who did not fit tended to be exceptions, some of them important exceptions, but nonetheless explainable.

For example, Tom Paine, perhaps the most influential of all the eighteenth-century democrats, also advocated commercial development; while John Taylor, a leading advocate of the anti-commercial agrarian mystique, had little sympathy for democracy.[25] It is significant, however, that neither Paine's economics nor Taylor's political ideas were well known to their contemporaries; that it was the formers' political ideas and the latter's economics which were praised and followed, or denounced and opposed, depending upon the point of view.

Important differences also separated urban democrats from agrarian democrats. City democrats, many of whom had migrated from the countryside, had some anti-commercial biases, but these biases were less intense and certainly less in touch with their felt needs than those of their rural counterparts. City democrats were also less anti-intellectual and less susceptible to evangelical Protestantism than agrarian democrats. To be sure, revivals did have some urban support, but they were definitely more congenial to the social conditions of the countryside than to those of the city. Moreover, while both groups were committed to the democratic process, it was for different reasons. Agrarians wanted to keep the government as weak and inactive as possible, whereas city democrats wanted to control the government for the positive purpose of obtaining benefits like protective tariffs and free public education for themselves.[26]

Both Benjamin Austin and William Duane were urban democrats. Austin was not hostile to commerce and often argued that his proposals for legal and judicial reform could easily be put to good use by his state's mercantile community. In fact Austin did little to cultivate an influence in agrarian areas, and since no matter how hard he tried, he could not carry Boston at election time or convince any of the other commercial areas to support his proposals, he never achieved political power in Massachusetts. He remained throughout his life simply a prolific and articulate propagandist whose ideas were effectively used by rural politicians more in touch with the realities of their day.[27] Duane was more realistic than Austin about the need for rural support; but even he, with all his hostility toward lawyers, an independent judiciary, and the English common law, retained grave reservations about some of the radical proposals for judicial reform.[28]

So long as they were out of power, city democrats and country democrats often worked together; once in power, however, they divided over the kinds of policies to be pursued. This occurred in Pennsylvania, where the Duane–Leib city democrats and the Snyder–Boileau country democrats worked together until Snyder's victory in 1808, at which time the differences between the two groups became apparent, and the Snyderites easily proved more powerful. City democrats tended to be more articulate, but it was in the countryside, where the great majority of Americans lived during the early national period, that the real political strength of the democrats lay.[29]

Another anomaly arose from the fact that the leadership for the attack upon the national judiciary was supplied by a small but politically important group of Old Republican planters. Coming mainly from economically declining areas on the eastern shore of Maryland, from eastern Virginia, and from the landlocked areas of North Carolina, these planters had been bypassed by the emerging entrepreneurial spirit and they actively opposed the further commercialization and industrialization of America. Like agrarian democrats, they believed in a weak central government, but that was the extent of their democracy, for on the local level they generally were not sympathetic to the radical program of judicial reform.[30] Other planters were ambivalent about the entrepreneurial spirit, denouncing it as they pursued it; the great majority of the planters, however, were businessmen who actively and willingly engaged in the money-making process: borrowing and lending on credit, buying slaves, raising crops for market, speculating in western lands, favoring the establishment of banks sympathetic to their need for long-term credit, and supporting the moderate position on judicial reform.[31]

During the period 1775–1815 the workingmen and Old Republican planters were no more than important exceptions, and the main and fundamental line of division during these years was between a provincial, anti-intellectual, agrarian democracy on the one hand, and a highly rationalized, elite-directed commercial society on the other. Furthermore, the basic divisions in American society not only coincided, they also reinforced each other. A large part of the population in agrarian areas had only recently arrived from Europe and tended to think of government, all government, in Old World terms of corruption and class rule. Using Old World standards to judge American society, agrarians believed the Good Society, as they understood it, had already been achieved or nearly achieved. Hence, they tended to take conservative, defensive, sometimes quasi-paranoic stances on most social and economic questions. Moreover, it was natural in many ways for people living in what was essentially a non-commercial economy to want a weak, inactive, and frugal government which would for the most part leave them alone. Finally, people in agrarian areas, almost always less educated and less worldly-wise than their commercial counterparts, were more susceptible to the emotional and anti-intellectual appeals of evangelical ministers. These ministers, whose constant warnings that the pursuit of wealth and luxurious living would lead to a corruption of the soul, provided a kind of intellectual and emotional justification for the agrarian way of life and even helped to foster the belief among yeoman farmers that their way of life was morally superior to any other. Conversely, almost all well-to-do and educated people lived in commercial areas. They generally had no use for the radical proposals of eighteenth-century democrats or for the anti-intellectual rantings of revivalist preachers; and the knowledge that a large, perhaps dominant, portion of the population viewed their way of life as contemptible and corrupt hardly endeared them to the democratic process. The commercial-minded also believed that much needed to be done to achieve the Good Society; and they tended to be dynamic and progressive on economic and social issues.

Clearly the division between commercial elitists and agrarian democrats involved more than a conflict between different parts of the same country in different stages of economic development. It involved two different ways of life, two different value systems, two different approaches to the same problem.[32] Agrarian democrats, with their high propensity toward evangelical religion, thought of issues in highly emotional, absolutist, moral and political terms. Things to them were either aristocratic or democratic, equal or unequal, good or bad, right or wrong; moreover, they believed those who opposed them had evil motives and engaged in conspiracies. In contrast, commercial elitists thought in the more broadly conceived and flexible categories of political economy, emphasizing the importance of stability, harmony, efficiency, uniformity, and order. The two groups, when debating an issue, spoke at each other rather than to each other.

V

The rise of the Jeffersonians to power cannot be explained simply in terms of a conflict between commercial elites and agrarian democrats, however. Commercial-minded men dominated the Federalist party, but large numbers of planters and artisans and a growing number of merchants could also be found in the Republican party. This was because, in its origin at least, the Republican party had no real connection with the more fundamental division between agrarian and commercial interests, the issues which first brought it into existence being a consequence of internal differences within the commercial community itself.[33]

But the presence of commercial-minded men in the Republican party, especially in positions of leadership, also arose because many politicians were not really motivated by any kind of principle. They appealed for agrarian support simply in order to get elected; because holding office meant political power, and political power during the early national period, when there were only vaguely defined nepotism and conflict-of-interest laws, meant political appointments for friends and relatives and special privileges in terms of land grants and bank charters. On this level the struggle tended to be between established elitists, who were most often to be found in the Federalist party, and aspiring elitists,—usually men of recently acquired wealth—who most often were to be found in the Republican party.[34]

There is no question but that the radicalism of a great many political leaders in the Republican party never went beyond their rhetoric. The French *chargé d'affaires,* Louis Guillaume Otto, recognized this in 1786, when he wrote that there existed in America "a class of men denominated 'gentlemen,' and although many of these men have betrayed the interests of their order to gain popularity, there reigns among them a connection so much more intimate as they almost all of them dread the efforts of the people to despoil them of their possessions." [35] Levi Lincoln similarly recognized this in 1802, when he complained that in Massachusetts "a large majority of the citizens of this state are Republicans. But unsustained by those who ought to be their leaders." [36]

The all too frequent manipulation of large segments of the electorate by self-seeking politicians was a hard fact of American political life during the first decade of the nineteenth century. Thus, in 1805, "Philander Rathburn," a Massachusetts Federalist, warned the voters of his state to be wary of Republicans who "no sooner . . . had effected their design of displacing others and establishing themselves," than they "with brazen front turned upon their heel, deserting their late pretensions and professions, and did in fact . . . enhance the burthens of their credulous friends, the farmers and mechanics, who had just raised them to place and power." [37] The Federalists only rarely pandered to the passions and prejudices of the people, but they repeatedly accused their more successful Republican opponents of being "designing demagogues," "warm hypocrites," "base lying wretches," and "men of deception" who knew all kinds of "tricks to delude." [38]

Once the deep divisions in the Republican party came out into the open, radical Jeffersonians also began to complain about the activities of unprincipled politicians, frequently using the same language as the Federalists. For example, during the fight over the Pennsylvania Constitution in 1805, "The Poor Man's Friend" bemoaned the activities of men in "pursuit of popularity" whose

> private sentiments . . . are best ascertained by contrasting their private actions with their public declarations. Whatever men may declare to the public in order to obtain popular favor private interest is always kept in view to insure their own ease and convenience. Hence we find that the zeal for the public good . . . and eager desire to serve the people originates in private ambition, and an insatiable desire to grow rich at the public expense.

The same writer believed that the cause for this situation lay in the fact that "the poorer class of citizens," were:

> More unsuspicious, the more credulous, than those in better condition, consequently more easily led astray by the insidious and hypocritical cant of designing knaves. The mass of men are credulous, and apt to put faith in any plausible tale that may get circulation, without inquiring the object or purpose of it. We find numbers in society ever ready to take advantage of this credulity, and turn it to their own account.[39]

Who were the "Mass of Men," the poorer class of citizens referred to by this writer? No group fits this description better than the agrarian-minded. Indeed, it is in the nature of agrarian society that much of the explanation for the differences that existed between leaders and followers in the Republican party is to be found. This is because people living in areas outside the mainstream of the market economy were too marginal econom-ically and too apathetic and uneducated politically to produce a large and effective leadership class of their own; while the people who had the wealth, time, and education to be political leaders were invariably commercial-minded. The dilemma which this posed for agrarians, a dilemma which they never successfully resolved, was succinctly put by a radical advocate of judicial reform in Kentucky:

> As the time for us to elect delegates is almost at hand, what shall we do, or what shall we not do? This is the question— shall we choose farmers, Lawyers or Magistrates to represent us? A due dilemma! On all sides there is danger.—farmers perhaps are too ignorant; Lawyers too full of quibble and mischief; and magistrates too aspiring and designing,—the magistrate can fix the pay for his own services as high as he pleases. The lawyer enhances his own fees; but the farmer none of these, O baleful ignorance! how prostrate are thou! [40]

Jesse Higgins, the author of *Sampson Against the Philistines or the Reformation of Lawsuits,* was in substantial agreement with this analysis. Concluding his appeal for the establishment of arbitration boards, he added a stern warning to his supporters to be careful of their opponents:

> If they discover that you are too strong for them they will pretend to come over to you, and join you; and if you elect any of them, they will delay and protract the reform, by pretending difficulties, and by dividing you, some under one pretence, and some for another; or if anything is carried with their consent, there will be some leaven thrown into it, which will spoil it in a short time. You must therefore beware of false brethren, and elect none, whatever may be his politics or his professions, who has not been a known friend to adjustment, that is justice and honesty.[41]

VI

The conflict between commercial elitism and agrarian democracy, each with a different kind of religious base and complicated by a continuing struggle between "ins" and "outs" on the leadership level, goes a long way to explain the differences between radicals and moderates on judicial reform. But it may even do more than this. Taken together with the work of other historians on politics and society during the early national period, an understanding of the significance of the judiciary struggle during the first decade of the nineteenth century also gives some added insight into the nature and direction of the development of American democracy between 1776 and 1840.

XVII
The Meaning of the Jeffersonian Ascendancy

No major problem in early American history has received as much attention from historians as the growth of democracy. Most of this work has centered around two main problems: whether or not the Revolution was a democratic movement, and the meaning of Andrew Jackson's election in 1828. Although some historians have studied the development of political parties during the 1790's, the significance of Jefferson's election in 1800 and its relationship to the advance of democracy in America has not received the attention it deserves. This is unfortunate. Not only is the period 1789–1815 important in itself to an understanding of the development of American democracy, but it also provides a valuable perspective from which to interpret the meaning of the Revolution and serves as an important prologue to developments of the Jacksonian era.

I

One way of understanding the meaning of Jeffersonian Democracy is to view it as the final phase of the American Revolution. It is one of the most regrettable aspects of the highly specialized nature of American historiography that students of the early national period have tended to consider the years 1789–1815 as an entity apart from the Revolution. Few historians who have written of the Confederation era take their stories beyond 1788, while those historians writing about the years immediately following the adoption of the Constitution pay little attention to those years immediately preceding it.[1] Actually there is a great deal of natural unity to the period 1775–1815. Bounded on both sides by wars with Great Britain, these years in America are marked by an attempt to come to terms with the implications of the Revolution. Most of the political leaders during these years were, in one way or another, involved in the Revolution; and most of the disagreements that occurred among them arose over their inabilities to agree upon the meaning of that event. Writing in 1786, Benjamin Rush noted, "we have only finished the first act of the great drama. We have changed our forms of government, but it remains yet to effect a Revolution in our principles, opinions and manners so as to accommodate them to the forms of government we have adopted."[2] It was this accommodation that dominated the politics of the following decades and was still going on when Jefferson took office as President in 1801.

If there is any consensus among historians about the nature of the American Revolution—and it is by no means clear that there is—it is that the Revolution was democratic in result though not in origin.[3] This was apparent in two separate but related ways. First, as a consequence of independence the king's authority was overthrown, and the structure of politics was altered completely. Prior to 1776 the fact that the great majority of the people had the right to vote had little practical effect on the existing power structure. The career of Thomas Hutchinson of Massachusetts illustrates this. A member of the General Court until 1749, when he made himself unpopular with his constituents by advocating anti-inflationary measures, Hutchinson never won another election, yet the House of Representatives immediately elected him to the upper house of the legislature. During the 1760's he was Lieutenant Governor of Massachusetts, Chief Justice of the Supreme Court, Commander of the Militia, and Probate Judge of Suffolk county; and in 1772 he became governor of the colony, having been appointed to all these positions by the king. Moreover, Hutchinson's ability to attain high posts in the government for himself was made even more spectacular as he filled other important offices with friends and relatives. His brother-in-law Andrew Oliver held positions as a member of the Governor's council, Secretary of the Province, and Judge of the Inferior Court of Common Pleas of Essex county. One of his sons sat in the General Court as Salem's representative, and two other relatives, Peter Oliver and Benjamin Lynde, were judges of the Superior Court. A few prominent families dominated the politics of the other colonies in the same manner. In short, colonial America was ruled by a small group of men who, through the royal connection, or what was more typical, through oligarchic domination of the local system, often in opposition to the royal governor and his faction of favorites, controlled the governor's councils, sat on the Superior and county courts, served as justices of the peace and senior militia officers, and also tended to control the election of representatives to colonial assemblies.[4]

This changed with independence, as the elimination of the royal connection and the establishment of republican government made the people the sovereign source of political authority in America. It did not, of course, mean the end of machine politics. But it did mean that in the future political power could be held for long periods of time only with the consent and support of the people. It made elections important, and it ushered in the age of the demagogue. During the 1780's this was most clearly manifested by the activities of John Hancock, George Clinton, and Patrick Henry, who completely changed the tone and style of American politics and who, to varying degrees, achieved positions of enormous power in their respective states by playing upon the hopes and fears of the people.[5]

Second, the constitutional debate with England touched off a genuine intellectual revolution in American political thought. Before 1760 the colonists had generally been too busy making their way in the New World to give much attention to abstract and theoretical questions of the rights of the ruled and their rulers.[6] But England's attempt to tighten up its colonial system during the 1760's, and America's determination to resist it, forced the colonists to think along constitutional and ideological lines. Consequently, as the debate developed over the next decade, Americans began to become aware of and to explore the complicated meanings of such concepts as "sovereignty," "constitution," and "representation." [7] What is especially significant about all this, however, is that innovative political thought did not stop with the Declaration of Independence, but continued and became increasingly radical as Americans debated among themselves about the kinds of political and economic systems under which they wished to live.

It was the interaction of these two deevlopments—the enlarged power of the ballot and the highly politicized nature of society following independence—that was at the heart of the democratic trust of the American Revolution.

Many people were unhappy about the democratic potential of the Revolution and attempted to mitigate its effect. The result was a series of political battles on the state level during the late 1770's and throughout the 1780's involving the writing of state constitutions, the location of state capitals, state fiscal and land policies, the treatment of loyalists, and the confiscation of loyalist estates. Although the political alignments on these questions could be complicated, with personal differences, vested interests, and sundry local considerations playing important, sometimes even dominant, roles, the basic division in most of the states tended to be agrarian democrats versus commercial elitists. The initial outcome of those struggles varied from state to state, but the general direction was clear; for even in such states as Massachusetts and South Carolina where elite-minded groups had emerged from the Revolution in firm control, there was by the middle of the 1780's a real fear of agrarian legislation and social upheaval.[8]

The vulnerability of the state governments to popular control was a principal motive behind the movement for a strong national government.[9] In 1781 a serious attempt, which had even included the possibility of a military takeover, had been made to increase the powers of the Confederation government so that it could act as a check upon the irresponsible actions of democratic state governments.[10] This attempt failed, but the efforts to create a strong national government continued until the Constitution was ratified. To be sure, the struggle over the adoption of the Constitution was a very complicated one, but once local and particularistic interests are accounted for, the underlying division appears again to have been between cosmopolitan, commercial, and elite-minded Americans on the one hand, and provincial, agrarian, and democratic Americans on the other.[11]

The adoption of the Constitution, with its numerous restraints upon the political and economic activities of the states, was an important victory for the American commercial community. But the Constitution as written and ratified was only a frame of government; actual policies still had to be formulated and implemented. It was at this point that the unity of the American business community began to break down; for while merchants, bankers, artisans, planters and speculators had put up a united front against agrarian groups hostile to their commercial way of life, they were not in agreement about the particular kinds of economic policies which the national government should adopt. An early indication of this disunity was the skirmish which took place between Southern planters and Northern financial interests over Hamilton's proposals to fund the national debt at face value and to assume all the state debts. But the struggle, while intense, was easily compromised and did not create permanent divisions.[12]

Much more serious was the division in the American business community over foreign policy questions, which over the course of the 1790's was to lead to the establishment of political parties.[13] On one side were the great majority of American merchants, who, as a result of experiences during the 1780's, had come to believe that their self-interest, and the future of American economic growth, lay in the establishment and maintenance of close commercial ties with Great Britain. This group, led by Alexander Hamilton, believed that nothing should be done to disrupt or jeopardize America's relation with England, even if it meant compromising America's political independence and allowing economic domination by Great Britain. On the other side were men who were also nationalists, but who were not anglophiles and who had doubts about parts or all of Hamilton's economic program. This group was made up of that very small part of the American mercantile community which did not have close financial ties with England; and commercial farming interests, especially planters, led by James Madison, who were opposed to having the American economy controlled by a single country. The origins of the planters' attitude—and it was this group that dominated the leadership of the Republican party—lay in their experiences during the colonial period and even after independence, when dependence upon English and Scottish merchants forced them to sell their crops cheaply and to pay high prices for services, loans, and manufactured goods, thereby keeping the planters in a condition of perpetual debt. The commercial agricultural community in America wanted to see commerce extended to as many nations other than England as possible, in order to raise prices through competitive bidding for their crops. Madison argued that to do this it would be necessary to build up an American merchant marine and place discriminatory duties on English ships. Only in this way, he believed, would it be possible to combat Great Britain, which "has bound us in commercial mannacles, and very nearly defeated the object of our independence." [14]

Although the conflict between Hamilton and Madison over the future course of American economic development began simply as a division within the American commercial community, it was immediately complicated by the outbreak of the French Revolution. At first most Americans hailed the overthrow of the *ancien régime:* the French Declaration of the Rights of Man and the Citizen set forth objectives similar to those of the Declaration of Independence and indicated that an important world power had embarked upon a republican experiment in liberty similar to America's. However, the execution of Louis XVI and the rise of Jacobinism quickly alienated those Americans who had been determined to suppress the radical implications of their own Revolution. But not all Americans were willing to turn their backs on the French Revolution, even after it entered its most radical phase. Extreme democratic-minded Americans continued to support it enthusiastically, their point of view finding expression in many of the Democratic-Republican societies founded to demonstrate America's support of the French Revolution.

The proponents of a radical kind of popularistic democracy, having played an important role in state politics during the

1780's and having formed an essential—even dominant—part of the Anti-Federalist coalition in the struggle over the adoption of the Constitution, did not simply cease to exist after the battle of 1787–88.[15] Despite the fact that they had been defeated in 1788, betrayed by many of their leaders, disappointed by the kinds of amendments that were grafted upon the Constitution, and generally excluded from positions in the new national government, agrarian democrats nevertheless remained a potent political force and added an important dimension to the political battles of the last decade of the eighteenth century.[16]

The continued significance of the agrarian democratic persuasion during the 1790's complicated matters for commercial interests hostile to Hamilton's foreign policy. The essential difference between Hamilton and Madison was that one was pro-British while the other was anti-British. Yet there were exigencies—the alliance of 1778 with France, the outbreak of war between France and England, and Washington's neutrality proclamation—that forced Madison and his followers to adopt a pro-French position. But they did this only reluctantly and in such a way as to disassociate themselves as much as possible from the more radical, agrarian democratic elements who began to re-enter politics on a large scale in 1793–94: Jefferson, Madison, and their followers either held themselves aloof or tried to control the proceedings of the Democratic-Republican societies, reacted cooly to Citizen Genêt's advances, were unsympathetic to the Whisky Rebellion (though equally critical of the repressive manner in which it was put down), did their best to avoid personal attacks upon President Washington's character, and, perhaps most important of all, during the crucial battle over Jay's Treaty backed down rather than support amendments to the Constitution limiting the powers of the executive.[17]

In 1797, when John Adams became President and Thomas Jefferson Vice President, an attempt was made to form a coalition of moderates from both parties by achieving a rapprochment between the two leaders, but it failed.[18] Still, it was only after Hamilton and the High Federalists, with the initial co-operation of Adams, passed the Alien and Sedition Acts and began to place the country on a war footing, that the moderate and commercial

Madisonian Republicans, fearing that Hamilton planned to make use of the army to destory his internal political opposition and put an end to the Republic, entered into an open alliance with the more extreme democratic elements.[19]

Consequently, beginning in the spring of 1798 the Republicans' opposition to Federalist measures took on a new intensity and urgency. They uncompromisingly assaulted and denounced their opponents' centralizing policies, and they increasingly resorted to extremist rhetoric to distinguish themselves from the Federalists. Moreover, through the adoption of the Virginia and especially the Kentucky resolutions, the Republican party appeared to imply that it now favored changes in the Constitution which would restore the balance of power to the states. Often referred to as the "Spirit of 1798," this open and deliberate embracing of the Anti-Federalist point of view by many people who had supported the adoption of the Constitution contributed significantly to Jefferson's election in 1800.

The Republican party at the time of Jefferson's inauguration was not a homogeneous group with a single point of view. It was rather a diverse coalition whose only real bond was opposition to the Federalists. Indeed, two of the most important groups in the coalition, commercial farmers and agrarian democrats, had very little in common and were even political enemies on many local issues. Because of this it was by no means clear what Jefferson's victory in 1800 signified. Some Republicans expected it to mean a thorough overhauling of the Constitution and a change in the administration of the national government in a democratic, agrarian, states' rights direction. Others, viewing themselves as protectors of the constitutional settlement of 1788, hoped it would only mean that changes in the area of foreign policy and in some of the government's personnel.[20]

It is a mistake, therefore, to argue, as some historians have done, that the true nature of Jeffersonian democracy is to be found only in the "Spirit of 1798," and that the Republican Party, while victorious at the polls, nevertheless failed to implement its program after it came to power in 1800.[21] To many of the more moderate members of the party the "Spirit of 1798" was at best a necessary evil, a means to the end of saving the country from High Federalist extremism. These moderate Republicans never had any intention of implementing many of their campaign promises. For the moderates, the meaning of Jeffersonian democracy is to be found in Jefferson's inaugural address and in his policy of conciliating his political enemies and harmonizing the different interests in the country. There were other Republicans, however, who viewed Jefferson's election as a divinely inspired event and who did wish to see the principles of the "Spirit of 1798" put into practice. Given the fundamental irreconcilability of these two points of view, it is not surprising that the most important political battles of the first decade of the nineteenth century took place between the moderate and radical wings of the Republican party.

II

The rapid, and in some parts of the country almost immediate, demise of the Federalist party after 1800 only served to heighten the differences between radicals and moderates within the Republican party. By 1805, following Jefferson's overwhelming victory in the presidential election of 1804 and the Republican party's rise to power in most of the states, the two wings had begun to fight their battles in full view of the public. An astute Federalist newspaper in an article entitled "Whence so much Third-partyism in States where democracy gains the ascendancy?" described the difficulties of the moderate and eventually dominant wing of the Republican party in this manner:

> There are among the leaders of the democrats, many men who have sense enough to know that the principles they advance, in opposition to federalism, tend to the subversion of order and the destruction of society. They sin against light, knowingly and willfully.—But as there is no other way of putting down federalism and putting them selves up, they ostensibly unite with the real jacobins, and make with them a common cause. When they succeed, they well know that adherence to their declared opinions would ruin society and whelm themselves in the general destruction. Hence they are disposed to attempt some restraint, upon the very vice and passions they have

cherished. They begin to adopt many of the salutary maxims of the federalists, but the floodgates they have opened are not easily shut. They find their pupils in violence and insubordination unmanageable, and are in turn denounced by them as tyrants, aristocrats and oppressors.[22]

The struggle between radicals and moderates for control of the Republican party took place on the national level during Jefferson's first administration. Battles were fought not only over how patronage should be dispensed and what to do about the Federalist-controlled judiciary, but also over other issues. On fiscal policy the radicals wished to indict the previous administrations for corruption, scale down and perhaps even repudiate part of the national debt, and abolish the first Bank of the United States. The moderates, on the other hand, wished only to reduce government spending, pay off the national debt as quickly as possible, and neutralize the political activities of the national bank.[23] The radicals wished to change the Constitution in order to make its wording more precise, the judiciary and senate more amenable to popular control, and the states more powerful. Most moderates really did not want to see any changes made in the Constitution, if only because they feared that once they started to make changes they would not be able to control the kinds of changes made. "I confess I do not like tampering with established systems or forms of Government," wrote Thomas McKean, "and would rather submit to small real injuries under them, than set everything afloat. I never desire to see any more Revolutions, and pant after tranquility, peace and sociability." [24] Such thinking made many moderates reluctant to even support the seemingly harmless and necessary Twelfth Amendment.[25] The two wings of the party also split over the kind of reception to be given the aged but still popular Tom Paine, who returned to America in 1804. The radicals wanted him to be given a hero's welcome and did so in many of the newspapers under their control; but Jefferson and the moderate-controlled national administration did not pay him a great deal of attention and even went so far as to have Sam Adams and William Duane request him to stop writing controversial newspaper articles on religious subjects.[26]

Radicals and moderates also battled on the state level. The

timing and intensity of these struggles varied from state to state and depended most importantly upon the relative strength of the Federalists and the ability of agrarians and radicals to organize and articulate their demands. In Kentucky and Georgia, where the Federalists were weak and agrarians active, the divisions in the Republican party had already become apparent during the 1790's, thus foreshadowing the struggles that were to take place in most of the other states after 1800. The rise to power of the Jeffersonians coincided with a new wave of constitution writing and numerous unsuccessful attempts to rewrite older constitutions, which forced radicals and moderates to declare themselves on just how democratic they wanted the fundamental law of their state to be.

Banking was another issue. For all their hostility to banks during the 1790's, the Jeffersonians, once in power, established more state banks than the Federalists had ever thought of creating.[27] Much of this was deliberate on the part of the moderates and bitterly opposed by the radicals. True, it still remains to be proved that the alignments on the banking issue were the same or similar to those on judicial and legal reform, but there is strong impressionistic evidence to indicate that they were. For example, commenting on an electoral campaign in Virginia, where there was no real judiciary struggle but where there was a bitter fight over the establishment of a bank, Samuel Smith wrote in 1805, "It is a struggle . . . between those who would carry Democracy to lengths dangerous to civil society . . . and those whose good sense, talents, and abilities, produce the present state of things and wish to proceed no further in reform." [28]

This mixed picture makes it impossible to explain the significance of Jeffersonian Democracy simply in terms of Jefferson's election in 1800. A series of full-scale political battles had to be fought within the Republican party during the first decade of the nineteenth century before the meaning of Jefferson's election became clear. The real meaning of Jeffersonian Democracy, it would seem, is to be found in the political triumph of the moderate Republicans and their eventual amalgamation with the moderate wing of the Federalist party. This represented a victory of moderation over the extremism of the ultra-nationalist, neo-mercantile wing of the Federalist party on the one hand, and the particularistic, Anti-Federalist–Old Republican wing of the Democratic-Republican party on the other. It meant, as one moderate wrote, that a successful defense had been made against all attacks upon the true principles and institutions of the American Revolution whether "under the mask of Federalism, artfully employed to disguise monarchy; or in the garb of Democracy, unworthily employed as a cover for anarchy." [29] For the over-all development of American democracy it meant the preservation of a government that was to be responsive but not directly and immediately controlled by the people.

There is a remarkable unity to the period 1776–1815. The constitutional struggles of the 1780's were over the question of how powerful the legislature should be, those of the 1790's involved the executive branch primarily, and so it was, in a way, natural for the final phase of the constitutional struggle to center on the judiciary. As John Adams noted in 1815, "the last twenty years of the last century, and first fifteen years of this may be called the age of Revolutions and Constitutions." [30]

III

It yet remains to explore the significance of the triumph of the moderate Republicans after 1800. Did it simply ensure the preservation of the constitutional settlement of 1788 and pave the way for the adoption of Federalist policies under Republican control? Or did Republican policies represent something different from those of the Federalists and help establish a new set of political and economic forces on the American scene? The answer is very much the latter; for to argue, as so many historians have done, that all the Republicans in power did was to out-federalize the Federalists is to fundamentally misunderstand the significance of the years of the Jeffersonian ascendancy.

Politically, the Jeffersonian ascendancy meant that for the first time since the country had embarked upon its "experiment in liberty" the official sources of power were completely under the control of people who were unqualifiedly committed to a republican form of government. While it is true that the overwhelming majority of the Federalists had shared this commitment, a small and powerful group in the Federalist party had shown a decided willingness to make use, among other things, of the army to thwart majority rule when circumstances warranted. Centered around Robert Morris during the early 1780's and around Alexander Hamilton during the 1790's, these High Federalists were probably the most influential and dynamic minority that America has ever known. They had no counterpart in the Republican Party. In short, the Jeffersonian triumph of 1800 probably secured the liberal tradition in America.[31]

In like manner the Republican party also contained a point of view that was not to be found in the Federalist party. For agrarian democrats invariably became Jeffersonians. They may not have been very important politically during Washington's administrations, but their influence increased sharply between 1798 and 1800, and they played an important role in the political battles of the first decade of the nineteenth century. The fact that the Federalists were no longer politically very important after 1800 allowed the moderate and radical Republicans to become the dominant political forces in the country, and, as a result, the tone, style and content of American politics shifted in a decidedly democratic direction.

Another important difference between the Federalists and moderate Republicans was in their attitudes toward massive popular participation in politics. Neither group thought it a good thing to appeal to the passions and prejudices of the public. But the moderate Republicans, never willing to publicly denounce the concept of majority rule, were prepared for and capable of playing the game of democratic politics when circumstances required. The Federalists, on the other hand, publicly denied the ability of the people to govern themselves, stressed the need for elitist guidance, and never were able to successfully practice the art of popular politics. This is an important point because it helps explain why, as moderate and radical Republicans battled each other during the first decade of the nineteenth century, voter participation reached new highs in most states. It also helps explain why political democracy was an established fact of life, on a theoretical if not always a practical level, well before the Jacksonians came to power.[32]

Even though the moderate Republicans were more willing than

the Federalists to play upon the hopes and fears of the electorate in order to obtain and maintain power, they nonetheless shared with the Federalists the prevalent eighteenth-century view that party politics was a bad thing. Madison had pointed out in *The Federalist* No. 10 that any kind of faction could be dangerous to the life of the republic, and that a majority faction was the most dangerous faction of all. Jefferson put it differently in his first inaugural address when he claimed, "We are all republicans— we are all federalists," but he meant much the same thing. The most important part of the moderate Jeffersonian political program, therefore, was that of putting an end to the first American party system, which had developed during the 1790's. And in 1817, as James Monroe's first administration ushered in the "Era of Good Feelings," it appeared as if they had succeeded.

There were also important differences between the economic policy of the Federalists and that of the moderate Republicans. The economic policies of the Federalist party when it was in power spoke to the needs of the American mercantile community and its English connections. Because this group represented at best only a small percentage (10 per cent would be a very liberal estimate) of the American population, Federalist policies, by necessity, became tied to maintaining an elite-directed political order. The moderate Republicans, on the other hand, placed special emphasis upon the agricultural sector of the economy as the base from which the country was to undergo its economic growth; and because such a large portion of the population was involved in agricultural pursuits, the moderate Republicans were able to operate successfully, though not always happily, within a democratic framework of politics.

Closely related to all this were the attitudes of the two groups towards the settlement and economic development of the west. The Federalists had never been happy about the flood of settlers that began to move across the mountains after the Revolution. Indeed, they feared its consequences, for as new states entered the union they overwhelmingly supported the Republican party. While in power, therefore, the Federalists did their best to retard the settlement of the west: they only sold land in large lots and charged high prices; they attempted, in one of those happy conjunctions of interest and humanity, to do justice to Indian claims; and they only reluctantly, in deference to political necessity, put pressure on Spain to open the Mississippi to American navigation. In contrast, the moderate Republicans encouraged the growth and development of the west: they reduced the size of tracts of land needed for a minimum purchase, and, until 1820, sold much of the national domain to settlers on credit; they treated the Indians in the old northwest and southwest very harshly, and eventually removed those who remained to the Missouri river; and they adopted a very aggressive stance toward the New World possessions of France and Spain, which led first to the Louisiana Purchase and then to the acquisition of Florida.[33]

Moderate Republicans also were aware that real dangers existed in the too rapid settlement of the west. For if settlement were allowed to take place in an indiscriminate and haphazard fashion, the number of people outside the market economy would increase. Many people in post-Revolutionary America recognized that this could be dangerous, because there existed a great gulf, one that could be harmful to the very fabric of society, between those who were and those who were not part of the cash nexus. To offset this danger, Jeffersonian land policy attempted, though unsuccessfully, to bring about a controlled and orderly settlement of the west, and harshly treated the large number of squatters who settled on the unsurveyed part of the public domain.[34]

To ensure the commercialization of the west, moderate Republicans also favored a system of internal improvements. One demonstration of this was the provision made at the time of Ohio's admission as a state, that part of the proceeds from the sale of its public lands be used to help build the national road. Another was Jefferson's call, in his second inaugural address, for an amendment to the constitution which would allow the Federal government to apply the surplus revenue *"in time of peace* to rivers, canals, roads, arts, manufactures, education and other great objects within each state."* He repeated this request even more strongly in his sixth annual address to Congress. In 1808 Gallatin presented an elaborate plan for a national system of internal improvements which provided for a complex of roads and canals to link to country together, North to South, and East to West. A series of circumstances prevented Gallatin's plan from being brought to fruition by the Federal government, but it nevertheless represented one of the greatest hopes of moderate Republicans and was eventually implemented through an alliance of public and private enterprise at the state and national level. Nor was it entirely fortuitous that the steamboat, which was to do so much to spread the market economy through the west, was first effectively developed in America by Robert Fulton, under the sponsorship of Robert R. Livingston, an important agricultural-minded moderate Republican from New York.[35]

Although moderate Republicans placed primary emphasis upon the development of commercial agriculture, they were neither antagonistic nor indifferent to the other sectors of the economy.[36] "You may be assured not a man in the administration is an enemy to commerce," wrote Jacob Crowninshield, an important merchant and moderate Republican from Massachusetts. "I will not say so much of their opposers. The Govt. may mistake what is the real interest of Commerce, but surely Mr. Jefferson has done enough to show that he has no hostile views to the Commercial interest." [37] The main thrust of the moderate Republican economic policy was to make the United States as self-sufficient as possible. To this end the administration was generally sympathetic to what it believed were the proper needs of the American mercantile community. "It is material," Jefferson asserted, "to the safety of Republicanism to detach the mercantile interest from its enemies and incorporate them into the body of its friends. A merchant is naturally a Republican, and can be otherwise only from a vitiated state of things." [38] The economic hopes of moderate Republicans came to partial fulfillment during the closing year of Madison's second administration, when a protective tariff was passed, the second Bank of the United States was established, and the Bonus Bill of 1817 was approved by both Houses, only to be vetoed by Madison for constitutional, not policy reasons.

Here then was another important difference between the moderate Republicans and the Federalists. The latter believed that American economic growth was dependent upon close ties with England, while the former stressed American self-sufficiency through the development of an internal market. What is especially important about this is that American economic growth between 1800 and 1828 generally took place in the way moderate Republicans envisioned it would: American agricultural staples brought in foreign capital; American industries, fostered by a protective tariff, gradually provided cheap manufactured goods and a domestic market for agricultural surpluses; the economic system thus generated was made possible by a series of roads and canals; and the domestic economy was regulated and a stable currency maintained by the second Bank of the United States.[39]

The moderate Jeffersonians, during the years of their ascendancy, created a new political and economic synthesis from the old dichotomies of the Revolution. For in the years immediately following independence most people generally believed that business enterprise and democracy were incompatible; what the moderate Jeffersonians did was to democratize business enterprise.

IV

During the years 1816 to 1819 an incomplete but nonetheless genuine fulfilment of the Jeffersonian belief in the harmony of interests took place as most Americans evinced an unbounded faith in the country's economic prosperity and a general lack of concern with politics. This came to an end with the Panic of 1819, when America underwent its first major national depression. The psychological shock was enormous, and what followed was a resurgence of radical and Old Republican principles, a decade of political strife and tension culminating in the election of 1828, and the re-establishment of a two-party system of politics.

Attempting to find the origins of the party divisions that took place between 1828 and 1848, some historians have argued that they can be traced back to the Federalist-Jeffersonian struggles of the 1790's.[40] Other historians have denied the existence of any connection between the first and second American party systems.[41] What has not been adequately appreciated, however, is the extent of the continuity between the moderate Republicans and the National Republicans and Whigs, on the one hand, and the agrarian democratic, radical, Old Republican wing of the Republican party and Jacksonian Democrats on the other.

One indication of the continuity between radical Jeffersonians and Jacksonians and between moderate Republicans and Whigs is to be found in the similarity of the categories of thought used in the various debates over judicial reform and in the debates over banking reform, which was the key issue on both the national and state levels during the 1830's. Advocates of a moderate kind of judicial reform and defenders of a stable and well-regulated currency argued primarily in terms of political economy, whereas the advocates of a radical kind of judicial reform and hard money proponents argued mainly in political and moral terms.

Also, while the continuity between the two sets of groups took place most clearly on an ideological level, there also exists a kind of tenuous connection between the personnel involved. Many of the most prominent Whigs—Henry Clay, Nicholas Biddle, and John Quincy Adams—had at one time been moderate Republicans, while most surviving radicals and Old Republicans—William Duane, Felix Grundy, and John Randolph—tended to espouse the Jacksonian cause.

Recognizing that a real and definite, though imperfect, connection existed between the bi-factional party battles of the first decade of the nineteenth century and the two-party battles of the 1830's helps explain some of the paradoxes of the Jackson era. In particular, it helps explain why Whigs and Democrats could both claim to be good Jeffersonians; and why the party battles of the 1830's involved democracy but did not pose a threat to democracy. For what was involved was a contest between the positive state economic democracy of the moderate-Republican-sponsored American system and the negative popularistic political democracy of the agrarian, radical, and Old Republican wing of the Jeffersonian party.[42]

Notes

CHAPTER I

1. Thomas Jefferson to Thomas Nelson, 16 May 1776, Julian P. Boyd (ed.), *The Papers of Thomas Jefferson* (17 vols., Princeton, 1950–), I, 292.
2. John Adams to George Wythe, 1776, C. F. Adams (ed.), *The Works of John Adams* (10 vols., Boston, 1850–56), IV, 200.
3. Bernard Bailyn (ed.), *Pamphlets of the American Revolution* (4 vols., Cambridge, Mass., 1965–), I, 90–138; George M. Dutcher, "The Rise of Republican Government in the United States," *Political Science Quarterly* LV (June 1940), 199–216.
4. Gordon S. Wood, *The Creation of the American Republic, 1776–1787* (Chapel Hill, 1969); J. R. Pole, *Political Representation in England and the Origins of the American Republic* (New York, 1966); E. P. Douglass, *Rebels and Democrats* (Chapel Hill, 1955).
5. Roscoe Pound, *Organization of the Courts* (Boston, 1940), 53–90; Erwin C. Surrency, "The Courts in the American Colonies," *American Journal of Legal History* 11 (July, October, 1967), 253–76, 347–76; Leonard Labaree, *Royal Government in America* (New York, 1958), 373–419; Evarts B. Greene, *The Provincial Governor in the English Colonies of North America* (Gloucester, Mass., 1966), 133–44; Arthur M. Schlesinger, "Colonial Appeals to the Privy Council," *Political Science Quarterly* XXVIII (June, September, 1913), 279–97, 433–50.
6. Robert J. Taylor, *Western Massachusetts in the Revolution* (Providence, 1954), 27–32; Charles S. Sydnor, *American Revolutionaries*

in the Making (New York, 1962), 74–85; Solon J. Buck and Elizabeth H. Buck, *The Planting of Civilization in Western Pennsylvania* (Pittsburgh, 1939), 435; Pound, *Organization of the Courts,* 88–89.

7. It is worth pointing out that while those historians who argue that America was democratic before the Revolution have based their arguments on the study of suffrage and representation, they have not treated the judiciary.

8. Richard M. Brown, *The South Carolina Regulators* (Cambridge, Mass., 1963); John S. Bassett, "Regulators of North Carolina, 1765–1771," American Historical Association, *Annual Report* (1894), 141–212; Milton M. Klein, "Prelude to Revolution in New York: Jury Trials and Judicial Tenure," *William and Mary Quarterly* 17 (October 1960), 439–62; Bailyn (ed.), *Pamphlets of the American Revolution,* I, 48–49, 66–68, 249–55; Jack P. Greene, *The Quest for Power* (Chapel Hill, 1964), 330–43; Bernard Knollenberg, *Origins of the American Revolution, 1759–1776* (New York, 1960), 71–74; Taylor, *Western Massachusetts in the Revolution,* 52–74; Emory G. Evans, "Planter Indebtedness and the Coming of the Revolution in Virginia," *William and Mary Quarterly* XIX (October 1962), 527–33; Charles Grier Sellers, Jr., "Making a Revolution: The North Carolina Whigs, 1765–1775," J. Carlyle Sitterson (ed.), *Studies in Southern History* (Chapel Hill, 1957), 27–46.

9. Wood, *Creation of the American Republic,* 159–61; W. C. Webster, "Comparative Study of the State Constitutions of the American Revolution," *Annals of the American Academy of Political and Social Science* IX (1897), 380–420; W. C. Morey, "The First State Constitutions," *ibid.,* IV (1893–94), 201–32; J. Paul Selsam, "A History of Judicial Tenure in Pennsylvania," *Dickinson Law Review* XXXVIII (April 1934), 169–83.

10. Wood, *Creation of the American Republic,* 127–255; Merrill Jensen, "Democracy and the American Revolution," *Huntington Library Quarterly* XX (August 1957), 321–41.

11. Wood, *Creation of the American Republic,* 393–467; Charles Grove Haines, *The American Doctrine of Judicial Supremacy* (New York, 1959), 88–121.

12. Richard D. Spaight to James Iredell, 12 August 1787, Griffith J. McRee (ed.), *Life and Correspondence of James Iredell* (2 vols., New York, 1857), II, 168–70.

13. James Iredell to Richard D. Spaight, 26 August 1787, ibid., II, 168–70.

14. I. Crawford Biggs, "The Power of the Judiciary over Legislation," North Carolina Bar Association, *Proceedings* (1915), 13–18; H. B. Dawson (ed.), *Arguments and Judgement of the Mayors Court . . . in a Cause between . . . Rutgers and Waddington* (Morrisania, 1886); Richard B. Morris (ed.), *Select Cases of the Mayors Court of New York City, 1674–1784* (Washington, D.C., 1935), 302–27; James M. Varnum, *The Case Trevett against Weeden . . . 1786. Also the Case of the Judges of Said Court* (Providence, 1787); John Winslow, *The Trial of the Rhode Island Judges: An Episode Touching Currency and Constitutional History* (Brooklyn, 1887).

15. J. F. Jameson, "The Predecessor of the Supreme Court," Jameson (ed.), *Essays in the Constitutional History of the United States* (Boston, 1898), 1–45; Robert J. Steamer, "The Legal and Political Genesis of the Supreme Court," *Political Science Quarterly* LXVII (December 1962), 565–66.

16. Max Farrand (ed.), *The Records of the Federal Convention of 1787* (4 vols., New Haven, 1911), I, 21, 124–27, 244–45, 292, 317, 341; II, 45–46, 136, 433.

17. Article II, sections 2 and 3; Article III.

18. Gouverneur Morris to Timothy Pickering, 22 December 1814, Farrand (ed.), *The Records of the Federal Convention of 1787*, III, 420.

19. "The Address and Reasons of Dissent of the Minority of the Convention of the State of Pennsylvania to their Constituents," John B. McMaster and F. D. Stone (eds.), *Pennsylvania and the Federal Constitution, 1787–1788* (Lancaster, 1888), 475.

20. Charles Warren, "New Light on the History of the Federal Judiciary Act of 1789," *Harvard Law Review* XXXVII (November 1923), 54–56.

21. Ibid., 49–132; Ralph Lerner, "The Supreme Court as Republican Schoolmaster," Philip B. Kurland (ed.), *The Supreme Court Review* (1967), 127–80.

22. Max Farrand, "The First Hayburn Case," *American Historical Review* 13 (January 1908), 281–85; Charles Warren, *The Supreme Court in United States History* (2 vols., Boston, 1926), I, 72–84, 91–123.

23. Warren, *Supreme Court,* I, 85–90.

24. William N. Chambers, *Political Parties in a New Nation* (New York, 1963); Richard Hofstadter, *Idea of a Party System: The Rise of Legitimate Opposition in the United States, 1780–1840* (Berkeley, 1969).

25. Warren, *Supreme Court,* I, 91–168.

26. Theodore Sedgwick to Rufus King, 15 November 1799, Charles R. King (ed.), *Life and Correspondence of Rufus King* (10 vols., New York, 1896), III, 146–47.

27. Kathryn Turner, "Federalist Policy and the Judiciary Act of 1801," *William and Mary Quarterly* XXII (January 1965), 9–14.

28. Ibid., 15–22; Erwin C. Surrency, "The Judiciary Act of 1801," *American Journal of Legal History* II (1958), 53–65; Max Farrand, "The Judiciary Act of 1801," *American Historical Review* V (1899–1900), 682–86.

29. Gouverneur Morris to Robert R. Livingston, 20 February 1801, Jared Sparks (ed.), *The Life of Gouverneur Morris* . . . (2 vols., Boston, 1832), 153–54; Kathryn Turner, "The Midnight Judges," *University of Pennsylvania Law Review* CIX (1960–61), 494–523.

30. Turner, "Federalist Policy and the Judiciary Act of 1801," *William and Mary Quarterly* XXII (January 1965), 22–32.

CHAPTER II

1. John Randolph to Joseph Hooper Nicholson, 26 July 1801, Nicholson Papers, Library of Congress (LC).

2. William Branch Giles to Thomas Jefferson, 1 June 1801, Jefferson Papers, LC.

3. St. George Tucker to James Monroe, 7 January, 25 February 1801, Monroe Papers, LC. See also: James Monroe to Thomas Jefferson, 3, 18 March, 30 April (not sent) 1801; Jefferson Papers, LC; William Branch Giles to Thomas Jefferson, 16 March 1801, ibid.; Stevens Thomas Mason to James Monroe, 5 July 1801, Monroe Papers, LC.

4. *Examiner* (Richmond), 20 October 1801; *National Intelligencer* (Washington), 26 October 1801; *American Commercial Daily Advertiser* (Baltimore), 26 October 1801; Henry H. Simms, *Life of John Taylor* (Richmond, 1932), 100–101; David J. Mays, *Edmund Pendleton, 1721–1803, A Biography* (2 vols., Cambridge, 1952), II, 331–36.

5. John Hunter to James Madison, 16 April 1801, Madison Papers, LC.

6. Alexander J. Dallas to Albert Gallatin, 14 June 1801, Gallatin Papers, New York Historical Society (NYHS); see also: Benjamin Rush to Thomas Jefferson, 12 March 1801, L. H. Butterfield (ed.), *Letters of Benjamin Rush* (2 vols., Princeton, 1951), II, 831–33; Elijah Boardman to Thomas Jefferson, 1 March 1801, Jefferson Papers, LC; John Stuart to Thomas Jefferson, 9 March 1801, ibid.

7. Albert Gallatin to Thomas Jefferson, 10 August 1801, Henry Adams

(ed.), *The Writings of Albert Gallatin* (3 vols., Philadelphia, 1879), I, 33. See also: Chandler Price to William Jones, 9 February 1803, Uselma Clark Smith Collection, Historical Society of Pennsylvania (HSP).

8. James Sullivan to William Eustis, 13 January 1802, Thomas C. Amory, *Life of James Sullivan; with Selections from His Writings* (2 vols., Boston, 1859), II, 94–95.

9. Wilson Cary Nicholas to James Madison, 1 May 1801, Madison Papers, LC.

10. Albert Gallatin to Thomas Jefferson, 12 September 1801, Adams (ed.), *Writings of Gallatin*, I, 47–49; Thomas McKean to Thomas Jefferson, 10 August 1801, Jefferson Papers, LC; Thomas Leiper to Thomas Jefferson, 8 March 1801, ibid.; James Warren to Thomas Jefferson, 4 March 1801, ibid.

11. Merrill D. Peterson, *The Jefferson Image in the American Mind* (New York, 1960).

12. For my view of Jefferson I am most indebted to the following works: Dumas Malone, *Jefferson and His Time* (4 vols., Boston, 1948–70); Elisha P. Douglass, *Rebels and Democrats* (Chapel Hill, 1955), 287–316; Leonard Levy, *Legacy of Suppression* (Cambridge, Mass., 1960), 299–307; R. R. Palmer, "The Dubious Democrat: Thomas Jefferson in Bourbon France," *Political Science Quarterly* LXXII (September 1957), 388–404; Bernard Bailyn, "Boyd's Jefferson: Notes For a Sketch," *New England Quarterly* XXXIII (September 1960), 380–400; William D. Grampp, "A Re-Examination of Jeffersonian Economics," *The Southern Economic Journal* XII (January 1946), 263–82; Morton Borden, "Thomas Jefferson," in Borden (ed.), *America's Ten Greatest Presidents* (Chicago, 1961), 57–80.

13. Julian P. Boyd (ed.), *The Papers of Thomas Jefferson* (17 vols., 1950–), I, 343, 351, 361; Thomas Jefferson to George Wythe, ? June 1776, ibid., I, 410; Thomas Jefferson to James Madison, 15 March 1789, ibid., XIV, 659; Charles Warren, *The Supreme Court in United States History* (2 vols., 1926), I, 163–64, 167.

14. Thomas Jefferson to James Madison, 26 December 1800, Paul L. Ford (ed.), *The Works of Thomas Jefferson* (12 vols., New York, 1905), IX, 161–62.

15. Alexander Hamilton to James A. Bayard, 16 January 1801, Henry Cabot Lodge (ed.), *The Works of Alexander Hamilton* (12 vols., New York, 1904), X, 413.

16. John Marshall to C. C. Pinckney, 4 March 1801, Richard J. Hooker (ed.), "John Marshall on the Judiciary, the Republicans, and

Jefferson, March 4, 1801," *American Historical Review* LIII (April 1948), 518–20.

17. [William P. Van Ness] Aristides, *An Examination of the Various Charges Exhibited Against Aaron Burr* (New York, 1803), 50.

18. John Dawson to James Monroe, 23 February 1801, James Monroe Papers, LC.

19. Thomas Jefferson to John Dickinson, 23 July 1801, Ford (ed.), *Works of Jefferson,* IX, 280–82.

20. Thomas Jefferson to Joseph Fay, 22 March 1801, Jefferson Papers, LC; Thomas Jefferson to Moses Robinson, 23 March 1801, ibid.; Thomas Jefferson to Thomas McKean, 24 July 1801, Ford (ed.), *Works of Jefferson,* IX, 282–84; Thomas Jefferson to Henry Knox, 27 March 1801, ibid., IX, 236–38.

21. Thomas Jefferson to David Denniston and James Cheetham, 6 June 1801, Jefferson Papers, LC.

22. Thomas Jefferson to Joseph Priestley, 19 June 1802, Ford (ed.), *Works of Jefferson,* IX, 381.

23. Thomas Jefferson to Gideon Granger, 13 August 1800, ibid., IX, 139.

24. Charles O. Lerche, Jr., "Jefferson and the Election of 1800: A Case Study in the Political Smear," *William and Mary Quarterly,* V (October 1948), 467–91; Thomas Jefferson to James Monroe, 7 March 1801, Ford (ed.), *Works of Jefferson,* IX, 202–5; Thomas Jefferson to John Dickinson, 6 March 1801, ibid., IX, 201–2; Thomas Jefferson to Joseph Priestley, 21 March 1801, ibid., IX, 218–19; Thomas Jefferson to Nathaniel Miles, 22 March 1801, ibid., IX, 221–22; Thomas Jefferson to Samuel Adams, 29 March 1801, ibid., IX, 239–40; Thomas Jefferson to Thomas McKean, 2 February 1801, McKean Papers, HSP. See Thomas McKean to Thomas Jefferson, 10 January, 19 March 1801, Jefferson Papers, LC; John Beckley to Albert Gallatin, 15 February 1801, Gallatin Papers, NYHS; W. C. Nicholas to J. Breckinridge, 20 January 1801, Breckinridge Papers, LC.

25. Thomas Jefferson to Walter Jones, 31 March 1801, Andrew A. Lipscomb (ed.), *The Writings of Thomas Jefferson* (20 vols., Washington, D.C., 1905), X, 255–56.

26. James Madison to N. P. Trist, ? May 1832, Gaillard Hunt (ed.), *The Writing of James Madison* (9 vols., New York, 1900–1910), IX, 479.

27. Entry of 27 December 1818, C. F. Adams (ed.), *Memoirs of John Quincy Adams* (12 vols., Philadelphia, 1874–77), IV, 492.

28. Thomas Jefferson to George Logan, 11 May 1805, Ford (ed.), *Works of Jefferson,* X, 143.

29. Thomas Jefferson to James Monroe, 7 March 1801, ibid., IX, 202–3.

30. Ibid., IX, 193–200; Nathan Schachner, *Thomas Jefferson, A Biography* (New York, 1957), 662–64.

31. William Branch Giles to James Madison, 22 February 1809, Madison Papers, LC; John Armstrong to Robert R. Livingston, 5 March 1801, Livingston Papers, NYHS; *Aurora* (Philadelphia), 23 March 1801; *National Intelligencer* (Washington), 6, 22 April, 1, 4 May 1801.

32. Thomas Jefferson to James Madison, 29 August 1803, Madison Papers, LC; Thomas Jefferson to William Wirt, 3 May 1811, Lipscomb (ed.), *The Writings of Thomas Jefferson*, XII, 55–56; Robert R. Livingston to Thomas Jefferson, 31 May 1801, Jefferson Papers, LC; William Duane to James Madison, 10 May 1801, Madison Papers, LC; William Duane to Albert Gallatin, 13 December 1801, Gallatin Papers, NYHS.

33. William Johnson to Samuel Harrison Smith, 21 November 1800, J. Henley Smith Papers, LC; *National Intelligencer* (Washington), 13, 18 March 1801; Margaret Bayard Smith, *First Forty Years of Washington Society* (New York, 1906), 9.

34. Thomas Jefferson to Abigail Adams, 13 June 1804, Lester Cappon (ed.), *The Adams-Jefferson Letters* (2 vols., Chapel Hill, 1959), I, 270; Thomas Jefferson to James Monroe, 7 March 1801, Ford (ed.), *Works of Jefferson*, IX, 202–4; Thomas Jefferson to William Findley, 24 March 1801, ibid., IX, 224–26; Thomas Jefferson to Benjamin Rush, 24 March 1801, ibid., IX, 229–32.

35. Thomas Jefferson to Benjamin Smith Barton, 14 February 1801, ibid., IX, 177–78; Thomas Jefferson to James Monroe, 7 March 1801, ibid., IX, 202–4; Thomas Jefferson to Horatio Gates, 8 March 1801, ibid., IX, 205–6; Thomas Jefferson to Henry Knox, 27 March 1801, ibid., IX, 236–38; Thomas Jefferson to Elbridge Gerry, 29 March 1801, ibid., IX, 240–44; Thomas Jefferson to Gideon Granger, 29 March 1801, ibid., IX, 244–47; Noble Cunningham, *The Jeffersonian Republicans in Power* (Chapel Hill, 1963), 12–16; Leonard White, *The Jeffersonians: A Study in Administrative History, 1801–1829* (New York, 1951), 347–54.

36. Thomas Jefferson to William Branch Giles, 23 March 1801, Ford (ed.), *Works of Jefferson*, IX, 247–48; Thomas Jefferson to Thomas Mann Randolph, 12 March 1801, Jefferson Papers, LC; White, *Jeffersonians*, 353–54.

37. The singular letter is: Thomas Jefferson to Archibald Stuart, 8 April 1801, Ford (ed.), *Works of Jefferson*, IX, 247–48. The ideas expressed in this paragraph rest on a wide variety of sources too

numerous to cite fully. Some of the most important are: Thomas Jefferson to Theodore Foster, 9 May 1801, ibid., IX, 251–53; Thomas Jefferson to the Senate, 6, 27 April, 1802, Jefferson Papers, LC; Thomas Jefferson to James Jackson, 28 May 1801, ibid.; Thomas Jefferson to Levi Lincoln, 17 April 1801, ibid.; Levi Lincoln to Thomas Jefferson, 8, 16 April 1801, ibid.; David Leonard Barnes to Thomas Jefferson, 18 May 1801, ibid.; Nathaniel Macon to Thomas Jefferson, 20 April, 1 May 1801, ibid.; Charles Pinckney to Thomas Jefferson, 26 May 1801, ibid.

CHAPTER III

1. *Columbian Centinel* (Boston), 18 March 1801; *Aurora* (Philadelphia), 4 March 1801; Robert Troup to Rufus King, 23 March 1801, Charles R. King (ed.), *Life and Correspondence of Rufus King* (10 vols., New York, 1896), II, 409.

2. David Jones to Thomas Jefferson, 2 July 1801, Jefferson Papers, LC; see also: David Denniston and James Cheetham to Thomas Jefferson, 1 June 1801, ibid.; Republicans of Connecticut to Levi Lincoln, 4 June 1801, ibid.; Elbridge Gerry to Thomas Jefferson, 4 May 1801, Chauncey Ford (ed.), *Some Letters of Elbridge Gerry of Massachusetts, 1784–1804* (Brooklyn, 1896), 24; William Duane to Albert Gallatin [1801], Gallatin Papers, NYHS.

3. John Randolph to Joseph Hooper Nicholson, 26 July 1801, Nicholson Papers, LC; see also: William Branch Giles to Thomas Jefferson, 16 March 1801, ibid.; Stevens Thomas Mason to James Monroe, 5 July 1801, Monroe Papers, LC.

4. Typical was an editorial in the *Washington Federalist*, 1 June 1801, condemning the President for apostasy from the principles of his inaugural address; "That speech was but a net to ensnare popularity; a shadowy deceptive basis for the reposing confidence of unguarded federalism. . . . Mr. Jefferson comes forward with the smile of French philanthropy in his countenance, *We are all Federalists, We are all Republicans,* dropping from his tongue; his right hand weaving with gestures of liberality and affection; and his left concealed under his cloak, grasping a bundle of *Sir, your services are no longer needed.*" See also: *Columbian Centinel* (Boston), 11 April 1801; *Gazette of the United States* (Philadelphia), 11 April 1801; John Rutledge to Theodore Sedgwick, 10 May 1801, Sedgwick Papers, Massachusetts Historical Society (MHS); Henry Lee to Rufus King, 18 June 1801, King (ed.), *Life and Correspondence of Rufus King*, III, 475–76.

5. Thomas Jefferson to Elias Shipman and others, a committee of the Merchants of New Haven, 12 July 1801, Ford (ed.), *Works of Jefferson*, IX, 270–74.

6. Albert Gallatin to Thomas Jefferson, 10 August 1801, Adams (ed.), *Writings of Gallatin*, I, 32–34; *Washington Federalist*, 13 July 1801; Warren Jones to James Madison, 13 September 1801, Madison Papers, LC; Entry of 15 August 1801 in Diary of Thomas Rodney, Rodney Family Papers, LC; Levi Lincoln to Thomas Jefferson, 28 July 1801, Jefferson Papers, LC; Cunningham, *Jeffersonian Republicans in Power*, 24–25.

7. Wilson Cary Nicholas to Thomas Jefferson, 24 June 1801, Jefferson Papers, LC.

8. Thomas Jefferson to Albert Gallatin, 14 August 1801, Adams (ed.), *Writings of Gallatin*, I, 32–34.

9. Harrison Gray Otis to John Rutledge, 18 October 1801, Rutledge Papers, University of North Carolina (UNC); John Rutledge to Theodore Sedgwick, 24 September 1801, Sedgwick Papers, MHS.

10. George Cabot to Oliver Wolcott, 3 August 1801, Henry Cabot Lodge, *Life and Letters of George Cabot* (Boston, 1877), 321; *Washington Federalist*, 5, 10 August 1801; *Gazette of the United States* (Philadelphia), 17 August 1801; *Columbian Centinel* (Boston), 29 July 1801.

11. Thomas Jefferson to Robert R. Livingston, 31 May 1801, Ford (ed.), *Works of Jefferson*, IX, 257–58; Thomas Jefferson to William Duane, 23 March 1801, ibid., 255–58; Levi Lincoln to Alexander J. Dallas, 25 March 1801, Jefferson Papers, LC; David Denniston and and James Cheetham to Thomas Jefferson, 22 October 1801, ibid.; Thomas Jefferson to James Madison, 19 July, 22 August 1801, Madison Papers, L.C; James Madison to Alexander J. Dallas, 20 July 1801, ibid.; *Washington Federalist*, 14, 21 October 1801, 29 January 1802; *Connecticut Courant* (Hartford), 2, November 1801.

12. *National Intelligencer* (Washington), 12 June, 23 October 1801; *Washington Federalist*, 10 July 1801; Charles Warren, *The Supreme Court in United States History* (2 vols., Boston, 1926), I, 194–98.

13. *National Intelligencer* (Washington), 18 November 1801.

14. *Aurora* (Philadelphia), 3 July 1801.

15. John Collins to John Breckinridge, 4 January 1802, Breckinridge Papers, LC. See also: *National Intelligencer* (Washington), 19 August 1801; *The Guardian of Freedom* (Frankfort, Kentucky), 13, 20 November 1801.

16. Ford (ed.), *Works of Jefferson*, IX, 321–42.

17. Thomas Jefferson to Joseph Bloomfield, 5 December 1801, Jefferson

Papers, LC. See also: Thomas Jefferson to Horatio Gates, 20 December 1801, ibid.; Thomas Jefferson to Thomas McKean, 19 February 1803, McKean Papers, HSP.

18. This is reproduced in Albert J. Beveridge, *The Life of John Marshall* (4 vols., Boston, 1919), III, 605–6, 52–53.

19. Roger Griswold to John Rutledge, 14 December 1801, Rutledge Papers, UNC. On this same point also see: James A. Bayard to John Rutledge, 20 December 1801, ibid.; Roger Griswold to David Daggett, 1 January 1802, William Griswold Lane Collection, Yale University (YU); Killian K. Van Rensselaer to John Sanders, 20 December 1801, Sanders Papers, NYHS; William Cranch to Noah Webster, 21 December 1801, Noah Webster Papers, New York Public Library (NYPL); Manasseh Culter to Thomas Burnham, 14 December 1801, W. P. and J. P. Cutler (eds.), *Life, Journal and Correspondence of Manasseh Cutler* (2 vols., New York, 1888), II, 50; *Washington Federalist*, 16 December 1801.

20. *National Intelligencer* (Washington) 21 December 1801; *Aurora* (Philadelphia) 22 December 1801; *New York Evening Post*, 23 December 1801.

21. Stevens Thomas Mason to James Monroe, 21 December 1801, Monroe Papers, LC; John Breckinridge to James Monroe, 24 December 1801, ibid.; Caesar A. Rodney to ?, 15 February 1802, Galloway–Maxcy–Markoe Papers, LC; George Clinton to Philip Van Cortlandt, January 1802, Van Cortlandt–Van Wyck Papers, NYPL; William Cranch to William Smith Shaw, 30 December 1801, Miscellaneous Bound Collection, MHS; *Washington Federalist*, 21, 22 December 1801.

22. Thomas Jefferson to John Dickinson, 18 December 1801, Jefferson Papers, LC.

23. Manasseh Cutler to Charles Torrey, 22 February 1802, W. P. and J. P. Cutler (eds.), *Life, Journal and Correspondence of Manasseh Cutler,* II, 86–87; James Hillhouse to Simeon Baldwin, 11 February 1802, *Life and Letters of Simeon Baldwin* (New Haven, n.d.), 436; *Annals of Congress,* 7:1, 110–11, 113, 161; *Gazette of the United States* (Philadelphia), 29 January 1802; *Independent Chronicle* (Boston), 2 January 1802; *The Republican; or Anti-Democrat* (Baltimore), 12 January 1802; *Washington Federalist,* 21 February 1802.

24. *Annals,* 7:1, 21, 25–30.

25. Thomas Jefferson to Thomas Mann Randolph, 9 January 1802, Jefferson Papers, LC.

26. John Randolph to St. George Tucker, 15 January 1802, John Randolph Papers (microfilm), University of Virginia (UVA); John

Randolph to James Monroe, 12 January 1802, Monroe Papers, NYPL; John Taylor to John Breckinridge, 22 December 1801, Breckinridge Papers, LC; John Taylor to Wilson Cary Nicholas, 5 September 1801, Coolidge Papers, MHS; Dr. Samuel Mitchill to Mrs. Mitchill, 10 January 1802, "Some Letters of Dr. Samuel Mitchill," *Harpers Magazine* LVIII (April 1879), 743–44.

27. John Rutledge to Theodore Sedgwick, 11 January 1802, Sedgwick Papers, MHS; *Annals*, 7:1, 30–41, 46–58, 59–145.

28. Stevens Thomas Mason to James Monroe, 27 January 1802, Monroe Papers, LC; John Rutledge to Harrison Gray Otis, 25 September 1801, Otis Papers, MHS; John Rutledge to James A. Bayard, 21 November 1801, Miscellaneous Personal Papers, LC; Henry W. DeSaussure to John Rutledge, 13 January 1802, Rutledge Papers, UNC; John Randolph to Joseph H. Nicholson, 26 July 1802, Shippen Family Papers, LC; John H. Morison, *Life of the Honorable Jeremiah Smith* (Boston, 1845), 147n.; *Annals* 7:1, 138–145.

29. *Annals* 7:1, 145–50; Stevens Thomas Mason to James Monroe, 27 January 1802, Monroe Papers, L.C; William Jones to Caesar Rodney, 27 January 1802, Rodney Papers, Historical Society of Delaware (HSD); Entry of 28 January 1802 in Diary of Thomas Worthington, Worthington Papers, LC; *Aurora* (Philadelphia), 1 February 1802; Ebenezer Elmer to ?, 19 January 1802, Simon Gratz Colection, HSP; W. H. Hill to Duncan Cameron, 28 January 1802, Cameron Papers, UNC.

30. Entry of 17 January 1802 in Diary of Gouverneur Morris, Morris Papers, LC; Matthew L. Davis (ed.), *Memoirs of Aaron Burr* (2 vols., New York, 1837), II, 80; Uriah Tracy to Aaron Burr, 29 March 1802, Burr Correspondence, American Antiquarian Society (AAS); James Jackson to Thomas Jefferson, 28 December 1801, Jefferson Papers, LC. For a different interpretation of Burr's role see Nathan Schachner, *Aaron Burr* (New York, 1961), 210–14.

31. *Philadelphia Gazette and Daily Advertiser,* 16 February 1802.

32. *Annals* 7:1, 152–53; *Aurora* (Philadelphia), 1, 3 February 1802; *Gazette of the United States* (Philadelphia), 30 January, 1, 3 February 1802; *Independent Chronicle* (Boston), 15 February 1802; *Farmers Weekly Gazette* (Walpole, N.H.), 15 February 1802; *Columbian Centinel* (Boston), 10 February 1802; George Logan and James Ross to Alexander Dallas and Thomas McKean, Jr., February 1802, Dallas Papers, HSP.

33. Alexander J. Dallas to Aaron Burr, 3 February 1802, Davis (ed.), *Memoirs of Aaron Burr,* 11, 81–83.

34. Archibald Roane to David Campbell, 13 February 1802, David

Campbell Papers, Duke University (DU); Henry W. DeSaussure to
John Rutledge, 17 February 1802, Rutledge Papers, UNC; David
Bullock to Wilson Cary Nicholas, 22 February 1802, Nicholas Papers,
LC; T. Rutherford to Wilson Cary Nichols, 28 February 1802,
ibid.

35. James Hillhouse to Simeon Baldwin, 18 February 1802, Simeon
Baldwin Papers, YU; *Annals,* 7:1, 155–60; 183; Thomas Jefferson to
James Monroe, 3 February 1802, Jefferson Papers, LC; Thomas
Jefferson to Thomas Mann Randolph, 3 February 1802, ibid.;
Aurora (Philadelphia), 15 February 1802.

36. Henry Dearborn to James Bowdoin, 3 March 1802, *Bowdoin–
Temple Papers,* 224–26; John Clopton to James Monroe, 2 March
1802, Monroe Papers, NYPL; *Annals,* 7:1, 362–65, 476–77, 480, 510–
11, 518, 521–22, 523–949. Morton Borden, *The Federalism of James
A. Bayard* (New York, 1955), 106–25.

37. Thomas Jefferson to Thomas Mann Randolph, 21 February 1802,
Jefferson Papers, LC.

38. James A. Bayard to Richard Bassett, 8 March 1802, Bayard Papers,
LC.

39. Gouverneur Morris to Nicholas Low, 12 February 1802, Morris
Papers, LC; James Hillhouse to Simeon Baldwin, 10, 11 February
1802, Baldwin Family Papers, YU; *Columbian Centinel* (Boston),
20 February, 6, 17 March 1802; *The Republican; or Anti-Democrat*
(Baltimore), 10, 16 February 1802; *New York Evening Post,* 22
February 1802.

40. Thomas Jefferson to M. Volney, 20 April 1802, Jefferson Papers, LC.

41. Entry of 11 March 1802, Diary of Gouverneur Morris, Morris
Papers, LC; Gouverneur Morris to Robert R. Livingston, 20 March
1802, ibid.

42. T. Law to William Eustis, 4 August 1802, Eustis Papers, LC. See
also J. Dawson to Alexander J. Dallas, 4 March 1802, Dallas Papers,
HSP; *Columbian Centinel* (Boston), 13 March 1802; *Washington
Federalist,* 16 March 1802; *Farmer's Museum of Literary Gazette*
(Walpole, N. H.), 23 March 1802.

CHAPTER IV

1. For Federalist divisions before 1800 see: Manning J. Dauer, *The
Adams Federalist* (Baltimore, 1953); Stephen Kurtz, *The Presidency of John Adams* (Philadelphia, 1957). For an interpretation
of Federalist divisions after 1800 which is different from mine see:
David H. Fischer, *The Revolution of American Conservatism, The*

Federalist Party in the Era of Jeffersonian Democracy (New York, 1965).

2. George Cabot to Timothy Pickering, 14 February 1804, Lodge (ed.), *Life and Letters of George Cabot,* 341.

3. *Annals of Congress,* 7:1, 41.

4. Fisher Ames to Christopher Gore, 13 December 1802, Ames (ed.), *Works,* I, 310.

5. William Plumer to Jeremiah Smith, 23 December 1803; John H. Morison (ed.), *The Life of Jeremiah Smith* (Boston, 1845), 213–15.

6. Kurtz, *Presidency of John Adams,* 219–38; Lyman Butterfield, "The Reconciliation of Jefferson and Adams," *Yale Review* XL (Winter 1959), 297–319; Levi Lincoln to Thomas Jefferson, 28 July 1801, Jefferson Papers, LC; Matthew Lyon to Thomas Jefferson, 4 April 1801, ibid.; James Gunn to John Rutledge, 16 March 1801, Rutledge Papers, UNC.

7. For my interpretation of Marshall I am most indebted to: Albert Beveridge, *Life of John Marshall* (4 vols., New York, 1916–19); Edward S. Corwin, *John Marshall and the Constitution* (New York, 1919), 25–52; Saul K. Padover, "The Political Ideas of John Marshall," *Social Research* XXVI (April 1956), 47–70; W. Mellville Jones (ed.) *Chief Justice John Marshall* (Ithaca, 1956); Robert K. Faulkner, *The Jurisprudence of John Marshall* (Princeton, 1968).

8. John Stokes Adams (ed.), *An Autobiographical Sketch by John Marshall* (Ann Arbor, 1937), 9–10.

9. Theodore Sedgwick to Rufus King, 11 May 1800, King (ed.), *Life and Correspondence of Rufus King,* III, 237.

10. Beveridge, *Marshall,* II, 374–84.

11. Fisher Ames to Christopher Gore, 18 December 1798, Ames (ed.) *Works of Fisher Ames,* I, 246.

12. Timothy Pickering to Rufus King, 5 January 1801, King (ed.), *Life and Correspondence of Rufus King,* III, 367; James McHenry to Oliver Wolcott, 22 January 1801, George Gibbs, *Memoirs of the Administrations of Washington and John Adams, edited from the Papers of Oliver Wolcott* (2 vols., New York, 1846), II, 469; Warren, *Supreme Court,* I, 172n.

13. Jonathan Dayton to William Paterson, 20 January 1801, cited in Gertrude S. Wood, *William Paterson of New Jersey* (Fairlawn, N.J., 1933), 166–67; James Hillhouse to Simeon Baldwin, 31 January 1801, Baldwin, *Life and Letters of Simeon Baldwin,* 43; Warren, *Supreme Court,* I, 175; Kathryn C. Turner, "The Appointment of Chief Justice Marshall," *William and Mary Quarterly* XVII (April 1960), 143–63.

14. For a different interpretation, one that strongly emphasizes the differences between Jefferson and Marshall, see Julian P. Boyd, "The Chasm that Separated Thomas Jefferson and John Marshall," Gottfried Dietze (ed.), *Essays on the American Constitution* (Englewood Cliffs, N.J., 1964), 3–20.

15. *Washington Federalist,* 3 March 1802; *New York Evening Post,* 7 July 1802; *Virginia Gazette and General Advertiser* (Richmond), 1 May 1802; *Republican; or Anti-Democrat* (Baltimore), 4 March 1802; *Farmer's Museum or Literary Gazette* (Walpole, N.H.), 16 March 1802; Warren, *Supreme Court* I, 210–11.

16. Roger Griswold to ?, 26 February 1802, Lane Collection, YU; See also: James Hillhouse to Simeon Baldwin, 4 February 1802, Baldwin Family Papers, YU; Ebenezer Matoon to Thomas Dwight, 11 February 1802, Dwight–Howard Papers, MHS; James Bayard to Andrew J. Bayard, 21 January 1802, Donnan (ed.), *Papers of James Bayard,* 146.

17. *Aurora* (Philadelphia), 16 January 1802.

18. *Annals,* 7:1, 181, 529–30, 606, 648–50, 737, 924.

19. *Annals,* 7:1, 178–80, 531, 552–53, 558, 585–90, 650–63, 759–60; S. Morse to Ephraim Kirby, 2 March 1802, Kirby Papers, DU; *Independent Chronicle* (Boston), 15 February 1802.

20. *Annals,* 7:1, 529–30, 579, 648–50, 767–94; Caesar A. Rodney to Thomas Jefferson, 20 March 1802, Jefferson Papers, LC; James Monroe to Thomas Jefferson, 12 February, 14 March 1802, ibid.; William R. Davie to Thomas Jefferson, 20 March 1802, ibid.

21. *Annals,* 7:1, 201, 205, 207; Thomas Jefferson to Thomas Mann Randolph, 28 March 1802, Jefferson Papers, LC.

22. William Cranch to Richard Cranch, 4 April 1802, Miscellaneous Bound Collection, MHS; *Annals,* 7:1, 1232–36.

23. James Monroe to Thomas Jefferson, 25 April 1802, Monroe Papers, LC.

24. *Annals,* 7:1, 1236.

25. James Bayard to Richard Bassett, 19 April 1802, Donnan (ed.), *Papers of James Bayard,* 153; Oliver Wolcott to Roger Griswold, 23 March 1802, Lane Collection, YU; entries of 3, 5 April 1802, Diary of Gouverneur Morris, Morris Papers, LC; James Bayard to John Rutledge 4 April 1802, Rutledge Papers, UNC; William Tilghman to Jeremiah Smith, 22 May 1802, Morison (ed.), *Life and Letters of Jeremiah Smith,* 148–49; Jeremiah Smith to William Tilghman, 7 June 1802, ibid., 149–50; *Oracle of Dauphin* (Harrisburg), 7 June 1802.

26. Samuel Chase to William Paterson, 6 April 1802, Samuel Chase Miscellaneous Manuscripts, NYHS.
27. Samuel Chase to William Paterson and John Marshall, 24 April 1802, Paterson Papers, Bancroft Transcripts, NYPL.
28. John Marshall to William Paterson, 6 April 1802, ibid.
29. John Marshall to William Paterson, 19 April 1802, ibid.
30. John Marshall to William Paterson, 3 May 1802, ibid.
31. William Paterson to William Cushing, 6 May 1802, ibid.; William Cushing to William Paterson, 29 May 1802, Cushing Miscellaneous Manuscripts, NYHS; William Paterson to John Marshall, 11, 18 June 1802, ibid.; There was a sixth Supreme Court Justice, Alfred Moore, but I have located no evidence relative to his opinion on this subject.
32. Entry of 24 April 1802, Diary of Gouverneur Morris, Morris Papers, LC; Borden, *The Federalism of James A. Bayard*, 125.
33. Ibid.
34. George Cabot to Oliver Wolcott, 21 October, 20 December 1802, Lodge (ed.), *Life and Letters of George Cabot*, 327–29; Henry W. DeSaussure to John Rutledge, 21 September 1802, Rutledge Papers, UNC. For Bassett's protest, which was widely republished and commented upon, see: *Aurora* (Philadelphia), 26, 27 August, 11 September, 4 October 1802; *New York Evening Post*, 2, 3, 4 September 1802; *Independent Chronicle* (Boston), 2, 6, 9 September 1802; *Virginia Gazette and General Advertiser* (Richmond), 4, 8 September 1802; *National Intelligencer* (Washington), 27 August 1802. See also Linda K. Kerber, "Oliver Wolcott: Midnight Judge," The Connecticut Historical Society, *Bulletin* 32 (January 1967), 25–30.
35. *National Intelligencer* (Washington), 4 October, 1 November, 17 December 1802; *Independent Chronicle* (Boston), 7 October 1802; *National Aegis* (Worcester, Mass.), 6 October 1802.
36. *Independent Chronicle* (Boston), 11, 21, 28 October 1802; Levi Lincoln to Thomas Jefferson, 29 October 1802, Jefferson Papers, LC; Benjamin Austin, *Constitutional Republicanism in Opposition to Fallacious Federalism* (Boston, 1803), No. LXXI, 295–302.
37. Cranch, 299–308.
38. William Plumer to Edward St. Loe Livermore, 21 December 1802, Plumer Papers, LC.
39. George Cabot to Oliver Wolcott, 20 December 1802, Lodge (ed.), *Life and Letters of George Cabot*, 328–29.
40. *Aurora* (Philadelphia), 24 November 1802; *National Intelligencer* (Washington), 17 December 1802.

41. *Independent Chronicle* (Boston), 8 November 1802; see also: *Pittsfield Sun*, 6 December 1802.

42. *Annals*, 7:2, 427–40, 31–78; *National Aegis* (Worcester, Mass.), 16 February 1803; *Pittsfield Sun*, 21 March 1803; *Klines Carlisle Gazette*, 9 February 1803.

43. *National Intelligencer* (Washington), 1 December 1802.

44. 1 Cranch, 309.

45. For example, see Beveridge, *Marshall*, III, 101–56.

46. The best historical treatment of the case is to be found in Warren, *Supreme Court*, I, 231–68. My only criticism of Warren is that he blunted his major insight by not pushing his thesis far enough.

47. *National Intelligencer* (Washington), 11, 13 May 1803; *Aurora* (Philadelphia), 23, 26, 30 April, 23 May 1803; *Independent Chronicle* (Boston), 16 June 1803; Warren, *Supreme Court*, I, 264–66.

48. Beveridge, *Marshall*, III, 605–6; Charles A. Beard, *Economic Origins of Jeffersonian Democracy* (New York, 1915), 454–55; Warren, *Supreme Court*, I, 264–66.

49. A different assessment of Jefferson's attitude toward the decision is to be found in Adrienne Koch, *Jefferson and Madison, The Great Collaboration* (New York, 1964), 227–34; and Sidney Hook, *The Paradoxes of Freedom* (Berkeley, 1962), 68–74.

50. Warren, *Supreme Court*, I, 246–48; see also: William Cranch to Richard Cranch, 23 February 1803, Cranch Papers, MHS.

51. *Washington Federalist*, 25 February 1803; *Charleston Courier*, 30 March 1803; William Cranch to Richard Cranch, 23 February 1803, Cranch Papers, MHS.

52. *Independent Chronicle* (Boston), 10 March 1803; *Annals*, 7:2, 425, 613, 143.

53. *Providence Gazette*, 26 June 1802; *National Intelligencer* (Washington), 19 July 1802; Caesar A. Rodney to Joseph H. Nicholson, 16 February 1803, Nicholson Papers, LC.

CHAPTER V

1. For much that follows I am indebted to Lynn Turner, "The Impeachment of John Pickering," *American Historical Review* 54 (April 1949), 485–507.

2. Beveridge, *Marshall*, III, 165n.

3. *Message From the President Enclosing Documents Relative to John Pickering* (Washington, 1803).

4. Article II. Section 4.

5. William Plumer to James Sheafe, 13 December 1802, Plumer Papers, LC; *Charleston Courier,* 22 March 1803.
6. Entry of 7 January 1804, Everett S. Brown (ed.), *William Plumer's Memorandum of Proceedings in the United States Senate, 1803–1804* (New York, 1923), 101; Lynn Turner, *William Plumer of New Hampshire, 1759–1850* (Chapel Hill, 1962), 122–24.
7. *Annals of Congress,* 7:2, 460, 544, 641–42, 645. For the lack of cohesion in the Republican majority at this time see William Barry Grove to John Steele, 25 February 1803, Wagstaff (ed.), *Papers of John Steele,* I, 368–69.
8. Thomas Jefferson to Thomas Cooper, 29 November 1802, Jefferson Papers, LC.
9. William Plumer to T. W. Thompson, 18 February 1803, William Plumer, Jr. (ed.), *Life of William Plumer* (Boston, 1857), 253.
10. Entry of 5 January 1804, *Plumer Memorandum,* 101.
11. William Plumer to Jeremiah Mason, 15 February 1804, Plumer Papers, LC.
12. Entry of 3 March 1804, C. F. Adams (ed.), *Memoirs of John Quincy Adams* (12 vols., Philadelphia, 1874–77), I, 299–300.
13. *Annals,* 8:1, 333.
14. Ibid. 334–43; Timothy Pickering to Stephen Higginson, 6 January 1804, Pickering Papers, MHS.
15. Entry of 3 March 1804, C. F. Adams (ed.), *Memoirs of John Quincy Adams,* I, 300; *Annals,* 8:1, 300; 345; *Independent Chronicle,* (Boston), 12 April 1804.
16. *Annals,* 8:1, 355, 359–61, 362; entry of 10 March 1804, C. F. Adams (ed.), *Memoirs of John Quincy Adams,* I, 302–3.
17. *Annals,* 8:1, 364.
18. Ibid. 366; entry of 12 March 1804, C. F. Adams (ed.), *Memoirs of John Quincy Adams,* 1, 308–9; entry of 10 March 1804, *Plumer Memorandum,* 173; William Plumer to John Park, 13 March 1804, Plumer Papers, LC.
19. Timothy Pickering to Theodore Lyman, 24 March 1804, Pickering Papers, LC. See also: Timothy Pickering to Rufus King, 3 March 1804, *Life and Letters of Rufus King,* IV, 362–63.
20. John Quincy Adams to John Adams, 8 March 1804, W. C. Ford (ed.), *Writings of John Quincy Adams* (5 vols., New York, 1914), III, 110; Timothy Pickering to Rufus King, 3 March 1804, *Life and Correspondence of Rufus King,* IV, 362–63.
21. *Annals,* 8:1, 367.
22. William Plumer to Theodore Lyman, 17 March 1804, Plumer

Papers, LC; John Quincy Adams to John Adams, 8 March 1804, Ford (ed.), *Writings of John Quincy Adams*, III, 106–14.

23. Timothy Pickering to Theodore Lyman, 11 February 1804, *Life and Letters of George Cabot*, 444. See also *The Republican Argus* (Northumberland, Pa.), 18 March 1803.

24. Federalists became more convinced than ever that the Republican attack on the judiciary was motivated by selfish reasons when Sherburne, one of the witnesses against Pickering, was appointed his successor. *Farmers Museum* (Walpole, N.H.), 14 April, 12 May 1804; *Newburyport Herald*, 20 January, 10 May 1804; Turner, *Plumer*, 131.

25. Timothy Pickering to Theodore Lyman, 14 March 1804, Henry Adams (ed.), *Documents Relating to New English Federalism, 1800–1815* (Boston, 1877), 359.

26. *Annals*, 8:1, 1182; James Stephenson to Moses Rawlings, 6 January, 24 March 1804, Rawlings Papers, Maryland Historical Society (MdHS).

27. Edward S. Corwin, "Samuel Chase," Allen Johnson and Dumas Malone (ed.), *Dictionary of American Biography* (*D.A.B.*, 20 vols., New York, 1928–36), IV, 34–37.

28. Samuel Chase to Governor Thomas Sims Lee, 22 August 1794, "Samuel Chase and the Grand Jury of Baltimore County," *Maryland Historical Magazine* VI (June 1911), 131–37.

29. James McHenry to George Washington, 14 June 1795, Bernard C. Steiner, *The Life and Correspondence of James McHenry* (Cleveland, 1907), 159. See also: William Vans Murray to James McHenry, 24 December 1795, ibid., 160; George Washington to Alexander Hamilton, 29 October 1795, John C. Fitzpatrick (ed.), *The Writings of George Washington* (39 vols., Washington, D.C., 1939–44), XXXIV, 349; George Washington to James McHenry, 28 January 1796, ibid., XXIV, 428–29; Oliver Wolcott Sr., to ?, 15 February 1796, George Gibbs (ed.), *Memoirs of the Administrations of Washington and John Adams, Edited from the Papers of Oliver Wolcott, Secretary of the Treasury* (2 vols., New York, 1846), I, 300.

30. [Thomas Cooper], *An Account of the Trial of Thomas Cooper, of Northumberland; on a Charge of Libel against the President of the United States* . . . (Philadelphia, 1800); Dumas Malone, *The Public Life of Thomas Cooper, 1783–1839* (New Haven, 1926), 121–30.

31. Francis Wharton, *State Trials of the United States during the Administrations of Washington and Adams* . . . (Philadelphia, 1849), 637–41.

32. Wharton, *State Trials*, 688–721; Smith, *Freedom's Fetters*, 334–58.

33. *Report of the Trial of the Honorable Samuel Chase* . . . (Baltimore, 1805), 22, 44, 63–64, 219, 223.

34. *American Commercial Daily Advertiser* (Baltimore), 18 August 1801; *Aurora* (Philadelphia), 15 January 1801.

35. John Adams to John Marshall, 30 July, 7 August 1800, C. F. Adams (ed.), *Works of John Adams*, IX, 66, 71–72.

36. Thomas Jefferson to Cyrus Griffin, 7 July 1802, Jefferson Papers, LC; see also: Cyrus Griffin to Thomas Jefferson, 15 July, 1802, ibid.

37. Samuel Chase to John F. Mercer, 6 March 1803, J. C. Wylie (ed.), "Letters of Some Members of the Old Congress," *Pennsylvania Magazine of History and Biography* XXIX (April 1905), 205–6.

38. *Annals*, 8:2, 675–76.

39. Thomas Jefferson to Joseph H. Nicholson, 13 May 1803, Jefferson Papers, LC; see also Caesar A. Rodney to Thomas Jefferson, 7 July 1803, ibid.

40. Nathaniel Macon to Joseph H. Nicholson, 26 July, 6 August 1803, Nicholson Papers, LC.

41. *National Intelligencer* (Washington), 20 May 1803; *Aurora* (Philadelphia), 24, 27 May 1803; *American and Commercial Daily Advertiser* (Baltimore), 13 June 1803; *Annals*, 8:1, 88–95; Timothy Pickering to Richard Peters, 6 January, 7 February 1804, Peters Papers, HSP; Timothy Pickering to Stephen Higginson, 6 January 1804, Pickering Papers, MHS; Erastus Root to DeWitt Clinton, 7 January 1804, Clinton Papers, CU; Roger Griswold to Oliver Wolcott, Jr., 8 January 1804, William Griswold Lane Papers, YU; *Newburyport Herald*, 24 January 1804.

42. Adams, *Randolph*, 94–96; *Annals*, 8:1, 1237–39.

43. Robert Goodloe Harper to James A. Bayard and Alexander Hamilton, 22 January 1804, Legal Men of Pennsylvania Collection, HSP; Joseph Hopkinson to Samuel Chase, 20 January, 14 March 1804, ibid.; Samuel Chase to Richard Peters, 22 January 1804, Peters Papers, HSP; James Winchester to Samuel Chase, 26 January 1804, Chase Papers, MdHS; Samuel Chase to William Paterson, 13 January 1804, Chase Misc. Mss., NYHS.

44. Richard Peters to Timothy Pickering, 24 January 1804, Peters Papers, HSP.

CHAPTER VI

1. John Randolph to Joseph H. Nicholson, 17 December 1800, Nicholson Papers, LC. On Randolph's life see: William Cabell Bruce, *John Randolph of Roanoke* (2 vols., New York, 1922); and Henry Adams, *John Randolph* (New York, 1882).

2. John Randolph to Joseph H. Nicholson, 1 January 1801, Nicholson Papers, LC.

3. John Randolph to James Monroe, 3 January, 15 June 1803, 28 February 1804, Monroe Papers, LC; John Randolph to Joseph H. Nicholson, 31 October 1802, Nicholson Papers, LC; Norman Risjord, *The Old Republicans* (New York, 1965), 18–39.

4. Cunningham, *Jeffersonian Republicans in Power*, 73–76; John Rutledge to Theodore Sedgwick, 11 January 1802, Sedgwick Papers, MHS; *Annals*, 7:1, 312.

5. Thomas Jefferson to Caesar A. Rodney, 31 December 1802, 24 February 1804, Jefferson Papers, LC.

6. Samuel Taggart to the Reverend John Taylor, 13 January 1804, George Haynes (ed.), "Letters of Samuel Taggart, Representative in Congress, 1803–1814," American Antiquarian Society *Proceedings*, new series, 33 (April 1923), 125; Roger Griswold to Oliver Wolcott, 11 March 1804, Lane Collection, YU; Cunningham, *Jeffersonian Republicans in Power*, 76–77.

7. The ideological and constitutional dimensions of the debate over the kinds of governments to establish in the territories obtained by the Louisiana purchase is a subject much in need of analysis. Some help along these lines may be found in: James E. Scanlon, "A Sudden Conceit: Jefferson and the Louisiana Government Bill of 1804," *Louisiana History* IX (Spring 1968), 139–62; Lowell H. Harrison, *John Breckinridge: Jeffersonian Republican* (Louisville, 1969), 164–70; Dumas Malone, *Jefferson the President: First Term, 1801–1805* (Boston, 1970), 348–63; Everett Somerville Brown, *The Constitutional History of the Louisiana Purchase* (Berkeley, 1920), 72–73, 79, 85–88.

8. Entry of 26 January 1803, *Plumer Memorandum*, 122–23.

9. Thomas Jefferson to George Clinton, 2 December 1803, DeWitt Clinton Papers, CU.

10. John Randolph to Thomas Jefferson, 30 November 1803, Jefferson Papers, LC; Thomas Jefferson to John Randolph, 1 December 1803, Ford (ed.), *Works of Jefferson*, X, 53–54; John Eppes to Thomas Jefferson, 14 April 1803, Edgehill–Randolph Papers, UVA.

11. Samuel Taggart to the Reverend John Taylor, 13 January 1804, "Letters of Samuel Taggart," American Antiquarian Society, *Proceedings*, 125; Erastus Root to DeWitt Clinton, 7 January 1804, Clinton Papers, CU; *Annals*, 8:2, 88–95.

12. Joseph H. Nicholson to William Jones, 24 April 1804, Uselma Clarke Smith Collection, HSP; Adams, *History*, II, 194–200; Harry Ammon, "James Monroe and the Election of 1808 in Virginia,"

William and Mary Quarterly XX (January 1963), 33–39; Paul Goodman, *The Democratic-Republicans of Massachusetts, Politics in a Young Republic* (Cambridge, 1964), 129–30; Sanford Higginbotham, *The Keystone in the Democratic Arch* (Harrisburg, 1952), 49–102; Delbert Harold Gilpatrick, *Jeffersonian Democracy in North Carolina*, 1789–1816 (New York, 1931–67), 127–78.

13. C. Peter Magrath, *Yazoo, Law and Politics in the New Republic* (Providence, 1966), 1–49; Brant, *James Madison, Secretary of State*, 233–40; Adams, *Randolph*, 31, 72, 89–106; Charles H. Haskins, "The Yazoo Land Companies," American Historical Association, *Papers* (Washington, 1891).

14. *Annals*, 8:1, 1102–4, 1107–15.

15. Baldwin, *Life and Letters of Simeon Baldwin*, 346–47; William Plumer to John Park, 15 February 1804, Plumer Papers, LC.

16. Oliver Wolcott to Roger Griswold, 3 March 1804, Lane Collection, YU; Schachner, *Aaron Burr*, 241–44.

17. Gideon Granger to DeWitt Clinton, 27 March 1804, Clinton Papers, CU; John Taylor to Wilson Cary Nicholas, 28 May 1804, Edgehill–Randolph Papers, UVA.

18. DeWitt Clinton to Morgan Lewis, 26 June 1804, Clinton Papers, NYHS; E. K. to James Kent, 10 April 1804, Kent Papers, LC. The administration, it is clear, watched the election very closely: J. Bailey to Thomas Jefferson, 9 June 1804, Jefferson Papers, LC; Samuel Mitchill to James Madison, 3 May 1804, Madison Papers, LC.

19. *Annals*, 8:2, 85, 726–63; ibid., 8:1, 1237–40.

20. *Annals*, 8:2, 86–92; Adams, *Randolph*, 94–98.

21. Adams, *History*, II, 208–10.

22. Entry of 26 November 1804, *Plumer Memorandum*, 203–4; Charles Carrol to Robert G. Harper, 12 January 1805, Harper–Pennington Papers, MdHS.

23. Uriah Tracy to James Gould, 10 December 1804, Gould Papers, Pierpont Morgan Library (PML); entries of 20, 24 December 1804, C. F. Adams (ed.), *Memoirs of John Quincy Adams*, I, 321–25; entry of 26 November 1804, *Plumer Memorandum*, 204.

24. Samuel Case to Roger Griswold, 8 November 1804, Lane Collection, YU; David M. Randolph to Samuel Chase, 25 December 1804, Chase Papers, MdHS; Edmund Lee to Samuel Chase, 29 January 1805, ibid.

25. *Annals*, 8:2, 92–100; entry of 2 January 1805, *Plumer Memorandum*, 236–39; T. Lowndes to Uriah Tracy, February 1805, Rutledge Papers, UNC.

26. Adams, *Randolph*, 90–93; entry of 2 February 1805, *Plumer Memorandum*, 269.

27. Samuel Taggart to the Reverend John Taylor, 4 January 1805, Haynes (ed.). "Letters of Samuel Taggart," American Antiquarian Society, *Proceedings*, 146; Cunningham, *Jeffersonian Republicans in Power*, 79.

28. Entry of 2 February 1805, *Plumer Memorandum*, 269–70; *National Aegis* (Worcester), 14 August 1805; *New England Palladium* (Boston), 15 February 1805; J. Fairfax McLaughlin, Matthew Lyon, *The Hampden of Congress* (New York, 1900), 453–57.

29. Samuel Taggart to the Reverend John Taylor, 20 January 1805, Haynes (ed.), "Letters of Samuel Taggart," American Antiquarian Society, *Proceedings*, 150.

30. Entry of 1 February 1805, C. F. Adams (ed.), *Memoirs of John Quincy Adams*, I, 343; Adams, *History*, II, 217.

31. *The North Carolina Journal* (Halifax), 4 February 1805; Archibald Roane to David Campbell, 26 February 1805, Campbell Papers, DU; *New York Evening Post*, 11 January 1805; *Connecticut Courant* (Hartford), 30 January 1805; Borden, *Bayard*, 145–46.

32. Entry of 19 February 1806, Adams (ed.), *Memoirs of John Quincy Adams*, I, 413.

CHAPTER VII

1. Uriah Tracy to James Gould, 4 February 1805, Tracy Papers, PML; *Annals*, 8:2, 100–101; William Plumer to James Sheafe, 9 January 1805, Plumer Papers, LC; Schachner, *Aaron Burr*, 264–65.

2. *Annals*, 8:2, 101–51.

3. *Annals*, 8:2, 151–52; entries of 7, 8 February 1805, C. F. Adams (ed.), *Memoirs of John Quincy Adams*, I, 347–48.

4. Entry of 9 February 1805, *Plumer Memorandum*, 280; Adams, *Randolph*, 100–101; *Annals*, 8:2, 153–65.

5. *Annals*, 8:2, 165–93.

6. Ibid., 193–221; entry of 11 February 1805, *Plumer Memorandum*, 282–83.

7. *Annals*, 8:2, 221–37.

8. Ibid., 237–57; entry of 15 February 1805, *Plumer Memorandum*, 290.

9. *Annals*, 8:2, 262–67; entry of 16 February 1805, *Plumer Memorandum*, 291; Beveridge, *Marshall*, III, 192–96.

10. *Annals*, 8:2, 291–96.

11. Timothy Pickering to Rufus King, 15 February 1805, King (ed.), *The Life and Correspondence of Rufus King*, IV, 439; Samuel Taggart to the Reverend John Taylor, 18 February 1805, Haynes

(ed.), "Letters of Samuel Taggart," *American Antiquarian Society, Proceedings,* 158–59; Ralph Izard to Mrs. Izard, 20 February 1805, Izard Family Papers, LC; Charles Carroll to Robert Goodloe Harper, 28 February 1805, Harper–Pennington Papers, MdHS; *Newburyport Herald,* 12 February 1805.

12. *Annals,* 8:2, 354–429; Alva Burton Konkle, *Joseph Hopkinson* (Philadelphia, 1931), 102–10; Samuel Taggart to the Reverend John Taylor, 23 February 1805, "Letters of Samuel Taggart," American Antiquarian Society, *Proceedings,* 164; entry of 21 February 1805, *Plumer Memorandum,* 297; entry of 20 February 1805, C. F. Adams (ed.), *Memoirs of John Quincy Adams,* I, 356.

13. *Annals,* 8:2, 429–84.

14. Entry of 23 February 1805, *Plumer Memorandum,* 300.

15. Entry of 27 February 1805, C. F. Adams (ed.), *Memoirs of John Quincy Adams,* I, 359; *Annals,* 8:2, 641–64; Henry St. George Tucker to St. George Tucker, 3 March 1805, Tucker–Coleman Papers (microfilm), UVA.

16. *Annals,* 8:2, 664–69.

17. Entry of 1 March 1805, C. F. Adams (ed.), *Memoirs of John Quincy Adams,* I, 364.

18. George Clinton to Pierre Van Cortlandt, 3 March 1805, Van Cortlandt Papers, NYPL; *Boston Repertory,* 5 March 1805.

19. John Quincy Adams to John Adams, 8 March 1805, Ford (ed.), *Writings of John Quincy Adams,* III, 108–11; Archibald Roane to David Campbell, 26 February 1805, Campbell Papers, DU; entry of 2 March 1802, *Plumer Memorandum,* 311–12; Samuel L. Mitchill to Mrs. Mitchill, 1 March 1805, *Harper's Magazine* LVIII (April 1879), 749.

20. William Plumer to Daniel Plumer, 25 February 1805, Plumer Papers, LC.

21. John Randolph to Joseph H. Nicholson, 30 April 1805, Nicholson Papers, LC. See also Creed Taylor to Charles Clarke, 17 February 1805, Taylor Papers, UVA.

22. Thomas Jefferson to Wilson Cary Nicholas, 26 March 1805, Ford (ed.), *Works of Jefferson,* X, 137–38. See also Thomas Jefferson to George Logan, 11 May 1805, Logan Papers, HSP.

23. Adams, *History,* II, 204–6; William Duane to Joseph Clay, 12 December 1805, Clay Papers, NYPL; John H. Saylen to James Monroe, 2 August 1806, Monroe Papers, LC; John Taylor to James Monroe, 27 February 1806, ibid.; William Duane to Thomas Jefferson, 12 March 1806, Jefferson Papers, LC. "As to the heads of departments approving or disapproving the acquittal of Judge Chase,"

wrote James Madison, "they did not I believe intermeddle during the trial with a subject exclusively belonging to another department and now that the constitutional decision has taken place, it would be evidently improper for themselves to pronounce for public use their opinion of the issue, however little disposed they may be to reserve, beyond the rules of official decorum." James Madison to ?, 29 May 1805, Madison Papers, LC.

24. John Randolph to St. George Tucker, 30 January 1805, John Randolph Papers (microfilm), UVA.

25. Rufus King to Timothy Pickering, 18 February 1805, King (ed.), *Life and Correspondence of Rufus King*, IV, 440.

26. Entry of 1 March 1805, C. F. Adams (ed.), *Memoirs of John Quincy Adams*, I, 365.

27. John Randolph to Joseph H. Nicholson, 9 March, 8 November 1805, Nicholson Papers, LC; Eldrid Simkins to Creed Taylor, 30 April, 20 July 1805, Taylor Papers, UVA.

28. *National Intelligencer* (Washington), 5 May 1805; Samuel Chase to Rufus King, 13 March 1805, King (ed.), *Life and Correspondence of Rufus King*, IV, 444–46.

29. *Annals*, 8:2, 68–61; Gordon L. Thomas, "Aaron Burr's Farewell Address," *Quarterly Journal of Speech* XXXIX (October 1953), 273–820.

30. Louis Marie Turreau to Charles-Maurice de Talleyrand, 9 March 1805, quoted in Adams, *History*, II, 406–7; Gideon Granger to Rufus Easton, 16 March 1805, W. V. N. Bay, *Reminiscences of the Bench and Bar of Missouri* (St. Louis, 1878), 598; Aaron Burr to Theodosia Alston, 10 March 1804, Davis, *Burr's Memoirs*, II, 359–60; James Ripley Jacobs, *Tarnished Warrior, Major James Wilkinson* (New York, 1938), 209–17.

31. Entry of 1 March 1805, C. F. Adams (ed.), *Memoirs of John Quincy Adams*, I, 364.

32. *Newburyport Herald*, 15 March 1805; John Randolph to Joseph H. Nicholson, 29 March 1805, Nicholson Papers, LC; John Randolph to Caesar A. Rodney, 30 March 1805, Rodney Papers, DHS.

33. Entry of 1 March 1805, *Plumer Memorandum*, 310–11.

34. Samuel Chase to Joseph Hopkinson, 10 March 1805, Chase Papers, NYPL; *Annals*, 8:2, 1213–14.

CHAPTER VIII

1. Michael G. Kammen, "Colonial Court Records and the Study of Early American History: A Bibliographical Review," *American*

Historical Review LXX (April 1965), 732–39; Stanley N. Katz, "Looking Backward: The Early History of American Law," *The University of Chicago Law Review* 33 (Summer 1966), 867–84.

2. On the condition of the bench and bar in America in the years immediately following the Revolution see: Francis R. Aumann, *The Changing American Legal System* (Columbus, 1940), 67–93; Anton-Hermann Chroust, *The Rise of the Legal System in America* (2 vols., Norman, 1965), II, 3–91; Charles Warren, *History of the American Bar* (Boston, 1913), 211–365; Perry Miller, *The Life of the Mind in America from the Revolution to the Civil War* (New York, 1965), 99–265; Roscoe Pound, *The Formative Era of American Law* (Boston, 1938), 38–81.

3. J. Hector St. John de Crèvecoeur, *Letters from an American Farmer* (New York, 1957), 135.

4. The quotations that follow are taken from the 1819 edition in the Library of Congress.

5. Entry of 23 December 1787, "Diary of John Quincy Adams," Massachusetts Historical Society, *Proceedings,* 2nd series, XVI, 358–59.

6. Chroust, *The Rise of the Legal Profession in America,* II, 18–20; John Bach McMaster, *A History of the People of the United States* (5 vols., New York, 1884), I, 344–48.

7. *American Law Review,* 40 (1906), 437; William Plumer, Jr., *Life of William Plumer* (Boston, 1856), 150–56; Chroust, *Rise of the Legal Profession in America,* II, 39–41; Roscoe Pound, *The Spirit of the Common Law* (Boston, 1963), 113.

8. Quoted in Thomas R. Meehan, "Courts, Cases, and Counselors in Revolutionary and Post-Revolutionary Pennsylvania," *Pennsylvania Magazine of History and Biography* XCI (January 1967), 3–34.

9. William Brockenbrough to Joseph Cabell, 8 June 1801, Cabell Papers, UVA.

10. Quoted in W. R. Fee, *The Transition from Aristocracy to Democracy in New Jersey, 1789–1829* (Somerville, New Jersey, 1933), 108.

11. William Hooper to James Iredell, 6 July 1785, McRee (ed.), *Life of James Iredell,* II, 125–26.

12. Louis B. Wright and Marion Tinling (ed.), *Quebec to Carolina in 1785–1786, Being the Travel Diary and Observations of Robert Hunter, Jr., A Young Merchant of London* (San Marino, 1943), 48–49.

13. Raymond Blackard, "Requirements for Admission to the Bar in Revolutionary America," *Tennessee Law Review,* XV (1938), 116–27.

14. Thomas Jefferson to John Garland Jefferson, 11 June 1790, Boyd (ed.), *The Papers of Thomas Jefferson*, XVI 480.
15. Alfred Z. Reed, *Training for the Public Profession of the Law* (New York, 1921), 116–18.
16. D. C. Kelbourn, *The Bench and Bar of Litchfield Connecticut, 1709–1809* (Litchfield, 1909), 181–214.
17. William Kent, *Memoirs and Letters of James Kent, LLD* (Boston, 1898), 112–17.
18. Quoted in John Belton O'Neall, *Biographical Sketches of the Bench and Bar of South Carolina* (2 vols., Charleston, 1859), I, 35.
19. Chroust, *Rise of the Legal Profession in America*, II, 74–76.
20. For Wythe's legal career, see: Lyon G. Tyler, "George Wythe," William Draper Lewis (ed.), *Great American Lawyers* (8 vols. Philadelphia, 1907–9), I, 51–90; John Sanderson, *Biography of the Signers of the Declaration of Independence* (Philadelphia, 1847), 633–41; B. B. Minor (ed.), *Wythe's Decisions of Cases in Virginia by the High Court of Chancery* . . . (Richmond, 1852), VII–XL; L. S. Herrink, "George Wythe," *The John P. Branch Historical Papers* III (June 1912), 283–313.
21. Quoted in David J. May, *Edmund Pendleton*, I, 228; *The Repertory* (Boston), 25 July 1806.
22. Thomas Jefferson to Ralph Izard, 17 July 1788, Boyd (ed.), *Papers of Thomas Jefferson*, XIII, 372.
23. Boyd (ed.), *Papers of Thomas Jefferson*, II, 492–507; 653–61.
24. Minor (ed.), *Wythe's Decisions*, XXII.
25. Ibid., XXI; *Commonwealth v. Caton et. al.*, 4 Call 5.
26. Thomas Jefferson to James Madison, 26 July 1780, Boyd (ed.), *Papers of Thomas Jefferson*, III, 507; John Brown to William Preston, 6 July 1780, "Glimpses of Old College Life," *William and Mary Quarterly* IX (October 1900), 80; Richard Henry Lee to Arthur Lee, 31 August 1780, James C. Ballagh (ed.), *The Letters of Richard Henry Lee* (2 vols., New York, 1914), II, 199.

CHAPTER IX

1. For much of the material in this and the following chapter, I am indebted to: Humphrey Marshall, *History of Kentucky* (2 vols., Frankfort, 1824); Mann Butler, *A History of the Commonwealth of Kentucky* (Louisville, 1834); William Esley Connelly and E. M. Coulter, *History of Kentucky* (5 vols., Chicago, 1922); Thomas Perkins Abernathy, *Three Virginia Frontiers* (Gloucester, 1962), 63–96.

2. Harry Innes to Jefferson, 27 August 1791, Jefferson Papers, LC. On conditions in Kentucky in 1792, see: E. M. Coulter, "Early Frontier Democracy in the First Kentucky Constitution," *Political Science Quarterly* XXXIX (December 1924), 665–77; Pratt Byrd, "The Kentucky Frontier in 1792," *The Filson Club History Quarterly* XXV (July, October, 1951), 181–203, 286–94; John D. Barnhart, *Valley of Democracy, The Frontier versus the Plantation in the Ohio Valley, 1775–1818* (Bloomington, 1953), 80-90.

3. Samuel M. Wilson, "The 'Kentucky Gazette' and John Bradford Its Founder," *The Papers of The Bibliographical Society of America* 31 (1937), 131–32.

4. For references to Paine see: *Kentucky Gazette* (Lexington), 19 November 1791, "H.S.B.M." 7 January, 4 February 1792; Arthur Campbell to Isaac Shelby, 20 March 1792, Durrett Collection, University of Chicago (UC). On Burgh see: "H.S.B.M.," *Kentucky Gazette* (Lexington), 26 November 1791, 18 February 1792.

5. Ibid., 15 October 1791.

6. Ibid., 24 December 1791.

7. Ibid., 7 January 1792.

8. Ibid., 15 October 1791; "Rob the Thrasher," ibid., 17, 24 December 1791.

9. Ibid., 18 February 1792.

10. Ibid., 24 September, 1, 8 October, 3, 10 December 1791, and 4 February 1792.

11. Ibid., 24 September, 1 October 1791; "The Disinterested Citizen," ibid., 22, 29 October, 31 December 1791, and 25 February 1792; "Little Brutus," ibid., 17, 24 December 1791; "X.Y.Z." ibid., 18 February 1792.

12. "The Disinterested Citizen," ibid., 11 February 1792, 1 October 1791.

13. "A.B.C." ibid., 4 February 1792; "X.Y.Z." ibid., 18 February 1792.

14. "Felte Firebrand," ibid., 12 November 1791; "The Disinterested Citizen," ibid., 22 October 1791.

15. "A.B.C.," ibid., 1 October 1791; ibid., 8 October 1791.

16. "Salamandar," ibid., 24 December 1791.

17. Ibid., 26 November 1791; "The Medlar"; ibid., 19 November 1791

18. Ibid., 15 October 1791.

19. "The Committee of Bourbon County," ibid., 15 October 1791.

20. Ibid., 15, 22 October 1791, 11 February 1792; "H.S.B.M.," ibid., 24 December 1791.

21. "H.S.B.M.," ibid., 19, 26 November 1791; "Philip Philips," ibid., 3 December 1791; "Torismond," ibid., 28 January 1792.

22. "A.B.C.," ibid., 8 October, 10 December 1791; "Felte Firebrand," ibid., 12 November 1791; "A Citizen," ibid., 17 December 1791; "X.Y.Z.," ibid., 14 January 1792.

23. H. Marshall, *History*, I, 353–96.

24. On George Nicholas see: High Blair Brigsby, *The History of the Virginia Federal Convention of 1788* (2 vols., Richmond, 1890), II, 281–98; Huntley Dupre, "The Political Ideas of George Nicholas," *Register Kentucky State Historical Society* 39 (July 1941), 201–23; Richard H. Caldemeyer, "The Career of George Nicholas" (Unpublished dissertation, University of Indiana, 1951).

25. Hubbard Taylor to James Madison, 17 December 1791, James Padgett (ed.), "The Letters of Hubbard Taylor to President James Madison," *Register of the Kentucky State Historical Society* 36 (April, July, October, 1938), 97.

26. "Speech in the Kentucky Convention," George Nicholas Papers, Durrett Collection, UC.

27. Ibid.

28. "House of Representatives"; "Senate"; "Governor"; "Right of Suffrage"; "Appointments to Office"; "Expense, Land Tax, Loan Office, etc."; "Religious Liberty and Tests"; "Bill of Rights"; "Slaves"; all in ibid.

29. The quotes that follow are taken from "Courts," ibid.

30. Article V, section 4.

31. Mss Journal of the Kentucky House of Delegates, June 1792, 7; also reprinted in *Kentucky Gazette* (Lexington), 23 June 1792.

32. H. Marshall, *History*, II, 24–27.

33. *Journal of the House of Representatives*, June 1792, 18, 33.

34. Hubbard Taylor to James Madison, 9 July 1792, *Register of the Kentucky Historical Society* (1938), 110–11; *Journal of the Senate*, June 1792, 9, 23, 24, 25; *Journal of the House*, June 1792, 13, 14, 29, 30.

35. *Journal of the Senate*, November 1793, 5; *Journal of the House*, June 1792, 32–33; Jon Mckinley to L. Draper, Fall 1846 (Memorandum of conversation), Boone Papers, Draper Collection, 12 C 47 (1–2), Wisconsin Historical Society (WHS), (microfilm).

36. *Journal of the House*, June, 1792, 18, 30; November 1793, 34; November 1794, 8, 10.

37. Connelly and Coulter, *History of Kentucky*, I, 318–46.

38. H. Marshall, *History*, II, 333.

39. W. R. Jillson, *The Kentucky Land Grants* (Louisville, 1925); Connelly and Coulter, *History of Kentucky*, I, 212–20.

40. Francois Andre Michaux, "Travels to the West of the Alleghany

Mountains," Reuben Gold Thwaites (ed.), *Early Western Travels, 1748–1846* (32 vols., Cleveland, 1934), III, 227–28.

41. Samuel W. Wilson, *The First Land Court of Kentucky, 1779–1780* (Louisville, 1923).
42. *1 Hughes Reports,* 134–69.
43. *Kentucky Gazette* (Lexington), 6 December 1794; "Tyrannoctonos," ibid., 31 January, 14 February 1795; "A Member of the Assembly," *Stewart's Kentucky Herald* (Frankfort), 14 July 1795.
44. *Journal of the House,* November 1794, 49, 64, 66–67, 68–71, 79, 81; Hubbard Taylor to James Madison, 3 February 1795, *Register of the Kentucky Historical Society,* (1938), 118–19; H. Marshall, *History,* II, 161–68.
45. H. Marshall, *History,* II, 156–57, 169.
46. *Kentucky Sessional Laws of 1795* (Frankfort, 1796), Chapter XV, Evans #30656.
47. Marshall, *History,* II, 175–76.

CHAPTER X

1. Article XI.
2. "A Plain Republican," *Kentucky Gazette* (Lexington), 8 June, 10 August, 19 October 1793; "Reuben Searchy," ibid., 16 March 1793, 1 March 1794; "Patrician," ibid., 27 April 1793; "Herald," ibid., 9 February 1793; "A Farmer," ibid., 29 December 1792, 2 February 1793; "Democratic Society of Kentucky in Bourbon County," ibid., 12 April 1794, 4, 11 October 1794; "Fools Will be Meddling," ibid., 18 October 1794.
3. Butler, *History of Kentucky,* 262; Charles Gano Talbert, *Benjamin Logan, Kentucky Frontiersman* (Lexington, 1962), 282–94; A. E. Martin, *The Anti-Slavery Movement in Kentucky Prior to 1850* (Louisville, 1918), 18–33.
4. *Journal of the House,* February 1797, 5–10; *Kentucky Session Laws,* February 1797, 194–95.
5. Quoted in Lowell H. Harrison, "John Breckinridge and the Kentucky Constitution of 1799," *Register of the Kentucky Historical Society* 57 (July 1959), 212.
6. *Journal of the House,* 101–2, 106, 155–62, 191–95, 199; *The Mirror* (Washington, Ky.), 24 February 1798; *Kentucky Gazette* (Lexington), 28 February 1798; H. Marshall, *History,* II, 233–36.
7. On Breckinridge see the following articles by Lowell H. Harrison: "John Breckinridge: Western Statesman," *Journal of Southern History,* XVIII (May, 1952), 137–51; "A Young Virginian: John

Breckinridge," *The Virginia Magazine of History and Biography* 71 (January 1963), 19–34; "A Virginian Moves to Kentucky, 1793," *William and Mary Quarterly* XV (April 1958), 201–13. Most, but not all, of this material has been brought together in Lowell Harrison, *John Breckinridge: Jeffersonian Republican* (Louisville, 1969).

8. Robert B. McAfee, "The Life and Times of Robert B. McAfee and His Family and Connections," *Register Kentucky State Historical Society* 25 (January, May, September, 1927), 218–19.

9. John Breckinridge to Isaac Shelby, 11 March 1798, Durrett Collection, UC.

10. "A Republican," *Stewart's Kentucky Herald* (Frankfort), 10 April 1798; *Kentucky Gazette* (Lexington), 14 March 1798.

11. "An Impartial Citizen," *Stewart's Kentucky Herald* (Frankfort), 24 April 1798; also in *Kentucky Gazette* (Lexington), 25 April 1798.

12. "Honestus," *Stewart's Kentucky Herald* (Frankfort), 1 May 1798; see also "A Friend to Order," ibid., 1 May 1798.

13. "A Republican," *Stewart's Kentucky Herald* (Frankfort), 10 April 1798.

14. "A Voter," ibid., 17 April 1798; William Warfield to John Breckinridge, 22 April 1798, Breckinridge Papers, LC.

15. "A Republican," *Stewart's Kentucky Herald* (Frankfort), 10 April 1798; "A Centinel," *Kentucky Gazette* (Lexington), 23 May 1798; A. E. Martin, *Anti-Slavery in Kentucky*, 18–33; Bernard Mayo, *Henry Clay* (Cambridge, Mass., 1937), 64–79; Levi Purviance, *The Biography of Elder David Purviance* (Dayton, 1848), 17–44.

16. "A Voter," *Stewart's Kentucky Herald* (Frankfort), 17 April 1798; "A Friend to Senates," *Kentucky Gazette* (Lexington), 25 April 1798; "Cassius," ibid., 2 May 1798; H. Marshall, *History*, II, 246–47.

17. H. Marshall, *History*, II, 252.

18. James Brown to Jefferson, 15 September 1798, Jefferson Papers, LC; Ethelbert Dudley Warfield, *The Kentucky Resolutions of 1798* (New York, 1887), 21–48.

19. Adrienne Koch and Harry Ammon, "The Virginia and Kentucky Resolutions: An Episode in Jefferson's and Madison's Defense of Civil Liberties," *William and Mary Quarterly* V (April 1948), 147–76.

20. *Kentucky Gazette* (Lexington), 1, 21 August 1798; *The Palladium* (Frankfort), 9, 27 August, 18 September 1798; Warfield, *Kentucky Resolutions of 1798*, 21–48; James Morton Smith, "The Grass Roots Origins of the Kentucky Resolutions," *William and Mary Quarterly* XXVII (April 1970), 221–45.

21. W. C. Nicholas to Jefferson, 4 October 1798, Jefferson Papers, LC; W. C. Nicholas to Breckinridge, 10 October 1798, Breckinridge Papers, LC.

22. Warfield, *Kentucky Resolutions of 1798*, 74–96; *The Mirror* (Washington, Ky.), 30 November 1798; John Adair to James Wilkinson, 14 December 1798, Durrett Collection, UC.

23. Hopkins to Breckinridge, 8 December 1798, Breckinridge Papers, LC; George Nicholas, *A Letter from George Nicholas of Kentucky to His Friend in Virginia Justifying the Conduct of the Citizens of Kentucky as to Some of the Late Measures of the General Government and Correcting Certain False Statements Which Have Been Made in the Different States of the Views and Action of the People of Kentucky* (Philadelphia, 1799).

24. Hopkins to Breckinridge, 8 December 1798, Breckinridge Papers, LC; Hubbard Taylor to James Madison, 3 January 1799, *Register of the Kentucky State Historical Society* (1938), 217.

25. *Kentucky Gazette* (Lexington), 31 January, 11 April 1799; *The Mirror* (Washington, Ky.), 3 April 1799; George Nicholas to John Breckinridge, 20 January 1799, Breckinridge Papers, LC.

26. "A Voter who does not wish to be a Committeeman," *The Palladium* (Frankfort), 21 March, 4 April 1799.

27. Connelley and Coulter, *History of Kentucky*, I, 400–402; Lowell Harrison, "John Breckinridge and the Kentucky Constitution of 1799," *Register of the Kentucky Historical Society* (July 1959), 227–33.

28. "Notes on the Debates," 30 July–2 August 1799, Breckinridge Papers, LC; Joseph H. Parks, *Felix Grundy* (Baton Rouge, 1940), 12–13.

29. Ninian Edwards, *History of Illinois from 1788 to 1833 and Life and Times of Ninian Edwards* (Springfield, 1870), 16–17.

30. Ninian Edwards to His Father, 12 October 1799, Ninian Edwards Papers, Chicago Historical Society (CHS).

31. Breckinridge to Samuel Meredith, 7 August 1796, Breckinridge Papers, LC; H. Marshall, *History*, II, 178–82; Connelley and Coulter, *History of Kentucky*, I, 488–89.

32. Parks, *Grundy*, 1–12; James Brown to Henry Clay, 27 February 1806, Hopkins (ed.), *Papers of Henry Clay*, I, 221.

33. Henry Clay to John Breckinridge, 18 December 1800, Hopkins (ed.), *The Papers of Henry Clay*, I, 145; *Kentucky Gazette* (Lexington), 17 November, 15 December 1800, 2 February 1801.

34. *The Palladium* (Frankfort), 20 November 1801.

35. Ibid., 11 December 1801.

36. Ibid., 27 November 1801.

37. Ibid., 27 November 1801.
38. Ibid., 11 December 1801.
39. *Stewart's Kentucky Herald* (Frankfort), 17 March 1801.
40. "A Citizen," *The Palladium* (Frankfort), 14 July 1801; ibid., 27 November, 4 December 1801.
41. *Kentucky Gazette* (Lexington), 12 January 1801.
42. *The Palladium* (Frankfort), 4 December 1801.
43. Ibid., 3 February 1801; Thomas Todd to Breckinridge, 9 November 1801, Breckinridge Papers, LC.
44. Parks, *Grundy*, 16–17; Marshall, *History*, II, 179; *The Guardian of Freedom* (Frankfort), 20 November 1801; *Kentucky Gazette* (Lexington), 27 November 1801; B. Howard to Breckinridge, 15 December 1801, Breckinridge Papers, LC; S. Hopkins to Breckinridge, 21 November, 20 December 1801, ibid. Transcripts of the debate can be found in *The Palladium* (Frankfort), 20, 27 November, 4, 11 December 1801, and the *Kentucky Gazette* (Lexington), 11, 18, 25 December 1801, 1 January 1802.
45. Parks, *Grundy*, 47.
46. S. Hopkins to Breckinridge, 26 January 1803, Breckinridge Papers, LC.
47. *The Palladium* (Frankfort), 18 November, 30 December 1802, 6 January 1803; *Guardian of Freedom* (Frankfort), 22 December 1802; *Kentucky Gazette* (Lexington), 25 January, 2 February 1803.
48. Lucius P. Little, *Ben Hardin: His Times and Contemporaries, with Selections from his Speeches* (Louisville, 1887), 469.
49. Marshall, *History*, II, 350–52.
50. "Hibernian," *Kentucky Gazette* (Lexington), 27 March, 17 April 1804; Mayo, *Clay*, 96–97; Butler, *History of Kentucky*, 301.

CHAPTER XI

1. The secondary materials for Pennsylvania politics during the period 1799–1808 are unusually good. The ones I have found most useful are: William M. Meigs, "Pennsylvania Politics Early in This Century," *Pennsylvania Magazine of History and Biography* XVII (No. 4, 1893), 462–90; James H. Pelling, "Governor McKean and the Pennsylvania Jacobins, 1799–1808," ibid., LIV (October 1930), 320–54; Elizabeth K. Henderson, "The Attack on the Judiciary in Pennsylvania, 1800–1810," ibid. LXI (April 1937), 113–36; Glen LeRoy Bushey, "William Duane, Crusader for Judicial Reform," *Pennsylvania History* V (July 1938), 141–56; Russel J. Ferguson, *Early Western Pennsylvania Politics* (Pittsburgh, 1938), 176–209; Sanford

W. Higginbotham, *The Keystone in the Democratic Arch: Pennsylvania Politics, 1800–1816* (Harrisburg, 1952).

2. James Hedley Pelling, "The Public Life of Thomas McKean, 1734–1817" (Unpublished doctoral dissertation, The University of Chicago, 1929); David Paul Brown, *The Forum: or Forty Years Full Practice at the Philadelphia Bar* (2 vols., Philadelphia, 1856), I, 320–49; William Vans Murray to John Quincy Adams, 3 December 1799, "Letters of William Vans Murray," American Historical Association, *Report* (1912), 628; John Adams to Christopher Gadsden, 16 April 1801, C. F. Adams (ed.), *Works of John Adams*, IX, 584.

3. Raymond Walters, Jr., *Alexander James Dallas* (Philadelphia, 1943); Brown, *Forum*, I, 529–41; Oliver Wolcott to Alexander Hamilton, 1 April 1799, John C. Hamilton (ed.), *Works of Alexander Hamilton* (7 vols., New York, 1850–51), VI, 406; James A. Bayard to Alexander Hamilton, 8 March 1801, ibid., VI, 523; Thomas Leiper to Thomas Jefferson, 11 February 1801, Jefferson Papers, LC.

4. John M. Coleman, "Thomas McKean and the Origin of an Independent Judiciary," *Pennsylvania History* XXXIV (April 1967), 111–30; Thomas McKean to Thomas Jefferson, 10 August 1801, Jefferson Papers, LC; Alexander J. Dallas to Albert Gallatin, 14 June, 18 August 1801, Gallatin Papers, NYHS; Albert Gallatin to Thomas Jefferson, 10, 17 August 1801, Jefferson Papers, LC; William Duane to Thomas Jefferson, 18 October 1802, ibid.; *Aurora* (Philadelphia), 6, 8, 9, 10, 12, 15 February 1802; Higginbotham, *Keystone in the Democratic Arch*, 40–43.

5. Claude G. Bowers, "William Duane," *D.A.B.*, V, 467–68; Allen C. Clark, "William Duane," Columbia Historical Society, *Records*, IX, 19–21; Smith, *Freedom's Fetters*, 277–306, By far the best and fullest treatment of Duane's career is Kim T. Phillips, "William Duane, Revolutionary Editor" (Unpublished doctoral dissertation, University of California, Berkeley, 1968).

6. Michael Leib to Caesar A. Rodney, 19 May 1803 [1808?], Gratz Collection, HSP; James H. Peeling, "Michael Leib," *Dictionary of American Biography*, XI, 149–50.

7. Harry M. Tinkcom, *Republicans and Federalists in Pennsylvania, 1790–1801* (Harrisburg, 1950), 220–24; *Gazette of the United States* (Philadelphia), 6, 14, 16, 28 August 1799; *Aurora* (Philadelphia), 1, 3 February, 1, 22, 24 December 1802; Alexander J. Dallas to Albert Gallatin, 30 March 1802, Gallatin Papers, NYHS.

8. Alexander J. Dallas to Albert Gallatin, 4 April 1805, Gallatin Papers, NYHS.

9. Thomas McKean to Thomas Jefferson, 10 August 1801, Jefferson

Papers, LC; Albert Gallatin to Thomas Jefferson, 21 March 1803, ibid.; Thomas Hockley to Moses Austin, 1 September 1801, Eugene C. Barker (ed.), "The Papers of Moses and Stephen Austin," American Historical Association, *Report* (1919), II, 77.

10. Higginbotham, *Keystone in the Democratic Arch*, 25–47.

11. *Pennsylvania Archives*, 4th series, IV, 460–61; *Aurora* (Philadelphia), 27 September 1802.

12. *Pennsylvania Archives*, 4th series, IV, 461, 478; Higginbotham, *Keystone in the Democratic Arch*, 51; *Oracle of Dauphin* (Harrisburg), 28 March 1803.

13. See Senate Journals and House Journals, 1799–1801; see also Henderson, "The Attack on the Judiciary in Pennsylvania," *Pennsylvania Magazine of History and Biography* LXI (1937), 117–18.

14. James H. Peeling, "Simon Snyder," *D.A.B.*, XVII, 389–90; John Binns, *Recollections of the Life of John Binns* (Philadelphia, 1854), 347–49.

15. Higginbotham, *Keystone in the Democratic Arch*, 81–82.

16. John D. Wade, "John Binns," *D.A.B.*, II, 282–83; Binns, *Recollections*, 78–139.

17. *Pennsylvania Archives*, 4th series, IV, 496–500.

18. For a copy of the Arbitration Bill see *Republican Argus* (Northumberland), 25 March 1803; Higginbotham, *Keystone in the Democratic Arch*, 52–53.

19. *Pennsylvania Archives*, 4th series, IV, 519–22.

20. Brown, *Forum*, I, 344–55.

21. Thomas McKean to Thomas Jefferson, 4 February 1803, McKean Papers, HSP.

22. Ferguson, *Early Western Pennsylvania Politics*, 115–16.

23. Ibid., 168–71.

24. Higginbotham, *Keystone in the Democratic Arch*, 54.

25. Thomas Lloyd, *The Trial of Alexander Addison* (Lancaster, 1803); *Kline's Carlisle Weekly Gazette*, 26 January 1803; *Pittsburgh Gazette*, 22 January 1803; *Gettysburgh Gazette*, 4, 11 February 1803.

26. Thomas McKean to Thomas Jefferson, 4 February 1803, McKean Papers, HSP; *Kline's Carlisle Weekly Gazette*, 6 April 1803; *Oracle of Dauphin* (Harrisburg), 7 February 1803; *Aurora* (Philadelphia), 29 March 1803.

27. Higginbotham, *Keystone in the Democratic Arch*, 55–57; William Hamilton (ed.), *Report of the Trial and Acquittal of Edward Shippen, Esquire Chief Justice, and Jasper Yeates and Thomas Smith Esquires, Assistant Justices, of the Supreme Court of Penn-*

sylvania, On an Impeachment Before the Senate of the Common-wealth, January 1805 (Lancaster, 1805), 6–8; Edward Shippen to Jasper Yeates, 13 February 1804, Legal Men of Pennsylvania Collection, HSP.

28. *Aurora* (Philadelphia), 31 March 1803.

29. Higginbotham, *Keystone in the Democratic Arch,* 55–58.

30. *Republican Argus* (Northumberland), 15, 22, 29 July, 5, 12, 19, 26 August, 2, 9, 16 September 1803; "Littleton," Nos. I-VII, *Aurora* (Philadelphia), 23, 26, 30 April, 2, 3, May 1803; "Philadelphiensis," ibid., 10 May 1803; "Arastus," ibid., 11, 13 May 1803.

31. *Kline's Carlisle Weekly Gazette,* 3 August 1803; C. R. Wilson to Thomas Rodney, 10 May 1803, C. A. Rodney Papers, NYPL; James Hopkins to Alexander J. Dallas, 28 May 1803, Dallas Papers, HSP; *The Oracle of Dauphin* (Harrisburg), 4 October 1802; Nathaniel B. Boileau to Jonathan Roberts, 10 December 1802, Roberts Papers, HSP; Higginbotham, *Keystone in the Democratic Arch,* 53–65.

32. *Frederick Town Herald,* 30 April 1803; *Gazette of the United States* (Philadelphia), 12, 16 February 1802; *Gettysburg Gazette,* 1 July 1803; *The Oracle of Dauphin* (Harrisburg), 28 January 1804.

33. *Oracle of Dauphin* (Harrisburg), 31 March 1804; *Sprig of Liberty* (Gettysburg), 3 February 1804; *Republican Argus* (Northumberland), 2, 9 March, 27 April, 25 May, 1 June 1804; Thomas McKean to Thomas McKean, Jr., 15 March 1804, McKean Papers, HSP.

34. Thomas McKean to Thomas McKean Jr., 29 March 1804, McKean Papers, HSP; Thomas McKean to Thomas Jefferson, 18 February 1805, Jefferson Papers, LC; Higginbotham, *Keystone in the Democratic Arch,* 66–67.

35. *Aurora* (Philadelphia), 6 April 1804; *Gazette of the United States* (Philadelphia), 22 December 1804; Thomas McKean to Thomas Jefferson, 16 February 1805, McKean Papers, HSP; Walters, Dallas, 129.

36. "Moderator," Nos. I–IV, *Pennsylvania Correspondent and Farmers Adventurer* (Doylestown), 4, 11, 18, 25 September, 9 October 1804; *Freeman's Journal* (Philadelphia), September–November 1804; *Aurora* (Philadephia), September–November 1804; William Duane to Joseph H. Nicholson, 20 October 1804, Uselma Clarke Smith Collection, HSP.

37. For the full proceedings of the trial see: William Hamilton, *Report of the Trial of E. Shippen, J. Yeates and T. Smith . . . before the Senate of the Commonwealth . . . .*

38. William Barton to ?, 28 January 1805, Dallas Papers, HSP; John

Hopkins to Alexander J. Dallas, 28 January 1805, ibid., HSP; Thomas McKean to Thomas Jefferson, 18 February 1805, Jefferson Papers, LC.

39. *Aurora* (Philadelphia), 30 January 1805; *Oracle of Dauphin* (Harrisburg), 2 February 1805.

CHAPTER XII

1. Alexander J. Dallas to Albert Gallatin, 26 January 1805, Gallatin Papers, NYHS.
2. "Amicus," *Aurora* (Philadelphia), 9, 20 February 1805; ibid., 23 February 1805; Nathaniel Boileau to Alexander J. Dallas, 25 March 1805, Dallas Papers, HSP; Nathaniel Boileau to Jonathan Roberts, 1 March 1805, Roberts Papers, HSP; *Crawford Weekely Messenger* (Meadville), 20 March 1805; *Sprig of Liberty* (Gettysburg), 18 March 1805.
3. *Freeman's Journal* (Philadelphia), 28 February 1805.
4. Ibid., 18, 23 March 1805; John Kean to Alexander J. Dallas, 20 March 1805, Dallas Papers, HSP.
5. *Aurora* (Philadelphia), 3, 5 June 1805; Also reprinted in *Dauphin Guardian* (Harrisburg), 15 June 1805; *Crawford Weekly Messenger* (Meadville), 10 July 1805. For the most careful treatment of the episode see Higginbotham, *Keystone in the Democratic Arch*, 84–86.
6. *Pennsylvania Archives*, 4th series, IV, 560–66.
7. *Aurora* (Philadelphia), 5 April 1805; Higginbotham, *Keystone in the Democratic Arch*, 87–89.
8. Thomas McKean to Thomas McKean, Jr., 6 April 1805, McKean Papers, HSP; *Lancaster Journal*, 6 April 1805.
9. For the radical point of view at this time see: *Aurora* (Philadelphia), May–October 1805; *Republican Argus* (Northumberland), May–October 1805; *Commonwealth* (Pittsburgh), 24 July–October 1805; *Crawford Weekly Messenger* (Meadville), 7 August 1805; "Hamden," *Sprig of Liberty* (Gettysburg), 26 September 1805; "Democritus," *Dauphin Guardian* (Harrisburg), 13, 27 July, 31 August 1805.
10. Philip S. Foner (ed.), *The Complete Writings of Thomas Paine* (2 vols., Binghamton, New York, 1945), II, 995, 1006.
11. Ibid., II, 1004.
12. Jesse Higgins, *Sampson Against the Philistines, or the Reformation of Lawsuits; and Justice made Cheap, Speedy, and Brought Home to Every Man's Door; Agreeably to the Principles of the Ancient Trial By Jury, Before the Same Was Innovated by Judges and Lawyers,* 2nd. edition (Philadelphia, 1805), iv; H. C. Conrad, *His-*

tory of the State of Delaware (3 vols., Wilmington, 1908), II, 528–30.
13. *Sampson Against the Philistines,* iv., 12.
14. Ibid., 30, 16.
15. Ibid., 30.
16. Ibid., 38.
17. Ibid., 111.
18. *Freeman's Journal* (Philadelphia), 28 May 1805.
19. "Philanthropist," *Pennsylvania Correspondent* (Doylestown), 11
    June 1805; "Juvenis," Nos. I–IV, ibid., 11, 18 June, 2 July, 5 Au-
    gust 1805; "A Farmer," ibid., 12 August 1805; "A Democratic-
    Republican," ibid., 23 April 1805; *Dauphin Guardian* (Harrisburg),
    20 July, 14 September 1805; "A Citizen," ibid., 29 June 1805;
    "Subscriber," ibid., 22 June 1805; *Crawford Weekly Messenger*
    (Meadville), 31 July 1805; "Miles Et Civis," ibid., 4, 11, 26 Sep-
    tember, 6 October 1895; Andrew Gregg to Joseph Heister, 9 August
    1805, Gratz Collection, HSP.
20. Walters, *Dallas,* 138–40.
21. George M. Dallas (ed.), *Life and Writings of Alexander James
    Dallas* (Philadelphia, 1871), 211–17.
22. Ibid., 221, 222.
23. Ibid., 233.
24. *Dauphin Guardian* (Harrisburg), 14 September 1805; Hugh Henry
    Brackenridge to Alexander J. Dallas, 20 May 1805, Dallas Papers,
    HSP; *Crawford Weekly Messenger* (Meadville), 4 September 1805;
    Ferguson, *Early Western Pennsylvania Politics,* 185–95.
25. *Dauphin Guardian* (Harrisburg), 14 September 1805; *Freeman's
    Journal* (Philadelphia), 21 September, 3, 4 October 1805; Higgin-
    botham, *Keystone in the Democratic Arch,* 97–98.
26. *Pennsylvania Correspondent* (Doylestown), 23, 30 September 1805;
    John Rutledge to Robert G. Harper, 13 August 1805, Harper
    Papers, LC, *Dauphin Guardian* (Harrisburg), 29 June 1805; Tarle-
    ton Bates to Frederick Bates, 17 October 1805, Elvert M. Davis
    (ed.), "The Letters of Tarleton Bates," *Western Pennsylvania
    History Magazine* XII (January 1929), 52.
27. Albert Gallatin to Jean Badollet, 25 October 1805, Henry Adams,
    The Life of Albert Gallatin (Philadelphia, 1879), 331.
28. John Dickinson to Thomas McKean, 27 October 1805, McKean
    Papers, HSP; Thomas McKean to John Dickinson, 28 November
    1805, ibid.; William Findley to Thomas McKean, 24 December
    1805, ibid.
29. *Pennsylvania Archives,* 4th series, IV, 566–68, 571.
30. Higginbotham, *Keystone in the Democratic Arch,* 107–8.

31. Alexander J. Dallas to Albert Gallatin, 21 December 1805, Adams, *Gallatin*, 333.

32. Horace Binney, *The Leaders of the Old Bar in Philadelphia* (Philadelphia, 1859), 51; Thomas McKean to Thomas McKean, Jr., 4 January 1806, McKean Papers, HSP.

33. William Tilghman to Thomas McKean, 20 February 1806, McKean Papers, HSP.

34. Brown, *Forum*, I, 379–95.

35. *Pennsylvania Archives*, 4th series, IV, 604–6, 606–7, 612–19; Henderson, "The Attack on the Judiciary in Pennsylvania," *Pennsylvania Magazine of History and Biography*, LXI, 129–35.

36. Higginbotham, *Keystone in the Democratic Arch*, 103–270.

CHAPTER XIII

1. Robert J. Taylor, *Western Massachusetts in the Revolution* (Providence, 1954); Theophilus Parsons, *Memoir of Theophilus Parsons, Chief Justice of the Supreme Judicial Court of Massachusetts* (Boston, 1859), 162–63.

2. "Decius," *Independent Chronicle* (Boston), 30 January 1804.

3. Ibid.

4. William Sullivan, *An Address to the Members of the Bar of Suffolk, Massachusetts* (Boston, 1825); Frank W. Grinnell, "The Constitutional History of the Supreme Judicial Court of Massachusetts from the Revolution to 1813," *Massachusetts Law Quarterly* (May, 1917), II, 474–76.

5. Theophilus Parsons, *Memoir of Theophilus Parsons*, 192–93; *Independent Chronicle* (Boston), 26 December 1803, 30 January 1804.

6. Quoted in Grinnell, "The Constitutional History of the Supreme Judicial Court of Massachusetts," *Massachusetts Law Quarterly* (May 1917), 497–98; Theophilus Parsons, *Memoir of Theophilus Parsons*, 213–14.

7. This report is reprinted in its entirety in Grinnell, "The Constitutional History of the Supreme Court of Massachusetts," *Massachusetts Law Quarterly* (May 1917), 478–79.

8. *Acts and Laws of the Commonwealth of Massachusetts* (Boston, 1897), 1799, Chapter 82, 1800, Chapter 71.

9. Theodore Sedgwick to Harrison Gray Otis, 7 January 1804, Otis Papers, MHS; *Independent Chronicle* (Boston), 21 February 1803.

10. *Newburyport Herald*, 4 December 1804.

11. *Acts and Laws of the Commonwealth of Massachusetts* (Boston, 1898), 975–76; Samuel Eliot Morison, *The Life and Letters of*

Harrison Gray Otis, Federalist 1765–1848, 2 vols. (Boston and New York, 1918), I, 258–59.

12. Richard E. Welch, Jr., *Theodore Sedgwick, Federalist: A Political Portrait* (Middleton, Conn., 1965).

13. Fisher Ames to Christopher Gore, 24 Februray 1803, Ames, *Works*, I, 321.

14. Theodore Sedgwick to Theodore Sedgwick, Jr., 13 March 1803, Sedgwick Papers, MHS.

15. The quotations that follow are taken from Theodore Sedgwick to Harrison Gray Otis, 7 February, 27 May 1803, 7 January, 24 May 1804, Harrison Gray Otis Papers, MHS; "The Letter from the Court to Governor Strong in 1804," Grinnell, "The Constitutional History of the Supreme Judicial Court in Massachusetts," *Massachusetts Law Quarterly* (May 1917), 501–6. This last letter was signed by Francis Dana, Simeon Strong, Samuel Sewall, George Thatcher, and Theodore Sedgwick, and it was probably composed by Sedgwick. See also the two proposed judiciary bills in the *New England Palladium* (Boston), 29 January 1805, also most likely written by Sedgwick. For expressions of similar points of view on judicial reform, though not clearly by Sedgwick, see: *Columbian Centinel* (Boston), 12, 16, 19, 23, 30 April, 3, 7, 10, 17 May 1806; Isaac Parker to Henry Knox, 24 February 1804, Henry Knox Papers, MHS.

16. *Acts and Laws*, 1803, Chapter 154.

17. Ibid.

18. Ibid., 1804, Chapter 105.

19. Ibid., 1805, Chapter 80.

20. *Columbian Centinel* (Boston), 10 May 1806; *Newburyport Herald*, 4 December 1804; Parsons, *Memoirs*, 200–201; Theodore Sedgwick to Harrison Gray Otis, January 1804, Otis Papers, MHS.

21. *Independent Chronicle* (Boston), 30 January 1804.

22. *Pittsfield Sun*, 13 December 1806; *National Aegis* (Worcester), 6 March 1805.

23. *National Aegis* (Worcester), 27 February 1802.

24. *Independent Chronicle* (Boston), 25 February 1802.

25. Ibid., 24 September 1804; *National Aegis* (Worcester), 26 September 1804; Robinson, *Jeffersonian Democracy in New England*, 117.

26. *Pittsfield Sun*, 20 January 1803; *Independent Chronicle* (Boston), 5 May 1803; entry of 14 July 1803, Bentley, *Diary*, III, 33.

27. *Independent Chronicle* (Boston), 14 February 1803. "The Republicans should not try Courts of Justice so called unnecessarily." Entry of 2 July 1803, Bentley, *Diary*, III, 30.

28. *Pittsfield Sun*, 30 April, 14 July 1804; *Independent Chronicle* (Boston), 30 August 1804.

29. Grinnell, "The Constitutional History of the Supreme Judicial Court of Massachusetts," *Massachusetts Law Quarterly* (May 1917), 508–10.

30. *National Aegis* (Worcester), 2 March 1803; *Independent Chronicle* (Boston), 10 March, 18 April 1803.

31. *Independent Chronicle* (Boston), 31 January 1803; *National Aegis* (Worcester), 4 May 1803.

32. *Independent Chronicle* (Boston), 24 February 1803; *Pittsfield Sun*, 21 March 1803.

33. "Algernon Sidney," *National Aegis* (Worcester), 24 October 1804; "Agricola," *Independent Chronicle* (Boston), 30 August, 6 December 1804.

34. Fisher Ames to Christopher Gore, 24 February 1803, Ames, *Works*, I, 321; *Independent Chronicle* (Boston), 12 November 1804.

35. *Independent Chronicle* (Boston), 1 March 1804; see also ibid., 26 January, 23 February 1804.

36. Ibid., 20 June 1803.

37. *Acts and Laws* 1803, Chapter 125; *Independent Chronicle* (Boston), 1 March 1804.

38. "Zenas," *Pittsfield Sun*, 24 October 1803; "Justice," *Western Star* (Stockbridge), 12 November 1803.

39. "Camden," *Pittsfield Sun*, 19 December 1803.

40. "Zenas," ibid., 5 December 1803.

41. "Camden," ibid., 19 December 1803; see also "Remarks on the Judiciary," *Independent Chronicle* (Boston), 26 December 1803.

42. *National Aegis* (Worcester), 24 October 1804; also see ibid., 6 April 1803; *Independent Chronicle* (Boston), 12 November 1804; *Eastern Argus* (Portland), 4 January 1804.

43. L. F. Greene (ed.), *The Writings of the Late Elder John Leland* (New York, 1845), 289–91.

44. For example, see "Hawley," *National Aegis* (Worcester), 12 December 1804, 24 July 1805; *Columbian Centinel* (Boston), 12 July 1806.

45. *Independent Chronicle* (Boston), 30 January 1804.

46. Ibid., 21 February 1803.

47. Ibid., 11 June 1804.

48. "A Yeoman," Ibid., 27 August 1804; see also ibid., 21 February 1803, 1 March, 21 June 1804.

49. *Eastern Argus* (Portland), 28 June 1805.

50. "Decius," *Independent Chronicle* (Boston), 30 January 1804.

51. Ibid., 2 January 1804.

52. Ibid., 21 February 1803.
53. Ibid., 10 February 1806.
54. Ibid., 24 November 1806; see also ibid., 9 October–1 December 1806.
55. Ibid., 10 February 1806.
56. Ibid., 21 February 1803.
57. "Decius," ibid., 31 January 1804.
58. *Hampshire Gazette* (Northampton), 6 November 1805.
59. *Eastern Argus* (Portland), 1 November 1805; *New England Palladium* (Boston), 15, 26 March 1805, 1 December 1807; "Acirema," *Massachusetts Spy* (Worcester), 19 February 1806; "The Republican, No. VI," *The Repertory* (Boston), 3 August 1804; *Newburyport Herald*, 1 February 1805.
60. Thomas Dwight to John Williams, 19 May 1803, Dwight–Howard Papers, MHS.
61. "The Republican," Nos. IX and XIV, *The Repertory* (Boston), 17 August, 7 September 1804.
62. *Eastern Argus* (Portland), 1 November 1805; "The Republican," No. VII, *The Repertory* (Boston), 10 August 1804.
63. Theophilus Parsons to Governor Caleb Strong, 5 June 1806, Grinnell, "The Constitutional History of the Supreme Judicial Court of Massachusetts," *Massachusetts Law Quarterly* (May 1917), 478–79.
64. "Government of Law," *The Repertory* (Boston), 22 March 1804; "The Republican," No. VI, ibid., 3 August 1804; "Acirema," *Boston Gazette*, 13 February 1806; *Columbian Centinel* (Boston), 12 April 1806.
65. "The Caravansary," No. XVIII, *The Repertory* (Boston), 18 December 1804. "Justice, to be anything, must be stronger than government, or at least stronger than the popular passions." Fisher Ames to Thomas Dwight, 25 January 1804, Ames, *Works*, I, 337–38.
66. *Boston Gazette*, 13 February 1806.
67. *Columbian Centinel* (Boston), 12 April 1806.
68. *New England Palladium* (Boston), 1 January 1805.
69. Theodore Sedgwick to Theodore Sedgwick, Jr., 17 May 1804, Sedgwick Papers, MHS.
70. *New England Palladium* (Boston), 5 March 1805.
71. "The Republican," No. XIV, *The Repertory* (Boston), 7 September 1804.
72. *New England Palladium* (Boston), 5 March 1805.
73. *Columbian Centinel* (Boston), 12 April 1806.

CHAPTER XIV

1. I have been greatly aided in my understanding of Massachusetts politics during the Jeffersonian era by the following works: William A. Robinson, *Jeffersonian Democracy in New England* (New Haven, 1916); Anson Ely Morse, *The Federalist Party in Massachusetts to the Year 1800* (Princeton, 1909); and especially Paul Goodman, *The Democratic-Republicans of Massachusetts* (Cambridge, Mass., 1964).

2. Samuel Eliot Morison, "Elbridge Gerry, Gentleman-Democrat," *New England Quarterly* II (January 1929), 6–32.

3. Jacob Eustis to William Eustis, 27 December 1802, William Eustis Papers, LC; James Bowdoin to Henry Dearborn, April 1802, Massachusetts Historical Society, *Collections,* ser. 7, vol. VI (Boston, 1907), 230–31; *Independent Chronicle* (Boston), 15 April, 3 June 1802; Goodman, *The Democratic-Republicans,* 70–127, 128–30.

4. Richard Birdsall, "The Reverend Thomas Allen: Jeffersonian Calvinist," *New England Quarterly* XXX (June 1947), 147–65; Lyman H. Butterfield, "Elder John Leland, Jeffersonian Itinerant," *Proceedings of the American Antiquarian Society,* N.S. LXII (1952), 155–242; *Pittsfield Sun,* 13 December 1802.

5. Lawrence Boyd Evans, "John Bacon," *D.A.B.,* I, 478–79; Goodman, *Democratic-Republicans,* 81.

6. Massachusetts Historical Society, *Proceedings,* 2nd ser., IV, 63; Samuel Eliot Morison, "Benjamin Austin," *D.A.B.,* I, 431–32; see above, Chapter VIII, Section I.

7. Christopher Gore to Rufus King, 26 March 1806, King (ed.), *Life and Correspondence of Rufus King,* IV, 511.

8. Benjamin Austin, Jr., *Constitutional Republicanism in Opposition to Fallacious Federalism* (Boston, 1803), 6.

9. "The New England Man," No. IV, *The Repertory* (Boston), 3 August 1804; *Massachusetts Spy* (Worcester), 4 April 1804; William A. Robinson, "Levi Lincoln," *D.A.B.* XI, 262–64.

10. Levi Lincoln to Thomas Jefferson, 28 July 1801, Jefferson Papers, LC; Robinson, *Jeffersonian Democracy in New England,* 33n.

11. Levi Lincoln to Thomas Jefferson, 16 October 1802, 15 March 1803, Jefferson Papers, LC.

12. Thomas C. Amory, *Life of James Sullivan; with Selections from His Writings,* 2 vols. (Boston, 1859), *passim.*

13. James Sullivan to William Eustis, 13 January 1802, ibid., II, 97.

14. James Sullivan to Henry Dearborn, 11 May 1804, ibid., II, 135–38;

James Sullivan, *The Path of Riches: An Inquiry into the Origins and Uses of Money* (Boston, 1792).

15. Goodman, *The Democratic-Republicans*, 128–30; Henry Knox to Jefferson, 16 March 1801, Jefferson Papers, LC; Levi Lincoln to Jefferson, 28 July 1801, ibid.; Benjamin Waterhouse to William Eustis, 20 February 1803, William Eustis Papers, LC; Timothy Pickering to Stephen Higginson, 16 April 1800, J. F. Jameson (ed.), "Letters of Stephen Higginson, 1783–1804," American Historical Association *Annual Report* (1896), I, 836; Lodge, *Life and Letters of George Cabot,* 311–13.

16. Jacob Eustis to William Eustis, 30 October 1802, Eustis Papers, LC; Aaron Hill to William Eustis, 23 January 1803; Elbridge Gerry to Thomas Jefferson, 9 August 1802, Jefferson Papers, LC; Levi Lincoln to Thomas Jefferson, 28 July 1802, ibid.

17. Jacob Eustis to William Eustis, 10 February 1803, Eustis Papers, LC; N. Fellows to William Eustis, 12 February 1803, ibid.; Aaron Hill to William Eustis, 23 January 1803, ibid.; *Pittsfield Sun,* 28 February 1803.

18. *Independent Chronicle* (Boston), 15 April 1802.

19. Ibid., 11 April 1803; *National Aegis* (Worcester), 13 April 1803; John Bacon to Thomas Jefferson, 11 April 1803, Jefferson Papers, LC.

20. James Sullivan to Henry Dearborn, 11 May 1804, Amory, *Sullivan,* II, 135.

21. *Independent Chronicle* (Boston), 10 May 1804; *Columbian Centinel* (Boston), 26 February 1806; Goodman, *The Democratic-Republicans,* 130.

22. Levi Lincoln to Thomas Jefferson, 9 March 1805, Jefferson Papers, LC.

23. *Independent Chronicle* (Boston), 11, 14 February 1805; *Eastern Argus* (Portland), 1 February 1805; Christopher Gore to Rufus King, 10 March 1805, King (ed.), *Life and Correspondence of Rufus King,* IV, 448–49; entries of 4 November 1804, 5, 6 March 1805, William Bentley, *Diary of William Bentley,* 4 vols. (Salem, 1905–14), III, 122, 144; Benjamin Austin to Thomas Jefferson, 21 November 1804, Jefferson Papers, LC.

24. Levi Lincoln to Thomas Jefferson, 2 June 1805, Jefferson Papers, LC. See also *New England Palladium* (Boston), 5 March, 5 April 1805; *National Aegis* (Worcester), 5 June 1805.

25. "A.," *Independent Chronicle* (Boston), 7 April 1806.

26. "Civis," *Eastern Argus* (Portland), 20 September 1805.

27. "Brutus," *Independent Chronicle* (Boston), 7 April 1806; "Fair Play," *Eastern Argus* (Portland), 21 March 1806.

28. Levi Lincoln to Thomas Jefferson, 30 July 1805, Jefferson Papers, LC; see also ibid., 6 November 1805.

29. Levi Lincoln to Thomas Jefferson, 2 June 1805, ibid.; William Eustis to Thomas Jefferson, 10 June, 17 August 1805, ibid.; *Columbian Centinel* (Boston), 26 February 1806; *New England Palladium* (Boston), 14 March 1806; entry of 10 December 1808, Bentley, *Diary*, III, 401.

30. Josiah Dwight to Harrison Gray Otis, 18 November 1805, Otis Papers, MHS; *The Repertory* (Boston), 23 August 1805, 1 April 1806; *New England Palladium* (Boston), 25 March 1806; *National Aegis* (Worcester), 10 July 1805; Levi Lincoln to Thomas Jefferson, 9 March 1805, Jefferson Papers, LC; Mannaseh Cutler to Timothy Pickering, 15 February 1806, Pickering Papers, MHS.

31. Edward St. Loe Livermore to Timothy Pickering, 26 January 1806, Pickering Papers, MHS; Edward St. Loe Livermore to Theodore Sedgwick, 1 February 1806, Sedgwick Papers, MHS.

32. Edward Stanwood, "The Massachusetts Election of 1806," Massachusetts Historical Society, *Proceedings*, Ser. 2, XX (January 1906), 12–19; Levi Lincoln to Thomas Jefferson, 17 June 1806, Jefferson Papers, LC; James Sullivan to Thomas Jefferson, 21 April, 20 June 1806, ibid.; Amory, *Sullivan*, II, 158–60; *Columbian Centinel* (Boston), 14 June 1806.

33. *The Repertory* (Boston), 26 August, 1806.

34. Theophilus Parsons, *Memoir of Theophilus Parsons* (Boston, 1859), 193–94; Theodore Sedgwick to Harrison Gray Otis, 16 May 1806, Otis Papers, MHS; J. Upham to Theodore Sedgwick, 25 May 1806, Sedgwick Papers, MHS; J. Hooker to Theodore Sedgwick, 28 May 1806, ibid.; Timothy Bigelow to Theodore Sedgwick, 2 June 1806, ibid.; Isaac Parker to Theodore Sedgwick, 25 July 1806, ibid.; Theodore Sedgwick to Theodore Sedgwick, Jr., 9 December 1806, ibid.; Richard E. Welch, Jr., "The Parsons-Sedgwick Feud and the Reform of the Massachusetts Judiciary," *Essex Institute Historical Collections* XCII (April 1956), 171–87.

35. Charles Fairman, "Theophilus Parsons," *D.A.B.*, XIV, 273–74; Isaac Parker, *Sketch of the Character of the Late Chief Justice Parsons* (Boston, 1813), 8–12; Frank Gaylord Cook, "Theophilus Parsons," in William Draper Lewis, *Great American Lawyers*, 10 vols. (Philadelphia, 1908), II, 49–146; Fisher Ames to Christopher Gore, 5 October 1802, Ames, *Works*, I, 299–301.

36. Theophilus Parsons to John Jay, 5 May 1800, H. P. Johnston (ed.),

Correspondence and Public Papers of John Jay (4 vols., New York, 1890–93), IV, 268–69.

37. W. W. Story (ed.), *Life and Letters of Joseph Story*, 2 vols. (Boston, 1851), I, 130; Parsons, *Memoirs*, 232; Theophilus Parsons to Governor Strong, 5 June 1806, Grinnell, "The Constitutional History of the Supreme Judicial Court in Massachusetts," *Massachusetts Law Quarterly* (May 1917), 538–40.

38. Entry of 19 March 1803, Bentley, *Diary*, III, 16–17.

39. W. W. Story, (ed.), *Life and Letters of Joseph Story*, I, 130; Gerald T. Dunne, "Joseph Story: The Germinal Years," *Harvard Law Review*, 75 (February 1962), 707–54; George Edward Woodbine, "Joseph Story," *D.A.B.*, XVIII, 102–8; Jacob Crowninshield to Richard Crowninshield, 25 January 1803, Jacob Crowninshield Papers, Peabody Museum (PM); Jacob Crowninshield to Benjamin Lynde Oliver, 22 December 1805, ibid.

40. W. W. Story (ed.), *Life and Letters of Joseph Story*, I, 128.

41. Ibid., 130–35.

42. Christopher Gore to Theodore Sedgwick, 28 June 1806, Sedgwick Papers, MHS.

43. *Pittsfield Sun*, 16, 23 August 1806, reprinted in *Independent Chronicle* (Boston), 15, 19 January 1807.

44. Charles Warren, *Jacobin and Junto* (Cambridge, 1931), 183–214; Amory, *Sullivan*, II, 163–89; Christopher Gore to Rufus King, 5 August 1806, King (ed.), *Life and Correspondence of Rufus King*, IV, 538; entry of 4 August 1804, Bentley, *Diary*, III, 242.

45. *Independent Chronicle* (Boston), 8, 25 December 1806; entries of 6, 10 December 1806, Bentley, *Diary*, III, 266.

46. *Independent Chronicle* (Boston), 25 September 1806.

47. Samuel Sewall to Joseph Story, 20 January 1807, Joseph Story Papers, LC. See also Samuel Sewall to Joseph Story, 2 January 1807, ibid.; Theodore Sedgwick to Joseph Story, 5 January 1807, Sedgwick Papers, MHS.

48. *The Repertory* (Boston), 23 January 1807; *Newburyport Herald*, 27 January 1807. For a copy of the bill see *New England Palladium* (Boston), 23 January 1807.

49. *New England Palladium* (Boston), 17 March 1807; *Columbian Centinel* (Boston), 4 April 1807.

50. Amory, *Sullivan*, II, 199–200.

51. *Columbian Centinel* (Boston), 6 June 1807; entries of 6, 8 June 1807, Bentley, *Diary*, III, 299.

52. *Columbian Centinel* (Boston), 27 June 1807; Amory, *Sullivan*, II, 207–9; Goodman, *Democratic-Republicans*, 150.

53. "Jack Nips," *Pittsfield Sun,* 31 October 1804; "The Examiner," No. 81, *Independent Chronicle* (Boston), 18 June 1807; Moses Greenleaf to Eleazer Jenks, 10 February 1807, Edgar C. Smith, *Moses Greenleaf, Maine's First Mapmaker* (Bangor, 1902), 88.

54. John Bacon to Thomas Jefferson, 21 October 1807, Jefferson Papers, LC; James Sullivan to Thomas Jefferson, 7 December 1807, ibid.

55. *New England Palladium* (Boston), 29 January 1808; W. W. Story (ed.), *Life and Letters of Joseph Story,* I, 138–39; Theodore Sedgwick to Joseph Story, 9 December 1807, Joseph Story Papers, LC.

56. *Columbian Centinel* (Boston), 27 January 1808; *The Repertory* (Boston), 29 January 1808.

57. Entry of 24 February 1808, Bentley, *Diary,* III, 346.

58. Fisher Ames to Timothy Pickering, 10 March 1806, Ames, *Works,* I, 370; Goodman, *The Democratic-Republicans,* 118–27.

59. David Cobb to Charles Hare, 2 March 1806; Frederick S. Allis (ed.), *William Bingham's Maine Lands, 1790–1820,* Colonial Society of Massachusetts, *Collections,* 2 vols. (Boston, 1954), II, 1193–94; *Eastern Argus* (Portland), 28 March 1806; *Columbian Centinel* (Boston), 12 November 1806; *Independent Chronicle* (Boston), 1 May 1806; Robinson, *Jeffersonian Democracy in New England,* 42–46.

60. Benjamin Whitwell to Theophilus Parsons, 13 August 1804, University Collection, CU.

61. Harrison Gray Otis to Charles Willing Hare, 22 June 1805, Allis, *Bingham's Maine Lands,* II, 1189.

62. Hare's Report to Trustees, 11 February 1807, ibid., II, 1215–16.

63. Moses Greenleaf to Eleazer Jenks, 10 February 1807, Edgar C. Smith, *Moses Greenleaf, Maine's First Map-Maker* (Bangor, 1902), 88.

64. Goodman, *The Democratic-Republicans,* 157–58; *Acts and Laws,* 1809, Chapter 84.

65. George F. Talbot, "General John Chandler of Monmouth, Maine with Extracts from His *Autobiography*," Maine Historical Society *Collections,* series I, IX (1887), 200–201.

66. Ibid.

67. Amory, *Sullivan,* II, 272–77; Christopher Gore to Rufus King, 25 December 1807; King (ed.), *Life and Correspondence of Rufus King,* V, 41–42.

68. Goodman, *The Democratic-Republicans,* 159.

69. Ibid.

70. Ibid., 158–61; David Cobb to Charles W. Hare, 22 August 1810, Allis (ed.), *Bingham's Maine Lands,* II, 1233.

71. Parsons, *Memoirs*, 206–30; Parker, *Theophilus Parsons*, 14–18; Grinnell, "The Constitutional History of the Supreme Judicial Court in Massachusetts," *Massachusetts Law Quarterly* (May 1917), 524–36.

CHAPTER XV

1. Noble Cunningham, "Who Were the Quids?" *Mississippi Valley Historical Review* L (September 1963), 252–63.
2. Thomas Jefferson to Thomas Cooper, 9 July 1807, Jefferson Papers, LC.
3. John Taylor to James Monroe, 26 October 1810, Monroe Papers, LC.
4. Thomas Jefferson to Barnabas Bidwell, 5 July 1806, Jefferson Papers, LC.
5. Ibid.; John Randolph to George Hay, 3 January 1806, John Randolph Papers, LC (photostat); Michael Leib to Caesar A. Rodney, 1 April 1806, Gratz Collection, HSP; Risjord, *The Old Republicans*, 72–95; Harry Ammon, "James Monroe and the Election of 1808 in Virginia," *William and Mary Quarterly*, XX, 38–39.
6. Adrienne Koch, *Jefferson and Madison, The Great Collaboration* (New York, 1964), 174–232; Irving Brant, "James Madison and His Times," *American Historical Review* LVII (July 1952), 853–70.
7. *United States Gazette* (Philadelphia), 11 December 1801; *Hampshire Gazette* (Northampton), 30 December 1801; John Taylor to Wilson Cary Nicholas, 14 April, 14 May, 16 June 1806, Edgehill-Randolph Papers, UVA; John Randolph to James Monroe, 16 September 1806, Monroe Papers, LC; Littleton H. Tazewell to James Monroe, 8 October 1808, ibid.; John Adair to Mark Hardin, 13 March 1806, Hardin Collection, CHS; Michael Leib to C. A. Rodney, 19 May 1803 (08?), Gratz Collection, HSP.
8. Entry of 8 April 1806, Plumer, *Memorandum*, 478.
9. John Randolph to James M. Garnett, 4 September 1806, transcript John Randolph Papers, LC.
10. John Randolph to James Monroe, 20 March 1806, Monroe Papers, LC; Thomas Jefferson to Barnabas Bidwell, 5 July 1806, Jefferson Papers, LC; Anderson, *Giles*, 101–2; Risjord, *The Old Republicans*, 64–65.
11. James Brown to Thomas Jefferson, 25 July 1806, Jefferson Papers, LC; John Smith to Thomas Jefferson, August 1806, ibid.; Nathaniel Macon to Joseph Hooper Nicholson, 15, 21 April 1806, Nicholson Papers, LC; John Taylor to Wilson Cary Nicholas, 14 April 1806, Edgehill–Randolph Papers, UVA; William Duane to Joseph Clay,

12 December 1805, Clay Papers, NYPL; Risjord, *Old Republicans*, 72–95; Cunningham, *Jeffersonian-Republicans in Power*, 86–88.

12. Harry V. Ames, "The Proposed Amendments to the Constitution of the United States During the First Century of Its History," American Historical Association, *Annual Report* (1896), II, 144–64.

13. Albert Gallatin to Thomas Jefferson, 15 February 1804, Jefferson Papers, LC.

14. Gaillard Hunt, "Office Seeking During Jefferson's Administration," *American Historical Review*, III, 282; William Plumer to James Sheafe, 22 March 1804, Plumer Papers, LC; John B. O'Neall, *Bench and Bar of South Carolina*, I, 74.

15. Donald G. Morgan, *Justice William Johnson, The First Dissenter* (Columbia, 1954), 3–41.

16. Albert Gallatin to Thomas Jefferson, 15 February 1804, Jefferson Papers, LC.

17. Robert E. Cushman, "Henry Brockholst Livingston," *D.A.B.*, XI, 312–13; Edwin B. Livingston, *The Livingstons of Livingston Manor* (New York, 1910), 344.

18. Entry of 17 December 1806, *Plumer Memorandum*, 532; *United States Gazette* (Philadelphia), 25 December 1806; Alfred F. Young, *The Democratic-Republicans of New York* (Chapel Hill, 1967), 177, 218, 222, 225, 238, 283, 358–59, 481–88, 494.

19. *Annals*, 9:2, 27, 1260–62. In Kentucky over 400 cases were pending. Henry Clay to Harry Innes, 16 January 1807, Hopkinson (ed.), *Papers of Henry Clay*, I, 271, 268–69.

20. John Randolph to Joseph Hooper Nicholson, 17 February, 4 March 1807, Nicholson Papers, LC; Warren, *Supreme Court*, I, 300–301.

21. *Biographical Encyclopaedia of Kentucky* (Cincinnati, 1878), 195; George W. Goble, "Thomas Todd," *D.A.B.*, XVII, 574–75; Mayo, *Henry Clay*, 273.

22. Joseph Story to Samuel P. Fay, 25 February 1808, W. W. Story (ed.), *Life and Letters of Joseph Story*, I, 167.

23. Quoted in Warren, *Supreme Court*, I, 301.

24. Morgan, *William Johnson*, 287–98.

25. Warren, *Supreme Court*, I, 400–419; Morgan D. Dowd, "Justice Story and the Politics of Appointment," *The American Journal of Legal History* IX (October 1965), 265–85; Joseph Story to Nathaniel Williams, 30 November 1811, Story (ed.), *Life and Letters of Joseph Story*, I, 201.

26. William Plumer to Robert Goodloe Harper, 26 November 1811, Plumer Papers, LC.

27. Robert Smith to John Smith, 26 July 1811, Smith Papers, LC; Warren, *Supreme Court*, I, 423. Duvall is not listed in the *Diction-*

ary of American Biography, though some material may be found in *The Biographical Dictionary of the American Congress*.

28. Donald M. Roper, "Judicial Unanimity and the Marshall Court— A Road to Reappraisal," *American Journal of Legal History* IX (Apirl 1965), 118–34.

29. Francis N. Thorpe (ed.), *Federal and State Constitutions*, III, 1686–1712; Samuel Tyler, *Memoir of Roger Brooke Taney* (Baltimore, 1872), 57–58; Carroll T. Bond, *The Court of Appeals of Maryland, A History* (Baltimore, 1928), 87–98; *Maryland Herald and Elizabeth Town Advertiser*, 12 February 1801.

30. William Pinkney to Ninian Pinkney, 21 July 1801, Rev. William Pinkney (ed.), *Life of William Pinkney* (New York, 1853), 41; *Whittington v. Polk*, 1 Harris and Johnson, 241; William Hopper to Joseph H. Nicholson, 17 April 1802, Nicholson Papers, LC; John Randolph to Joseph H. Nicholson, 25 July 1802, Shippen Family Papers, LC; *American and Commercial Daily Advertiser* (Baltimore), 2 February 1801; *Republican; or Anti-Democrat* (Baltimore), 8 March 1802.

31. *American Commercial Daily Advertiser* (Baltimore), 25 February 1801; "A Farmer," *Maryland Gazette* (Annapolis), 27 January, 29 September 1803; Benjamin Galloway to Thomas Jefferson, 19 July 1803, Jefferson Papers, LC.

32. 1804 Chapter 55; John Leads Bozman, *A New Arrangement of the Courts of Justice of the State of Maryland Proposed* (1802).

33. *Easton Republican Star*, 30 September 1806; J. R. Heller III, "Democracy in Maryland, 1790–1810" (unpublished senior thesis, Princeton, 1959), 79–91; James M. Phalen, "William Kilty," *D.A.B.*, X, 375–76.

34. Guion Griffis Johnson, *Ante-Bellum North Carolina, A Social History* (Chapel Hill, 1937), 616–25.

35. *Raleigh Register*, 21 July, 15 December 1806; "Lycurgus," *Raleigh Minerva*, 24 August 1806.

36. *Raleigh Register*, 9 June, 29 September, 24 November, 15, 22 December 1806; *North Carolina Journal* (Halifax), 11 November 1805.

37. "Responser," *Raleigh Register*, 21 July 1806.

38. Ibid., 9 June, 15 December 1806; *Raleigh Minerva*, 2 December 1805; Robert Williams to John Steele, 28 April 1806, Wagstaff (ed.), *The Papers of John Steele*, II, 473–74.

39. "A District Court Suitor," *Raleigh Minerva*, 16 June 1806; "An Old Farmer," ibid., 23 June 1803, 15 December 1806; "Publius," *Raleigh Register*, 29 September, 8, 22 December 1806.

40. "Citizen," *Raleigh Register*, 7 July 1806.

41. "Poor Farmer," ibid., 28 July 1806; "Corrector," ibid., 16 June 1806; "Old Farmer," *Raleigh Minerva*, 23 June 1806.
42. "Country Squire," *Raleigh Minerva*, 13 October 1806.
43. Ibid., 25 August 1806; *Raleigh Register*, 9 June, 25 August 1806; *North Carolina Journal* (Halifax), 15 December 1806.
44. *Raleigh Register*, November–February 1806–07; *North Carolina Journal* (Halifax), 15 December 1806.
45. *Raleigh Minerva*, 17 December 1807; *Raleigh Register*, 26 November 1807.
46. William T. Utter, "Judicial Review in Early Ohio," *Mississippi Valley Historical Review* XIV (June 1927), 3–24; and, by the same author, "Ohio and the English Common Law," ibid., XVI (December 1929), 321–33; Carl F. Prince, *New Jersey's Jeffersonian Republicans* (Chapel Hill, 1964), 113–16; Lynn Turner, *William Plumer*, 225–26, 244–45, 255–56, 262; Morison, *Jeremiah Smith*, 268–72.
47. J. Harold Ennis, "William Henry DeSaussure," *D.A.B.*, V, 253–54; O'Neall, *Biographical Sketches of the Bench and Bar of South Carolina*, I, 243–52; Horton, *James Kent*, 137–41; William Kent, *Memoirs and Letters of James Kent* (Boston, 1898), 120–21.

CHAPTER XVI

1. For my understanding of the nature of eighteenth century democracy I am particularly indebted to Merrill Jensen, "Democracy and the American Revolution," *Huntington Library Quarterly* XX (August 1957), 321–41; Roy N. Lokken, "The Concept of Democracy in Colonial Political Thought," *William and Mary Quarterly* XVI (October 1959), 568–80; Elisha P. Douglass, *Rebels and Democrats* (Chapel Hill, 1955), 10–33; Robert W. Shoemaker, " 'Democracy' and 'Republic' as understood in Late Eighteenth Century America," *American Speech*, XLI (May 1966), 83–95.
2. Cecelia M. Kenyon, in an article entitled "Men of Little Faith: The Anti-Federalists on the Nature of Representative Government," *William and Mary Quarterly*, XII (January 1955), 43, has argued that people who favored limited government were not democratic, because "they lacked both the faith and the vision to extend their principles nationwide." But fear of man's corruptibility was also shared by those opposed to democracy, only it was directed at a different target. It seems to me that if a study were made of the persuasion of those who favored and of those who opposed the democratic process in the post-Revolutionary era, it would be shown that democrats emphasized the fear of misrule by those in power while their opponents addressed themselves to the terrors of

majority rule. Optimism of man's ability to govern himself played only a very small role in eighteenth-century political thought. See especially Richard Hofstadter, *The American Political Tradition* (New York, 1948), 3–17.

3. In fact, frequently, though not always, it was the opponents of democracy who most actively supported liberal and humanitarian reform movements. Douglass, *Rebels and Democrats,* 311–16.

4. George M. Dutcher, "The Rise of Republican Government in the United States," *Political Science Quarterly* LV (June 1940), 199–216; Louis Hartz, *The Liberal Tradition in America* (New York, 1955), 35–86; Louise Burnham Dunbar, "A Study of Monarchical Tendencies in the United States from 1776–1801," *University of Illinois Studies in the Social Sciences* X (March 1922).

5. See the items cited in note 1. See also J. R. Pole, "Historians and the Problem of Early American Democracy," *American Historical Review* LXVII (April 1962), 626–46.

6. Good examples of democratic activity are to be found in: Jensen, "Democracy and the American Revolution," *Huntington Library Quarterly* (August 1947), 334–38; Chilton Williamson, *American Suffrage from Property to Democracy, 1760–1860* (Princeton, 1960), 84–115; Staughton Lynd, "Who Should Rule at Home? Dutchess County, New York in the American Revolution," *William and Mary Quarterly* XVIII (July 1961), 354–57; Robert J. Taylor, *Western Massachusetts in the Revolution* (Providence, 1954), 75–102.

7. For examples of Paine's influence in Kentucky, Massachusetts, and Pennsylvania see: *Kentucky Gazette* (Lexington), 19 November 1791; "H.S.B.M.," ibid., 7 January, 4 February 1792; Arthur Campbell to Isaac Shelby, 20 March 1792, Durrett Collection, University of Chicago (UC); Levi Lincoln to Thomas Jefferson, 6 December 1802, 9 March 1805, Jefferson Papers, LC; Philip S. Foner, *The Complete Writings of Thomas Paine* (2 vols., Binghamton, 1945), II, 992–1007. I seriously question Miss Cecelia Kenyon's claim that Paine's political ideas did not have any influence after 1776. "Where Paine Went Wrong," *The American Political Science Review,* XLV (December, 1951), 1086–99.

8. For the struggle over judicial reform see chapters 7–13 above. On the struggle over constitutional reform in the states 1790–1815 see: John D. Barnhart, *Valley of Democracy,* 66–160; Chilton Williamson, *American Suffrage,* 158–81; Fletcher Green, *Constitutional Development in the South Atlantic States, 1776–1860* (New York, 1966), 142–201.

9. For what follows I am very much indebted to Alan Heimert,

*Religion and the American Mind, From the Great Awakening to the
Revolution* (Cambridge, 1966), *passim;* Richard Hofstadter, *Anti-
Intellectualism in American Life* (New York, 1963), 55–141; William
G. McLaughlin, "The American Revolution as a Religious Revival:
The Millennium in One Country," *New England Quarterly* XL
(March 1967), 99–110.

10. Heimert, *Religion and the American Mind,* 510–52.
11. Ibid., 5.
12. Quoted in ibid., 180.
13. Leland, *Writings,* 292.
14. Barnhart, *Valley of Democracy,* 292, notes 7–11.
15. Paul Hummel Eller, "Revivalism and the German Churches in
    Pennsylvania, 1783–1816" (Unpublished dissertation, University of
    Chicago, 1933); C. H. Maxson, *The Great Awakening in the
    Middle Colonies* (Chicago, 1920).
16. *Newburyport Herald,* 26 October 1804.
17. Lee Benson, *Turner and Beard* (Glencoe, 1960), 214–38, is the
    clearest theoretical statement of this analytical tool. Manning J.
    Dauer, *The Adams Federalists* (Baltimore, 1953); Jackson T. Main,
    The Anti-Federalists, Critics of the Constitution, 1781–1788 (Chapel
    Hill, 1961); and Charles Sellers and Henry May, *A Synopsis of
    American History* (Chicago, 1963), 65–146, are good examples of the
    meaningful way in which this thesis may be applied to the early
    national period. It was first stated in an empirical study by Orin
    Grant Libby, *The Geographical Distribution of the Vote of the
    Thirteen States on the Federal Constitution, 1787–1788* (Madison,
    1894). Thomas P. Govan, "Agrarian and Agrarianism: A Study in
    the Use and Abuse of Words," *Journal of Southern History* XXX
    (February 1964), 35–47, is a survey of the different ways in which
    historians have used these words.
18. It of course does not follow that all non-commercial areas favored
    a radical kind of judicial reform, or for that matter even voted
    Republican. Much depended on how an area was settled, the
    availability of newspapers, the quality of leadership, and the extent
    of politicization. Western New York, western Maryland, and Maine
    are examples of non-politicized agrarian areas that supported Fed-
    eralists during the 1790's.

    For my understanding of agrarian or non-rational legal thought
    I have benefited greatly from Max Rheinstein (ed.), *Max Weber
    on Law in Economy and Society* (Cambridge, 1966).
19. On this point see especially James Willard Hurst, *Law and the
    Conditions of Freedom in the Nineteenth-Century United States*

(Madison, 1967), and R. Kent Newmyer, *The Supreme Court Under Marshall and Taney* (New York, 1968), 56–88.

20. W. P. Strickland (ed.), *Autobiography of Peter Cartwright, The Backwoods Preacher* (New York, 1857), 25–26.

21. Richard C. Wade, *The Urban Frontier* (Cambridge, 1959), 18–22; Bernard Mayo, "Lexington, Frontier Metropolis," in Eric F. Goldman (ed.), *Historiography and Urbanization* (Baltimore, 1941), 21–42.

22. *Dauphin Guardian* (Harrisburg), 14 September 1805; Hugh Henry Brackenridge to Alexander J. Dallas, 20 May 1805, Dallas Papers, HSP; *Crawford Weekly Messenger* (Meadville), 4, 11 September 1805; Ferguson, *Early Western Pennsylvania Politics,* 185–95; Elizabeth Henderson, "Some Aspects of Sectionalism in Pennsylvania, 1790–1812" (unpublished doctoral dissertation, Bryn Mawr College, 1935).

23. An important exception to the argument that the Federalist party in Massachusetts drew its strength only from commercial communities is the fact that Worcester county, backward and undeveloped economically, generally went Federalist. But this can be explained mainly on the ground that it was the home county of Caleb Strong, who was popular with his neighbors, and who built up a very powerful personal connection. Federalists, other than Strong, usually ran behind Republicans in Worcester county. *Independent Chronicle* (Boston), 8 May 1806. For a different interpretation of the social sources of Massachusetts politics during the early national period, see James M. Banner, Jr., *To the Hartford Convention* (New York, 1970).

24. Goodman, *Democratic-Republicans of Massachusetts,* 70–127.

25. Harry H. Clark (ed.), *Six New Letters of Paine* (Madison, 1939), introduction; Manning J. Dauer and Hans Hammond, "John Taylor, Democrat or Aristocrat?" *Journal of Politics* VI (November 1944), 381–43.

26. Staughton Lynd and Alfred F. Young, "After Carl Becker: The Mechanics and New York City Politics, 1774–1801," *Labor History* V (1964), 215–76; Staughton Lynd, "Capitalism, Democracy and the United States Constitution: The Case of New York," *Science and Society* XXVII (Fall 1963), 385–414; Main, *The Anti-Federalists,* 266–68. For an interesting treatment of working men's attitudes toward the good society during the Jackson era, see Edward Pessen, *Most Uncommon Jacksonians* (Albany, 1967).

27. See chapters on Massachusetts.

28. See chapters on Pennsylvania.

10

29. Jesse Higgins to Jonathan Roberts and Matthew Roberts, 8 May 1807, Roberts Paper, HSP; Samuel Maclay to Jonathan Roberts, 2 February 1808, ibid.; Jonathan Roberts to Jonathan Roberts, Sr., 8 January 1808, ibid.; Higginbotham, *Keystone in the Democratic Arch,* 121–46.

30. Risjord, *The Old Republicans,* 3–10.

31. Aubrey C. Land, "Economic Base and Social Structure: The Northern Chesapeake in the Eighteenth Century," *Journal of Economic History* XXV (December 1965), 639–54; and, by the same author, "Economic Behavior in a Planting Society: The Eighteenth-Century Chesapeake," *Journal of Southern History* XXXIII (November 1967), 469–85.

32. To be sure, as Louis Hartz and Richard Hofstadter have pointed out, almost all Americans were in agreement upon the concepts of the sanctity of private property and the importance of republican government. Nevertheless it is equally clear that there existed deep ideological differences over the kind of country that commercial-minded and agrarian-minded groups wanted to see America become.

33. This aspect of the problem will be treated more fully in Chapter 17.

34. See especially the following works by Paul Goodman: *The Democratic-Republicans of Massachusetts, passim;* "Social Status of Party Leadership: The House of Representatives, 1797–1804," *William and Mary Quarterly* XXV (July 1968), 465–74; "The First American Party System," in William Nisbet Chambers and Walter Dean Burnham (eds.), *The American Party Systems, Stages of Political Development* (New York, 1967), 56–89. See also David Hachett Fischer, *The Revolution of American Conservatism, The Federalist Party in the Era of Jeffersonian Democracy* (New York, 1965), 203–11; Staughton Lynd, *Anti-Federalism in Dutchess County, New York* (Chicago, 1962), esp. 6–7.

35. Louis Guillaume Otto to Comte de Vergennes, 10 October 1786, in George Bancroft, *History of the Formation of the Constitution,* 2 vols. (New York, 1882), II, 399–400.

36. Levi Lincoln to Thomas Jefferson, 30 July 1805, Jefferson Papers, LC.

37. *Massachusetts Spy, or Worcester Gazette,* 18 December 1805.

38. *The Repertory* (Boston), 4 May 1804, 31 July 1804; *New England Palladium* (Boston), 18 December 1805.

39. *Crawfordsville Weekly Messenger* (Meadville, Pa.), 4 September 1805.

40. *Kentucky Gazette* (Lexington), 27 April 1793.
41. Jesse Higgins, *Sampson Against the Philistines,* 75.

CHAPTER XVII

1. One of the first historians to emphasize the continuity of issues before and after 1788 was Charles A. Beard. See in particular his *Economic Origins of Jeffersonian Democracy* (New York, 1915). Since the early 1950's an increasing number of scholars has emphasized the influence of the Revolution on the period following 1788. For example: John D. Barnhart, *Valley of Democracy, The Frontier Versus the Plantation in the Ohio Valley, 1775–1815* (Bloomington, 1953); E. James Ferguson, *The Power of the Purse, A History of American Public Finance, 1776–1790* (Chapel Hill, 1961); Curtis P. Nattels, *The Emergence of a National Economy, 1775–1815* (New York, 1962); Chilton Williamson, *American Suffrage from Property to Democracy* (Princeton, 1960).
2. Benjamin Rush to Richard Price, 25 May 1786, in Lyman Butterfield (ed.), *Letters of Benjamin Rush,* 2 vols. (Princeton, 1951), I, 388.
3. Scholars who share this point of view, though little else, are: Merrill Jensen, "Democracy and the American Revolution," *Huntington Library Quarterly* XX (August 1957); Cecelia Kenyon, "Republicanism and Radicalism in the American Revolution: An Old Fashioned Interpretation," *William and Mary Quarterly* XIX (April 1962), 153–182; Richard B. Morris, "Class Struggle and the American Revolution," *William and Mary Quarterly* XIX (July 1962), 3–29; Bernard Bailyn (ed.), *Pamphlets of the American Revolution,* 4 vols. (1965–?), I, 169–90. Important exceptions to this point of view are Robert E. Brown, *Middle Class Democracy in Massachusetts* (Ithaca, 1955) and *Virginia 1705–1786: Democracy or Aristocracy* (East Lansing, 1964); also Daniel J. Boorstin, *The Genius of American Politics* (Chicago, 1953), 66–98.
4. Malcolm Freiberg, "How to Become a Colonial Governor: Thomas Hutchinson of Massachusetts," *The Review of Politics* 21 (October 1959), 646–56; Ellen E. Brennan, *Plural Office-Holding in Massachusetts, 1760–1780* (Chapel Hill, 1945), 32–35; Robert J. Taylor, *Western Massachusetts in the Revolution* (Providence, 1954), 11–26; Charles S. Sydnor, *Gentlemen Freeholders* (Chapel Hill, 1952); Jack P. Greene, "Foundations of Political Power in the Virginia House of Burgesses, 1720–1776," *William and Mary Quarterly* XVI (Octo-

ber 1959), 485–506; Oscar Zeichner, *Connecticut's Years of Controversy, 1750–1776* (Chapel Hill, 1949), 3–19; David S. Lovejoy, *Rhode Island Politics and the American Revolution, 1760–1776* (Providence, 1958), 5–31; Leonard W. Labaree, *Conservatism in Early American History* (Ithaca, 1959), 1–31; Frederick B. Tolles, *Meeting House and Counting House* (Chapel Hill, 1948), 109–43; Carl L. Becker, *History of Political Parties in the Province of New York, 1760–1776* (Madison, 1960), 5–22.

5. Jackson T. Main, "Government by the People, the American Revolution and the Democratization of the Legislatures," *William and Mary Quarterly* XXIII (July 1966), 391–407, and *The Upper House in Revolutionary America 1763–1788* (Madison, 1967). See also Moses Coit Tyler, *Patrick Henry* (Ithaca, 1962), 214–356; E. Wilder Spaulding, *His Excellency George Clinton, Critic of the Constitution* (New York, 1938), 86–183; Herbert S. Allan, *John Hancock: Patriot in Purple* (New York, 1948) 175–296.

6. Daniel J. Boorstin, *The Americans: The Colonial Experience* (New York, 1958).

7. Bernard Bailyn (ed.), *Pamphlets of the American Revolution*, I, 90–202; Gordon S. Wood, "Rhetoric and Reality in the American Revolution," *William and Mary Quarterly* XXIII (January 1966), 3–32; Wood, *The Creation of the American Republic, passim*.

8. Jackson T. Main, *The Anti-Federalists*, 21–71; "Sections and Politics in Virginia, 1781–1787," *William and Mary Quarterly* XII (January 1955), 96–112; "Political Parties in Revolutionary Maryland, 1780–1787," *Maryland Historical Magazine* 62 (March 1967), 1–27; Robert East, "The Massachusetts Conservatives in the Critical Period," in Richard Morris (ed.), *The Era of the American Revolution* (New York, 1965), 349–91; Jensen, *The New Nation* (New York, 1950), 259–326.

9. For example, see Edmund Randolph's opening speech to the Philadelphia Convention of 1787: He said, "our chief danger arises from the democratic parts of our state constitutions. . . . None of the state constitutions have provided a sufficient check against the democracy." In another place Randolph noted that the evils of the confederation period were to be found "in the turbulence and follies of democracy: that some check therefore was to be sought for against this tendency of our Governments." Elbridge Gerry noted, "The evils we experience flow from the excess of democracy." George Mason complained of "the oppressions and injustice experienced among us from democracy." And Madison: "No agrarian attempts have yet been made in this country, but symp-

toms of a leveling spirit, as we have understood, have sufficiently appeared in a certain quarter to give notice of the future danger." Max Farrand (ed.), *The Records of the Federal Convention of 1787*, I, 26–27, 48, 51, 101, 422–23.

10. E. James Ferguson, *The Power of the Purse*, 109–76; Jensen, *The New Nation*, 28–84; Forrest McDonald, *We the People* (Boston, 1965), 1–32.

11. Main, *The Anti-Federalists*, Conclusion; Benson, *Turner and Beard*, 214–28.

12. Ferguson, *Power of the Purse*, 289–326; Whitney Bates, "Northern Speculations and Southern State Debts: 1790," *William and Mary Quarterly*, XIX (January 1962), 30–48; Noble Cunningham, *The Jeffersonian Republicans, The Formation of Party Organization, 1789–1801* (Chapel Hill, 1957), 3–32.

13. There appears to be a general consensus among historians of the early national period on this point. See Joseph N. Charles, *The Origins of the American Party System* (New York, 1961), 91–140; William N. Chambers, *Political Parties in a New Nation, The American Experience 1776–1809* (New York, 1963), 34–129; Cunningham, *The Jeffersonian Republicans of Massachusetts*, 74–69; Young, *The Democratic Republicans of New York*, 345–442; Prince, *New Jersey's Jeffersonian Republicans*, 41–69; Harry Ammon, "The Formation of the Republican Party in Virginia, 1789–1796," *Journal of Southern History*, XIX (August 1953), 283–310.

14. *Annals*, 1:1, 238; Paul Varg, *Foreign Policies of the Founding Fathers* (East Lansing, 1963), 70–94; Merrill Peterson, "Thomas Jefferson and Commercial Policy, 1783–1793," *William and Mary Quarterly* XXII (October 1965), 584–610; McDonald, *E. Pluribus Unum*, 68–77.

15. It has recently become fashionable to deny the existence of Anti-Federalist sentiment after the adoption of the Constitution. See the works cited in note 13. Young's book on New York is the only exception.

16. I do not mean to claim that the Anti-Federalists existed as an organizational entity on the national level, for they did not. Rather I am arguing that their ideas continued to be attractive to a large segment of the electorate. Moreover, on the state level there are some indications that the alignments of the 1780's may have continued on into the early 1790's. Norman Risjord, "The Virginia Federalists," *Journal of Southern History* XXXIII (November 1967), 486–517; Young, *The Democratic-Republicans of New York*, 109–66. The story of what happened to the Anti-Federalists during the

1790's has yet to be told. That their point of view still existed can be seen by examining the rhetoric of the Democratic-Republican societies. On this point see particularly Eugene Link, *Democratic-Republican Societies, 1790–1800* (New York, 1942), esp. chapters III and V. Many of Link's interpretations are questionable, but his is nonetheless an important book because it shows the continued existence of extreme democratic ideas during the 1790's.

17. Cunningham, *The Jeffersonian-Republicans,* 62–66; Alexander DeConde, *Entangling Alliance* (Durham, 1958), 283–310; Irving Brant, *James Madison, Father of the Constitution, 1787–1800* (Indianapolis, 1950), 416; Stephen G. Kurtz, *The Presidency of John Adams* (Philadelphia, 1957), 40–45.

18. Lyman H. Butterfield, "The Dream of Benjamin Rush; the Reconciliation of Jefferson and Adams," *Yale Review* XL (Winter 1951), 297–319; Kurtz, *Presidency of John Adams,* 218–38; Dauer, *The Adams Federalists,* 112–19; Alexander DeConde, *The Quasi-War* (New York, 1966), 12.

19. Risjord, *The Old Republicans,* 11–17; Dumas Malone, *Jefferson and the Ordeal of Liberty* (Boston, 1962), 359–424.

20. There is no direct organizational connection between the Federalists and Anti-Federalists of 1787–1788 and the Federalists and Republicans of the 1790's. But impressionistic evidence would seem to indicate strongly that almost all the Federalists of the 1790's had favored the adoption of the Constitution; although not everyone who favored the adoption of the constitution became Federalists, for many, like Madison, went into the Republican party. Likewise, almost all Anti-Federalists, with only a few important exceptions (Patrick Henry, Luther Martin, and Samuel Chase), mostly on the leadership level, became Republicans. So that there would appear to be some connection between political alignments before and after the adoption of the Constitution, though it is not a simple direct and lineal one.

21. Henry Adams, *History of the United States of America During the Administrations of Thomas Jefferson and James Madison, 1801–1816,* 9 vols. (New York, 1891–96); Richard Hofstadter, "Thomas Jefferson: The Aristocrat as Democrat," in *The American Political Tradition* (New York, 1957), 18–44. It is also the standard interpretation found in most college textbooks.

22. *The Repertory,* (Boston), 11 October 1805.

23. Adams, *History of the United States, 1801–1816,* I, 237–43; Risjord, *The Old Republicans,* 37–38; Raymond Walters, *Albert Gallatin,* 143–54; 170–84; Alexander Balinky, *Albert Gallatin, Fiscal Theories and Policies* (New Brunswick, 1958), 17–127; Bray Hammond, *Banks*

and *Politics in America from the Revolution to the Civil War* (Princeton, 1957), 114–43, 197–226. Jeffersonian fiscal policy is a subject much in need of further research.

24. Thomas McKean to Uriah Tracy, 14 January 1804, McKean Papers, HSP.

25. Jacob Crowinshield to George W. Prescott, 15 November 1803, Alexander C. Washburn Collection, MHS; Samuel Smith to Timothy Pickering, 29 December 1803, Pickering Papers, MHS; Lolabel House, *A Study of the Twelfth Amendment of the Constitution of the United States* (Philadelphia, 1901).

26. Tom Paine to the Editor of the National Intelligencer, 1 January 1803, Foner (ed.), *Complete Writings of Tom Paine*, 1432–33; Tom Paine to Samuel Adams, 1 January 1803, ibid., 1434–38; Tom Paine to Thomas Jefferson, 12 January 1803, ibid., 1439; Gideon Granger to William Eustis, 18 November 1802, William Eustis Papers, LC; William Duane to Thomas Jefferson, 27 November 1802, Jefferson Papers, LC; Levi Lincoln to Thomas Jefferson, 6 December 1802, ibid.; Alfred Owen Aldridge, *Man of Reason* (Philadelphia, 1959), 273–79.

27. Hammond, *Banks and Politics*, 144–96; Goodman, *The Democratic-Republicans of Massachusetts*, 170–81; Gilpatrick, *Jeffersonian Democracy in North Carolina*, 149–52; Prince, *New Jersey's Jeffersonian Republicans*, 151, 158, 165–67, 172–73, 252.

28. Samuel Smith to ?, 14 December 1805, Samuel Smith Papers, LC.

29. *Freeman's Journal* (Philadelphia), 25 March 1805.

30. Quoted in Peter Gay, "The Enlightenment," in C. Vann Woodward (ed.), *The Comparative Approach to American History* (New York, 1968), 42. For a penetrating study of the coming of the War of 1812 as a crisis in republicanism see Roger H. Brown, *The Republic in Peril: 1812* (New York, 1964).

31. It seems to me that Louis Hartz, in *The Liberal Tradition in America,* a truly brilliant book, has greatly underestimated the threat of a military takeover that existed in America during the last two decades of the eighteenth century.

32. For a different interpretation, which, in my opinion, greatly over-emphasizes the importance of the Federalist Party after 1800, see Fischer, *The Revolution of American Conservatism*, 182–99.

33. Payson Jackson Treat, *The National Land System, 1785–1820* (New York, 1967); Reginald Horsman, *Expansion and American Indian Policy, 1783–1812* (East Lansing, 1967).

34. Treat, *National Land System*, 101–43; Benjamin Horace Hibbard, *A History of the Public Land Policies* (Madison, 1965), 144–51.

35. See especially Joseph H. Harrison. "The Internal Improvement

Issue in the Politics of the Union, 1783–1825." (Unpublished doctoral dissertation, University of Virginia, 1954), 135–200. See also Carter Goodrich, "National Planning of Internal Improvements," *Political Science Quarterly,* LXIII (March 1948), 16–44.

36. Much too much has been made of Jefferson's agrarianism. It only lasted for a short time and does not seem to be very important during the years he was President. As for Madison, he never appears to have been an agrarian. William D. Grampp, "A Re-examination of Jeffersonian Economics," *The Southern Economic Journal,* XII (January 1946), 263–82; Joseph J. Spengler, "The Political Economy of Jefferson, Madison, and Adams," in David Kelly Jackson (ed.), *American Studies in Honor of William Kenneth Boyd* (Durham, 1940), 3–59; Joseph Dorfman, *The Economic Mind in American Civilization, 1606–1865,* I, 433–46.

37. Jacob Crowninshield to Captain Nathaniel Silsbee, 13 January 1805, Crowninshield Papers, PM.

38. Thomas Jefferson to Albert Gallatin, 12 July 1803, Ford (ed.), *Works of Jefferson,* X, 15–16.

39. Douglass C. North, *The Economic Growth of the United States, 1790–1860* (Englewood Cliffs, 1961).

40. For example see: Arthur M. Schlesinger, Jr., *The Age of Jackson* (Boston, 1950), 267–82; Louis Hartz, *The Liberal Tradition in America,* 89–113.

41. Lee Benson, *The Concept of Jacksonian Democracy, New York as a Test Case* (Princeton, 1961), 4–11; Richard P. McCormick, *The Second American Party System* (Chapel Hill, 1966), 3–16.

42. Marvin Meyers in *The Jacksonian Persuasion* (Stanford, 1960), 13, describes the party battles of the 1820–1840 period as between the Whigs, who spoke to the "explicit hopes of Americans," and Jacksonians, who "addressed their diffuse fears and resentments." Lee Benson, *Concept of Jacksonian Democracy,* 104–9, says much the same thing when he claims the Whigs advocated a positive liberal state while the Jacksonians wanted a negative liberal state. For an interpretation somewhat similar to mine, though with much less stress on ideological factors, see Lynn Marshall, "The Strange Stillbirth of the Whig Party," *American Historical Review* LXXII (January 1967), 445–68. Finally, see the perceptive treatment in Peterson, *The Jefferson Image,* 17–111.

Bibliography

MANUSCRIPTS

American Antiquarian Society (AAS)
    Burr Correspondence (Photostat)

Chicago Historical Society (CHS)
    Ninian Edwards Papers
    Hardin Collection

Columbia University (CU)
    DeWitt Clinton Papers (Microfilm)
    University Collection

Duke University (DU)
    David Campbell Papers
    Ephraim Kirby Papers

Historical Society of Delaware (HSD)
    Rodney Family Papers

Historical Society of Pennsylvania (HSP)
    Alexander J. Dallas Papers
    Simon Gratz Collection
    Legal Men of Pennsylvania Collection
    George Logan Papers
    Thomas McKean Papers

Richard Peters Papers
Jonathan Roberts Papers
Uselma Clark Smith Collection

Library of Congress (LC)
James A. Bayard Papers
Breckinridge Family Papers
William Eustis Papers
Galloway–Maxcy–Markoe Papers
Robert Goodice Harper Papers
Izard Family Papers
Thomas Jefferson Papers
James Kent Papers
James Madison Papers
Miscellaneous Personal Papers
James Monroe Papers
Gouverneur Morris Papers
Wilson Cary Nicholas Papers
Joseph H. Nicholson Papers
William Plumer Papers
John Randolph Papers
Rodney Family Papers
Shippen Family Papers
John Cotton Smith Papers
J. Henley Smith Papers
Samuel Smith Papers
Joseph Story Papers
Thomas Worthington Papers

Maryland Historical Society (MdHS)
Samuel Chase Papers
Harper–Pennington Papers
Moses Rawlings Papers

Massachusetts Historical Society (MHS)
Coolidge Collection
William Cranch Papers
Dwight–Howard Papers
Henry Knox Papers
Harrison Gray Otis Papers
Miscellaneous Bound Collection

Timothy Pickering Papers
Theodore Sedgwick Papers

New York Historical Society (NYHS)
Samuel Chase Miscellaneous Manuscripts
DeWitt Clinton Papers
William Cushing Miscellaneous Manuscripts
Albert Gallatin Papers (Microfilm)
Robert R. Livingston Papers
John Sanders Papers

New York Public Library (NYPL)
Samuel Chase Papers
Joseph Clay Papers
James Madison Papers
James Monroe Papers
William Paterson Papers, Bancroft Transcrip
C. A. Rodney Papers
Noah Webster Papers
Pierre Van Cortlandt Papers
Van Cortlandt–Van Wyck Papers

Peabody Museum (PM)
Jacob Crowninshield Papers

Pierpont Morgan Library (PML)
James Gould Papers
Uriah Tracy Papers

University of Chicago (UC)
Durrett Collection
Mss. Journal of the Kentucky House of Delegates, June 1792 (microfilm)
Mss. Journal of the Kentucky Senate (microfilm)
George Nicholas Papers

University of North Carolina (UNC)
Duncan Cameron Papers
John Rutledge Papers

University of Virginia (UVA)
Joseph Cabell Papers
Wilson Cary Nicholas Papers

Edgehill–Randolph Papers
John Randolph Papers (microfilm)
Creed Taylor Papers
Tucker–Coleman Papers (microfilm)

Wisconsin Historical Society (WHS)
Draper Collection (microfilm)

Yale University (YU)
Simeon Baldwin Papers
William Griswold Lane Collection
John Cotton Smith Papers

NEWSPAPERS

Connecticut
Connecticut Courant (Hartford)

District of Columbia
National Intelligencer
Washington Federalist

Kentucky
The Guardian of Freedom (Frankfort)
Kentucky Gazette (Lexington)
The Mirror (Washington
The Palladium (Frankfort)
Stewart's Kentucky Herald (Frankfort)

Maryland
American Commercial Daily Advertiser (Baltimore)
Easton Republican Star
Frederick Town Herald
Maryland Gazette (Annapolis)
Maryland Herald and Elizabeth Town Advertiser
The Republican; or Anti-Democrat (Baltimore)

Massachusetts
Boston Gazette
Columbia Centinel (Boston)
Eastern Argus (Portland, Me.)
Hampshire Gazette (Northampton)

Independent Chronicle (Boston)
Massachusetts Spy (Worcester)
National Aegis (Worcester)
Newburyport Herald
New England Palladium (Boston)
Pittsfield Sun
The Repertory (Boston)
Western Star (Stockbridge)

New York
New-York Evening Post

New Hampshire
Farmers Weekly Gazette (Walpole)

North Carolina
North Carolina Journal (Halifax)
Raleigh Minerva
Raleigh Register

Pennsylvania
Aurora (Philadelphia)
Commonwealth (Pittsburgh)
Crawford Weekly Messenger
Dauphin Guardian (Harrisburg)
Freeman's Journal (Philadelphia)
Gazette of the United States (Philadelphia)
Gettysburg Gazette
Klines Carlisle Gazette
Lancaster Journal
Oracle of Dauphin (Harrisburg)
Pennsylvania Correspondent and Farmers Adventurer (Doylestown)
Philadelphia Gazette and Daily Advertiser
Pittsburgh Gazette
The Republican Argus (Northumberland)
Sprig of Liberty (Gettysburg)

Rhode Island
Providence Gazette

South Carolina
> *Charleston Courier*

Virginia
> *Enquirer* (Richmond)
> *Examiner* (Richmond)
> *Virginia Gazette and General Advertiser* (Richmond)

PAMPHLETS AND ESSAYS

Austin, Benjamin. *Constitutional Republicanism in Opposition to Fallacious Federalism.* Boston, 1803.

Austin, Benjamin. *Observations on the Pernicious Practice of the Law by Honestus.* Boston, 1786, 1819.

Bozman, John Leeds. *A New Arrangement of the Courts of Justice of the State of Maryland Proposed.* 1802.

Cooper, Thomas. *An Account of the Trial of Thomas Cooper of Northumberland; on a Charge of Libel against the President of the United States. . . .* Philadelphia, 1800.

Dawson, H. B. (ed.). *Arguments and Judgment of the Mayor's Court . . . in a Cause between . . . Rutgers and Waddington.* Morrisania, 1886.

Hamilton, William (ed.). *Report of the Trial and Acquittal of Edward Shippen, Esquire, Chief Justice, and Jasper Yeates and Thomas Smith Esquires, Assistant Justices of the Supreme Court of Pennsylvania. On an Impeachment Before the Senate of the Commonwealth, January 1805.* Lancaster, 1805.

Higgins, Jesse. *Sampson Against the Philistines, or the Reformation of Lawsuits; and Justice Made Cheap, Speedy, and Brought Home to Every Man's Door; Agreeably to the Principles of the Ancient Trial by Jury, Before the Same was Innovated by Judges and Lawyers.* Philadelphia, 1805.

Lloyd, Thomas. *The Trial of Alexander Addison.* Lancaster, 1803.

Message from the President Enclosing Documents Relative to John Pickering. Washington, 1803.

Nicholas, George. *A Letter from George Nicholas of Kentucky to His Friend in Virginia Justifying the Conduct of the Citizens of Kentucky as to Some of the Late Measures of the General Government and Correcting Certain False Statements Which Have Been Made in the Different States of the Views and Action of the People of Kentucky.* Philadelphia, 1799.

Parker, Isaac. *Sketch of the Character of the Late Chief Justice Parsons.* Boston, 1813.

Report of the Trial of the Honorable Samuel Chase. . . . Baltimore, 1805.

Sullivan, James. *The Path of Riches: An Inquiry into the Origins and Uses of Money.* Boston, 1792.

Sullivan, William. *An Address to the Members of the Bar of Suffolk, Massachusetts.* Boston, 1825.

[Van Ness, William P.] Aristides. *An Examination of the Various Charges Exhibited Against Aaron Burr.* New York, 1803.

Varnum, James M. *The Case Trevett against Weeden . . . 1786. Also the Case of the Judges of Said Court.* Providence, 1787.

PUBLISHED SOURCES

Acts and Laws of the Commonwealth of Massachusetts. Boston, 1897.

Adams, C. F. (ed.). *Memoirs of John Quincy Adams,* 12 vols. Philadelphia, 1874–77.

Adams, C. F. (ed.). *The Works of John Adams,* 10 vols. Boston, 1850–56.

Adams, Henry (ed.). *Documents Relating to New England Federalism, 1800–1815.* Boston, 1877.

Adams, Henry (ed.). *The Writings of Albert Gallatin,* 3 vols. Philadelphia, 1879.

Adams, John Stokes (ed.). *An Autobiographical Sketch by John Marshall.* Ann Arbor, 1937.

Allis, Frederick S. (ed.). *William Bingham's Maine Lands, 1780–1820.* Colonial Society of Massachusetts, *Collections,* 2 vols. Boston, 1954.

Ames, Seth (ed.). *Works of Fisher Ames,* 2 vols. Boston, 1854.

Amory, Thomas C. *Life of James Sullivan; With Selections from His Writings,* 2 vols. Boston, 1859.

Bailyn, Bernard (ed.). *Pamphlets of the American Revolution,* 4 vols. Cambridge, 1965–?

Baldwin, Simeon E. *Life and Letters of Simeon Baldwin.* New Haven, 1918.

Ballagh, Henry C. (ed.). *The Life and Letters of Richard Henry Lee.* 2 vols. New York, 1914.

Barker, Eugene C. (ed.). "The Papers of Moses and Stephen Austin," American Historical Association, *Report* (1919), II.

Bentley, William. *The Diary of William Bentley,* 4 vols. Salem, 1905–14.

Binns, John. *Recollections of the Life of John Binns.* Philadelphia, 1854.

Bowdoin, James. *The Bowdoin and Temple Papers.* Massachusetts Historical Society, *Collections,* ser. 6, vol. 9; ser. 7, vol. 6 (1897, 1907).

Boyd, Julian P. (ed.). *The Papers of Thomas Jefferson,* 17 vols. Princeton, 1950–?.

Brown, Everett S. (ed.). *William Plumer's Memorandum of Proceedings in the United States Senate, 1803–1807.* New York, 1923.

Butterfield, L. H. (ed.). *Letters of Benjamin Rush,* 2 vols. Princeton, 1951.

Cappon, Lester (ed.). *The Adams–Jefferson Letters,* 2 vols. Chapel Hill, 1959.

"Samuel Chase and the Grand Jury of Baltimore County," *Maryland Historical Magazine,* VI (June 1911).

Clark, Harry H. (ed.). *Six New Letters of Paine.* Madison, 1939.

Cranch, William. *Reports of Cases Argued and Adjudged in the Supreme Court of the United States. . . . 1801, 1803–1815.* New York, 1812–16.

Crevecoeur, J. Hector St. John de. *Letters from an American Farmer.* New York, 1957.

Cutler, W. P., and J. P. Cutler (eds.). *Life Journal and Correspondence of Manasseh Cutler,* 2 vols. New York, 1888.

Dallas, George M. (ed.). *Life and Writings of Alexander James Dallas.* Philadelphia, 1871.

Davis, Elvert M. (ed.). "The Letters of Tarleton Bates." *Western Pennsylvania History Magazine,* XII (January 1929).

Davis, Matthew L. (ed.). *Memoirs of Aaron Burr,* 2 vols. New York, 1837.

Debates and Proceedings in the Congress of the United States, vols. 1–19. Washington, D.C., 1834–53.

Donnan, Elizabeth (ed.). *Papers of James A. Bayard, 1796–1815.* Washington, 1913.

Farrand, Max (ed.). *The Records of the Federal Convention of 1787,* 4 vols. New Haven, 1911.

Fitzpatrick, John C. (ed.). *The Writings of George Washington,* 39 vols. Washington, D.C., 1939–44.

Foner, Philip S. (ed.). *The Complete Writings of Thomas Paine,* 2 vols. Binghamton, 1945.

Ford, Chauncey (ed.). *Some Letters of Elbridge Gerry of Massachusetts, 1784–1804.* Brooklyn, 1896.

Ford, Paul L. (ed.). *The Works of Thomas Jefferson*, 12 vols. New York, 1905.

Ford, Worthington C. (ed.). "Letters of William Vans Murray to John Quincy Adams, 1797–1803," American Historical Association, *Annual Report* (1912).

Ford, Worthington C. (ed.). *Warren–Adams Letters*, 2 vols. Boston, 1917, 1925.

Ford, Worthington C. (ed.). *Writings of John Quincy Adams*, 5 vols. New York, 1914.

Gibbs, George (ed.). *Memoirs of the Administration of Washington and John Adams, edited from the Papers of Oliver Wolcott*, 2 vols. New York, 1846.

"Glimpses of Old College Life," *William and Mary Quarterly*, IX (October 1900).

Greene, L. F. (ed.). *The Writings of the Late Elder John Leland*. New York, 1845.

Handlin, Oscar (ed.). *The Popular Sources of Political Authority*. Cambridge, 1966.

Haynes, George (ed.). "Letters of Samuel Taggart, Representative in Congress, 1803–1814," American Antiquarian Society *Proceedings*, New Series, 33 (April 1923).

Hooker, Richard J. (ed.). "John Marshall on the Judiciary, the Republicans, and Jefferson, March 4, 1801," *American Historical Review*, LIII (April 1948).

Hopkins, James F. (ed.). *The Papers of Henry Clay*, 3 vols. Lexington, 1959–?.

Hunt, Gaillard (ed.). *The Writings of James Madison*, 9 vols. New York, 1900–1910.

Jameson, J. F. (ed.). "Letters of Stephen Higginson, 1783–1804," American Historical Association, *Annual Report* (1896), I.

Kent, William. *Memoirs and Letters of James Kent, LLD*. Boston, 1898.

Kentucky Sessional Laws of 1795. Frankfort, 1796.

King, Charles R. (ed.). *Life and Correspondence of Rufus King*, 10 vols. New York, 1896.

Lodge, Henry Cabot. *Life and Letters of George Cabot*. Boston, 1877.

Lodge, Henry Cabot (ed.). *The Works of Alexander Hamilton*, 12 vols. New York, 1904.

"The Life and Times of Robert B. McAfee and His Family and Connections," *Register of the Kentucky State Historical Society*, 25 (January, May, September, 1927).

McMaster, John B., and F. D. Stone (eds.). *Pennsylvania and the Federal Constitution, 1787–1788*. Lancaster, 1888.

McRee, Griffith J. (ed.). *Life and Correspondence of James Iredell*, 2 vols. New York, 1857.

Marshall, Humphrey. *History of Kentucky*, 2 vols. Frankfort, 1824.

Minor, B. B. (ed.). *Wythe's Decisions of Cases in Virginia by the High Court of Chancery.* . . . Richmond, 1852.

"Some Letters of Dr. Samuel Mitchill," *Harpers Magazine*, LVIII (April 1879).

Morison, John H. (ed.). *The Life of Jeremiah Smith*. Boston, 1845.

Morris, Richard B. (ed.) *Select Cases of the Mayors Court of New York City, 1674–1784*. Washington, 1935.

Padgett, James (ed.). "The Letters of Hubbard Taylor to President James Madison," *Register of the Kentucky State Historical Society*, 36 (April, July, October, 1938).

Parsons, Theophilus. *Memoir of Theophilus Parsons, Chief Justice of the Supreme Judicial Court of Massachusetts*. Boston, 1859.

Pennsylvania Archives. 4th series, 12 vols. Harrisburg, 1900–1902.

Pinkney, William (ed.). *Life of William Pinkney*. New York, 1853.

Plumer, William (ed.). *Life of William Plumer*. Boston, 1857.

Saunders, William L. (ed.). *The Colonial Records of North Carolina*, 10 vols. Raleigh, 1886–1890.

Smith, Margaret Bayard. *First Forty Years of Washington Society*. New York, 1906.

Sparks, Jared (ed.). *The Life of Gouverneur Morris* . . . , 2 vols. Boston, 1832.

Steiner, Bernard C. *The Life and Correspondence of James McHenry*. Cleveland, 1907.

Story, W. W. (ed.). *Life and Letters of Joseph Story*, 2 vols. Boston, 1851.

Strickland, W. P. (ed.). *Autobiography of Peter Cartwright, The Backwoods Preacher*. New York, 1857.

Talbot, George F. "General John Chandler of Monmouth Maine with Extracts from His *Autobiography*," Maine Historical Society, *Collections*, Series I, IX (1887).

Taylor, Robert J. (ed.). *Massachusetts, Colony to Commonwealth, Documents on the Formation of its Constitution, 1775–1780*. Chapel Hill, 1961.

Thorpe, Francis N. (ed.). *Federal and State Constitutions*, 7 vols. Washington, 1909.

Thwaites, Reuben Gold (ed.). *Early Western Travels, 1748–1846*, 32 vols. Cleveland, 1934.

Tyler, Samuel. *Memoir of Roger Brooke Taney.* Baltimore, 1872.

Wagstaff, H. M. (ed.). *The Papers of John Steele,* 2 vols. Raleigh, 1924.

Wharton, Francis. *State Trials of the United States During the Administrations of Washington and Adams.* . . . Philadelphia, 1849.

Wright, Louis B., and Marion Tinling (eds.). *Quebec to Carolina in 1785–1786, Being the Travel Diary and Observations of Robert Hunter, Jr., A Young Merchant of London.* San Marino, 1943.

Wylie, J. C. (ed.). "Letters of Some Members of the Old Congress," *Pennsylvania Magazine of History and Biography,* XXIX (April 1905).

ARTICLES AND ESSAYS

Ames, Harry V. "The Proposed Amendments to the Constitution of the United States During the First Century of its History," American Historical Association, *Annual Report* (1896), II.

Ammon, Harry. "The Formation of the Republican Party in Virginia, 1789–1796," *Journal of Southern History,* XIX (August 1953).

Ammon, Harry. "James Monroe and the Election of 1808 in Virginia," *William and Mary Quarterly,* XX (January 1963).

Bailyn, Bernard. "Boyd's Jefferson: Notes for a Sketch," *New England Quarterly,* XXXIII (September 1960).

Bassett, John S. "Regulators of North Carolina, 1765–1771," American Historical Association, *Annual Report* (1894).

Bates, Whitney. "Northern Speculations and Southern State Debts: 1790," *William and Mary Quarterly,* XIX (January 1962).

Biggs, I. Crawford. "The Power of the Judiciary over Legislation," North Carolina Bar Association, *Proceedings* (1915).

Birdsall, Richard. "The Reverend Thomas Allen: Jeffersonian Calvinist," *New England Quarterly,* XXX (June 1957).

Blackard, W. Raymond. "Requirements for Admission to the Bar in Revolutionary America," *Tennessee Law Review,* XV (1938).

Borden, Morton. "Thomas Jefferson." In Morton Borden (ed.). *America's Ten Greatest Presidents.* Chicago, 1961.

Boyd, Julian P. "The Chasm that Separated Thomas Jefferson and John Marshall." In Gottfried Dietze (ed.). *Essays on the American Constitution.* Englewood Cliffs, 1964.

Brant, Irving. "James Madison and His Times," *American Historical Review,* LVII (July 1952).

Bushey, Glen LeRoy. "William Duane, Crusader for Judicial Reform," *Pennsylvania History,* V (July 1938).

Butterfield, Lyman H. "Elder John Leland, Jeffersonian Itinerant." American Antiquarian Society, *Proceedings*, N.S. LXII (1952).

Butterfield, Lyman. "The Reconciliation of Jefferson and Adams," *Yale Review*, XL (Winter 1951).

Byrd, Pratt. "The Kentucky Frontier in 1792," *The Filson Club History Quarterly*, XXV (July, October, 1951).

Clark, Allen C. "William Duane," Columbia Historical Society, *Records*, IX.

Coleman, John M. "Thomas McKean and the Origin of an Independent Judiciary," *Pennsylvania History*, XXXIV (April 1967).

Coulter, E. Merton. "Early Frontier Democracy in the First Kentucky Constitution," *Political Science Quarterly*, XXXIX (December 1924).

Cunningham, Noble. "Who Were the Quids?" *Mississippi Valley Historical Review*, L (September 1963), 252–63.

Dauer, Manning J., and Hans Hammond. "John Taylor, Democrat or Aristocrat?" *Journal of Politics*, VI (November 1944).

Dowd, Morgan D. "Justice Story and the Politics of Appointment," *The American Journal of Legal History*, IX (October 1965).

Dutcher, George M. "The Rise of Republican Government in the United States," *Political Science Quarterly*, IV (June 1940).

Dunbar, Louise Burnham. "A Study of Monarchical Tendencies in the United States from 1776–1801," *University of Illinois Studies in the Social Sciences*, X (March 1922).

Dunne, Gerald T. "Joseph Story: The Germinal Years," *Harvard Law Review*, 75 (February 1962).

Dupre, Huntley. "The Political Ideas of George Nicholas," *Register, Kentucky State Historical Society*, 39 (July 1941).

East, Robert. "The Massachusetts Conservatives in the Critical Period." In Richard B. Morris (ed.). *The Era of the American Revolution*. New York, 1965.

Evans, Emory G. "Planter Indebtedness and the Coming of the Revolution in Virginia," *William and Mary Quarterly*, XIX (October 1962).

Farrand, Max. "The First Hayburn Case," *American Historical Review*, 13 (January 1908).

Farrand, Max. "The Judiciary Act of 1801," *American Historical Review*, V (1899–1900).

Goodman, Paul. "The First American Party System." In William Nisbet Chambers and Walter Dean Burnham (ed.). *The American Party System, Stages of Political Development*. New York, 1967.

Goodman, Paul. "Social Status of Party Leadership: The House of

Representatives, 1797–1804," *William and Mary Quarterly*, XXV (July 1968).

Goodrich, Carter. "National Planning of Internal Improvements," *Political Science Quarterly*, LXIII (March 1948).

Govan, Thomas P. "Agrarian and Agrarianism: A Study in the Use and Abuse of Words," *Journal of Southern History*, XXX (February 1964).

Grampp, William D. "A Re-Examination of Jeffersonian Economics," *The Southern Economic Journal*, XII (January 1946).

Greene, Jack P. "Foundations of Political Power in the Virginia House of Burgesses, 1720–1776," *William and Mary Quarterly*, XVI (October 1959).

Grinell, Frank W. "The Constitutional History of the Supreme Judicial Court of Massachusetts from the Revolution to 1813," *Massachusetts Law Quarterly* (May 1917), II.

Harrison, Lowell H. "John Breckinridge and the Kentucky Constitution of 1799," *Register of the Kentucky Historical Society*, 57 (July 1959).

Harrison, Lowell H. "John Breckinridge: Western Statesman," *Journal of Southern History*, XVIII (May 1952).

Harrison, Lowell H. "A Virginian Moves to Kentucky, 1793," *William and Mary Quarterly*, XV (April 1958).

Harrison, Lowell H. "A Young Virginian: John Breckinridge," *Virginia Magazine of History and Biography*, 71 (January 1963).

Henderson, Elizabeth K. "The Attack on the Judiciary in Pennsylvania, 1800–1810," *Pennsylvania Magazine of History and Biography*, LXI (April 1937).

Herrink, L. S. "George Wythe," *The John P. Branch Historical Papers*, III (June 1912).

Hunt, Gaillard. "Office-Seeking during Jefferson's Administration," *American Historical Review*, III (January 1898).

Jameson, J. F. "The Predecessor of the Supreme Court." In J. F. Jameson (ed.). *Essays in the Constitutional History of the United States.* Boston, 1898.

Jensen, Merrill. "Democracy and the American Revolution," *Huntington Library Quarterly*, XX (August 1957).

Kammen, Michael G. "Colonial Court Records and the Study of Early American History: A Bibliographical Review," *American Historical Review*, LXX (April 1965).

Katz, Stanley N. "Looking Backward: The Early History of American Law," *The University of Chicago Law Review*, 33 (Summer 1966).

Kenyon, Cecelia M. "Men of Little Faith: The Anti-Federalists on the Nature of Representative Government," *William and Mary Quarterly*, XII (January 1955).

Kenyon, Cecelia M. "Republicanism and Radicalism in the American Revolution: An Old Fashioned Interpretation," *William and Mary Quarterly*, XIX (April 1962).

Kenyon, Cecelia M. "Where Paine Went Wrong," *The American Political Science Review*, XLV (December 1951).

Kerber, Linda R. "Oliver Wolcott: Midnight Judge," The Connecticut Historical Society, *Bulletin*, 32 (January 1967).

Koch, Adrienne, and Harry Ammon. "The Virginia and Kentucky Resolutions: An Episode in Jefferson's and Madison's Defense of Civil Liberties," *William and Mary Quarterly*, V (April 1948).

Land, Aubrey C. "Economic Base and Social Structure: The Northern Chesapeake in the Eighteenth Century," *Journal of Economic History*, XXV (December 1965).

Land, Aubrey C. "Economic Behavior in a Planting Society: The Eighteenth-Century Chesapeake," *Journal of Southern History*, XXXIII (November 1967).

Lerche, Charles O., Jr. "Jefferson and the Election of 1800: A Case Study in the Political Smear," *William and Mary Quarterly*, V (October 1948).

Lerner, Ralph. "The Supreme Court as Republican Schoolmaster." In Philip B. Kurland (ed.). *The Supreme Court Review*. Chicago, 1967.

Lillich, Richard B. "The Chase Impeachment," *American Journal of Legal History*, 4 (January 1960).

Lokken, Roy N. "The Concept of Democracy in Colonial Political Thought," *William and Mary Quarterly*, XVI (October 1959).

Lynd, Staughton, and Young, Alfred F. "After Carl Becker: The Mechanics and New York City Politics, 1774–1801," *Labor History*, V (1964).

Lynd, Staughton. "Capitalism, Democracy and the United States Constitution: The Case of New York," *Science and Society*, XXVII (Fall 1963).

Lynd, Staughton. "Who Should Rule at Home? Dutchess County, New York, in the American Revolution," *William and Mary Quarterly*, XVIII (July 1961).

McLaughlin, William. "The American Revolution as a Religious Revival: The Millennium in One Country," *New England Quarterly*, XL (March 1967).

Main, Jackson T. "Government by the People, the American Revolution and the Democratization of the Legislatures," *William and Mary Quarterly*, XXIII (July 1966).

Main, Jackson T. "Political Parties in Revolutionary Maryland, 1780–1787," *Maryland Historical Magazine*, 62 (March 1967).

Main, Jackson T. "Sections and Politics in Virginia, 1781–1787," *William and Mary Quarterly*, XII (January 1955).

Matthews, Donald R. "United States Senators and the Class Structure," *Public Opinion Quarterly*, XVIII (October 1954).

Mayo, Bernard. "Lexington, Frontier Metropolis." In Eric Goldman (ed.). *Historiography and Urbanization*. Baltimore, 1941.

Meehan, Thomas R. "Courts, Cases, and Counselors in Revolutionary and Post-Revolutionary Pennsylvania," *Pennsylvania Magazine of History and Biography*, XCI (January 1967).

Meigs, William M. "Pennsylvania Politics Early in this Century," *Pennsylvania Magazine of History and Biography*, XVII (No. 4, 1893).

Morey, W. C. "The First State Constitutions," *Annals of the American Academy of Political and Social Science*, IV (1893–94).

Morison, Samuel Eliot. "Elbridge Gerry, Gentleman-Democrat," *New England Quarterly*, II (January 1929).

Morison, Samuel Eliot. "The Struggle over the Adoption of the Constitution of Massachusetts, 1780," *Massachusetts Historical Society Proceedings*, L (1916–17).

Morris, Richard B. "Class Struggle and the American Revolution," *William and Mary Quarterly*, XIX (July 1962).

Padover, Saul K. "The Political Ideas of John Marshall," *Social Research*, XXVI (April 1956).

Palmer, R. R. "The Dubious Democrat: Thomas Jefferson in Bourbon France," *Political Science Quarterly*, LXXII (September 1957).

Pelling, James H. "Governor McKean and the Pennsylvania Jacobins, 1799–1808," *Pennsylvania Magazine of History and Biography*, LIV (October 1930).

Peterson, Merrill D. "Henry Adams on Jefferson the President," *Virginia Quarterly Review*, 39 (Spring, 1963).

Peterson, Merrill, D. "Thomas Jefferson and Commercial Policy, 1783–1793," *William and Mary Quarterly*, XXII (October 1965).

Pole, J. R. "Historians and the Problem of Early American Democracy," *American Historical Review*, LXVII (April 1962).

Risjord, Norman. "The Virginia Federalists," *Journal of Southern History*, XXXIII (November 1967).

Roper, Donald M. "Judicial Unanimity and the Marshall Court—A Road to Reappraisal," *American Journal of Legal History*, IX (April 1965).

Scanlon, James E. "A Sudden Conceit: Jefferson and the Louisiana Government Bill of 1804," *Louisiana History*, IX (Spring, 1968).

Shoemaker, Robert W. "'Democrat' and 'Republican' as Understood in Late Eighteen Century America," *American Speech*, XLI (May 1966).

Sellers, Charles Grier, Jr. "Making a Revolution: The North Carolina Whigs, 1756–1775." In J. Carlyle Sitterson (ed.). *Studies in Southern History*. Chapel Hill: 1957.

Selsam, J. Paul. "A History of Judicial Tenure in Pennsylvania," *Dickinson Law Review*, XXXVIII (April 1934).

Smith, James Morton. "The Grass Roots Origins of the Kentucky Resolutions," *William and Mary Quarterly*, XXVII (April 1970), 221–45.

Spengler, Joseph J. "The Political Economy of Jefferson, Madison, and Adams." In David Kelly Jackson (ed.). *American Studies in Honor of William Kenneth Boyd*. Durham: 1940.

Stanwood, Edward. "The Massachusetts Election of 1806," Massachusetts Historical Society, *Proceedings*, Ser. 2, XX (January 1906).

Steamer, Robert J. "The Legal and Political Genesis of the Supreme Court," *Political Science Quarterly*, LXVII (December 1962).

Surrency, Erwin C. "The Courts in the American Colonies," *American Journal of Legal History*, 11 (1967).

Surrency, Erwin C. "The Judiciary Act of 1801," *American Journal of Legal History*, II (1958).

Thomas, Gordon L. "Aaron Burr's Farewell Address," *Quarterly Journal of Speech*, XXXIX (October 1953).

Turner, Kathryn C. "The Appointment of Chief Justice Marshall," *William and Mary Quarterly*, XVII (April 1960).

Turner, Kathryn. "Federalist Policy and the Judiciary Act of 1801," *William and Mary Quarterly*, XXII (January 1965).

Turner, Kathryn. "The Midnight Judges," *University of Pennsylvania Law Review*, CIX (1960–61).

Turner, Lynn. "The Impeachment of John Pickering," *American Historical Review*, 54 (April 1949).

Utter, William T. "Judicial Review in Ohio," *Mississippi Valley Historical Review*, XIV (June 1927).

Utter, William T. "Ohio and the English Common Law," *Mississippi Valley Historical Review*, XVI (December 1929).

Warren, Charles. "Earliest Cases of Judicial Review of State Legislation by Federal Courts," *Yale Law Journal*, XXX (November 1922).

Warren, Charles. "New Light on the History of the Federal Judiciary Act of 1789," *Harvard Law Review*, XXXVII (November, 1923).

Webster, W. C. "Comparative Study of the State Constitutions of the

American Revolution," *Annals of the American Academy of Political and Social Science,* IX (1897).

Welch, Richard E., Jr. "The Parsons-Sedgwick Feud and the Reform of the Massachusetts Judiciary," Essex Institute Historical *Collections,* XCII (April 1956).

Wilson, Samuel M. "The 'Kentucky Gazette' and John Bradford its Founder," *The Papers of the Bibliographical Society of America,* 31 (1937).

Wood, Gordon S. "Rhetoric and Reality in the American Revolution," *William and Mary Quarterly,* XXIII (January 1966).

Zeichner, Oscar. "The Loyalist Problem in New York after the Revolution," *New York History,* XXI (July 1940).

BOOKS

Abernethey, Thomas Perkins. *Three Virginia Frontiers.* Gloucester, 1922.

Adams, Henry. *History of the United States of America During the Administrations of Thomas Jefferson and James Madison, 1801–1816,* 9 vols. New York, 1891–96.

Adams, Henry. *John Randolph.* New York, 1882.

Adams, Henry. *The Life of Albert Gallatin.* Philadelphia, 1879.

Aldridge, Alfred Owen. *Man of Reason.* Philadelphia, 1959.

Alexander, Edward P. *A Revolutionary Conservative, James Duane of New York.* New York, 1938.

Allan, Herbert S. *John Hancock, Patriot in Purple.* New York, 1948.

Aumann, Francis R. *The Changing American Legal System.* Columbus, 1940.

Balinky, Alexander. *Albert Gallatin, Fiscal Theories and Policies.* New Brunswick, 1958.

Bancroft, George. *History of the Formation of the Constitution,* 2 vols. New York, 1832.

Banner, James M. Jr. *To the Hartford Convention: The Federalists and the Origins of Party Politics in Massachusetts, 1789–1815.* New York, 1970.

Barnhart, John D. *Valley of Democracy, The Frontier versus the Plantation in the Ohio Valley, 1775–1818.* Bloomington, 1953.

Bates, Frank Green. *Rhode Island and the Formation of the Union.* New York, 1898.

Bay, W. V. N. *Reminiscences of the Bench and Bar of Missouri.* St. Louis, 1878.

Beard, Charles A. *Economic Origins of Jeffersonian Democracy*. New York, 1915.

Becker, Carl L. *History of Political Parties in the Province of New York, 1760–1776*. Madison, 1960.

Benson, Lee. *The Concept of Jacksonian Democracy, New York as a Test Case*. Princeton, 1961.

Benson, Lee. *Turner and Beard*. Glencoe, 1960.

Beverdge, Albert J. *The Life of John Marshall*, 4 vols. Boston, 1919.

Binney, Horace. *The Leaders of the Old Bar in Philadelphia*. Philadelphia, 1859.

Bond, Carroll T. *The Court of Appeals of Maryland, A History*. Baltimore, 1828.

Boorstin, Daniel J. *The Americans: The Colonial Experience*. New York, 1958.

Boorstin, Daniel J. *The Genius of American Politics*. Chicago, 1953.

Borden, Morton. *The Federalism of James A. Bayard*. New York, 1955.

Brennan, Ellen E. *Plural Office-holding in Massachusetts, 1760–1780*. Chapel Hill, 1945.

Brown, David Paul. *The Forum: or Forty Years Full Practice at the Philadelphia Bar*, 2 vols. Philadelphia, 1856.

Brown, Everett Somerville. *The Constitutional History of the Louisiana Purchase*. Berkeley, 1920.

Brown, Richard M. *The South Carolina Regulators*. Cambridge, 1963.

Brown, Robert E. *Middle Class Democracy in Massachusetts, 1691–1780*. Ithaca, 1955.

Brown, Robert E. *Virginia 1705–1786: Democracy or Aristocracy?* East Lansing, 1964.

Brown, Roger H. *The Republic in Peril: 1812*. New York, 1964.

Bruce, William Cabell. *John Randolph of Roanoke*, 2 vols. New York, 1922.

Brunhouse, Robert S. *The Counter-Revolution in Pennsylvania, 1776–1780*. Harrisburg, 1942.

Buck, Solon J., and Elizabeth H. Buck. *The Planting of Civilization in Western Pennsylvania*. Pittsburgh, 1939.

Butler, Mann. *A History of the Commonwealth of Kentucky*. Louisville, 1834.

Chambers, William N. *Political Parties in a New Nation*. New York, 1963.

Charles, Joseph N. *The Origins of the American Party System*. New York, 1961.

Chroust, Anton-Hermann. *The Rise of the Legal Profession in America*, 2 vols. Norman, 1965.

Connelley, William Esley, and E. M. Coulter. *History of Kentucky*, 5 vols. Chicago, 1922.

Conrad, H. C. *History of the State of Delaware*, 3 vols. Wilmington, 1908.

Corwin, Edward S. *John Marshall and the Constitution*. New York, 1919.

Cunningham, Noble. *The Jeffersonian Republicans in Power, 1801–1809*. Chapel Hill, 1963.

Cunningham, Noble. *The Jeffersonian Republicans, The Formation of Party Organization, 1789–1801*. Chapel Hill, 1957.

Cushing, H. A. *History of the Transition from Province to Commonwealth Government in Massachusetts*. New York, 1896.

Dauer, Manning J. *The Adams Federalists*. Baltimore, 1953.

DeConde, Alexander. *Entangling Alliance*. Durham, 1958.

DeConde, Alexander. *The Quasi-War*. New York, 1966.

DeMond, Robert O. *The Loyalists in North Carolina During the Revolution*. Durham, 1940.

Douglass, Elisha P. *Rebels and Democrats*. Chapel Hill, 1955.

Edwards, Ninian W. *History of Illinois from 1788 to 1833 and Life and Times of Ninian Edwards*. Springfield, 1870.

Faulkner, Robert K. *The Jurisprudence of John Marshall*. Princeton, 1968.

Fee, W. R. *The Transition from Aristocracy to Democracy in New Jersey, 1789–1829*. Somerville, 1933.

Ferguson, E. James. *The Power of the Purse, A History of American Public Finance, 1776–1790*. Chapel Hill, 1961.

Ferguson, Russell J. *Early Western Pennsylvania Politics*. Pittsburgh, 1938.

Fischer, David H. *The Revolution of American Conservatism: The Federalist Party in the Era of Jeffersonian Democracy*. New York, 1965.

Gilpatrick, Delbert Harold. *Jeffersonian Democracy in North Carolina, 1789–1816*. New York, 1931, 1967.

Goodman, Paul. *The Democratic-Republicans of Massachusetts, Politics in a Young Republic*. Cambridge, 1964.

Green, Fletcher. *Constitutional Development in the South Atlantic States, 1776–1860*. New York, 1966.

Greene, Jack P. *The Quest for Power*. Chapel Hill, 1964.

Grigsby, Hugh Blair. *The History of the Virginia Federal Convention of 1788*, 2 vols. Richmond, 1890.

Haines, Charles Grove. *The American Doctrine of Judicial Supremacy.* New York, 1959.

Hammond, Bray. *Banks and Politics in America from the Revolution to the Civil War.* Princeton, 1957.

Harrison, Lowell H. *John Breckinridge: Jeffersonian Republican.* Louisville, 1969.

Hartz, Louis. *The Liberal Tradition in America.* New York, 1955.

Haskins, Charles Homer. *The Yazoo Land Companies.* New York, 1891.

Heimert, Alan. *Religion and the American Mind, From the Great Awakening to the Revolution.* Cambridge, 1966.

Hibbard, Benjamin Horace. *A History of the Public Land Policies.* Madison, 1965.

Higginbotham, Sanford. *The Keystone in the Democratic Arch.* Harrisburg, 1952.

Hofstadter, Richard. *The American Political Tradition.* New York, 1948.

Hofstadter, Richard. *Anti-Intellectualism in American Life.* New York, 1963.

Hook, Sidney. *The Paradoxes of Freedom.* Berkeley, 1962.

Horsman, Reginald. *Expansion and American Indian Policy, 1783–1812.* East Lansing, 1967.

House, Lolabel. *A Study of the Twelfth Amendment of the Constitution of the United States.* Philadelphia, 1901.

Hurst, James Willard. *Law and the Conditions of Freedom in the Nineteenth-Century United States.* Madison, 1967.

Jacobs, James Ripley. *Tarnished Warrior, Major James Wilkinson.* New York, 1938.

Jensen, Merrill. *The New Nation.* New York, 1950.

Jillson, W. R. *The Kentucky Land Grants.* Louisville, 1925.

Johnson, Allen, and Dumas Malone (ed.). *Dictionary of American Biography,* 20 vols. New York, 1928–1936.

Johnson, Guion Griffis. *Ante-Bellum North Carolina, A Social History.* Chapel Hill, 1937.

Jones, W. Melville (ed.). *Chief Justice John Marshall.* Ithaca, 1956.

Kelbourn, D. C. *The Bench and Bar of Litchfield Connecticut, 1709–1809.* Litchfield, 1909.

Kerber, Linda K. *Federalists in Dissent: Imagery and Ideology in Jeffersonian America.* Ithaca, 1970.

Knollenberg, Bernard. *Origins of the American Revolution, 1759–1766.* New York, 1960.

Koch, Adrienne. *Jefferson and Madison, The Great Collaboration.* New York, 1964.

Konkle, Burton Alva. *Joseph Hopkinson.* Philadelphia, 1931.

Kurtz, Stephen. *The Presidency of John Adams.* Philadelphia, 1957.

Labaree, Benjamin W. *Patriots and Partisans, The Merchants of Newburyport, 1764–1815.* Cambridge, 1961.

Labaree, Leonard W. *Conservatism in Early American History.* Ithaca, 1959.

Lefler, Hugh T., and Albert R. Newsome. *North Carolina; The History of a Southern State.* Chapel Hill, 1954.

Levy, Leonard. *Legacy of Suppression.* Cambridge, 1960.

Lewis, William Draper (ed.). *Great American Lawyers,* 8 vols. Philadelphia, 1907–9.

Libby, Orin Grant. *The Geographical Distribution of the Vote of the Thirteen States on the Federal Constitution, 1787–1788.* Madison, 1894.

Link, Eugene. *Democratic-Republican Societies, 1790–1800.* New York, 1942.

Little, Lucius P. *Ben Hardin: His Times and Contemporaries, with Selections from His Speeches.* Louisville, 1887.

Livingston, Edwin B. *The Livingstons of Livingston Manor.* New York, 1910.

Lovejoy, David S. *Rhode Island Politics and the American Revolution, 1760–1776.* Providence, 1958.

McCormick, Richard P. *The Second American Party System.* Chapel Hill, 1966.

McDonald, Forrest. *We The People.* Boston, 1965.

McLaughlin, J. Fairfax. *Matthew Lyon, The Hampden of Congress.* New York, 1900.

McMaster, John Bach. *A History of the People of the United States,* 5 vols. New York, 1884.

Magrath, C. Peter. *Yazoo, Law and Politics in the New Republic.* Providence, 1966.

Main, Jackson T. *The Anti-Federalists, Critics of the Constitution, 1781–1788.* Chapel Hill, 1961.

Main, Jackson T. *The Upper House in Revolutionary America, 1763–1788.* Madison, 1967.

Malone, Dumas. *Jefferson and His Time,* 4 vols. Boston, 1948–70.

Malone Dumas. *The Public Life of Thomas Cooper, 1783–1839.* New Haven, 1926.

Martin, A. E. *The Anti-Slavery Movement in Kentucky Prior to 1850.* Louisville, 1918.

Maxson, C. H. *The Great Awakening in the Middle Colonies.* Chicago, 1920.

Mayo, Bernard. *Henry Clay.* Cambridge, 1937.

Mays, David J. *Edmund Pendleton, 1721–1803, A Biography*, 2 vols. Cambridge, 1952.

Miller, Perry. *The Life of the Mind in America from the Revolution to the Civil War.* New York, 1965.

Morgan, Donald G. *Justice William Johnson, The First Dissenter.* Columbia, 1954.

Morison, John H. *Life of the Honorable Jeremiah Smith.* Boston, 1845.

Morison, Samuel Eliot. *The Life and Letters of Harrison Gray Otis, Federalist 1765–1848*, 2 vols. Boston, 1918.

Morse, Anson Ely. *The Federalist Party in Massachusetts to the Year 1800.* Princeton, 1909.

Nettels, Curtis P. *The Emergence of a National Economy, 1775–1815.* New York, 1962.

Nevins, Allan. *The American States During and After the Revolution, 1776–1789.* New York, 1924.

Newmyer, R. Kent. *The Supreme Court Under Marshall and Taney.* New York, 1968.

North, Douglass C. *The Economic Growth of the United States, 1790–1860.* Englewood Cliffs, 1961.

O'Neall, John Belton. *Biographical Sketches of the Bench and Bar of South Carolina*, 2 vols. Charleston, 1859.

Parks, Joseph H. *Felix Grundy.* Baton Rouge, 1940.

Pessen, Edward. *Most Uncommon Jacksonians.* Albany, 1967.

Peterson, Merrill D. *The Jefferson Image in the American Mind.* New York, 1960.

Peterson, Merrill D. *Thomas Jefferson and the New Nation.* New York, 1970.

Pole, J. R. *Political Representation in England and the Origins of the American Republic.* New York, 1966.

Pound, Roscoe. *The Formative Era of American Law.* Boston, 1938.

Pound, Roscoe. *Organization of the Courts.* Boston, 1940.

Pound, Roscoe. *The Spirit of the Common Law.* Boston, 1963.

Prince, Carl F. *New Jersey's Jeffersonian Republicans.* Chapel Hill, 1964.

Purviance, Levi. *The Biography of Elder David Purviance.* Dayton, 1848.

Reed, Alfred Z. *Training for the Public Profession of the Law.* New York, 1921.

Rheinstein, Max (ed.). *Max Weber on Law in Economy and Society.* Cambridge, 1966.

Risjord, Norman. *The Old Republicans.* New York, 1965.

Robinson, Blackman. *William R. Davie.* Chapel Hill, 1957.

Robinson, William A. *Jeffersonian Democracy in New England*. New Haven, 1916.

Sanderson, John. *Biography of the Signers to the Declaration of Independence*. Philadelphia, 1847.

Schachner, Nathan. *Aaron Burr*. New York, 1961.

Schachner, Nathan. *Thomas Jefferson, A Biography*. New York, 1957.

Schlesinger, Arthur M., Jr. *The Age of Jackson*. Boston, 1950.

Sellers, Charles, and Henry May. *A Synopsis of American History*. Chicago, 1963.

Selsam, J. Paul. *The Pennsylvania Constitution of 1776: A Struggle in Revolutionary Democracy*. Philadelphia, 1936.

Simms, Henry H. *Life of John Taylor*. Richmond, 1932.

Smith, Edgar C. *Moses Greenleaf, Maine's First Mapmaker*. Bangor, 1902.

Smith, James M. *Freedom's Fetters*. Ithaca, 1956.

Spaulding, E. Wilder. *His Excellency George Clinton, Critic of the Constitution*. New York, 1938.

Spaulding, E. Wilder. *New York in the Critical Period, 1783–89*. New York, 1938.

Sydnor, Charles S. *American Revolutionaries in the Making*. New York, 1962.

Talbert, Charles Gano. *Benjamin Logan, Kentucky Frontiersman*. Lexington, 1962.

Taylor, Robert J. *Western-Massachusetts in the Revolution*. Providence, 1954.

Tinkcom, Harry M. *Republicans and Federalists in Pennsylvania, 1790–1801*. Harrisburg, 1950.

Tolles, Frederick B. *Meeting House and Counting House*. Chapel Hill, 1948.

Treat, Payson Jackson. *The National Land System, 1785–1820*. New York, 1967.

Turner, Lynn. *William Plumer of New Hampshire, 1759–1850*. Chapel Hill, 1962.

Tyler, Moses Coit. *Patrick Henry*. Ithaca, 1962.

Varg, Paul. *Foreign Policies of the Founding Fathers*. East Lansing, 1963.

Wade, Richard C. *The Urban Frontier*. Cambridge, 1959.

Walters, Raymond. *Albert Gallatin: Jeffersonian Financier and Diplomat*. New York, 1957.

Walters, Raymond, Jr. *Alexander James Dallas*. Philadelphia, 1943.

Warfield, Ethelbert Dudley. *The Kentucky Resolutions of 1798*. New York, 1887.

Warren, Charles. *History of the American Bar*. Boston, 1913.

Warren, Charles. *Jacobin and Junto.* Cambridge, 1931.
Warren, Charles. *The Supreme Court in United States History,* 2 vols. Boston, 1926.
Welch, Richard E., Jr. *Theodore Sedgwick, Federalist: A Political Portrait.* Middleton, 1965.
White, Leonard. *The Jeffersonians: A Study in Administrative History, 1801–1829.* New York, 1951.
Williamson, Chilton. *American Suffrage from Property to Democracy.* Princeton, 1960.
Wilson, Samuel W. *The First Land Court of Kentucky, 1779–1780.* Louisville, 1923.
Winslow, John. *The Trial of the Rhode Island Judges: An Episode Touching Currency and Constitutional History.* Brooklyn, 1887.
Wood, Gertrude S. *William Paterson of New Jersey.* Fair Lawn, 1933.
Wood, Gordon S. *The Creation of the American Republic.* Chapel Hill, 1969.
Woodward, C. Vann (ed.). *The Comparative Approach to American History.* New York, 1968.
Young, Alfred F. *The Democratic-Republicans of New York.* Chapel Hill, 1967.
Young, James S. *The Washington Community.* New York, 1966.
Zeichner, Oscar. *Connecticuts Year's of Controversy, 1750–1776.* Chapel Hill, 1949.

SECONDARY SOURCES: THESES AND DISSERTATIONS

Caldemeyer, Richard H. "The Career of George Nicholas." Unpublished Doctoral Dissertation, University of Indiana, 1951.
Eller, Paul Hummel. "Revivalism and the German Churches in Pennsylvania, 1783–1816." Unpublished Dissertation, University of Chicago, 1933.
Elsmere, Mary Jane Shaffer. "The Impeachment Trial of Justice Samuel Chase." Unpublished Doctoral Dissertation, University of Indiana, 1962.
Harrison, Joseph H. "The Internal Improvement Issue in the Politics of the Union, 1783–1825." Unpublished Doctoral Dissertation, University of Virginia, 1954.
Heller, J. E., III. "Democracy in Maryland, 1790–1810." Unpublished Senior Thesis, Princeton, 1959.
Henderson, Elizabeth. "Some Aspects of Sectionalism in Pennsylvania, 1790–1812." Unpublished Doctoral Dissertation, Bryn Mawr College, 1935.

Meehan, Thomas R. "The Pennsylvania Supreme Court in the Law and Politics of the Commonwealth, 1776–1790." Unpublished Doctoral Dissertation, University of Wisconsin, 1960.

Pelling, James Hedley. "The Public Life of Thomas McKean, 1734–1817." Unpublished Doctoral Dissertation, The University of Chicago, 1929.

Phillips, Kim T. "William Duane." Unpublished Doctoral Dissertation, University of California, Berkeley, 1968.

Index